INSURGENT
ENCOUNTERS

INSURGENT

Transnational Activism, Ethnography, & the Political

ENCOUNTERS

JEFFREY S. JURIS | ALEX KHASNABISH | EDITORS

Duke University Press   Durham and London   2013

© 2013 Duke University Press
All rights reserved
Printed in the United States of America on acid-free paper ∞
Designed by Courtney Leigh Baker
Typeset in Minion Pro by Tseng Information Systems, Inc.
Library of Congress Cataloging-in-Publication Data
Insurgent encounters : transnational activism, ethnography,
and the political / Jeffrey S. Juris and Alex Khasnabish, eds.
p. cm.
Includes bibliographical references and index.
ISBN 978-0-8223-5349-2 (cloth : alk. paper)
ISBN 978-0-8223-5362-1 (pbk. : alk. paper)
1. Political anthropology. 2. Ethnology—Political aspects.
3. Ethnology—Sociological aspects. 4. Political activists.
I. Juris, Jeffrey S., 1971– II. Khasnabish, Alex, 1976–
GN492.I578 2013
306.2—dc23
2012044746

For a just, democratic, and liberated world—one capable of holding many worlds, and to all those insurgent movements struggling to imagine and build them . . .

CONTENTS

Discrepant Paradigms

Transformational Knowledges

Subversive Technologies

ACKNOWLEDGMENTS

Any book project accumulates a list of debts, and this one is no exception, but before acknowledging these, a few words on how this project came together are in order. From its inception, this project has been a collaborative, long-term, and mutually supportive enterprise. The initial idea dates back to a conversation between Jeffrey Juris and Michal Osterweil in the fall of 2005, building on some of the exchanges facilitated by the Social Movements Working Group (SMWG) at the University of North Carolina, Chapel Hill. After several years of discussion and groundwork (and a change of editors to allow Michal to finish her dissertation), initial drafts were submitted in the fall of 2009, which served as the basis for a workshop held at Northeastern University on February 11–13, 2010, in order to comment on the chapters and to collectively discuss the structure of the volume. Since then, each of the chapters has gone through at least three additional rounds of revision before the volume draft was submitted in February 2011. Indeed, the process was as much a part of the intellectual and political ethic of this project as was the completed work.

Beyond our work as volume editors and contributors many others helped to bring this book into being. We would like to start by thanking the Department of Sociology and Anthropology, the Program in International Affairs, and the former College of Arts and Sciences (now the College of Humanities and Social Sciences and the College of Science) at Northeastern University for funding the public "Globalization and the Grassroots" symposium and workshop. We want to personally thank Steven Vallas, chair of the Department of Sociology and Anthropology; Dennis Sullivan, former director of the Program in International Affairs;

and Bruce Ronkin, former acting dean of the College of Arts and Sciences, for their financial and intellectual support of the project. We would also like to thank those members of Northeastern's Department of Sociology and Anthropology and the Program in International Affairs who participated in the public symposium: Denise Horn, Berna Turam, and Liza Weinstein, as well as the faculty of both units who served as gracious hosts during the event. And a special note of appreciation to Amy Lubitow for her tireless efforts in providing the logistical support without which the symposium and workshop would not have been possible. Finally, we are also grateful to Mariama White-Hammond, of Project Hip-Hop, who also took part in the symposium and helped to ground our discussions of globalization and transnational activism in the realities of everyday structural violence and inequality in urban Boston.

In terms of the intellectual development of the volume we would like to thank Jackie Smith for serving as a special guest discussant during the Northeastern workshop and Arturo Escobar for reading and commenting on a previous version of the introduction. We are also indebted to the SMWG at the University of North Carolina, Chapel Hill, for incubating early discussions regarding activism, ethnography, and transnational activism that helped to contribute to the idea for the volume. Many of the volume's contributors—including Maribel Casas-Cortés, Janet Conway, Vinci Daro, David Hess, Jeffrey Juris, Michal Osterweil, and Dana Powell—have either been members of the SMWG or have participated in SMWG workshops over the years. We are particularly grateful to Arturo Escobar and Dorothy Holland, among others, for their leadership of the SMWG as well as their intellectual inspiration and support. We would also like to thank all of the contributors for reading and commenting on earlier versions of each other's chapters; this was truly a collaborative effort. Of course we are also indebted to the social movements and activist comrades (together with and alongside of whom we have all worked and struggled) for their critical role in the development of the ideas and ethnographic analyses presented in this volume. Last, but by no means least, we would also like to express our gratitude to friends and family whose support, encouragement, forbearance, and patience make projects like this possible and struggles for social change and justice meaningful.

At Duke University Press we would like to thank Ken Wissoker for his steadfast support and intellectual guidance throughout this book's development, submission, and revision. We are also grateful to three anonymous reviewers for their invaluable comments and suggestions about the book as a whole, as well as individual chapters. The volume has been significantly improved as a result of their engaged, astute, and critical readings. Heartfelt thanks also go out to Jade Brooks for her willingness to answer our seemingly endless questions and to more generally shepherd us through the manuscript-preparation process.

A much earlier version of chapter 1, "Spaces of Intentionality: Race, Class, and Horizontality at the U.S. Social Forum," by Jeffrey S. Juris, appeared in *Mobilization* 13 (4): 353–72.

ABBREVIATIONS

AFM	Articulación Feminista Mercosur (Mercosur Feminist Alliance)
ANT	actor-network theory
APC	Association for Progressive Communications
A16	protest against the World Bank and International Monetary Fund in Washington, D.C., on April 16, 2000
ASSÉ	L'Association pour une Solidarité Syndicale Étudiante (Association for Student Union Solidarity)
CAD	computer-aided design
CFE	Carnival for Full Enjoyment
CIRCA	Clandestine Insurgent Rebel Clown Army
CNG	Consultative Network Group (of the Feminist Dialogues)
COP 15	Conference of the Parties (2009 UN Climate Change Conference in Copenhagen, with fifteen participants, as part of UN Framework Convention on Climate Change)
COP 16	Conference of the Parties (2010 UN Climate Change Conference in Cancun, with sixteen participants, as part of UN Framework Convention on Climate Change)

DAWN	Development Alternatives with Women for a New Era
ESF	European Social Forum
FCC	Federal Communications Commission
FD	Feminist Dialogues
FEMA	Federal Emergency Management Agency
FEMNET	African Women's Development and Communication Network
FLOSS	free/libre and open-source software
FS	free software
FSF	Free Software Foundation
FTAA	Free Trade Area of the Americas
G8	Group of Eight (the most powerful industrial countries, now G20)
GGJ	Grassroots Global Justice
GIM	global indigenous movement
IC	International Council (of the World Social Forum)
ICT	Information and Communication Technology

IMC	Independent Media Center
INB	Infernal Noise Brigade
IOC	Indian Organizing Committee (of the 2004 World Social Forum in Mumbai)
IS	International Secretariat (of the World Social Forum)
IWC	Indian Working Committee (of the 2004 World Social Forum in Mumbai)
IYC	International Youth Camp (of the World Social Forum)
LETS	Local Exchange Trading System
MPH	Make Poverty History
NBA	Narmada Bachao Andolan (Save the Narmada Movement)
NAFTA	North American Free Trade Agreement
NGO	nongovernmental organization
NIEO	New International Economic Order
NIIO	New International Information Order
NNWAG	National Network of Women's Autonomous Groups

NPC	National Planning Committee (of the United States Social Forum)
N30	protest and global day of action against the World Trade Organization summit meeting in Seattle on November 30, 1999
PAR	participatory action research
PGA	Peoples' Global Action
PMA	People's Movement Assembly
SMS	social movement studies
SMWG	Social Movements Working Group (at the University of North Carolina, Chapel Hill)
SOC	Southeast Organizing Committee (of the U.S. Southeast Social Forum)
STS	science and technology studies
TAN	transnational advocacy network
TSMO	transnational social movement organization
UFP	Union des Forces Progressistes (Union of Progressive Forces)

UFPA	Universidade Federal do Pará (Federal University of Para)
UFRA	Universidade Federal Rural da Amazônia (Federal Rural University of the Amazon)
UNESCO	United Nations Educational, Scientific, and Cultural Organization
UNFCCC	United Nations Framework Convention on Climate Change
UNPFII	United Nations Permanent Forum on Indigenous Issues
UNWGIP	United Nations Working Group on Indigenous Populations
USSF	U.S. Social Forum
WICEJ	Women's International Coalition for Economic Justice
WSF	World Social Forum
WTO	World Trade Organization

INTRODUCTION

Ethnography and Activism within Networked Spaces of Transnational Encounter

JEFFREY S. JURIS | ALEX KHASNABISH

A MOMENT

From December 30, 2006, to January 2, 2007, nearly two thousand activists from around the world, including large contingents from Spain, Italy, the United States, and Mexico, gathered in the Zapatista *caracol* (literally shell, refers to a meeting point and a regional seat of autonomous government) of Oventik for the first of a series of international gatherings between the Zapatista Pueblos and the Pueblos of the World. Unlike the Intergalactic Gathering for Humanity and against Neoliberalism in 1996, where the internationals and the Ejército Zapatista de Liberación Nacional (EZLN; Zapatista National Liberation Army) leadership dominated the discussions, this time the Zapatista base communities held center stage. For four days members of the Juntas de Buen Gobierno (Good Government Councils) from the five Zapatista caracoles recounted their successes and challenges over the past twelve years while implementing autonomy in their communities.[1] The internationals and activists from other parts of Mexico listened intently, for the most part, as the Zapatistas told of their experiences in diverse areas such as autonomous government, justice, health, education, and media. Beyond the scheduled workshops, visitors mingled informally, if uneasily at times, with each other and their indigenous hosts, sharing meals, holding impromptu discussions, planning future actions and events, and dancing late into the night. In many ways, this was a typical networked space of transnational encounter, similar to dozens of other gatherings that have taken place around the world since 1996, including many associated with global justice movements. However, there was something particularly romantic, mysterious, and radical about this one, not only the scores of masked Zapatistas seemingly appearing and disappearing in the highland Chiapas fog but also the fact that the meeting was held in autonomous territory, constantly under threat yet still beyond the full grasp of the capitalist market and the Mexican state.[2]

Of course, the encounter was also rife with contradictions, struggles, and tensions. Some of these came to the fore on the last day of the gathering, when, after hours and hours of listening to members of the Zapatista base communities, the visitors were finally given a chance to speak in response to a call for ideas and proposals regarding when, where, and how to organize the next Intergalactic Gathering. Most of the interventions were constructive, suggesting specific dates, places, and methods, and thanking the base communities for their hospitality, initiative, and inspirational model of anticapitalist struggle and autonomous organization. However, several speakers expressed their desire for a more interactive, dynamic, and participatory format. At one point, an activist from the Spanish state stood up, put a soda can on the table, and criticized the Zapatistas for selling Coca-Cola in their communities, concluding that this was "inconsistent." People in the crowd let out a loud gasp, as many were shocked by the boldness of the critique, while others applauded in enthusiastic approval. Indeed, the man publicly expressed what many European and North American participants had commented to each other privately.[3]

The Zapatistas remained silent, until the following July when Subcomandante Marcos spoke out during a presentation in San Cristóbal de las Casas prior to the second Encounter of the Zapatista Pueblos with the Pueblos of the World. After exhibiting an unmarked soda can and recounting what had taken place the previous January, Marcos, visibly upset, exclaimed, "Those who applauded didn't ask the spontaneous judge, jury, and executioner what brand of shoes and clothes he wore, or where and how he had attained the modern and expensive vehicle in which he came to judge and condemn the Zapatista struggle." He later clarified that the leaders' "silence . . . was an act of courtesy; it did and does not mean agreement with what that person said." Calming down somewhat, Marcos went on to provide a subtle analysis of what the silence of his *compañeros* actually meant. He explained that there are different kinds of anticapitalism, each valid and consistent: a consumer-based anticapitalism favored by many of those who visit the Zapatista communities; an anticapitalism that attacks the system at the point of distribution by promoting small businesses, street vendors, and cooperatives over large multinationals; and a production-oriented anticapitalism. Regarding the latter, Marcos explained that when a Zapatista sees a can of soda, she or he asks questions such as who made the can and who owns the factory where it was produced? The Zapatista opts to join forces with the workers who produced the can against the owners of the soda factory, practicing anticapitalism by "attacking the means of production." Marcos transformed a delicate tension into a teaching moment as a way to reflect on alternative forms of anticapitalist struggle, while highlighting the Zapatistas' open and inclusive ethic, expressed most recently in the Sexta Declaración de la Selva Lacandona (Sixth Declaration of the Lacandon Jungle).[4] As he exclaimed, "All anticapitalist efforts are respectable and important. . . . So go ahead and explain, educate, and advise[,] . . . but don't judge or condemn those who have decided to risk their lives . . . to destroy the system in which we are all enclosed, and that exploits, represses, and undervalues us."[5]

We begin with this brief ethnographic vignette in order to highlight and reflect on the importance of ethnography for understanding networked spaces of transnational encounter, and the wider social movements of which they are a part. On the one hand, ethnography, understood not just as a set of research methods including qualitative interviews and participant observation but also as a mode of analysis and writing, allows us to capture the subjective mood, feeling, and tone of such events. Ethnographic descriptions provide a vivid sense of actually "being there" (Geertz 1989) during transnational social movement actions and gatherings, contributing descriptive flesh to what might otherwise read as dry, distant, and disengaged analytic accounts. In this sense, the ethnographic vignette tries to bring the reader into the flow of events, recounting some of what was actually said and conveying a sense of the prevailing atmosphere and emotional climate. In many ways, this has long been seen as the role of ethnography, widely valued even among the most positivist social movement scholars.

However, as we argue in this volume, ethnography is not restricted to thick description. Rather, ethnographic analyses and accounts, particularly when they are politically engaged and carried out from within rather than outside grassroots movements for social change, are able to uncover important empirical issues and generate critical theoretical insights that are simply not accessible through traditional objectivist methods. For example, as evident in the account above, networked spaces of transnational activist encounter are rife with political and cultural tensions, conflicts, and power imbalances. In this sense, the tension between different forms of anticapitalism (see Santos 2007) and the power-laden dynamics associated with the critique of the Zapatistas by a Northern activist, and Marcos's impassioned response, are only rendered visible through ethnographic engagement. Against overly romanticized views of transnational activism, ethnography reveals the inevitable, yet productive, "friction" (Tsing 2005) that ensues in the encounter between activists from diverse movements, political contexts, and cultural backgrounds.

For the engaged ethnographer, the goal of producing such accounts is never only to uncover internal conflicts and tensions; the ethnographer also produces critical understandings that can help activists develop strategies to overcome obstacles and barriers to effective organizing. In this case, it is Marcos who makes an elegant plea for the importance of mutual understanding and "translation" (Tsing 2005; see also Santos 2006; Casas-Cortés, Osterweil, and Powell, this volume; and Juris, this volume) between different forms of struggle. As the following chapters demonstrate, activist engagements and positionalities are important for gaining access, but they also provide engaged ethnographers with critical purchase on key tensions and issues underlying processes and events and can help generate subsequent ethnographic accounts that speak to political strategy and tactics. The ethnographic vignette above thus reveals the strategic importance of activists themselves developing an ethnographic sensibility to more effectively negotiate the different understandings and visions within networked spaces of transnational encounter (see Juris 2008a).

Finally, the ethnographic mise en scène narrated above is networked and transnational in a particular sense, with important implications for politically engaged ethnography. On the one hand, it is a site that is linked to many other sites, both in Mexico and around the world, and thus has to be seen as a momentary concatenation of translocal processes, flows, and relations. It is a site that generates its own dynamics yet always points elsewhere: to other meanings, events, and places. On the other hand, place remains crucial, in terms of the particular nexus of meanings and relations associated with Zapatista caracoles and with respect to the place-based visions and practices that activists bring with them from their diverse locales. Grasping such dynamics requires not so much an ethnographic strategy that is multisited (although that can be a critical component) as one that is networked: attuned to the complex place-based meanings, flows, and sensibilities that interact within momentary spaces of encounter. The political significance of such transnationally networked ethnographies lies in their capacity to generate strategic insights related to the tensions, obstacles, and opportunities that emerge within networked spaces of transnational encounter.

TRANSNATIONAL ACTIVISM, ETHNOGRAPHY, AND THE POLITICAL

Ethnography as a methodology and epistemology has long been associated with a deep concern for the lived realities that comprise sociocultural contexts. However, our exploration of ethnography and activism within transnational spaces of encounter aims at something more. For us, ethnography is not simply a useful approach for understanding transnational activism. As a theory and a method of research that demands an explicit awareness of our being situated in place and in relation to other acting subjects, ethnography is also a form of knowledge that fundamentally challenges, even if it does not entirely overcome the (researching) subject–(researched) object binary (Juris 2007; see also the volume's conclusion). The role of social movements as knowledge producers (see Casas-Cortés, Osterweil, and Powell 2008, this volume; Conway 2005a; Escobar 2008; Hess 2007a) is suggested in the efforts on the part of the Zapatista base communities to articulate and communicate their emerging model of autonomous self-management in diverse spheres of social life, as well as in Marcos's astute analysis of alternative forms of anticapitalist practice.

Conventional social movement theory has analyzed the broad contours of contemporary activism with respect to dimensions such as resources, issue framing, and political opportunities (see, e.g., McAdam, McCarthy, and Zald 1996; Snow et al. 1986; Tarrow 1998). Such scholarship maps social movements onto a political landscape marked by modern institutions (the state, political parties, and electoral democracy) and power relations (citizenship, political influence, discourses of democracy, human rights, and sovereignty), thereby reducing these phenomena to existing political, epistemological, and ontological frameworks. When the terrain is expanded to the transnational level, dominant political and economic institutions and processes again serve as focal points for analysis (see Tarrow 2005). This approach reflects an underlying acceptance of capitalist modernity, liberal democracy, and individualism, values challenged by more radical movements, including many of those addressed in this volume. Of course such movements have promises and limitations, which we further address in the conclusion. Nonetheless, the way in which we view the causes, forms, and consequences of social movements has significant implications for how we understand their potential, the stakes involved, and the meaning of the political itself.

In this sense, social logics born out of a particular system of social, economic, and political power may come to arbitrate and evaluate the significance of struggles that seek to explicitly contest, subvert, and replace that system. While these predispositions can produce excellent scholarship about conventional movements that seek to wield influence and power within the nexus of dominant sociopolitical orders, such biases often obscure movements that aim to radically unsettle existing power structures while bringing new sociopolitical relationships, subjectivities, and imaginations into being. Even in cases where theorists have addressed the symbolic challenge posed by the so-called new social movements with respect to prevailing orders and underlying social logics (see Melucci 1996), these analyses tend to overstate the significance of symbolic and cultural transformation at the expense of the material realities of struggle and the complexities of lived experience (Fox and Starn 1997).

Ethnography's attention to everyday practices, cultural imaginaries, and emerging subjectivities allows us to grasp the complexity, contingency, and transformational potential of contemporary transnational movements. In this sense, the Zapatista model of autonomy has been particularly inspirational, resonating widely within transnational activist networks (Khasnabish 2008).[6] Nonetheless, when confronted with contradictions, ideal models often generate harsh critiques, as evidenced by the charge of inconsistency leveled against the Zapatistas. Ethnography can also help shed light on the importance of space and place within transnational movements (Conway 2004b; Escobar 2001, 2008; Routledge 2003a). The Zapatistas thus engage in a place-based struggle to maintain autonomous control of their territories as they reach out to other Mexican and international activists, creating novel spaces of transnational encounter.

The cycle of transnational activism sparked by the Zapatista uprising in 1994, which is often subsumed under the banner of *global justice movement*, is more ephemeral, rhizomatic, and dynamic than most conventional social movement analyses allow (Khasnabish 2007, 2008). The wave of Occupy movements that spread around the globe in 2011–12 displays many similar, yet also some distinct, characteristics (see Juris 2012, and the volume's conclusion). This book ventures into this shifting and uneven, yet vibrant, terrain of transnational action in order to highlight the contribution of ethnography to our understanding of transnational social movements. Previous volumes on transnational activism have included ethnographic chapters (see, e.g., Bandy and Smith 2005; Guidry, Kennedy, and Zald 2000), but none have had as their main focus the methods, perspectives, and theoretical insights generated by ethnography. Given the publication of several ethnographic studies in the late 2000s dealing with transnational social movements and activist networking, particularly in the context of the global justice movements (see Escobar 2008; Juris 2008a; Khasnabish 2008), it is a propitious moment to bring together, in a single volume, the work of both younger and more-established scholars engaged in the ethnographic study of what we call networked spaces of transnational encounter. Our goal is to convene a similarly transnationally networked group of scholar-activists to explore the intersections of the transnational, the sociopolitical practice of activists, and the academic labor of ethnographers.[7]

Before moving on to more deeply engage the issues, themes, and perspectives addressed in the chapters that follow, it is important to say a few words about the title of this book. This is, of course, a collection of contributions about encounters—between anthropology and struggles for social change, between scholarly and political commitments, between ethnographers and social movement actors, and between academics and activists—but what makes these encounters *insurgent*? Although we realize the language of insurgency is freighted with masculinist and militaristic overtones, we deploy it here because it suggests the clearing of a path for new forms of sociopolitical imagination and construction. An insurgency is always a provocation, a forceful intervention that aims not to constitute a singular new order from whole cloth but to radically destabilize authorized forms of power, knowledge, and organization and, in so doing, to create the space necessary for new acts of constitution (see Negri 1999). In this sense, the chapters seek to destabilize dominant understandings of social transformation, political possibility, knowledge production, and the relationship between immaterial intellectual labor and sociopolitical activism. But we also employ the language and imaginary of insurgency because we believe the engaged ethnographies collected here represent a form of critical social research that can contribute in multiple ways to social change as opposed to simply archiving, commenting on, or dissecting the efforts of grassroots social movements. This is not to suggest that such a contribution should be privileged or valorized over others, that our goals are always achieved, or that we have all the answers. Indeed, the significance of the insurgent encounters explored here lies in their capacity to elicit a critical exploration of the possibilities that emerge through the intersection of a politically committed, engaged ethnography and ongoing struggles for radical social change.

We employ the term *transnational* to refer to a scale that transcends, yet also incorporates, other levels of analysis, including the local, regional, and national. Transnational thus reflects the multiscalar nature of much contemporary activism. The transnational is lived and imagined; it is a social space made and remade through the activity and conjuring of institutions, collectivities, and individuals beyond the territorial, juridical, economic, political, and sociocultural limits of a single nation-state (Conway 2008a). In this sense, an ontological space is constituted and reconstituted at the intersection of the activities and subjectivities of disparate actors. The transnational is also a space of action and imagination, a new political horizon on which projects for social transformation are arrayed. As a scale that derives meaning, presence, and force from lived processes of articulation, the transnational—and the possibilities it offers for radical social change—has to be understood as an outcome of lived relationships. Ethnography, and its attention to everyday realities, is thus an indispensable tool for exploring transnational activism as well as the more general search for and articulation of new practices of knowledge production capable of generating democratic, liberatory, and just social futures.

With respect to activism, here we refer to an object of analysis and a mode of research. On the one hand, this volume is centrally concerned with exploring new forms of activism that are emerging in an increasingly globalized, digitally connected world. In this sense, the book presents numerous ethnographies of transnational activism. On the other hand, our concern with activism represents a commitment to a politically engaged form of ethnographic research, which not only generates knowledge that we hope can be useful for those with whom we study but also potentially constitutes a form of activism itself. In this sense, the volume showcases diverse modes of activist ethnography that vary according to disciplinary convention and political proclivity.

By ethnography, as mentioned above, we mean more than a set of research methods. Participant observation, open-ended interviews, and related qualitative techniques are necessary, but not sufficient, *sine qua nons* of ethnographic praxis. We also conceive of ethnography as an attitude, a perspective, and, above all, a specific mode of "epistemological encounter" (Kelty 2008, 18; see also M. Fischer 2003; Marcus 1998), involving an ethic of openness and flexibility and a willingness to allow oneself to become personally transformed through the research process. This approach to transnational social movements does not search for universal laws or test already formulated theories. Rather it generates new concepts and analyses in the process of ethnographic engagement.[8] We also refer to ethnography as a form of writing characterized by descriptive thickness and close attention to detail, context, and tone. At the same time, the chapters also reflect diverse disciplinary norms and practices: some employ a more humanistic mode of ethnographic writing characteristic of fields such as cultural anthropology or critical geography, while others approach ethnography less as a textual product than as a means for gathering observations and generating analysis, which tends to be the norm in qualitative sociology or political science (see Hess's chapter). Nonetheless, what all of the chapters share is a commitment to using ethnography as a tool for generating insights and understandings that are obscured by more objectivist approaches.

Our inclusion of "the political" in the book's subtitle points to the various ways the chapters interrogate, reformulate, and broaden the meaning of the political to encompass diverse strategies, discourses, and practices that not only challenge the distribution of power and resources within hegemonic political orders but also create new meanings, subjectivities, and alternative modes of socioeconomic, cultural, and political organization. Politics thus moves out from purely institutional domains to also inhabit the autonomous realms of social movement networks, grassroots communities, and the intimate spheres of everyday social life. A concluding conceptual note: although many of the contributions explore the dynamics of transnational activist networks, we offer the broader term *net-*

worked spaces of transnational encounter to make room for a wider array of phenomena, events, and processes than suggested by the network concept alone.[9] This notion of encounter dovetails with the logic of contemporary networked movements themselves, which involves the forging of horizontal connections across diversity and difference (Juris 2008a).

TOWARD THE ETHNOGRAPHY OF TRANSNATIONAL ACTIVISM

The earliest approaches to the study of transnational activism understood the emergence of cross-border political actors, including transnational social movements and advocacy networks, as a response to the rise of a global civil society (see Wapner 1996). These novel forms of political engagement were alternatively viewed through the prism of traditional social movement theory (Jackie Smith, Chatfield, and Pagnucco 1997) or a combination of international relations and network perspectives (Keck and Sikkink 1998). In their pathbreaking study, Jackie Smith and her colleagues employed the resource mobilization framework to characterize transnational social movements as distinguished "by the actors and resources they mobilize and in the extent to which they communicate, consult, coordinate, and cooperate in the international arena" (Jackie Smith, Chatfield, and Pagnucco 1997, 60). For their part, Margaret Keck and Kathryn Sikkink emphasized the novel role of *information politics* through which NGOs in fields such as human rights, environmentalism, and women's rights disseminate messages and apply pressure on foreign governments by circulating information within transnational advocacy networks (TANs) (1998). Subsequent volumes developed these themes further, bringing to bear additional ideas from the conceptual toolbox of social movement theory in order to analyze transnational collective action, including political opportunities, diffusion, and framing (della Porta, Kriesi, and Rucht 1999; Jackie Smith and Johnston 2002).

Although these early volumes broke important ground by highlighting the emerging transnational dimensions of collective action, they were limited in two important respects. First, they were primarily concerned with the role of formal NGOs and transnational social movement organizations (TSMOs), reflecting the influence of resource mobilization and international relations perspectives. This obscured the more diffuse formations, including informal collectives and affinity groups, that characterize contemporary transnational activism and the decentralized, dynamic, and rhizomatic nature of transnational movement networks. At the same time, orthodox theoretical perspectives obscured many of the key problems and themes revealed by ethnographic approaches, including the importance of power, political tension, and cultural struggle within transnational movements, as well as issues related to space, place, and knowledge production.

Meanwhile, other volumes paid more attention to the role of culture and identity within transnational movements (Cohen and Rai 2000; Guidry, Kennedy, and Zald 2000), but few of the individual contributions employed ethnographic approaches. The influential collection edited by Sonia Alvarez, Evelina Dagnino, and Arturo Escobar—*Cultures of Politics, Politics of Cultures* (1998)—featured a section on transnational activism that addressed the themes of globalization, culture, digital technologies, and scale, but these chapters, although ethnographic, were not based on longer-term fieldwork.

More recently, scholars from this early wave of research on transnational activism have begun to incorporate innovative frameworks, reflecting the cross-fertilization of ideas and the unique characteristics of contemporary transnational collective action. Joe Bandy and Jackie Smith's *Coalitions across Borders* is particularly noteworthy in this respect. In the book's introduction, the editors recognize the importance of informal modes of transnational coordination, although, as they suggest, sustained modes of cross-border coordination and cooperation often require more formalized structures (2005, 4). The question remains as to whether formal structures need to resemble traditional hierarchical organizations of the past (Juris 2008a). The example of the social forums suggests that they need not (Juris 2008a; Jackie Smith et al. 2007). Just as importantly, Bandy and Smith emphasize cultural and political conflict, power imbalances, resource inequalities, and related obstacles to transnational organizing.

Meanwhile, scholars such as Donatella della Porta and Sidney Tarrow have continued to use the dominant political process model to explain transnational activism (see Tarrow and della Porta 2005),[10] although they have begun to employ novel concepts and perspectives to analyze the distinctive characteristics of the global justice movements and related forms of transnational collective action. For example, della Porta (2005, 2007) has developed the idea of "tolerant" identities to understand the multiple, shifting attachments developed by global justice activists associated with loose, decentralized organizational forms. In *Globalization from Below* della Porta and her co-editors further explore these issues in their survey-based study of Italian global justice activists, as well as other critical themes, including computer-mediated communication, the rise of a new politics, and the search for new forms of democratic practice (della Porta et al. 2006). For his part, Tarrow (2005; see also Tarrow and McAdam 2005) has usefully applied notions such as scale shift, diffusion, and the internalization and externalization of protest to explain key mechanisms associated with transnational activism. Scholars such as Thomas Olesen (2005a) and Ruth Reitan (2007) have used a variety of these conceptual tools to analyze specific networks in the context of global justice and Zapatista solidarity activism. These and related approaches have greatly enhanced our understanding of the dynamics of transnational activism, but they too often neglect issues related to power, inequality, and cultural struggle that are more clearly revealed through the ethnographic encounter (but see Reitan 2007). Tellingly, in their summary of methodological innovations used to capture the new realities of transnational contention, Tarrow and della Porta refer to the Internet, activist surveys, and comparative research designs, but nowhere do they mention ethnography (2005, 234).

Beyond traditional social movement theory, the most influential macro-level approaches to the study of transnational collective action have come from scholars interested in the relationship between communication networks, new digital technologies, and distributed networked modes of organization (Arquilla and Ronfeldt 2001; Castells 1997; Hardt and Negri 2004).[11] Manuel Castells paved the way by identifying a "networking, decentered form of organization and intervention, characteristic of the new social movements, mirroring, and counteracting, the networking logic of domination in the information society" (1997, 362). Echoing Castells's analysis, Hardt and Negri made the even bolder claim that the networking logic of Empire has given rise to a new form of networked counter-power: the multitude—"an open and expansive network in which all differences can be experienced freely and equally, a network that provides the means of encounter so that we can work and live in common" (2004, xiii–xiv). However, it is important to remember that networks are also associated with imperial domination, repression, and informational capitalism. As Jackie Smith points out, "The opponents of the global 'movement of movements' . . . also share the network form" (2008, 34). Smith is

referring to networks of multilateral institutions, transnational corporations, and neoliberal governments. Yet, as Luis Fernandez argues, global
police formations assume a networked form as well (2008). Macro-level
approaches to transnationally networked activism have inspired ethnographic analyses that use similar perspectives and concepts in new and
innovative ways. Moreover, many activists themselves, particularly within
the global justice movements, have found ideas such as networks, rhizomes, Empire, and multitude useful in their own theorizing.

This brings us to the recent proliferation of ethnographic writing on
transnational collective action. Hilary Cunningham's analysis of transnational activism among (post)sanctuary activists in Tucson, Arizona, represents one of the first ethnographic accounts of cross-border organizing
(1999). Cunningham was particularly interested in the role of the imaginary, in her case how "the global" is constructed as an important part of
political identity and practice. She conducted research during two phases:
the height of the sanctuary movement in the 1980s and the postsanctuary
period of solidarity activism in the mid-1990s. She found that by the
latter period, postsanctuary activists had begun to incorporate many of
the terms and concepts that had been developed by social scientists, including the discourse of transnational social movements and global civil
society, raising an important *representational conundrum* with respect to
the role of analysis when native and analytic categories coincide (1999; see
also Escobar 2008; Riles 2000). Her research also uncovered trends related to transnational activism that would become increasingly apparent
over the next several years, including the widespread use of the Internet,
the rise of a flexible politics, and an expanded sense of global imagination
and possibility.

Transnational feminist organizing has provided a key theme and a
source of inspiration for much early ethnographic work on transnational
activism. Sonia Alvarez's essay on transnational feminist "webs" and the
tensions that arise when feminist movements "go global" was pioneering in this regard (1998). Through an analysis of parallel NGO-sponsored
women's forums held in conjunction with major UN conferences, as well
as the history and politics of feminism in Latin America, Alvarez explores
a growing rift between what she calls the "ethical-cultural" and "structural-
institutional" dimensions of second-wave feminism in the region. This
focus on plural feminisms and the cultural-political struggles between
them, particularly during emerging transnational spaces of encounter,

prefigures many of the themes we address here, including power imbalances and unequal access to cultural, material, and political resources.

Millie Thayer picked up on these issues in her analysis of transnational feminism in northeastern Brazil (2001, see also 2010). Against Manuel Castells's (1998) claim that certain places are becoming structurally irrelevant, Thayer argues that transnational forces are leading to new kinds of movement even in historically marginalized regions such as the Brazilian *sertão* (the semiarid region in the northeast of Brazil). In particular, transnational feminism has articulated local, regional, and transnational women's organizing in complex, and often contradictory, ways. Thayer's fine-grained ethnographic analysis highlights the processes of contestation, negotiation, and appropriation that characterize transnational gender politics. In her ethnographic account of the strategies and practices of an autonomous women's labor collective in Nicaragua, Jennifer Bickham Méndez similarly shows how local, national, and transnational processes articulate in complex ways (2005; see also Desai 2009; Moghadam 2005, 2008).

Other influential ethnographic analyses of transnational activism include Anna Tsing's highly acclaimed account of translation, difference, and the construction of globality among transnational forest activists in Indonesia (2005), and Arjun Appadurai's study of deep democracy and horizontal, global networking among urban activists in Mumbai (2002). However, transnational Zapatismo and global justice movements (including the World Social Forum process) have provided the most fertile terrain for the ethnographic analysis of transnational social movements in recent years, including work by many authors in this volume (Caruso 2004, 2005b, 2012; Casas-Cortés, Osterweil, and Powell 2008; Conway 2012; Escobar 2001, 2008; Graeber 2009; D. Hess 2007a, 2009; Juris 2004a, 2004b, 2005a, 2008a; Khasnabish 2007, 2008; Maeckelbergh 2009; Osterweil 2004a, 2004b; Pleyers 2008, 2011; Routledge 2008; Routledge and Cumbers 2009).

For example, Jeffrey Juris's ethnography of the global justice movements is, in part, a response to the macro-level theories of distributed network structure and technology within contemporary movements (2008a). Carving out a practice-based approach to networks, Juris argues that global justice movements involve an increasing confluence among network technologies, network-based organizational forms, and network-based political norms, mediated by activist practice. In this sense, the network, beyond technology and organizational infrastructure, has also become a widespread cultural ideal, a model of and for emerging forms of radical, directly democratic practice. The complex, dynamic relationship between imagination and political practice is also the principal focus of Alex Khasnabish's ethnographic study of the often unexpected, unpredictable consequences of the resonance of Zapatismo among diverse communities of activists in Canada and the United States (2008). Khasnabish's analysis explores the forms and consequences of Zapatismo's resonance for North American activists who, rather than simply "importing" Zapatismo, have encountered it through politico-cultural and technological processes of transmission and translation. And, having found their political imaginations radicalized, activists sought to ground this resonance in their own living fabric of struggle. At the same time, global justice networks are marked by tensions, power imbalances, and cultural struggles, particularly given the diversity of activists' cultural and political backgrounds and the existence of competing organizational logics, giving rise to what Juris calls the "cultural politics of networking" (2008a).

Actor-network theory (ANT) and complexity theory have also inspired recent ethnographic work on the global justice movements. Complexity theory, which emphasizes the recursive self-generation of complex, adaptive systems through myriad micro-level interactions, has become increasingly influential among activists and social theorists (see Chesters and Welsh 2006; Escobar 2001, 2008; Maeckelbergh 2009; Sterpka, this volume). In his recent ethnography of the Proceso de Comunidades Negras (Process of Black Communities) on Colombia's Pacific coast, including the group's participation in transnational global justice networks such as Peoples' Global Action, Arturo Escobar suggests that social movements possess complex, adaptive features (2008). Although the networks he studies are hybrid formations, involving aspects of hierarchy and more diffuse, horizontal "meshworks,"[12] they exhibit many features associated with the latter, as they are "based on decentralized decision making, self-organization, and heterogeneity and diversity," and develop "through their encounter with their environments, although conserving their basic organization, as in the case of autopoietic entities" (274). In other chapters, Escobar explores the role of place, culture, and power in the context of transnational organizing, and the critical role of social movements as producers of insurgent knowledges.

For his part, Paul Routledge has drawn on ANT to develop an analysis of the shifting patterns of connection, association, and translation within the Peoples' Global Action network based on ethnographic fieldwork in

Bangladesh (2008; see also Routledge and Cumbers 2009). Whereas ANT has been silent on issues of power and human agency, particularly given its view of reality as an effect of sociotechnical networks composed of heterogeneous chains of human and nonhuman elements (Callon 1991; Latour 1993; see also Escobar 2000; Juris 2004a), Routledge argues that power differentials and intentionality are central to shaping the contours of network association. In arguing for a corrective to ANT, this analysis resonates with many of the ethnographic themes we have highlighted, including the critical role of practice, culture, and power within networked spaces of transnational encounter. At the same time, as discussed below, such insights largely flow from a critically engaged position within the networks being examined.

Before moving on, it is important to specify two kinds of activism that fall outside of this volume's bounds. First, there has been a growing ethnographic literature on NGOs in anthropology and related fields, much of it concerned with issues related to globalization, development, and transnational civil society (see Bornstein 2003; Fisher 1997; Hemment 2007; Markowitz 2001; Riles 2000). NGO-based activism is an important dimension of contemporary politics, but its relation to neoliberalism has been hotly debated, with some scholars and activist groups even suggesting that NGOs are complicit with neoliberal rule (Hardt and Negri 2000; INCITE! 2007; Postero 2006; Speed 2007). Although some progressive NGOs participate in wider social movements, their position is frequently marked by their implication within and reliance on dominant architectures of power and funding. None of this is to say that NGOs cannot be significant vehicles for social change, only that there is an important distinction to be made between formal organizations and more noninstitutional, grassroots, and confrontational forms of mobilization.

Second, exciting research on the frontier of anthropology and science and technology studies (STS) has also addressed various types of activism in a global context. Whereas David Hess (2007a, 2009, this volume) has examined the more or less organized activity of localist movements in response to corporate globalization, other scholars, such as Kim Fortun (2001) and Christopher Kelty (2008), have explored more diffuse kinds of global activism not directly associated with collective political actors: the former concerned with environmental advocacy following the Bhopal disaster, and the latter revolving around a loose network of free software writers and activists. Fortun's experimental, self-reflexive ethnography of transnational advocacy is more focused on formal NGOs than grassroots movements, while Kelty's emphasis is less related to activism and social movements than to a set of discourses and practices surrounding free software as a recursive public. In contrast, this volume is concerned with expressly organized, oppositional, and grassroots activism that belongs more properly to the field of social movements.

NETWORKED SPACES OF
TRANSNATIONAL ACTIVIST ENCOUNTER

Covering an admittedly partial terrain of transnational activism, this volume takes up diverse analytic challenges guided by four key themes: emerging subjectivities; discrepant paradigms; transformational knowledges; and subversive technologies. Using each of these themes as a lens, the chapters render diverse dimensions of transnational activism and the knowledge work of ethnography in relation to such activism visible in provocative and illuminating ways.

Emerging Subjectivities

Michael Hardt and Antonio Negri (2000, 2004) have posited that through the global, neoliberal, and biopolitical order of Empire, a new revolutionary subjectivity is emerging: the multitude. Rather than a homogeneous, singular historical subject, the multitude is unified by a collective no (to global neoliberal capitalism and liberal democracy) and is marked by many yeses (to diverse alternatives to dominant political, economic, and social processes). Although the notions of multitude and Empire have generated considerable debate (see Brennan 2006; Bull 2005), we invoke these terms as a way of broaching the theme of subjectivity. As a space of encounter, action, and imagination, the transnational is also a space of subjectification.

The notion of the rhizome is another useful guidepost in our analysis of power and subjectivity. For Gilles Deleuze and Félix Guattari (1987), the rhizome requires us to do away with fixed lines and linearity. As a bulb or tuber possessing both shoots and roots, the rhizome's shape is unpredictable and capable of growth across multiple dimensions. The rhizome's process of becoming is influenced by its nonuniform capacity for growth and its engagement with its surroundings. In much the same way, transnational networks and movements are unpredictable, multiscalar, and multidimensional, as well as acephalous, segmented, and reticulate (Gerlach and Hine 1970), constituted by ongoing processes of becoming. Indeed, it is only in attending to the connections that comprise them and the nonisomorphic shapes they take that we can begin to understand their power and capacity to forge new subjectivities.

We also refer to subjectivities in the more concrete sense of diverse political identities based on gender, race, ethnicity, indigeneity, and other social categories. Contemporary social movements involve a multiplicity of subjects such as women, youth, indigenous people, gays and lesbians, students, the unemployed, squatters, landless workers, and so on. These subjectivities comprise what Raul Zibechi refers to in his writings on Latin America as new social movements "from below" (2010). Unlike traditional labor and socialist movements, these new political actors do not merely counteract dominant global networks; they are building a new politics of autonomy and self-management rooted in local territories and identities while also reaching out horizontally across diversity, difference, and geographic space to develop new forms of regional and transnational coordination.

The contributors to this volume explore emerging subjectivities as sites of liberation and foci of tension and conflict. How, asks Juris, does the creation of an intentional space at the U.S. Social Forum (USSF) enhance the visibility and inclusion of some subjects while deemphasizing others, and what is the political significance of this dynamic? Manisha Desai grapples with subjectivity as a scholar-activist critically reflecting on her positionality and on larger debates about scholar-activists and activist-scholars within a feminist space at the WSF. Tracing cross-border political subjectivities, Khasnabish explores the intersection of imagination and politics in a transnational encounter between Northern radicals and the discourse of Zapatismo: can such encounters and their resonances, asks Khasnabish, generate new political possibilities? Finally, Geoffrey Pleyers troubles conventional narratives that delimit the "success" of social struggles in narrowly institutional terms and instead illuminates forms of resistance to corporate globalization that focus on subjectivity, lived experience, and the articulation of alternative ways of being and doing.

Discrepant Paradigms

What comes of our attempts to critically and analytically engage movements for social change is contingent not only on the categories we adopt and our own familiarity with such movements but also on our ethical commitments, cultural backgrounds, and epistemological frameworks. In other words, the political and intellectual "paradigms" (Kuhn 1970) we bring to bear matter, not only analytically but also with regard to political effects. Following Sylvia Escárcega's contribution to this volume, we define a paradigm as the "set of assumptions, concepts, values, and practices that pertains to a specific yet nonbounded worldview of an imagined community of actors." Given that any paradigm imposes a sense of order or meaning, this definition allows us to see that a paradigm is capable of obscuring as much as it reveals. For instance, dominant social movement studies paradigms often narrowly define what counts as movement success by focusing on the impact of movements in the formal spheres of governance and policy (see Amenta and Caren 2004; Giugni, McAdam, and Tilly 1999).[13] In such a light, most movements follow a standard tragic narrative arc of emergence, contestation, and demobilization (see Tarrow 1998) that casts struggles for social transformation as plagued by socio-political entropy, always failing against the inevitability of their decline.

What would happen if we reject these paradigmatic assumptions and pursue alternative paradigms that unsettle hegemonic forms of politics and knowledge production? Operating from distinct ontological and epistemological premises, such paradigms could be described as discrepant for at least two reasons. First, they contest the authority of explanatory accounts that reduce radical challenges to dominant orders by narrating such challenges within the parameters of established frameworks. Second, rather than foreclosing horizons of possibility, these paradigms suggest the potential for alternative orders that are radically different. What if, asks Escárcega, instead of turning to well-worn techno-scientific models born of European modernity to address the global eco-social crisis, we attune ourselves to the alternative paradigms offered by indigenous peoples for living, working, and relating to Mother Earth? What if instead of paying attention to what is most visible, we attend to, as Vinci Daro exhorts, the encounters and possibilities that occur at the margins of political protest? What if, as Hess suggests, we take seriously the epistemological and ethico-political possibilities and challenges of engaging each other across disciplinary paradigms? Or, as Hess advises, what if we break out of the rigid dichotomy between local and global analytic frames? Such discrepant paradigms destabilize authorized frameworks, paving the way for the envisioning and articulation of new possibilities.

Transformational Knowledges

The knowledge categories we deploy affect how we understand social action. Indeed, our epistemological and ontological grounding has profound consequences for the way we represent the lives of others. Academic disciplines are by no means absolved of responsibility for the effects of their knowledge production (Lal 2002). Our volume specifically attempts to understand the work of subjects deeply invested in reimagining and reconstructing their worlds as they resist the violence of the neoliberal order.

This relates to the vital, yet often overlooked work of social movements that Ron Eyerman and Andrew Jamison refer to as "cognitive practice" (1991). In this sense, as Maribel Casas-Cortés, Michal Osterweil, and Dana Powell suggest in their chapter, social movements should be viewed as knowledge producers (see also Casas-Cortés, Osterweil, and Powell 2008; Conway 2005a; Escobar 2008; D. Hess 2007a; Santos 2008), which is one of the premises of the Social Movements Working Group (SMWG), founded in 2003 at the University of North Carolina, Chapel Hill. Contributors in this section critically assess various kinds of academic and movement knowledge and explore ways of knowing otherwise among engaged researchers participating in projects of social transformation. Giuseppe Caruso invites us to consider the contours of transformative ethnography, which aims to cultivate the conditions necessary for transformative action. In a similar vein, Paul Routledge considers the obligations and responsibilities of activist ethnographers, and in the process compels us to examine what it might mean for ethnographers to live up to commitments of solidarity with respect to urgent social justice struggles. Casas-Cortés, Osterweil, and Powell ask us to reflect on the methodological, epistemological, and political implications of their premise that movements are knowledge producers and that ethnographers are but one actor in a crowded field of knowledge production. Janet Conway similarly interrogates the potential contributions of ethnography to our understanding of transnational political dynamics, such as the social forum process: What can ethnography achieve within transnationally networked political spaces? What are its limitations?

Subversive Technologies

The networked spaces of transnational encounter we explore in this volume are thoroughly intertwined with new digital technologies. The Internet provides a key technological tool for the spaces, networks, and movements we consider; it also shapes their emerging visions, practices, and identities. With respect to the global justice movements, Juris has identified a powerful "cultural logic of networking," a set of "broad guiding principles, shaped by the logic of informational capitalism, which are internalized by activists and generate concrete networking practices" (2008a, 11). Although always uneven and contested, this logic emerges as global justice activists interact with new digital technologies in everyday social contexts. Although some scholars refer to wider social technologies in a Foucauldian sense (see Casas-Cortés, Osterweil, and Powell, this volume), the contributions in this section specifically address computer-related technologies. Even in this more restricted sense, technology is infused with questions of epistemology, power, and subjectivity. For example, activists use the Internet to communicate and coordinate with one another across vast distances, but they also employ digital technologies to experiment with innovative forms of collaborative practice within virtual and physical spaces. Online tools, such as movement-related forums, blogs, wikis, and emerging forms of social networking represent new modes of collectively producing and distributing knowledge in ways that reflect activists' emerging utopian subjectivities and ideals with respect to directly democratic practice, horizontal coordination, and the free and open flow of information (Juris 2005a, 2008a, 2012). Although new digital technologies may enhance the relative power of grassroots movements vis-à-vis the state, they also constitute sites for the expression of internal tensions and power struggles.[14]

Contributors to this section examine diverse technologies that operate across multiple scales and spaces. Jeffrey Juris, Giuseppe Caruso, Stéphane Couture, and Lorenzo Mosca ask what kinds of politics and exclusions are enacted in the use of free/libre and open-source software (FLOSS) within transnationally networked spaces, such as the social forums. M. K. Sterpka asks how we might better understand the aspirations and contributions of struggles for information freedom by critically examining pre-Internet civil society networks in historical and ethnographic contexts. Explicitly positioning herself in the midst of a transnationally networked, Internet-based social change project—Indymedia—Tish Stringer probes the possibilities for change when scholars work within the academy through their activism while also supporting social movements as academics.

This volume is situated within the post-1980s critique of ethnography and the reconfiguration of ethnographic fieldwork in two fundamental ways. First, it contributes to the recent expansion of scale and complexity in the construction of the "field." The critique of a single, bounded location for fieldwork cut off from wider processes and political economic trends was clearly articulated by George E. Marcus and Michael M. J. Fischer in their influential book *Anthropology as Cultural Critique* (1986). Their idea of a *multilocale* ethnography foreshadowed the recent emergence of multi-sitedness as a strategy for depicting a complex world characterized by increasing connectedness and translocal flows (Candea 2009). This expanding scale of fieldwork has given rise to a radical questioning of the idea of the "field" itself. The Malinowskian ideal of the ethnographic field site as a village coterminous with a discrete, bounded people and culture no longer holds water (if it ever did) in a world of complex transnational flows (Gupta and Ferguson 1997a). The difference between home and field is thus rendered blurry, requiring us to reconstruct the field anew (Amit 2000).

One strategy for reconstructing the field has been to demarcate a series of multiple sites that are connected by translocal flows of people, ideas, things, and conflicts (Marcus 1995). Such multisited strategies have been influential over the last decade and a half, yet they have also been criticized for their lack of "depth" (Falzon 2009), and their perhaps paradoxical tendency toward holism (Candea 2009). Given our focus on networked spaces of transnational encounter, the chapters in this volume all speak to issues of space, place, and scale—either directly or implicitly. However, the authors pursue a range of ethnographic strategies for doing so, involving varying degrees of emplacement and mobility. Some emphasize local places and how they interact with translocal forces, flows, and connections, constituting examples of what Michael Burawoy refers to as "global ethnographies." Others pursue multisited strategies (Marcus 1995), traveling within and through various networked spaces. However, most of the chapters feature a combination of ethnographic strategies, involving aspects of each of these ideal types. In this sense, studying networks that are locally situated yet globally connected calls for novel modes of networked ethnography (see Casas-Cortés, Osterweil, and Powell, and Sterpka, both in this volume). As Arturo Escobar puts it, this would "relate place-based, yet transnationalized, struggles to transnational networks," and "investigate the ways in which . . . actors relate to both places and spaces as they 'travel' back and forth" (2001, 163).

This volume should also be seen as a response to the crisis of ethnography in the wake of the Writing Culture critique of the 1980s, particularly the links between ethnography, colonialism, and power (Clifford and Marcus 1986). Any project with such a strong emphasis on ethnography has to confront inevitable questions regarding the power relations embedded in the ethnographic process. This is even more the case when engaging social movements that explicitly challenge unequal power relations in the context of broad-based struggles for social justice.

As Shannon Speed (2006, 2008) maintains, the recognition since the 1970s and 1980s of anthropology's history of colonial entanglement, together with the recognition of our situatedness as ethnographers and the potentially negative, if unintended, consequences of our ethnographic depictions of others (see Clifford and Marcus 1986; Marcus and Fischer 1986), has given rise to two reactions. Some anthropologists have responded to the crisis of representation via theoretical and textual experimentation, primarily engaging in self-reflexive cultural critique. Others have forged more collaborative, activist approaches involving a commitment to the human rights and political struggles of our interlocutors as well as an attempt to create more equitable relations of research. This second current has led to a proliferation of politically committed strategies: action research, engaged research, advocacy research, participatory action research, collaborative ethnography, and militant anthropology (Hale 2008; see also Burdick 1995; Lamphere 2004; Lassiter 2005; Low and Merry 2010; Mullins 2011; Sanford and Angel-Ajani 2006; Scheper-Hughes 1995). Marcus (2009) himself has noted a significant rise in the numbers of graduate students coming to anthropology to work on activist-oriented projects. Although the literature on engaged, activist modes of research has not always addressed similar debates among feminist scholars (Méndez 2008; see also Maguire 1996), this trend builds on decades of politically committed feminist research situated within and/or drawing inspiration from diverse feminist movements inside and outside of the academy (see Cancian 1992; Harding 2005; Mohanty 2003; Naples 2003). The trend is also related to recent efforts to challenge the continuing hegemony of universalist objectivism within a still largely white, Eurocentric university context (see Costa Vargas 2006; Wallerstein et al. 1996; Zuberi and Bonilla-Silva 2008).

The chapters in this volume are clearly linked to this second tradition. However, recent accounts have exaggerated the contrast between *activist research* and *cultural critique* (see, e.g., Hale 2006, 2008; Speed 2006, 2008). According to Charles Hale, *activist research* refers to a collaborative method involving explicit alignment with a group in struggle. While practitioners of *cultural critique* express political alignment through the content of the knowledge produced (and, we would add, the style of theory and writing), activist researchers enact their political engagements by establishing relationships with a politically organized movement or group (2006).[15] This distinction has two consequences. First, activist researchers have dual loyalties—one to the academy and another to a broader social struggle—while proponents of cultural critique "collapse these dual loyalties into one" (100). Second, the latter are often particularly concerned with generating theoretical and analytic complexity and sophistication, and thus tend to be averse to "the politically induced analytic closure that activist research often requires" (101). Even positivist methods reviled by postmodernists and politically engaged scholars may be precisely the kind of research that our allies request.[16] The contributors to this book share this schizophrenic yet productive sense of divided loyalties, but not necessarily the thrust toward theoretical and analytic closure, which may proscribe other modes of activist research (see also Osterweil 2008, and Casas-Cortés, Osterweil, and Powell, this volume).

When we situate ourselves within a particular network or struggle, and are thus a constitutive part of rather than an outside supporter of that struggle, our contributions as researchers become potentially less instrumental and more strategic (see Méndez 2008). Given that strategizing is inherently open-ended and exploratory, and often involves the kind of search for new analytic categories and theoretical approaches that Hale associates with cultural critique, a strict divide between activist research and cultural critique is not necessarily warranted. At the same time, in common with the tradition of cultural critique, the chapters that follow also share a commitment to self-reflexivity. Interestingly, the social movement networks considered here are by nature self-reflexive, engaged in the collaborative production and circulation of knowledge by and for the networks themselves (Juris 2008a). In this sense, activist research might also be seen as a creative process of collective theorization and knowledge production carried out from inside social movements. Stevphen Shukaitis and David Graeber capture this collaborative, exploratory spirit when they describe "a process of collective wondering and wandering that is not afraid to admit that the question of how to move forward is always uncertain, difficult, and never resolved in easy answers that are eternally correct" (2007, 11). Here *activist research* refuses analytic closure.

This is not to suggest that Hale's view of activist research is wrong, but rather that it points to one among many kinds of activist research. Grassroots communities are often in desperate need of strategically placed allies with access to cultural and material skills, tools, and resources. This kind of traditional solidarity should not be underestimated and is often a matter of life and death (see Sanford and Angel-Ajani 2006). In this volume, however, we stake out a different form of solidarity, one that is reciprocal rather than one way (Waterman 1998). In this sense, each of us is engaged in our own struggles and we each write from an embedded, if at times contradictory, position. Even when we stand in support of other groups, we do so as part of much wider networked spaces of encounter. We are interested in precisely the uneven, power-laden interactions and encounters between groups within these spaces (see Chesters and Welsh 2006). In this sense, studying the cultural logics and practices associated with a particular network requires acting within the network (Juris 2008a; Routledge 2008). Of course, there is a critical class- and power-related dimension to consider: acting and researching from within a network is often facilitated by our collaboration with middle-class actors with whom we are more likely to share a critical, intellectually oriented habitus.[17] The kind of activist research outlined by Hale is perhaps more appropriate to situations where we are working across class and power divides.

Andrew Mathers and Mario Novelli have noted a more general "process of re-engagement among academics" (2007, 230), which can be seen, in part, as a response to the rising poverty, inequality, and social suffering caused by neoliberal globalization (see Bourgois 2006). Calls for a public anthropology and sociology (Burawoy 2005; Lamphere 2004) attest to a growing desire among scholars for their research to be relevant. However, politically engaged research is not just about reaching a wider audience; it is also about how we conduct our research (Calhoun 2008; see also Hale 2008). On the one hand, political engagement means explicitly taking sides, recognizing that even the most seemingly objective accounts have an implicit politics. As Victoria Sanford argues, "activist scholarship reminds us that all research is inherently political—even, and perhaps especially, that scholarship presented under the guise of 'objectivity,' which is really no more than a veiled defense of the status quo" (2006, 14). On the other hand, political engagement also means working together with the subjects of our research. Hale puts it this way, "activist scholars work in dialogue, collaboration, [and] alliance with people who are struggling to better their lives" (2008, 5). Participatory action research (PAR), which involves the collective design and implementation of research between a researcher and an organization or community of stakeholders, represents a particularly radical example of this collaborative ethic (Greenwood 2008; see also Reitan 2007).

At the same time, even PAR is rooted in an a priori separation between research subject and object, regardless of how democratic the relationship between the two might be. This makes good sense for projects where there is a clear divide between the researcher and the group he or she is working with, but it is less appropriate when researchers are trying to understand a network, group, or struggle of which they are a part. In this case, a mode of situated, self-reflexive research is called for that seeks to overcome the divide between subject and object. As feminist scholars have long insisted (see Haraway 1988; Harding 2005; Sprague and Zimmerman 1993), this is not just a question of political utility but is also a matter of generating more adequate knowledge.

With regard to the operation of transnational social movements, for example, Juris (2007, 2008a) has argued that the only way to truly grasp the concrete logic of activist networking is to become an active practitioner. This kind of *militant ethnography* requires becoming directly involved in a particular struggle through activities such as organizing actions and events, facilitating meetings, staking out and supporting positions during discussions and debates, and risking one's body during mass actions. This leads to deeper cognitive understanding and also provides a sense of the embodied emotions generated by activist practice. If it is to be taken seriously, activist-oriented research of any kind has to justify itself in terms of the standards and criteria of the academy (Hale 2008), while simultaneously generating analytic and theoretical insights—regarding movement practices, cultures, and forms; internal relations of power and inequality; organizing strategies and tactics; and the nature of wider social, cultural, political, and economic contexts—that are useful to activists.

The relationship between knowledge production, the intellectual, and social change has long been a site of contestation. Ethnographers have been compelled to address the politics of knowledge precisely because our work is grounded in the lived realities of others. While questions about the ethnographic production of knowledge and related issues of representation surfaced in anthropological circles in the 1980s, critiques of ethnographic knowledge had been raised previously by feminists, indigenous peoples, and anticolonial struggles (L. Smith 1999). At the same time, many anthropologists have worked in a dedicated fashion with research participants and partners to bring tangible benefits to communities (Bourgois 2001; Burdick 1995, 1998; Farmer 2004; Scheper-Hughes 1995). In the past decade, discussion turned toward the subject of activism and the academy and the possibilities and challenges therein (see Casas-Cortés, Osterweil, and Powell 2008; Coté, Day, and de Peuter 2007; Graeber 2004; Hale 2008; Juris 2007, 2008a; Shukaitis and Graeber 2007). In this spirit, this volume seeks to explore the possibilities for elite provinces of knowledge production and dissemination to become sites of liberatory collaboration. What might a radically collaborative ethnography look like?[18] What does it promise and what are the obstacles and challenges to its realization?

Nonetheless, engaged, activist approaches to ethnography are not without their own challenges. These are of at least three varieties: tensions and obstacles in the field, contradictions between academic and activist spaces, and the difficulty of bridging academic and movement audiences. First, despite our best intentions, activist researchers and militant ethnographers often find themselves embroiled in complex arguments and power struggles. It is one thing to declare ourselves in support of a certain movement or group, but what if we disagree with a particular goal or course of action? As active participants it would seem that we should clearly stake out a particular position, but what happens if this undermines our role in the group? Just as difficult are situations where we find ourselves caught negotiating between competing factions (see Speed 2008). Neutrality might seem a desired course, but this is not always an option. In this sense, our goals and responsibilities as researchers and activists do not necessarily coincide.

Second, it is also often difficult to move back and forth between academic and activist spaces. Even when we are able to convince our activist collaborators of our political commitments, finding the time and energy to maintain our activist pursuits beyond the moment of field research, given the enormous pressures to teach and publish in the neoliberal university, is a major challenge. As Routledge (1996a) has pointed out, there is a significant gap between the moment of research, when we are active collaborators with our research hosts, and the moment of writing and publishing, when we are faced with vastly different incentives and institutional rewards (Juris 2008a). One way to negotiate this tension is to transform teaching and publishing into political acts. However, it is important to remember that there are multiple positionalities, multiple strategies for engaging movements, and multiple ways of negotiating the gulf between activist and academic spaces.

This suggests a final tension related to activist ethnography: the divide between academic and movement audiences. Tenure requires that we publish articles in peer-reviewed journals and books with university presses, yet these are often far removed from activist-oriented outlets and circuits of distribution. These distinct modes of knowledge production may lead to very different forms of knowledge. Furthermore, some activists, particularly those who are influenced by the free software movement (see Juris, Caruso, Couture, and Mosca, this volume), are opposed to any form of publication based on intellectual copyright. Of course many of us write for both academic and activist outlets, yet the hope remains that a book such as this can partially transcend the divide between activism and the academy. Whether or not this occurs depends on complex factors such as price, marketing strategy, and the possibility of more open distribution.

THE VOLUME AHEAD

We have tried to maintain a balance between up-and-coming and more-established scholars in this book. There is a fairly even distribution of men and women, but with the exception of two authors from the global South (Desai and Escárcega), the rest of the contributors are from Europe, Canada, or the United States. In terms of discipline, most are anthropologists by training, but there are also sociologists, geographers, and political scientists. This anthropological thrust is reflected in the more interpretivist ethnographic tradition expressed in this introduction. However, several authors employ a more social scientific approach and are more comfortable generalizing from particular ethnographic cases (e.g., Hess, this volume). Nonetheless, we share a commitment to working across disciplinary and epistemological boundaries. Moreover, although most of us are situated in the academy, we are all dedicated to bridging the gap between academic and activist work, while some of us are primarily engaged in independent research and activism.

Following this introduction is a section on emerging subjectivities. In his contribution, Juris explores the dynamics of race, class, and political subjectivity at the USSF. Through an ethnographic account of the 2007 USSF in Atlanta, Juris examines one high-profile attempt to confront the tension between directly democratic organization and the goal of racial and class diversity within radical social movements by establishing an *intentional* space. He argues that USSF organizers implemented an intentional organizing strategy by focusing on and specifically recruiting grassroots base-building groups. This strategy achieved a significant degree of racial and class diversity, but it deemphasized political and ideological diversity as larger NGOs, liberals, white radicals and anarchists, organized labor, and mainstream environmentalists and feminists were largely excluded from the organizing process. At the same time, given the strong desire among participants to overcome past exclusions, the privileging of intentionality over horizontality and openness was widely viewed as legitimate, even among those excluded from the organizing process.

In chapter 2, Khasnabish examines the transnational resonance of Zapatismo among activists in Canada and the United States. Pushing beyond a politics of solidarity to consider how transnational Zapatismo has generated new political imaginations and political subjectivities, Khasnabish argues for the utility of ethnographically informed analyses of radical expressions of political possibility. Drawing on fieldwork with North American activists inspired by the Zapatista struggle, Khasnabish probes the dynamics, promises, and pitfalls of a specific manifestation of the radical imagination. Since institutional transformation is a necessary but not sufficient element of social change, attending to the subjectivities emerging from social justice struggles makes analytic sense and facilitates the exploration of social movements as generators of radical sociopolitical possibility that exceed conventional measures of political success.

Based on participant observation at the Feminist Dialogues (FD) during the WSFs in Porto Alegre, Nairobi, and Bélem, in chapter 3 Desai analyzes the shifting spatial and power relations between and within the FD and the WSF. She examines how dialogue operates as a transnational feminist practice, arguing that although the FD is imagined as a dialogic space, it has produced limited exchanges—primarily among the organizers—and as dialogue became the predominant concern of activists, its original aims of making the WSF more feminist and energizing transnational feminist organizing were undermined. She also reflects on the relationship between feminist activism and feminist writing as a way to contribute to academic and activist transnational feminist practices by showing how our concepts and research strategies can contribute, albeit in a limited way, to diverse forms of political activism. In the section's final chapter, Pleyers employs a Tourainian lens to explore the subjectivities and grammars of experience emerging among distinct yet transnationally linked movements in Mexico, Argentina, and Belgium: the Zapatistas in Chiapas, alter-activists in Mexico City, the *piqueteros* (picketers) in Buenos Aires, and a social center in Liège. Pleyers argues that an ethnographic focus can elucidate the noninstitutional dimensions of such movements, including their favoring of horizontal and participatory organization, their reinvesting of local territories with meaning, and their privileging of learning by experience through ongoing processes of experimentation.

The chapters in the next section explore the dynamics of transnational social movements from diverse analytic perspectives related to activism and ethnography, suggesting the need for a shift toward nondualistic, noninstitutional, and noncentralizing frameworks. The chapters also deal with the discrepant paradigms proposed by movements. For example, in chapter 5 Escárcega provides an ethnographic analysis of the activities of the global indigenous movement, including network building, the development of common political agendas, and the negotiation of discourses on indigeneity. Escárcega argues that while in past decades indigenous struggles aimed to establish new relations with states and societies through legal instruments, indigenous intellectuals and activists today are participating in networked spaces of transnational encounter such as the UN and the social forums to establish new political alliances, empower new movement actors (e.g., indigenous women), and propose alternative cultural paradigms that transform our received understandings of humanity, nature, and the world.

In the next chapter Hess maintains that alternative economy movements should be considered alongside protest-based movements as part of a single family of antiglobalization movements. According to Hess, community-based or localist antiglobalization movements ought to be understood as neither local nor global but rather as simultaneously place-based and transnational. Hess then uses this discussion as a springboard for considering the larger methodological and theoretical issues addressed in this volume and in his own research, specifically the role of ethics in the ethnographic study of antiglobalization movements and the two cultures of ethnography, understood as a humanistic product and a method for social science research.

Daro then considers, in chapter 7, the dynamics of counter-summit protests against meetings of institutions such as the World Trade Organization (WTO) and the most powerful industrialized capitalist countries (the G8, now the G20) as transnational spaces where activists confront and negotiate power. Daro specifically addresses the significance of the local for how global justice activist convergences are "figured" by activists and nonactivists alike. Moving away from a concern with core protest actors to consider other participants—police, bystanders, local shop owners, and government officials—Daro develops an innovative approach to the study of protest events based on what she refers to as "edge effects": "the unpredictable, unintentional effects of interactions across social, political, and cultural boundaries, or edges, marked by different interpretive lenses and different relationships to global processes." Daro argues that shifts in the meanings and trajectories of activists' practices and alliances in *edge zones* during large protest actions merit ethnographic attention to reveal the complex dynamics that are often obscured by traditional approaches in the study of social movements.

The next section foregrounds the transformational knowledges arising at the intersection of contemporary social movement practice and ethnographic fieldwork. In chapter 8, Casas-Cortés, Osterweil, and Powell combine insights of experimental ethnography with a body of interdisciplinary work that conceives of social movements as knowledge producers. Based on fieldwork with Native American environmental justice movements and global justice collectives in Spain and Italy, Casas-Cortés, Osterweil, and Powell argue that the role of ethnography should be seen not in terms of explanation or representation but as translation and weaving, processes in which the ethnographer is one voice in a crowded field of knowledge producers. Ethnographic translation enables the ethnographer's participation in the creation of new and different worlds, constituting a vital form of political intervention.

In the next chapter Caruso develops an innovative model of transformative ethnography based on his experience as a mediator and his ongoing fieldwork with the social forum process. Transformative ethnography generates knowledge that is nonprescriptive, nondirective, and collaboratively generated as a process of recognition, adaptation, and transformation between multiple actors. Highlighting recurring patterns of concern, transformative ethnographers can contribute to processes of theory making and political deliberation toward transformative action within transnational networks. In so doing they are aware that, while patterns may emerge out of interaction, such interaction is mediated by cultural, social, and political differences and the frictions that arise from them.

In chapter 10, Routledge explores the dynamics of solidarity associated with activist ethnographies, involving an immersion in the field and in the practices being examined. This requires critical engagement with resisting others inside *embodied terrains of resistance*. Based on his years of engaged ethnographic research among transnational activists in places such as India, Bangladesh, and the United Kingdom, Routledge argues that activist ethnography is animated by a commitment to action, reflection, and empowerment—on the part of the ethnographer and of others who resist—to forge bonds of solidarity and challenge oppressive power relations.

In chapter 11, Conway considers the new forms of ethnographic knowledge that can be produced about the WSF as a transnational, movement-based, multisited process. Through an ethnographic analysis of the participation of indigenous movements in the WSF she makes five related arguments: (1) ethnographic approaches are able to ground the production of particular transnationalisms in concrete practices and places; (2) the ethnographic focus on locating and contextualizing practices and discourses within their own lifeworlds and in their own terms rightly considers the agents of these practices and discourses as subjects rather than objects and as producers of the transnational and of transnational social movements; (3) the production of knowledge about others has been problematized and politicized as a result of the epistemological and ethical debates about the practice of ethnography that have intensified over the last decade; (4) ethnographic sensitivity to lived realities allows social diversity to come more fully into view, troubling monolithic constructions and perceptions of homogeneity while helping to counter Eurocentrism and positivism; and (5) ethnography in and of itself is not analytically self-sufficient.

The final section explores the links between new, potentially subversive technologies, ethnography, and activism within networked spaces of transnational encounter. In her chapter, Sterpka examines a lesser-known history of transnational civil society computer organizing that began in the 1970s and laid the groundwork for contemporary struggles by establishing early on the role of networks, user protocols, and methods of engagement for online mobilization. Using historical and ethnographic analysis, Sterpka highlights the labor of a small group of transnational activists in the early days of computer-mediated communication as well as the formative phase of deep democratic politics that arose from a postcolonial critique of the global economy. Sterpka introduces the term *social emergence* to highlight continuities between activist practices and social studies of complexity, which are well suited to analyzing the communicative interactions of activists articulated through social networking and information systems, reinforcing an overall reticulate structure.

Moving to the contemporary period, in chapter 13, Stringer examines the rise of new modes of collaborative production inside the transnational Indymedia network, and addresses three related tensions associated with the use of technologies and the open, collaborative ethic of the Indymedia network. First she explores how Indymedia activists use "masks" as a response to surveillance and, paradoxically, as a way to maintain openness and visibility. She then considers the tensions associated with her relationship to the Indymedia network, which revolves around two competing poles: activism—being inside a movement—and the academy. In an attempt to bridge this dichotomy, Stringer constructs a hybrid position, which, like the mask, allows her to inhabit and speak to multiple communities. But this alternative position is also haunted by the figure of the snitch, one that is deeply problematic for academics circulating among and writing about political activists.

In chapter 14, Juris, Caruso, Couture, and Mosca conduct a collaborative transnational ethnographic exploration of the *cultural politics of technology* within the social forums by analyzing the political goals and struggles over FLOSS and wider technological infrastructures within the social forum process. The authors contend that conflicts over specific uses and configurations of computers, software, and technologies are cultural, reflecting distinct visions and understandings of what software and technology mean. In this sense, the authors argue that decisions about technological infrastructure are not primarily technical but rather political. While free software, in particular, can be seen as reflecting the open, collaborative, and nonproprietary nature of the forum, the authors also suggest that, similarly, struggles surrounding software and technology reflect conflicts over the nature of the forum itself. The conclusion then ties together the volume's principal themes while further exploring some of the political possibilities, limitations, and tensions of activist ethnography and the kinds of networked movements and spaces of encounter explored in the preceding chapters.

NOTES

1 The caracoles, regional seats of the new autonomous Zapatista governing councils called the Juntas de Buen Gobierno, were created in 2003 to replace the former *aguascalientes*, which were regional places of encounter for Zapatista communities and civil society. For more on the development and implementation of autonomy in the Zapatista communities, see Barmeyer 2009; Earle and Simonelli 2005; and Speed 2007. For a more general analysis of the Zapatista vision of indigenous autonomy, see Nash 2001.

2 This opening vignette is based on fieldwork carried out by Jeffrey S. Juris during the first two Gatherings of the Zapatista Pueblos with the Pueblos of the World, the first of which took place in Chiapas in the caracol of Oventik (December 30, 2006 to January 2, 2007), and the second in the caracoles of Oventik, Morelia, and La Realidad (July 20 to 29, 2007). Juris translated the quotes into English.

3 The critique of Zapatista communities for selling Coca-Cola is a common one among Northern activists, but it is generally not expressed in public forums. This issue has also stirred significant debate, as many in the solidarity community defend the Zapatistas, arguing that Coca-Cola is a sensible alternative given the shortage of potable water, and that the communities are governed democratically, so if members want to drink Coca-Cola, they have every right to do so.

4 The Sixth Declaration of the Lacandon Jungle is the most recent in a series of communiqués issued by the EZLN since the uprising began in 1994. The Sexta, as it is widely known in Spanish, was released in June 2005 after a long period of silence, and provided an analysis of the situation in Chiapas, Mexico, and the world followed by an explanation of the Zapatistas' anticapitalist vision, the rise of the caracoles and Juntas de Buen Gobierno, and the EZLN's plan for building alliances with other anticapitalist struggles in Mexico and internationally.

5 Within this quote, Marcos actually used the Spanish verb *enlatado*, which is translated as "enclosed" but literally means "canned" or "tinned," making a poetic play on the Spanish word for can, *lata*.

6　By also focusing on the movements, networks, and activist communities in the global North that have been influenced by Zapatista discourse and practice, Khasnabish (2008) provides an important corrective to previous approaches to transnational Zapatismo that have exclusively emphasized the strategic framing (Olesen 2005a) or marketing (Bob 2005) of the Zapatista rebellion from the perspective of the Zapatistas.

7　In invoking the transnational we are aware of the considerable scholarship and debate this phenomenon has generated at least since the mid-1990s (see, e.g., Schiller and Fouron 2001; Kearney 1995; Olesen 2005b; M. Smith and Guarnizo 1998).

8　Our approach to theory is similar to, but somewhat less universalizing than, Michael Burawoy's approach in his extended case method (1998). Whereas Burawoy employs particular case studies to test, reject, and/or extend existing theories, our goal is less to build a theoretical corpus than to develop new and/or adapt existing theoretical concepts in ways that help us to understand particular movements and that are also potentially useful to movements.

9　See J. Fox 2002 for a discussion of alternative forms of transnational political organization, including networks, coalitions, and movements, from the lowest to highest levels of integration (see Bandy and Smith 2005). Our notion of "networked space of transnational encounter" is even broader, making room for periodic or even momentary gatherings, actions, and events.

10　Political process theory holds that social movements emerge as a result of expanding political opportunities (institutional access, elite alignments, existence or lack of repression, etc.), which are seized upon by collective actors and sustained through mobilization structures (organizations, networks, channels of recruitment, etc.) and resonant cultural frames (McAdam, McCarthy, and Zald 1996).

11　The argument here is not that distributed network forms are entirely new in the context of grassroots social movements—Gerlach and Hine (1970) wrote many years ago about the networked structure of the Black Power movement as acephalous, segmentary, and reticulate (see Kim 2000)—but rather that new digital technologies significantly reinforce such networked structures, allowing them to operate at a greater distance and on a larger scale (Juris 2008a).

12　Juris (2004b, 2008a) has identified a similar tension between "horizontal networking" and "vertical command" logics.

13　Some of this literature also examines the cultural and biological consequences of social movements (see, e.g., Earl 2004; Guigni 2004, 2008), but the vast majority of work in this area focuses on policy-related outcomes.

14　The chapters assembled in this section take us from the "pre-history" of social movement organizing on the web through the years just before the Arab uprisings and Occupy movements, which, making innovative use of new social media such as Twitter and Facebook (see, e.g., Allagui and Kuebler 2011; Castells 2012; Juris 2012), appeared in 2011 as this volume was nearing completion and going to press.

15   For example, in her study of transnational activism among Indonesian forest activists, Anna Tsing (2005) employs a particular mode of storytelling and ethnographic writing as a form of resistance in itself. She explains, "I have used ethnographic fragments to interrupt stories of a unified and successful regime of global self-management" (271). Practitioners of various forms of activist research, including the authors in this volume, would question whether this is enough.

16   For example, Hale (2006) provides an account of his experience giving expert testimony in support of communal land claims by a Costa Rican indigenous group, the Awas Tingni. As he explains, "Community members asked us to make forceful and authoritative claims to the state and other powerful actors and to put social science to the service of their struggles" (113). Shannon Speed (2006, 2008) writes of similar experiences where she was called upon by a community in Chiapas to provide research to support its claims to indigenous identity. In the process, she had to confront a tension between the community's understanding of identity as fixed and continuous with the past and her anthropological approach to identity as socially constructed, unstable, and changing.

17   For some of us the decision to study with collaborators that have similar class backgrounds and levels of social privilege reflects a political decision to study horizontally in ways that avoid the complex power differentials and exploitative tendencies that often characterize traditional ethnographic research projects with marginalized groups (see Juris 2008a).

18   For a few preliminary examples, see Kelty 2009; Matsutake Worlds Research Group 2009; and Jackie Smith, Juris, and the Social Forum Research Collective 2008.

EMERGING
SUBJECTIVITIES

1

Spaces of Intentionality

Race, Class, and Horizontality at the U.S. Social Forum

JEFFREY S. JURIS

On July 1, 2007, the last day of the first-ever U.S. Social Forum (USSF) in Atlanta, a prominent indigenous leader from Ecuador began reading a statement from the Third Continental Assembly of Indigenous People during the People's Movement Assembly (PMA). The woman who had accompanied him on stage had taken up most of their allotted two minutes, so his time concluded before he was able to finish, and one of the two moderators, an African American woman, asked him to step down. She abruptly grabbed the microphone when he refused to stop. He continued for a short time, but soon left the stage in anger as many in the crowd chanted, "Let him speak, let him speak!" Ten minutes later several dozen indigenous people and their allies marched out of the theater, taking the stage shortly thereafter. The Ecuadoran explained to the audience, "We have to unite, organize, and defend ourselves. I did not want to disappear. I am tired of receiving these kinds of insults. In my country they think we are savages, but they say, 'you look so beautiful.' It cannot happen again at the social forums, not to women, not to indigenous people!" A Native North American leader went on to denounce the history of racist oppression and marginalization of his people, followed by a drumming circle meant to heal and restore the speaker's dignity. The moderator then returned to the stage and apologized for the offense, and everyone began to hug as the crowd chanted, "The People, United, Will Never Be Defeated!"

Since the first World Social Forum (WSF) was held in Porto Alegre, Brazil, in January 2001, the social forums have provided a platform for diverse movements, networks, and organizations to share information, develop common strategies, and build concrete alternatives to neoliberal globalization. Coming on the heels of mass actions in Seattle; Washington, D.C.; Quebec; and Prague, the first WSF allowed global justice activists to articulate positive visions of what they were fighting for. The forums have continued to facilitate movement building while also constituting pedagogical spaces and laboratories for new forms of radical democracy (Fisher and Ponniah 2003; Santos 2006). Meanwhile, what began as a singular event has since become a sustained process involving forums at local, regional, and global levels. As the forums intersect with diverse social, cultural, and political contexts, new issues and tensions come to the fore, reflecting the importance of place within the forum process (Conway 2008b).

Conflicts and struggles within and around the forums specifically reflect key tensions associated with particular organizing processes. The incident at the USSF described above points to important differences between the U.S. and other forums, particularly the European Social Forum (ESF), with respect to the conception and practice of open space. Unlike the WSF International Council (IC), which is based on formal membership, the ESF has been coordinated through an open committee composed of anyone who wants to participate. Given this process, conflicts have tended to emerge around openness and horizontality, while important issues of access and exclusion have remained muted. Since 2003, the USSF process has addressed another key contradiction in the practice of open space: the lack of racial and class diversity. The protest by indigenous peoples during the USSF was motivated by a deep sense of disrespect, yet also reflected the crucial role of identity, voice, and representation in the U.S. context.

Such differences raise key questions regarding the relationship between openness, inclusiveness, and horizontality. Popularized by grassroots autonomous movements in Argentina, the term *horizontality* refers to an increasingly widespread mode of political organizing characterized by nonhierarchical relations, decentralized coordination, direct democracy, and the striving for consensus (Sitrin 2006, vi). As I argue elsewhere, global justice movements are more generally characterized by a "horizontal networking logic" (Juris 2008a). At the same time, many movement sectors, particularly in the global North, have been criticized for their white, middle-class composition (see Martínez 2000; Starr 2004). In contrast, as many participants and observers have noted, the USSF was characterized by significant racial and class diversity (see Guerrero 2008; Ponniah 2008). As we shall see, the USSF's "intentional" organizing strategy helped generate a more inclusive space than previous forums. The participation and leadership of so many working-class people of color, who are among the most directly affected by corporate globalization, was groundbreaking and inspirational. At the same time, openness and horizontality were afforded far less importance.

This chapter addresses a long-standing tension between directly democratic forms of organization and the goal of racial and class diversity within radical social movements (see Epstein 1991; Lichterman 1996; Polletta 2002). Through an ethnographic account of the 2007 USSF in Atlanta, I examine one high-profile attempt to confront this challenge by establishing what I refer to as an "intentional" space.[1] I argue that the intentionality enacted by USSF organizers, which involved targeting and reaching out to grassroots base-building groups, achieved a high level of diversity in racial and class terms, but resulted in the exclusion of many other sectors from the organizing process, including larger NGOs, liberals, white radicals and anarchists, organized labor, and mainstream environmentalists and feminists. Racial and class diversity was thus achieved in practice by favoring a specific model of social change: grassroots organizing, or *movement-building*, within working-class communities of color, de-emphasizing the role of the forum as a "contact zone" for translation, sharing, and exchange among diverse movement sectors (Santos 2006). At the same time, given the strong desire among participants to overcome past exclusions, the privileging of intentionality over horizontality and openness was widely viewed as legitimate, even among those who were excluded from the organizing process. These findings have important implications for democratic practice.[2]

OPEN SPACE AND ITS DISCONTENTS

WSF organizers view the forum as an *open space*, an arena for diverse movements to exchange ideas and information, interact, and coordinate as they struggle to build another world (see Patomäki and Teivainen 2004; Sen 2003). Unlike a political party, no singular identity, program, or perspective holds sway (in theory), allowing multiple networks and groups to interact across their differences. The notion of open space reflects the inscription of a horizontal networking logic within the organizational architecture of the forum (Juris 2005b, 2008a). Given its goal of facilitating deliberation and debate around new ideas, practices, and alternatives to neoliberalism, scholars have characterized the forum as an emerging global public sphere (see Glasius 2005; Jackie Smith et al. 2007; Ylä-Anttila 2005). At the same time, there has been a heated debate about whether the forum should also be viewed as a civil society actor, providing a means for organizations and movements not only to communicate and coordinate with one another but also to articulate common positions and engage in collective action.

In Patomäki and Teivainen's (2004) formulation, the forum has been alternatively construed as a space or a movement, the former resonating with a Habermasian model of deliberative democracy, the latter reflecting a Gramscian emphasis on counter-hegemonic struggle (Glasius 2005). These competing visions reflect a struggle between *networking* and *command* logics constitutive of the forum process itself (Juris 2005b, 2008a). As Jay Smith (2005) suggests, this constitutive tension can also be expressed as an opposition between two conceptions of the public sphere: "discursive" and "agonistic," both of which are reflected in the principles and practice of the forum.

With respect to the former, the forum's open space ideal is often conceived along Habermasian lines as a discursive public sphere where rational-critical debate on public issues is conducted and where decisions are based on the quality of argumentation rather than social status (Calhoun 1992, 1). According to Jürgen Habermas (1989), the "lifeworld," or the sphere of autonomous personal relations guided by communicative interaction, should be shielded from the "system," which is rooted in the logic of money and power (see Calhoun 1992, 30). In this sense, the bourgeois public sphere was meant to be an "institutionalized arena of discursive interaction" (Fraser 1992, 110), where citizens could deliberate and produce critical discourses outside of the market and state. It was also to be open and accessible, and status inequalities would be bracketed (113). Leaving aside for the moment the intractability of inequality (see below), it is important to note that deliberative public spheres tend to deemphasize noncommunicative action (see Jay Smith 2005). In this sense, Habermas has more recently noted that opinion formation should be seen as distinct from the enactment of opinions, an activity reserved for the institutional political sphere (1996, 361–62). Moreover, publics are by definition self-organized: no single person or group can determine their direction or speak on their behalf (Warner 2002).

Although organizers clearly defined the forum as an agonistic space with respect to the World Economic Forum and neoliberalism, it was also seen as a space for movements to communicate with one another, share ideas, and debate alternatives. The WSF Charter of Principles, in particular, has a decidedly Habermasian bent (Jay Smith 2005), as it defines the forum as "an open meeting place for reflective thinking, democratic debate of ideas, formulation of proposals, free exchange of experiences, and interlinking for effective action."[3] Although the WSF encourages planning and coordination, the forum itself does not act. Instead it provides an open space for self-organized discourse and exchange. The charter specifically states that no one can speak in the name of the forum or all of its participants. Moreover, reflecting the Habermasian separation between system and lifeworld, the WSF is viewed as a space without internal struggle, and political parties and military organizations are excluded (Jay Smith 2005, 9). In practice, of course, the forum's open space ideal is often contradicted, as evidenced by the power struggles within various organizing committees, the support of the forums provided by political formations such as the Brazilian Partido dos Trabalhadores (Workers' Party), and the massive public rallies and speeches by leaders such as Luis Inácio da Silva (Lula) of Brazil and Hugo Chávez of Venezuela.

The contrasting view of the forum as a civil society actor reflects an alternative model of democratic practice that Chantal Mouffe (1999) calls "agonistic democracy" (see Jay Smith 2005). Without completely rejecting the deliberative view of the WSF, a focus on its agonistic dimensions reveals critical aspects of the forum that discursive perspectives often overlook. Indeed, as Colin Wright (2005) points out, a critique of the Habermasian public sphere can shed light on the weaknesses of the forum's open space approach. USSF organizers may not have explicitly theorized their actions in such terms, but their intentionality resonates with criticism of deliberative democracy for failing to take into account power relations and the structural and cultural exclusions that are a constitutive feature of public spheres, including the open space of the forum (see Ylä-Anttila 2005).

In the Habermasian public sphere, competing views are articulated as alternative normative claims to be judged by the rational strength of their supporting arguments, but for Mouffe social and political relations are always infused with power. From this perspective, democracy goes beyond deliberation to also encompass political conflict and struggle. As with discursive models of the public sphere, more simplistic conceptions of open space can be similarly criticized for positing a neutral space of rational-critical debate. As many observers have noted, the idea that internal power struggles are absent from the forum is both naive and may reinforce inequalities (Biccum 2005; Juris 2005b; Patomäki and Teivainen 2004; Wright 2005). An agonistic view of the forum means that, internally, diverse movement sectors are always involved in power struggles even as they work to build democratic alliances. Still, one can retain a more nuanced approach to open space as a guiding vision and a process entailing significant conflict and contradiction.

In terms of the relationship between the forum and the outside world, some organizers and participants have criticized the idea of open space for reproducing a liberal notion of civil society based on dialogue rather than collective action. These actors would like to see a greater emphasis on the forum's instrumental as opposed to its prefigurative goals (Juris 2008a; see also Polletta 2002). While recognizing the pedagogical role and the radically democratic spirit of the forum, they would also like to see the development of a common set of strategies and demands, as evidenced by repeated efforts to promote a forum-wide platform, including the G19 statement at the 2005 WSF in Porto Alegre and the Bamako Appeal at the polycentric WSF in Mali the following year.[4]

On another level, with respect to inclusiveness and access, public spheres always already involve significant exclusions, which reproduce prevailing structures of privilege and inequality. As Nancy Fraser suggests, contra Habermas, in highly stratified societies it is not possible to bracket status inequalities. Even if marginalized groups are formally admitted to the public sphere, informal protocols of style and interaction may continue to mark status differences, preventing them from participating on an equal footing. At the same time, subordinate groups often lack the material means to access public spheres, making it difficult for them to participate in the first place (1992, 120).

Such cultural and structural exclusions have also been at work within the forums (Ylä-Anttila 2005). With the exception of the 2004 WSF in

Mumbai and the 2007 WSF in Nairobi (and now the USSF), forum participants have been disproportionately lighter skinned and middle class (R. Álvarez et al. 2008). Such disparities can be partly explained in structural terms as resulting from an unequal access to resources. Indeed, the "tyranny of distance" prevents many poor people from traveling to the forums. As Christopher Chase-Dunn and his co-authors (2008) note, delegates at the various editions of the WSF have tended to come from the host country and surrounding regions. Exclusion has also worked along religious and cultural lines, a point that has been made in terms of Muslim participation (Caruso 2004; Daulatzai 2004). Despite formal openness, structures of privilege and inequality erect "invisible" barriers to participation that are masked by discourses of openness, making it likely that powerful groups will predominate (see Conway 2008b).

THE CONTRIBUTION OF THE USSF: FROM OPEN TO INTENTIONAL SPACE

As I made my way to the staging area before the start of the USSF opening march on June 27, 2007, Tom Goldtooth, the executive director of the Indigenous Environmental Network, was addressing the crowd: "Because we're first inhabitants we understand what racism is, we understand what genocide is, we understand what capitalism is!" Amy Walker, from the Eastern Band of Cherokee, followed Goldtooth, along with Reverend Joseph Lowery, a former civil rights leader who denounced racial and class domination. Thousands of protesters began filing in with colorful signs and T-shirts, representing diverse racial and ethnic communities. The large number of Latinos, African Americans, immigrants, and indigenous people was striking, particularly when compared with past forums and global justice protests in the United States. When the march began I moved to a spot on a nearby hill to watch the various blocs marching by: Grassroots Global Justice, Acorn, Jobs with Justice, Derechos para Todos (Rights for All), the People's Freedom Caravan, the Immokolee Workers, Critical Resistance, and other largely people-of-color groups dedicated to social, economic, and environmental justice. There were also immigrant rights, solidarity, and peace groups, and two anarchist samba bands. Despite the oppressive heat and humidity, the atmosphere was welcoming and festive (see figs. 1.1–1.4). The opening march set the tone for the rest of the forum, where people of color made up at least half, if not more, of

FIGURE 1.1.
Head of the opening march at the USSF on June 27, 2007.

FIGURE 1.2.
Stilt walkers convey key themes and messages at the USSF opening march.

Photos by Jeffrey S. Juris.

FIGURE 1.3.
Radical women's samba band plays during USSF opening march.

FIGURE 1.4.
Street theater performed before the USSF opening ceremony.

all participants, while young women of color assumed visible roles as presenters, plenary speakers, and organizers.

Given previous dynamics of participation within the forums, why was this one so different? How did the USSF achieve such a stunning level of racial and class diversity? These questions assume greater importance in the U.S. context, where the largely white complexion of past global justice actions has drawn criticism since the challenge "Where Was the Color in Seattle?" was issued following the anti–World Trade Organization protests (Martínez 2000; see also Starr 2004). As we shall see, the unprecedented diversity at the USSF resulted from an intentional strategy that reflected the more agonistic dimensions of the forum as well as critiques of the deliberative model of public space. Indeed, racial and class diversity was among the most notable contributions of the USSF, as was its role in linking U.S. movements to the global forum process in a more organized and visible way.

The USSF was a long time in coming. Whereas regional forums were first held in Europe, Asia, and Latin America in 2002, 2003, and 2004, respectively, the initial USSF did not take place until June/July 2007. For years activists at a global level had noted the lack of U.S. presence at the WSF. A review of the statistics, however, suggests that U.S. delegations have been among the largest, even if not on a per capita basis (see Hadden and Tarrow 2007, 221). From 2003 to 2006, for example, the United States had one of the top foreign delegations at every WSF, including the polycentric forum in Caracas.[5] In this sense, U.S. activists have gone to the WSF, but they have not had as visible a collective presence as other contingents. As it turns out, the delayed start of a national-level forum process in the United States was the result of a strategic decision, which will be examined below. At the same time, however, this lag should also be viewed in terms of a set of wider obstacles, including a public opinion less supportive of global justice movements than elsewhere, a discursive shift toward war and terrorism in the U.S. political context, and a greater focus on domestic concerns among U.S.-based movements (Hadden and Tarrow 2007).

The idea for a U.S. Social Forum had been discussed at prior forums, but the project ultimately coalesced under the stewardship of Grassroots Global Justice (GGJ), an alliance founded in June 2002 by a network of grassroots organizations that had gone to the WSF earlier that year. Also in 2002, the IC had asked Jobs with Justice and the Fifty Years Is Enough network, which were on the council, to organize a U.S. forum, but they responded that it was still premature given that the forums were largely unknown within grassroots communities.

GGJ organizers realized that without a coordinated effort to ensure diversity, the open space represented by a U.S. social forum would have informally excluded many historically marginalized groups. When the IC met in Miami in November 2003 during the mobilization against the Free Trade Area of the Americas (FTAA) Summit (and the annual Jobs with Justice meeting), GGJ finally agreed to look into the possibility of organizing a social forum in the United States. A pair of meetings was held in Washington, D.C., in April 2004, one for grassroots groups, who drafted a proposal for the USSF, and one for a larger array of organizations that had been involved in the IC and the WSF. A call then went out to mostly grassroots groups with the goal of forming a national coordinating committee of fifty organizations. By August 2004 only twenty-two organizations had applied, and all were accepted, the majority of which had bases in working-class people-of-color communities. From the beginning, USSF organizers developed a set of intentional strategies that sought to address many of the perceived shortcomings associated with the deliberative model of open space.

At the Moving the Movement Workshop on the first day of the USSF organizers recounted the effort that had been made to ensure that organizations from what they called the "grassroots base-building" sector would assume a lead role and have ownership of the process. As a member of GGJ and the National Planning Committee (NPC) later explained, "If we called for it [the USSF] back in 2002 we wouldn't have seen the diversity that we saw in 2007. There just wasn't enough awareness of the process, and those who were familiar with it tended to be folks who were more white, who came from the anarchist sector, who came from the policy and solidarity groups and some labor, so it would have looked more like Seattle. Not that that was bad, I mean that was a very significant and important historical event, but we felt it was important that it be broadened and deepened, so we pushed back on it" (personal interview, August 24, 2007).[6] USSF organizers thus recognized and addressed the structural barriers that prevent marginalized groups from participating in open spaces.

In the discourse and practice of USSF organizers, the term *grassroots* came to signify a particular kind of organization defined by a specific politics. At the risk of obscuring the political diversity inside the NPC, most, but not all, of the member organizations shared several important characteristics. First, there was a widespread commitment to grassroots organizing, where the goal is to help communities build sustainable organizations that empower their members, achieve tangible victories, and remain accountable to their base (Polletta 2002). This "communitarian" politics is defined by a sense of belonging to a community with a shared history and identity that confronts common challenges through formal organizations rooted in the conditions of daily social life (Lichterman 1996, 106–7). This is in sharp contrast to the highly institutionalized politics of mainstream labor, environmental, and other large nonprofit organizations, as well as the "personalized" politics of middle-class direct action activists, anarchists, and radical environmentalists, which involve a more diffuse sense of belonging, flexible modes of commitment, and an individualized style of grassroots participation (24). Second, and related to this point, the communities that are most directly affected by prevailing structures of exploitation and inequality are viewed as the principal agents of social change. In the United States these include working-class communities, people of color, indigenous peoples, youths, and gays and lesbians, among others. Middle-class and white activists also have an important role to play, but oppressed communities should be at the forefront. Third, whereas traditional community organizing strategies focus on pragmatic politics rooted in people's self-interest (Polletta 2002, 179), many of the organizations in the NPC were committed to building broader multiracial and multiclass movements led by oppressed people of color.[7] Finally, there was also a widespread emphasis on popular education, leadership development, and community empowerment as concrete strategies for building long-term structures of resistance and change.

During USSF workshops and interviews, organizers continually referred to their recruitment strategies in terms of intentionality, reflecting the grassroots politics outlined above. In this sense, USSF outreach specifically targeted working-class people of color. As one NPC member explained, "The intentionality comes in here in that the folks who were brought together in Grassroots Global Justice said if it's going to be in the U.S. it's got to be different. And so part of the difference was that we said we want to focus on grassroots base-building organizations, of and inside working-class communities of color" (personal interview, August 22, 2007). Rather than broadly circulating the initial call for the coordinating committee, the early recruitment strategy was directed. The NPC member continued, "This is where the intentionality comes in, because if we just sent out a broad call, you know, part of the open space is that you make it broad, whoever wants to come, but who would respond would be very different." Throughout the process, the outreach group continued to recruit grassroots people-of-color organizations as anchors within specific regions. This targeted strategy was open in a formal sense, although, the NPC member explained, "Our intentionality was that we might not have asked you to come in, not because we wanted to prevent you from coming, but we only had so many resources." As a result, the NPC would ultimately be led by historically marginalized groups, including people of color (85 percent), women (64 percent), people under the age of forty (51 percent), and those who are queer identified (15 percent) (Guerrero 2008, 179).

In addition to focusing on the grassroots base-building sector, the city of Atlanta was specifically chosen as a site for the USSF to highlight the history of struggle against racism and white supremacy. The USSF was initially scheduled for 2006, but when Hurricane Katrina hit, organizers decided to postpone the event. Organizers then created three bodies: the Organizing Committee in Atlanta, the NPC, and the Southeast Organizing Committee (SOC). Open working groups were also created around logistical tasks, including the website, media, program, outreach, and fundraising. In June 2006, the SOC held a Southeast Social Forum in Durham, North Carolina, which mobilized large numbers of working-class people of color. A similarly diverse Border Social Forum was held in El Paso/Ciudad Juárez the following October. In contrast, a major Northwest Social Forum was scheduled to take place in October 2004, but it was canceled when the Indigenous and Youth Programming Committees withdrew to protest their perceived marginalization (Guerrero 2008, 176).

Ultimately, organizers were pleased with the diversity and representation of the USSF, which included significant participation by grassroots base-building groups: antiracists, farmworkers, environmental justice activists, welfare rights organizations, anti-displacement and anti-gentrification groups, grassroots labor- and community-based organizations, immigrant rights activists, and queer liberationists. Other sectors also had a visible presence, including antiwar movements, fair trade networks, environmentalists, women's groups, direct action activists, anarchists, and alternative media and technology collectives, but the most prominent delegations involved organizations with a base among low-income people of color. As a result, participants included large numbers of working-class African Americans, Latinos, indigenous peoples, and, to a lesser extent, Asians, as well as white and middle-class activists.

USSF organizers also recognized that movements always involve power relations and struggle. Rather than allowing themselves to be dominated by more financially and politically powerful groups led by "white liberals" (Global Exchange and Greenpeace were frequently mentioned), grassroots base-building sectors made a strategic decision to build up their own power base. In addition to large nonprofit organizations, grassroots people-of-color groups also had to position themselves vis-à-vis other sectors: big labor, environmentalists, anarchists, and direct action groups. Organizers thus counter-posed "grassroots" not only to large bureaucratic organizations associated with the "non-profit industrial complex" (IN-CITE! 2007), but also to other kinds of grassroots formations that involve a more personalized politics practiced by many white, middle-class activists: direct action groups, anarchist collectives, and radical environmental groups. As an NPC member explained during the International Perspectives on the WSF session, "We were in Seattle and saw various axes of power: one was dominated by the AFL-CIO and other unions. Another was controlled by the ecologists. Another axis was controlled by a large number of NGOs with large budgets. There was also a fourth axis of power in the streets, which the press called anarchists, the black bloc, youth, or the Direct Action Network. We sent a delegation there from indigenous, African American, Asian, and Latino organizations. We realized we didn't have a platform of power, an identity within this process. . . . We then created a project, a plan for finding new ways of participating to give a voice to the grassroots in the struggle for global justice."

The formation of Grassroots Global Justice should be viewed in this context as part of the process of building a strong identity and power base among grassroots people-of-color organizations. Beyond the forums, this emerging grassroots sector also played a key role in the mobilization against the FTAA Summit in Miami in November 2003 by organizing a caravan and protest bloc called Root Cause. As organizers explained, this sector is underfunded, which presented a significant challenge in organizing the forum. The significant racial and class diversity that characterized the USSF thus resulted, in part, from a conscious and deliberate struggle for hegemony.

Organizers also stressed the movement-building role of the forum.

This is not to say they rejected open space, but they de-emphasized horizontality and openness. On one level, when I asked NPC members about the movement-versus-space debate they often refused to take sides. At the same time, although there were more than nine hundred self-organized workshops, many organizers stressed alliance building, popular education, and deliberate efforts to bring about a particular kind of social change. In this sense, each day of the workshops was organized around a different movement-building theme: consciousness, vision, and strategy. As an NPC member explained during the Moving the Movement workshop, "From the beginning we looked at this as a movement-building process. We looked at this event as just one little step in the road . . . of building the kind of movement that can get us to the point where we can respond to all the stuff going on in the world." In their outreach, organizers thus specifically targeted groups involved in *movement building*, by which they meant community organizing among grassroots communities of color. Although this strategy may have left out other sectors, it allowed organizers to plug into many already existing movements involving working-class people of color. The organizers' movement-building strategy thus helped them achieve a diverse forum in terms of race and class, but this came at the expense of a stronger emphasis on horizontal sharing and exchange across sectors.

Once again, this strategy involved a high degree of intentionality. As an NPC member suggested during the Moving the Movement session, "This is a very intentional process. . . . [I]t's a people-of-color movement, so we're talking about black folks, Latinos, indigenous folks, Asian folks. We led with a process of self-determination." In this sense, organizers promoted a particular vision of movement building rooted in oppressed communities. As a USSF document explains, "There is a strategic need to unite the struggles of oppressed communities and peoples within the United States (particularly black, Latino, Asian/Pacific-Islander and indigenous communities) to the struggles of oppressed nations in the Third World."[8] This model privileges community organizing, popular education, and leadership development. It also reflects an anti-imperialist, nationalist frame that views oppressed communities in the United States as "internal colonies." The statement continues, "The USSF should place the highest priority on groups that are actually doing grassroots organizing with working-class people of color, who are training organizers, building long-term structures of resistance." By reaching out to already existing grassroots people-of-color formations, such as environmental justice networks (see Faber 2005), the Right to the City alliance, and an emerging coalition of community-based workers' centers, organizers ultimately succeeded in turning out their base among working-class people of color.

INTENTIONALITY AND HORIZONTALITY

As I have been arguing, the significant racial and class diversity at the USSF resulted from a deliberate strategy, generating what I refer to as an *intentional space*. Although organizers did not entirely reject the open space model, they placed a greater emphasis on establishing a space with a particular racial and class composition, balance of power, and movement-building strategy. However, this commitment to inclusiveness and diversity was associated with a weaker commitment to horizontality and openness. As a result, racial and class diversity was achieved by privileging a strategy of grassroots organizing over a more open space of convergence among diverse sectors with distinct political visions, organizational practices, and strategies for social change.

Boaventura de Sousa Santos (2006) has argued that the social forums should be viewed as "contact zones," which establish planes of interaction and exchange among movements with distinctive knowledges, temporalities, subjectivities, scalar practices, and alternative visions of social and economic organization. Santos explains, "Such a task entails a wide exercise in translation to expand reciprocal intelligibility without destroying the identity of the partners of translation. The point is to create, in every movement or NGO, in every practice or strategy, in every discourse or knowledge, a *contact zone* that may render it porous and hence permeable to other NGOs, practices, strategies, discourses and knowledges" (133). In this sense, the intentional strategy of USSF organizers ensured that people of color, working-class communities, indigenous peoples, and other oppressed groups would be able to contribute their perspectives to the overall "ecology" of epistemologies and practices. At the same time, by privileging one strategy—grassroots organizing—over all others, racial and class diversity was achieved by downplaying the forum's wider role as a facilitator of translation across sectors.

Rather than a singular public sphere, Santos's view reflects a model of the forum as a multiplicity of spaces, an overarching arena promoting cross-fertilization among diverse "counterpublics" (Fraser 1992; see also

Lichterman 1996). This is precisely the promise of the USSF. As organizers recognized, however, the first step was to ensure that historically marginalized groups had a strong presence by implementing an intentional organizing strategy. At the same time, although this process led to a diverse, grassroots, and movement-oriented forum, it was less open than it might have been. Moreover, the NPC attempted to manage much of the content and tone of the forum, particularly during the more visible public moments. In this sense, the USSF was less a space for translation and exchange than a platform for expressing a particular kind of grassroots identity and politics. This was apparent in at least two fundamental ways.

First, the goal of ensuring that the USSF was led by grassroots base-building groups meant that other sectors were initially left out of the organizing process. On the one hand, the criteria to join the NPC limited membership to certain kinds of organizations. The two requirements were that groups had to be member based and they had to be involved in movement building. In other words, NPC member groups had to be communitarian organizations engaged in or providing support for grassroots organizing. Individuals, policy-oriented NGOs, intellectual and student groups, environmental organizations, and informal networks, including anarchists, direct action activists, and independent media practitioners, were largely excluded from the NPC. Rather than creating a wider space for dialogue and translation, communitarian politics were privileged over both bureaucratic forms of organization as well as more informal, personalized modes of commitment.[9]

On the other hand, the specific outreach strategy employed by the NPC primarily targeted grassroots base-building organizations rooted among working-class communities of color. This had the salutary effect of reversing traditional hierarchies, but at the same time a great deal of energy, creativity, and experience from other sectors may have been lost. When I asked an NPC member whether a completely open process where anyone could participate regardless of organizational affiliation, as in Europe, would work in the United States, she neatly summed up the contradiction between openness and diversity: "If we were to throw open the U.S. Social Forum, what you would get the first time would be activists, organizations with more capacity, maybe more intermediaries rather than base-building organizations, and it probably would be more white than not. This would provide the level of transparency and openness that people value, but would also replicate the very oppressions that prevent people from coming to the table" (personal interview, August 22, 2007). In this sense, the invisible exclusions of open space were replaced by more visible barriers.

A second way the tension between intentionality and openness was made visible had to do with the movement-versus-space dynamic. Organizers articulated a particular vision of social change based on building powerful movements through long-term community organizing, grassroots base building, and popular education. The organizers' ability to insert this model as the dominant paradigm helps explain why the USSF was able to attract so many groups that organize among working-class people of color, and thus why the forum was so diverse and inclusive. Moreover, this movement-building focus also helps explain the importance given to larger public moments as well as the specific composition, style, and tone of the plenaries and many of the workshops.

One result of emphasizing a particular kind of movement, however, was that less attention was paid to alternative strategies, tactics, and political visions. Which is more effective: community organizing, direct action, lobbying, or media work? Should social movements pursue state-oriented or autonomous strategies for social change? What are the relative strengths and weaknesses of vertical versus horizontal forms of organizing? How might these different strategies, tactics, and organizational forms work together within a broad-based movement? As one participant pointed out, "there was a great deal of racial diversity, but little ideological diversity" (personal interview, August 17, 2007). Put differently, the translation dynamic of the forum was muted. Beyond ideology, what was perhaps more notable was a lack of interaction between diverse strategies, political visions, and forms of commitment.

Another result of the particular movement-building strategy within the USSF was that more informal networks characterized by a personalized mode of politics, including a greater commitment to horizontality and autonomy, were less involved in the organizing process than has been the case elsewhere, particularly in Europe. Although the groups that spearheaded the USSF process are generally resource poor, most have traditional organizational structures, involving vertical leadership, formal membership, and paid staff supported by foundation funding. In many ways, they resemble the classic social movement organizations of resource mobilization theory. As Frances Fox Piven and Richard Cloward (1978) argue, however, formal organizations can dampen the spontaneity and militancy required to build mass movements. In this sense, there has been growing criticism of what some grassroots activists and observers now call the "non-profit industrial complex" (INCITE! 2007). At the global level, where formal organizations dominate the IC, informal networks have played a significant role by organizing youth camps and autonomous spaces outside, yet still connected to, the official forums (Juris 2005b). Although direct action, anarchist, and other groups committed to horizontal organizing did attend the USSF, they had little access to, and impact on, the organization of the event.

This helps to explain why movement building was emphasized over open space. This is not to say open space was absent: roughly nine hundred self-organized workshops covered a vast array of themes. Still, the plenaries and public events consistently stressed movement building as opposed to establishing a contact zone for sharing, exchange, and translation among groups with diverse political visions, ideological perspectives, tactical preferences, and strategies. By way of comparison, while the 2005 WSF in Porto Alegre was entirely self-organized, the USSF featured central plenary sessions where specific issues, strategies, and communities were highlighted. Even the workshops reflected an intentional strategy, as organizers were asked to engage issues of concern to grassroots communities and to address USSF goals with respect to young people as well as racial and class diversity.[10]

Moreover, on a logistical level, the greater involvement of informal, anarchist-oriented sectors, particularly groups such as Food Not Bombs or radical environmental networks with experience organizing action camps, may have helped organizers address the lack of affordable food and housing.[11] At the same time, these networks are usually dominated by white, middle-class youths with strong subcultural identities. As noted by many activists of color and white antiracist organizers, such countercultural groups tend to create environments that people of color find unwelcoming (see Martínez 2000; Starr 2004). Indeed, as Lichterman (1996) suggests, middle-class white radicals are more likely to emphasize alternative communities and lifestyles, while for activists of color, political activity is often rooted in their everyday networks of social relations. Whereas the former tend to prefer prefigurative, participatory forms of organization, working-class activists of color, who generally face more immediate concerns and lack the time and resources needed to take part in long meetings, often mobilize within formal community-based groups (see this volume's conclusion). Consequently, the greater participation of white radicals may have complicated efforts to achieve racial and class diversity. At the same time, if the USSF is to play a role as a contact zone for interaction and exchange among diverse practices, knowledges, and forms of commitment, other sectors will have to participate more fully in the organizing process, which will both require and facilitate a greater emphasis on translation.

CONCLUSION: IS ANOTHER POLITICS POSSIBLE?

I walked into a ballroom at the Renaissance Hotel in Atlanta on the morning of Friday, June 29, 2007. The room was packed with several hundred people, mostly young. Slightly less than half were people of color. The chairs were set up in concentric circles, and in a corner a few childcare volunteers were watching a group of kids. As I entered the room, two organizers handed me a paper with questions about horizontalism, intersectionality, "living the vision," and social transformation. The session began with a drum circle and chant. Facilitators then welcomed us to the "Another Politics Is Possible" initiative. "Another Politics Is Possible" was a study group, session, and track at the USSF, as well as a delegation of grassroots groups, childcare volunteers, and individuals—mostly mothers and women of color. The participating groups were mainly small, collectively run, and committed to building an alternative politics based on horizontality, autonomy, and self-management. The session explored prospects and challenges for developing nonhierarchical approaches to organizing and movement building in the United States.

We began by breaking into groups of three or four where we discussed questions such as, "How do you practice leadership development when you are trying to implement a horizontal structure and politics?" and "When and how do you decide to make demands of and organize against dominant institutions, or build an alternative to that institution?" Afterward, delegates from grassroots people-of-color collectives—the Immokolee Workers, the Garment Worker Center in Los Angeles, INCITE!, Sista II Sista, and the Center for Immigrant Families in New York City, among others—took turns responding to the larger group.

The session complicated the neat binary I have set up between open and intentional space. On the one hand, a relatively open space was created where groups could come together and share ideas and experiences regarding various approaches to social change. Moreover, the overall theme dealt with issues that had been obscured in the larger USSF. Indeed, several respondents challenged not only nonprofit structures but also the model of grassroots organizing. As one participant explained, "It might sound a little harsh, but in our organization we don't believe in organizers. We're animators and consciousness raisers in our community." A community organizer might respond that such informal roles do not ensure accountability, but for a horizontalist, accountability can derive from multiple sources, including nonbureaucratic structures and community trust (see this volume's conclusion). Others stressed intentionality by noting that "having a nonhierarchical or horizontal collective structure doesn't mean just having an open circle for everyone to come in. . . . [I]t means having very intentional, deliberate structures. . . . [I]f we just have an open space, our internalized privileges or oppressions or entitlements come out."

The "Another Politics Is Possible" session was an attempt to build a space that was horizontal *and* intentional, and where participants grappled with alternative visions. In this sense, there is no reason why a collectively run, self-managed process cannot create an intentional space. However, the tension between openness and intentionality is more complicated. The session was not completely open: organizers decided which questions to address, how to structure the discussion, and who would present publicly. In strict terms, creating a space is always intentional (see Nunes 2005). The relationship between intentionality and openness is better viewed, then, as a continuum rather than as a strict opposition.

As I have argued, the USSF succeeded where many previous forums have failed in building a process that was not only diverse in terms of race and class but was also led by grassroots organizations that have a base among working-class communities of color. In achieving this, the USSF confronted an important contradiction: as with broader public spheres, open spaces tend to reproduce exclusions due to structural barriers and power inequalities. In response, USSF organizers developed a vision for how the space of the USSF should look and took strategic steps to make that vision a reality by engaging in a more agonistic approach to democratic practice. However, efforts to generate inclusive spaces may contradict other values that are important to activists, such as openness and horizontality. Many sectors were left out of the organizing process, while the more visible, public moments of the USSF had a predetermined content, composition, and tone defined by the NPC. In this sense, the organizers' intentionality privileged grassroots organizing over alternative strategies. Racial and class diversity were thus achieved at the cost of downplaying the forum's role as a contact zone for translation, interaction, and exchange among diverse knowledges, visions, practices, and forms.

In comparative terms what is interesting is that few groups openly challenged the NPC regarding openness and horizontality, as has occurred regularly at the European and World Social Forums. I heard a few individual comments, but there were no actions such as the storming of the stage at the 2004 ESF in London (see Juris 2005b). Sessions such as "Another Politics Is Possible" or an anarchist workshop I attended, where one might expect critiques to have been raised, were silent on these issues. Instead there seemed to be agreement across sectors that the USSF was an opportunity to begin rebuilding a U.S.-based global justice movement by addressing past critiques of racial and class exclusion. As a white male activist explained in our breakout group at the "Another Politics Is Possible" session, "It's wise for groups to put boundaries and limits on it [the USSF organizing process] that are perhaps overly excessive, at least for now. We need to break down where we're coming from and we need to start fresh, and this is how we are starting fresh. Maybe it's not horizontal, maybe it's the opposite, but we'll work back toward the middle from there."

What activists implicitly recognized is that deliberative approaches to democracy often neglect the power imbalances as well as the structural and cultural exclusions that are constitutive of any public sphere. In this sense, for the USSF to become a truly open, democratic space and for it to fulfill its broader role as a contact zone between different movement knowledges, visions, and practices, proactive steps must be taken to ensure that historically marginalized groups can participate on a more or less equal footing. This suggests that intentional strategies that might otherwise be viewed as closed, top-down, and nondemocratic may in fact be widely recognized as legitimate if they are seen as advancing longer-term democratic goals. At some point, however, if other sectors are to remain committed to the USSF, they will demand a greater role in the organizing process. This will inevitably lead to questions about openness and horizontality.

Indeed, NPC members have since talked about the need to open up and bring in other sectors. As one organizer explained, "If we were going to fall short, if we're going to accept criticism, we're willing to live with the criticism that it wasn't broad enough in terms of bringing in these other sectors" (personal interview, August 24, 2007). Regarding future USSFs and subsequent iterations of the NPC, he continued, "We want to see broader diversity, but we also want to make sure the grassroots doesn't get overrun." One of the main challenges going forward will be precisely to move toward greater openness, while maintaining a certain level of intentionality so that working-class communities of color continue to have a strong presence. At the same time, it will also be important to build unity between people of color and an embattled white working class that has also borne the brunt of neoliberal globalization. Meanwhile, as the incident involving the African American moderator and indigenous speaker suggests, there are also significant differences and rifts to heal within and between people-of-color communities.

Finally, to bring in a greater diversity of sectors, it might help to think about the USSF less as a single space, and more, as mentioned above, in terms of a multiplicity of spaces that are self-organized and autonomously managed (see Juris 2005b). As Nancy Fraser (1992) has argued, in a highly stratified society with significant social inequality, multiple publics are required to overcome structural barriers and ensure participatory parity. Even in a theoretically egalitarian and multicultural society, however, a plurality of publics is still preferable to avoid cultural exclusions based on "filtering diverse rhetorical and stylistic norms through a single, overarching lens" (126). At the same time, an "additional, more comprehensive arena" would allow members of different publics to interact across their social, cultural, and political differences (126). The USSF represents precisely such an arena. In this sense, the NPC would become a space of coordination, allowing different political ideas, styles, and visions of the forum to flourish. Proactive measures may still be necessary to ensure grassroots participation, but recognizing and institutionalizing a plurality of spaces would allow the USSF to become more broad-based, participatory, and politically diverse.

While recognizing and facilitating a multiplicity of spaces within the USSF would enhance its radically democratic character and pedagogic function, proponents of a more agonistic democracy may well ask how this will advance concrete struggles for social and economic justice. Indeed, the WSF was initially created as a way to support the global struggle against neoliberalism. As others have pointed out though, there is no nec-essary contradiction between an organization's prefigurative goals, in this case the forum's role as a laboratory for radical democracy, and its more instrumental objectives (Breines 1982; Polletta 2002; see also Juris 2008a). Indeed, as Francesca Polletta (2002) suggests, participatory forms of or-ganization also have a critical strategic dimension: enhancing solidarity, facilitating learning, and generating innovation. For the USSF to help build a powerful, broad-based coalition for long-term social transforma-tion, it will have to not only include historically marginalized voices but also foster a wide sense of ownership among diverse movement sectors. The future of the USSF depends in large part on whether organizers are able to achieve this delicate strategic balance.

There have been some notable developments since the first USSF, al-though many similar dynamics remain in place. The second USSF was held in Detroit from June 22 to 26, 2010. About fifteen thousand people attended, and the social composition of the attendees was roughly similar to that of the Atlanta forum. The most visible difference in terms of the issues addressed in this chapter was the relatively more muted emphasis on intentionality. The composition of the NPC and of the evening ple-naries was still largely made up of people of color from grassroots base-building organizations, but there was little public discussion of the orga-nizing strategy. My sense is that the intentional strategy implemented in Atlanta is now hegemonic, and organizers did not feel it was necessary to stress publicly. In addition, the plenaries and opening and closing cere-monies and final PMA seemed less central in Detroit than had been the case in Atlanta. In general, they were relatively poorly attended compared to the size of the forum (a few thousand people at its height at the opening ceremony, perhaps half that at the closing ceremony and final PMA, and about five hundred to six hundred at the evening plenaries). In this sense, most attendees focused on their particular workshops and issue-based PMAS (a series of smaller thematic PMAS were held that fed into the final PMA on the last day), so that there were fewer large-scale performative platforms to communicate overarching discourses. If there was a prevail-ing theme it had more to do with the importance of the local context in Detroit given the depth of the crisis in that city and the need to support local grassroots movements.

Nonetheless, based on my experiences working with a local delegation of grassroots organizations from Boston and my discussions with NPC members during and after the 2010 USSF, the strategy of intentionality remained firmly in place. Interestingly, an earlier version of this chapter was passed around by several NPC members during the lead-up to Detroit and some of the arguments were echoed in discussions. In this sense, the goal of helping to spark critical, strategic debate was to some extent realized. At least one NPC member, a Latino man, voiced support for the essay's call for greater openness during the Detroit organizing process. It seems that there was little open opposition, but that in practice the overall movement-building strategy continued to focus on grassroots base-building groups with a membership rooted among working-class people of color. There is nothing wrong with a movement-building strategy that revolves around the construction of long-term, bottom-up power among the communities that are most affected by pressing social, economic, and environmental crises. Indeed, the strong participation and leadership by these sectors in Detroit, as in Atlanta, was extremely inspirational.

The issue continues to be whether the practice of emphasizing one movement-building strategy over others (e.g., public education and community base building on the part of formal nonprofit organizations over, say, direct action, labor organizing, international solidarity, policy work, self-organizing among informal collectives, etc.) and privileging a particular subjectivity (working-class people of color) over others (white working classes, middle classes, etc.) is the most effective way to build a mass movement that is large and broad enough to effect lasting change. To some extent, the USSF attracts a large number of participants from diverse sectors anyway, and the focus on base-building groups does help them not to feel overrun. Yet, to build a truly broad-based movement that people actually feel a part of, it is important to incorporate other sectors in the organizing process and the overall strategic vision.

What seems to have happened is the reproduction of a set of rigid subject positions, no longer based on particular identities, but rather involving broader categories such as "people of color" or "working class." Organizers have developed an analysis of intersectionality in terms of interlocking oppressions around axes such as race, class, gender, sexuality, physical ability, and so on. At the same time, the fluidity of particular identities is often subsumed within broader categories, while other subject positions, such as "white" or "middle class," are set in opposition to them. This reduces the lived complexity of identity (which, given the need to clearly and succinctly articulate complex political ideas and strategies, is to some extent unavoidable; indeed, I have reproduced many of the static categories used by organizers in this chapter), and it also makes it more difficult to build bridges across broad identity-based categories. The need to forge alliances among people-of-color (and other oppressed) groups is clearly recognized, but the importance of building coalitions that also include white working classes or middle classes is discursively muted. This is linked to a propensity to view social change as *necessarily* led by a privileged subject (the "proletariat" here is replaced by "working-class people of color"), which easily becomes a reified social category that can be represented and used to reinforce particular ideological claims and agendas. My critique is not about contesting the need to grapple with racial, class, gender, and other forms of privilege and exclusion. Indeed, I have elsewhere argued precisely that activists should more proactively address these dynamics in the context of the Occupy movements in the United States (see Juris et al. 2012). Rather, this is a call for greater ideological openness and a more complex treatment of political subjectivity.

One alternative might be a more flexible, Gramscian approach that affirms the need to build a counterhegemonic bloc composed of cross-racial and cross-class alliances, combined with an openness to multiple, shifting, and overlapping political subjectivities, which would include those constructed around race, class, gender, and sexuality, and also those not reducible to such categories (students, environmentalists, peace activists, solidarity activists, concerned citizens, anarchists, etc.). This is not to suggest that issues related to racism, class domination, patriarchy, heterosexism, white privilege, and so on are unimportant. On the contrary, the USSF has made significant strides on all of these terrains. I am instead arguing for a political strategy that recognizes the need to build a broad-based progressive front across multiple sectors and forms of movement building to struggle for social, political, and economic justice. With the Tea Party and the radical Right on the rise, this task seems more urgent than ever.

NOTES

1 I adapt the term *intentional space*, in part, from members of the NPC who frequently refer to "intentionality" to characterize their organizing strategy.
2 This chapter is based on participant observation at the USSF from June 27 to July 1, 2007, and follow-up interviews with members of the NPC. I carried out

previous research during the 2002 and 2005 gatherings of the WSF in Porto Alegre and the 2004 ESF in London.

3 WSF Charter of Principles, August 6, 2002, www.forumsocialmundial.org.br (accessed December 25, 2011).

4 See Bello 2007 and Whitaker 2007b for a more recent instantiation of this debate.

5 See www.ibase.org.br/userimages/relatorio_fsm2005_INGLES2.pdf (accessed December 27, 2011).

6 Interviewee names have been suppressed to protect anonymity.

7 For a summary statement of the "grassroots" politics of the NPC, see the "What We Believe" page of the 2007 USSF's website, www.ussf2007.org (accessed December 25, 2011).

8 Ibid.

9 However, not many groups from other movement sectors applied and no applicant was ever rejected. Meanwhile, the process eventually opened up, and a few non-base-building organizations did ultimately serve on the NPC, including Sociologists without Borders, the American Friends Service Committee, the 50 Years Is Enough Network, and the Ruckus Society.

10 In the end, members of the program group decided not to vet specific workshops, given the large number of proposals (personal interview, August 17, 2007).

11 NPC members did make an effort to secure alternative facilities, but they faced a shortage of meeting spaces in Atlanta and scheduling conflicts at the historically black colleges (personal interview, August 8, 2007).

2

Tracing the Zapatista Rhizome, or, the Ethnography of a Transnationalized Political Imagination

ALEX KHASNABISH

> Revolutionary movements do not spread by contamination but by *resonance*. Something that is constituted here resonates with the shock wave emitted by something constituted over there. A body that resonates does so according to its own mode. An insurrection is not like a plague or a forest fire—a linear process which spreads from place to place after an initial spark. It rather takes the shape of music, whose focal points, though dispersed in time and space, succeed in imposing the rhythm of their own vibrations, always taking on more density. To the point that any return to normal is no longer desirable or even imaginable.
>
> *The Invisible Committee,* The Coming Insurrection

On a beautiful, late summer day in 2004 I sat in a Lebanese restaurant in downtown Hamilton, Ontario. Across the table from me were Rick Rowley and Jacquie Soohen, two radical filmmakers based in New York City and part of a collective known as Big Noise Tactical. Rick and Jacquie were in Hamilton to screen their new activist documentary, *The Fourth World War,* a film that charts inspiring moments and struggles within the "movement of movements" that is widely referred to as the alter-globalization movement.[1] The three of us met that afternoon to share food and too much coffee so that I could interview them for my Ph.D. dissertation— "Zapatismo, Transnational Activism, and the Political Imagination"— about radical social change struggles, new imaginations of political possibility, and the new cycle of activism that began with the uprising of several thousand indigenous Mayan people in the far southeast of Mexico on the first day of January 1994 (see Khasnabish 2008).

The project emerged out of my fascination with the Zapatistas—a radical social change movement that had begun as an armed insurgency initiated by the Ejército Zapatista de Liberación Nacional (Zapatista National Liberation Army, EZLN) in the Mexican state of Chiapas on January 1, 1994. On the first day of the new year in 1994, several thousand indigenous Mayan insurgents—some armed with semiautomatic weapons, many others with nothing more than sticks—emerged from ten years of clandestine organizing and five centuries of resistance and persistence in the face of genocide, colonialism, and imperialism, and declared war on the federal executive of the Mexican Republic and the Mexican army. In statements issued during those first days of the new year, the insurgents of the EZLN declared that they had risen up in arms not to seize the state but to smash a corrupt, violent, and illegitimate system so that Mexicans could freely and democratically govern themselves. They called the North American Free Trade Agreement (NAFTA) a "death sentence" for the indigenous peoples of Mexico, but more than a rebellion for or against a particular kind of economic model, the Zapatistas articulated the rationale for their uprising in terms of justice, dignity, and democracy. As an insurgent calling himself Subcomandante Insurgente Marcos explained during an impromptu interview on January 1, 1994:

> What was needed was for someone to give a lesson in dignity, and this fell to the most ancient inhabitants of this country that is now called Mexico, but when they were here it did not have a name, that name. It fell to the lowest citizens of this country to raise their heads, with dignity. And this should be a lesson for all. We cannot let ourselves be treated this way, and we have to try and construct a better world, a world truly for everyone, and not only a few, as the current regime does. This is what we want. We do not want to monopolize the vanguard or say that we are the light, the only alternative, or stingily claim the qualification of revolutionary for one or another current. We say, look at what happened. That is what we had to do. We have dignity, patriotism and we are demonstrating it. You should do the same, within your ideology, within your means, within your beliefs, and make your human condition count. (Marcos 2002, 211–12)

The Zapatista uprising did not topple the government of President Carlos Salinas, nor did it manage to defeat the Mexican army, but in many ways the rebellion initiated by the Zapatistas would accomplish something as revolutionary—and far less predictable—as these goals. Indeed, as the dream of state-sponsored socialism lay for so many buried beneath the rubble of the Berlin Wall, what began as an armed uprising in the far southeast of Mexico would radically expand the horizon of political possibility on a global scale and spark a transnational "movement of movements." Beyond providing a powerful affirmation of the fact that, neoliberal dogma aside, resistance was indeed still possible in the midst of a "New World Order" at "the end of history,"[2] the Zapatistas would also provide the catalyst for a profound reimagining on a transnational scale of the possibilities for and paths toward radical social change at the end of the millennium.

As a young university student coming to political awareness and in desperate search of inspiration and hope amid a bleak political landscape in North America in the mid-1990s, the Zapatistas captivated my imagination, but it would be many years before I would physically enter Zapatista territory in rebellion and encounter the living reality of the Zapatista struggle on the ground in Chiapas. As a young, middle-class, heterosexual man living in southern Ontario, I bore the marks of privilege that structurally set me worlds apart from the struggle being waged in the far southeast of Mexico. But as a first-generation Canadian, a child of parents from the formerly Second (Latvia) and Third (Burma) Worlds, with a surname and complexion that often marked me as Other, and born into a family solidly middle class in terms of social capital but often living an economically precarious existence, I found something powerfully resonant in the Zapatista struggle. In this, I was certainly not alone.

I have written extensively about the significance of Zapatismo (the political practice and philosophy of the Zapatista movement) to activists transnationally and its relevance to new conceptions of struggle elsewhere (see Khasnabish 2008, 2010). Here I want to argue for the utility of ethnographically informed studies of radical explorations of political possibility such as Zapatismo. I draw broadly on my year of fieldwork with diverse activists in the United States and Canada who experienced the resonance of Zapatismo in order to ethnographically probe the dynamics, promises, and pitfalls of a specific manifestation of the radical imagination. By ethnography I refer not only to the methodology of participant observation, something I drew on quite sparsely, but also to the collection of narratives through open-ended interviews. The collection of stories has always been a key element of ethnographic engagement as a route to understanding other realities through the way they are explained by those who inhabit them. Focusing on the ways people narrate their own experiences and understandings of their own social realities also serves as a pathway to exploring how subjectivities—understandings of oneself and one's place in the world—are produced and reproduced. If social change is about more than simply institutional transformation, then attending to the subjectivities emerging out of struggles for social justice not only makes good analytic sense but also allows us to explore social movements as engines generative of potentially radical sociopolitical possibility outside more concrete and conventional measures of political success and failure.

This is my attempt to demonstrate the importance of critical and ethnographically informed explorations into the intersection of politics and the imagination in a transnationalized space. It is also an effort to articulate a jumping-off point for further politically committed, ethnographically grounded, collaborative research that participates unapologetically but critically in advancing struggles for radical social justice. The research I reflect on here, and the work that has since emerged out of it, is animated by the conviction that academic research can play an important role in supporting social struggles for radical social justice. This is not to privilege the site of the academy; rather, it is to assert that social movements produce knowledge, critical reflection, and theoretical insights about the world we collectively inhabit and how it might be changed (see Casas-Cortés, Osterweil, and Powell, this volume). Academic research can play a role in highlighting and helping to collect and circulate this socially transformative knowledge, but only when movements are taken seriously as living laboratories of struggle and transformation rather than studied like specimens under a microscope. Engaged and critical ethnographic research carried out in the spirit of affinity with struggles for social justice can also play a vital role in cultivating spaces and processes that facilitate critical and committed dialogue and debate among activists about issues that activists and organizers rarely have the opportunity to take up in the course of their day-to-day work.

For example, in the course of conducting this research, I was often surprised to receive unsolicited comments from my collaborators about the value of the project for their own work, particularly the process of facilitating a space for critical, reflexive deliberation about their social change efforts and their connections—or lack thereof—with the work of others. The collaborative research project that followed this one focuses on the radical imagination among activist collectives in Halifax, Nova Scotia, and is explicitly and intentionally geared toward creating spaces that allow for social change actors to express and share the radical imaginations animating their activist work while at the same time encountering the imaginations and work of others with whom they may have had no or little contact. In this way, ethnographically grounded research with those engaged in social struggle is well suited to actually contributing to such struggles instead of merely cataloguing them without forsaking the critical perspective academic research can bring to bear on social phenomena.

My current research is guided by a critical intellectual and political interest in exploring the radical imagination in terms of what it does and how it works as a dialogic process possible only within collective as opposed to individual bodies (see Haiven and Khasnabish 2011). This project is informed by the principle that such research can actively assist in convoking the radical imagination through the cultivation of collective spaces and processes of reflection, deliberation, and encounter that can in turn spur movements for social transformation. In an age of concerted attacks against critical scholarship and worldly intellectualism, the university has increasingly taken on the role of the knowledge factory, pushed by political and economic elites to produce market-ready "outcomes." The liberal conception of the academy and the academic vocation as goods in themselves that are necessary for enlightened social development and an engaged citizenry (a conception that itself relied on and entrenched forms of classed, racialized, and gendered privilege) has withered, sharing the fate of Keynesian social democratic welfarism in the face of an ascendant neoliberal politico-economic paradigm and a vicious neoconservative moralism.

Nevertheless, in spite of these transformations, the university remains one of the few "public" spaces left within an ever more privatized and securitized social fabric, and the position of the academic (at least in its nonprecarious manifestation) is one of the few that retains a degree of autonomy with respect to these dominant power relations. This is neither to valorize the role of the academic nor to condemn more positivist, less engaged forms of inquiry into and about social movements. In the first case, this autonomy—although by no means sacrosanct, always justly bestowed, or put to productive use—remains a place of possibility. In the second case, as pointed out in the introduction, the diverse body of social movement scholarship has generated significant, rigorous, and insightful analysis and useful pedagogical tools. However, the approach I am advocating here, without seeking to elevate the academy above other spaces, does seek to make use of the tools, resources, and location of the academy to experiment with nonvanguardist forms of research that attempt to contribute to rather than objectify struggles for social justice (see also Graeber 2007; Juris 2008a; Maeckelbergh 2009).

TRANSNATIONAL ZAPATISMO

In the year I spent conducting fieldwork for this project, which began in the fall of 2003, I had numerous conversations with diverse activists across Canada, the United States, and Mexico who shared with me stories of their encounters with Zapatismo and the wider significance of the transnational political reverberations of the Zapatista inspiration. I use the term *transnational* as a reference to a political space constituted beyond the national and the international without suggesting that it is anything so totalizing or comprehensive as "the global." This is by no means to suggest that the nation-state system is in decline or that national politics serves no constructive purpose. It is certainly not to imply that the transnational is an inherently liberatory space. On the one hand, governed by the interests of capital, the transnational becomes a way to take the logic of enclosure and exploitation to new heights. On the other hand, shaped and animated by radical struggles for sociopolitical and economic justice, the transnational is potentially a plane that transverses, transgresses, and offers paths beyond the dominating logic of the state, the nation, and the current world disorder. In this sense, the transnational is a scale and a plane of action, communication, and encounter constructed through the relationships that traverse it.

While the resonance of Zapatismo is a transnational phenomenon, I focus on the north of the Americas for three main reasons related to political geography and the significance of lived spaces. These reasons also shed light on the contributions of ethnographic approaches to understanding the significance of radical social struggles. First, while the elite-driven nation-state projects of Canada and the United States supposedly share a civilizational legacy with Western Europe, these nation-states and the populations inhabiting them, in addition to sharing a continent with Mexico, are physically, historically, politically, economically, and socially part of the Americas. The eco-social crises facing peoples around the world today necessitate critical analysis and collective action that recognizes global interconnection while remaining grounded in the shared spaces and places we inhabit. The second reason is the simple realization that the resonance of a political imagination can never be divorced from the context within which it occurs. In this sense, exploring the transnational resonance of Zapatismo among communities of activists in Canada and the United States allows for a much richer consideration of the role of context and history than a globe-spanning overview might. Finally, focusing on the United States and Canada as sites for the materialization of transnationalized Zapatismo derives from these states' preeminent positions in the global architecture of power.

TAKING IMAGINATION SERIOUSLY

The imagination as a site of power, possibility, and struggle has occupied the attention of critical theorists for some time. Some of the most provocative and insightful of these references come from a body of theory linked broadly to the Marxist tradition. In some of these cases, "the imagination" is not necessarily invoked as such. Guy Debord's deconstruction of the society of the spectacle is one such example (1994). But even in these cases what is clearly being invoked—even if only tacitly—is the imaginative life of systems of power and the paths beyond them. From the more classical work of theorists such as Ernst Bloch (1986), Guy Debord (1994), and Cornelius Castoriadis (1991) to the more contemporary and varied interventions offered by thinkers such as Susan Buck-Morss (2000), Michael Hardt and Antonio Negri (2000, 2004), George Katsiaficas (1987, 2006), and Paolo Virno (2003), the common thread binding this diverse field is its insistence on imagination. Imagination is understood as a collective and profoundly social rather than individual capacity that is at once deeply interwoven with the fabric of the prevailing sociohistorical conditions and, simultaneously, the rocket fuel for an escape velocity beyond the violence and exploitation of the capitalist status quo.

This ambivalence is part of the imagination's power but it also illustrates how the imagination cannot be viewed in a purely celebratory light.

As Castoriadis argues, for example, the radical imagination of the individual cannot be freed from the dominant power-laden structures of meaning making and signification in which it is enmeshed without first cultivating a space that would allow for a "reflective and deliberative instance" (1991, 163). Explaining this ambivalence, the liberal political theorist Charles Taylor describes the social imaginary not as a set of particular ideas but as that which "enables, through making sense of, the practices of a society" (2004, 2). Arjun Appadurai has made a similar argument about the imagination, contending that through new electronic media and the increased flow of peoples across borders, imagination today needs to be considered a "collective, social fact" resulting in a "plurality of imagined worlds" that can become the basis for collective social action (1996, 5). None of this means that imagination is a necessarily world-changing force; it can equally be a reactionary or conservative one. In the work of autonomist Marxists such as Negri, Hardt, and Virno, the imagination is a force that weaves its way—often ambiguously—through regimes of immaterial production, biopolitics, and the general intellect. Susan Buck-Morss illuminates the power and radical contingency of political imaginaries when she suggests that their significance "depends on the power structures in which people desire and dream, and on the cultural meanings they give to the changed situation" (2000, 277).

Much like desire and dream, the imagination is dependent on power structures, context, and larger signifying systems. In this regard, it is fair to say that there is a double movement to Zapatismo. Zapatismo can be understood as the political philosophy and practice of the Zapatista movement located physically, culturally, and politically in the far southeast of Mexico. It can also be understood as a new imagination of political struggle and possibility—a new way of envisioning and enacting projects for radical social change that does not advance a singular path, a privileged subject, or a specific endpoint. Counter-posed to the formalism of philosophy and the interpellating force of ideology, imagination is a much more collective, organic, and unfolding process. It is what the utopian Marxist theorist Bloch (1986) called the "Not-Yet," that which is not fully present or formed but still in the process of becoming and, as such, remains open to radical reconfiguration. Rather than a lens through which to make sense out of the world, radical imagination is a collective and collaborative force that emerges out of radical dialogue, practice, reflection, and circulation.

On a transnational plane, Zapatismo operates less as an established set of political ideas and practices and more as a constant provocation. In this sense, I am not suggesting that Zapatismo as a transnationalized imagination is equivalent to the realities of its practice on the ground in Zapatista communities in Chiapas. A distinction should be made between on-the-ground and transnationalized manifestations of Zapatismo. As soon as Zapatismo began to circulate through globalizing media circuits from solidarity delegation "report backs" to conventional corporate media to activist, academic, and artistic renderings of the movement, this transnationalized Zapatismo took on lives of its own, deeply linked but not coterminous with the praxis of Zapatismo grounded in the sociopolitical and cultural soil of Chiapas.

Over the year I spent tracing Zapatismo's resonance among collectives of activists in Canada and the United States, I encountered numerous politically powerful examples of the manifestation of Zapatismo's transnationalized political imagination. The activists with whom I worked are involved in a diversity of organizations and projects, including Big Noise Tactical, Building Bridges, the Chiapas Media Project, Food for Chiapas, Global Exchange, "hacktivists" from the University of Toronto, Mexico Solidarity Network, the Ontario Coalition against Poverty, Peoples' Global Action, the *smart*Meme Strategy and Training Project, activists involved in planning the Third Intercontinental Encuentro for Humanity and against Neoliberalism, and a variety of activists involved in political projects ranging from Latin American solidarity to community capacity-building projects.[3] The existence of these collectives, organizations, and projects can be read as material signs of the resonance of Zapatismo's transnationalized political imagination.

"THE POWER STRUCTURES IN WHICH PEOPLE DESIRE AND DREAM"

Some commentators have, in the years since the Zapatista uprising, dismissed the resonance of the Zapatista struggle transnationally as a facile romanticism, yet another iteration of an impulse on the part of those who are privileged enough to be shielded from the cutting edges of structural violence to uncritically valorize—and consume—"revolutionary" struggles that are always elsewhere (see Hellman 1999; Oppenheimer 2002). It must be acknowledged that this romanticism has certainly come into play with respect to Northern activists' views of the Zapatista movement and has indeed had negative consequences in some instances, so much so that the Zapatistas themselves have commented on the real problems romanticism can present for those on its receiving end.[4] Many of my own research partners spoke passionately about the consequences for people's struggles when romanticism runs up against reality. As Manuel Rozental, a physician and Colombian activist with the Canada-Colombia Solidarity Campaign, reflected during a conversation we had in the winter of 2003:

> It's fair and it's useful to get inspiration. . . . It's also good to learn from processes like [Zapatismo]. . . . But if it's relatively easy for an activist from the North to get there, why is it not obvious to someone from Canada that they could actually use some of their resources to get somebody from the South into Chiapas or to get people from Chiapas into the South somewhere else? . . . What do we see first when we get to San Cristóbal? What one of the Zapatistas calls "Zapatour," thousands of tourists that stand in the plaza and shout for the Zapatistas with expensive cameras. This is a holiday that provides meaning for the many in the North that feel themselves progressive but you don't see any indigenous people or people from popular movements and organizations. (Personal interview, December 10, 2003)

There are indeed consequences—some empowering, some highly problematic—to the resonance of radical imaginations. The reproduction of inequalities and violences expressed in terms of class, race, gender, sexual orientation, age, and ability can frequently be manifested concretely through the resonance of political imaginations. Rozental described just such an outcome. If such violences and inequalities are reproduced through the dynamics of resonance, struggles elsewhere can become fodder for an inherently capitalistic logic of commodification. In these cases, those shielded from the worst consequences of the eco-social crisis we currently face consume radical movements while those facing the cutting edges of this crisis do the actual work of struggling for radical transformation. In this dynamic, imagination is replaced by spectacle and spectators are produced. This act of movement fetishization alienates people from one another, substituting self-satisfying fantasies of radical politics for the work of building mass movements capable of actualizing social change.

Jessica Marques, an activist and organizer with the Mexico Solidarity Network, also expressed significant reservations about the implications of the resonance of political imaginations when they become highly idealized. Rather than the work of imagination, which is a collaborative product of encounter and dialogue, idealization substitutes representation for the living and complex reality of movements on the ground, subverting the critical awareness of the distance between representation and living realities that is necessary to avoid the fetishization of social change struggles. In this sense, the mediated connection that so many people in the global North have with the Zapatista movement—whether that mediation occurs through the work of organizations involved in transnational advocacy networks, Internet, video, DVDs, or textual sources—actually serves to reinforce the idealization rather than challenging it. Marques noted in this regard:

> I think there's definitely a tendency to idealize the movement and
> a lot of people I've found in their first trip to Chiapas are surprised
> to find that the Zapatistas are a people who are struggling to cre-
> ate the society that they talk about and they want. For example
> the Mayan people are a society that is very in touch with nature,
> they [have] within their religion a sensitivity toward nature and yet
> you'll see people kick a dog in a community and sometimes people
> from the U.S. are just shocked by that because we treat dogs as chil-
> dren in this country and they can't really get it through their head
> that that exists. There's a lot of ideas about women's rights issues;
> for example, the Zapatistas have a revolutionary law for women.
> Marcos actually said that the uprising that began in 1994 was the
> second Zapatista uprising and that the first was within the move-
> ment related to women's rights; however, that doesn't mean that
> there's equality across the board in the communities. There are still
> a lot of power struggles for women's rights. (Personal interview,
> February 19, 2004)

Being confronted by the incongruity between the living reality of people organizing themselves in struggle and the transnationalized representations of this struggle can be a moment of opportunity to begin building real relationships of solidarity based on the mutual recognition of dignity and humanity—complete with the explicit recognition of all the complexity and contradiction that implies. But when people react to this incongruity out of a sense of betrayal or profound disappointment at the shattering of their illusions, the consequences for the Zapatistas—and others like them—can be damaging indeed. As Stephan Dobson, a member of the Canadian Union of Public Employees, an academic, and a member of the planning committee for the Third Intercontinental Encuentro for Humanity and against Neoliberalism, noted to me during a conversation in the fall of 2003:

> I've seen [romanticization] in action [and] it's a problem of sustainability. People find out that it's not real or that they're dealing with the image rather than the really existing conditions. From my perspective, while you're imagining a better world how do you actualize it? My frustration with that kind of imagination way up here [is that it] strikes me as dogmatic idealism. It's always the revolution's elsewhere; Nicaragua was really the one when I was an undergraduate. Here it is, opportunity, it's happening, you have to be a part of it, you have to mobilize because it's the leading edge, it's something new, and it takes on all of the hopes and dreams and the aspirations and ambitions [of a generation]. But perhaps what I'm trying to get at with one of the things with the Third Encounter that always was falling out of sight was that those struggles [are] directly here. So while you have all this wonderful solidarity going on with Zapatistas, you've got a thousand Patricia Pats [a regiment of the Canadian Armed Forces] moving in on Oka.[5] No justice on stolen land. (Personal interview, October 31, 2003)

Dobson's comment about seeing romanticism as a problem of sustainability and the consequences of a "dogmatic idealism" are profoundly significant to any attempt to critically appreciate the possibilities and limitations of the radical imagination. These comments also serve as a signpost marking one of the most important contributions that ethnographically grounded approaches to exploring radical struggles for social change can make: namely, that it is only in attending to the way that imaginations are articulated, circulated, contested, and embodied that one can glean their true sociopolitical significance. As Dobson stresses here, one of the central challenges of mobilizing romanticism is not only that it can be betrayed but also that it must be continually reinvented or boredom ensues.

Does this then not begin to border on a desire to be entertained or stimulated by movements and struggles that, for the people who live them, are often quite literally about issues of life and death?

What is the political value of an encounter with a struggle if that encounter remains limited to satisfying the existential and political yearnings of those with whom the struggle finds resonance? At the same time, how do we measure the nonlinear effects of the circulation and resonance of a radical political imagination? What are the rhizomatic effects this resonance leaves in its wake? Cognizant of the warnings offered by my research partners, I nevertheless wish to posit a different interpretation of this romantic sentiment and the political imagination to which it is so often attached. One way to begin doing so is to cast an eye briefly toward history and remember that transnationalized Zapatismo is certainly not the first example of a rebel or revolutionary movement in one part of the world sparking the imaginations of activists located elsewhere. Indeed, as Peter Linebaugh and Marcus Rediker (2000) compellingly illustrate, the circulation and proliferation of powerfully liberatory and revolutionary ideas, and the human beings and social relationships that gave them form, were central—if all too often hidden or ignored—features of the rise of capitalism, the colonial enterprise, and the emergence of the modern world system. What is so striking about the circulation of these powerful revolutionary ideas, argue Linebaugh and Rediker, is that they were carried throughout the Atlantic world by those whom history has so often forgotten and despised—sailors, slaves, market women, laborers, criminals, pirates, indentured servants, and commoners. In the minds of the elites seeking to exercise their dominance over the emerging Atlantic economy, their own labors were of Herculean proportions, while the resistance struggles and lines of flight traced by common people marked them as a many-headed hydra (Linebaugh and Rediker 2000, 2–4). Propelled by processes of enclosure, criminalization, exploitation, resistance, and exodus and by traveling the emerging pathways of the nascent Atlantic capitalist economy, this motley, unruly multitude carried with it radical political imaginations that would persist despite the consolidation of the modern nation-state and the rise of capitalism by the early eighteenth century.

The circulation of radical imaginations of struggle was also a constituent feature of the rise of the politics of the New Left in the 1960s (see Katsiaficas 1987). In the overdeveloped or minority world, much of the revolutionary sloganeering and iconography of the New Left drew explicitly on the imaginary of the colonial militant as its impetus. The exhortation of student radicals engaged in the Students for a Democratic Society in the United States and, later, the Weather Underground to "bring the war home"—a direct reference to the guerrilla war being fought by the Vietcong against the U.S. war machine in Vietnam—is one such rhetorical invocation of this internationalized insurgent imagination. While, for some, Zapatismo and the Zapatista struggle functioned as fantasy facilitating the politically irrelevant romanticization and consumption of a revolutionary movement far distant from their own spaces and places, for others, the transnationalized political imagination of Zapatismo allowed a new dream of radical social change to flourish. More than this, it also shattered the illusion of the defeat of political possibility carefully cultivated by neoliberal elites at "the end of history."

A NORTHERN NODE IN THE ZAPATISTA RHIZOME

As I sat across the table from Rick Rowley and Jacquie Soohen in downtown Hamilton more than a decade after the Zapatista uprising and at the other end of the politico-economic space bound by NAFTA, the two radical filmmakers from Big Noise Tactical shared with me the significance of their own encounters with Zapatismo. Attending to this significance expressed in Rick's and Jacquie's own words opens a window to the Zapatista rhizome as well as the utility of ethnographic approaches to exploring the critical relationship between the radical imagination and radical social change struggles.

Rick, traveling through Central America and Mexico by bus with friends after high school, found himself in Mexico as the federal government was breaking its cease-fire with the EZLN in an attempt to capture key members of the Zapatista leadership and demonstrate the reliability of Mexico as a site for foreign investment. In Rick's words:

> We were heading north on buses and we arrived in Mexico City and ended up living in the south of the city in the university district, the UNAM, at this amazing moment when the country's on fire, there's a civil war in the South, there's movements emerging all over the country. No one in the [United] States had any idea that any of this was going on. I ended up staying for six months in Mexico City

. . . and became involved with the Zapatista solidarity movement there, so it was an amazing time to be alive. Every day we'd come down to buy [the Mexican Leftist daily newspaper] *La Jornada* and read the new communiqués from [the Zapatista spokesperson Sub-comandante] Marcos that came out. Every weekend there were demonstrations in the Zócalo sometimes as big as three hundred or five hundred thousand people, unlike anything I'd ever seen in the North. It was a party, we were dancing, there were huge puppets; it was an entire artistic, cultural, creative [experience]. It was every aspect of life being caught up in this feeling of change and open-ing and possibility. Even more amazing than that was the fact that we won, the demonstrations not just in Mexico City but uprisings throughout the rest of the country stopped the Mexican military from invading and ended the aggression. When we marched in the center of Mexico City, in the Zócalo in '95, we didn't march the way that people like us had marched in the '70s and the '80s, say-ing "we're against the war in the South; we support these people down there." We marched and said, "We are Zapatistas and the war is right here under our feet." That the Zapatistas have survived and won victories against this First World military armed with sticks and their word [is] because they've managed to tell a story about struggle that's an invitation to people to read themselves in as par-ticipants and not as observers on the outside. (Personal interview, September 20, 2004)

If Rick's story ended here, it could be read as an engaging but essentially voyeuristic political travelogue, an opportunity to step into and then out of someone else's struggle in a more politically minded variation on the rite of passage so often practiced by middle-class youths in the North as they proceed through the education system en route to their integration into the social machinery of capitalism. But Rick's story does not end there:

We returned to the United States as Zapatistas looking for what that might mean in the North and trying to learn from their ex-ample of struggle. You know, take it seriously, not just as an in-spiration but to learn from their tactics and their strategy. One of the things that was most resonant to us at that moment was the famous Zapatista line, "our word is our weapon." Armed with our word and sticks against this machine we're winning, and so we thought about what our word would look like in the North and we didn't think that communiqués and children's stories and poems in the Left-wing papers in the States was the move that would make sense. We thought video made sense as a language that could circulate, could move through these circuits of American culture. None of us had ever held video cameras before [or] had any film training, but we got credit cards and we bought cameras and went [back] down [to Zapatista territory in Chiapas] and started to shoot *Zapatista* [Big Noise Tactical's first documentary]. That was the beginning of Big Noise, the beginning of the work that followed, the work that I've done since then. We've never thought of ourselves as filmmakers, but as Zapatistas looking for forms of struggle that make sense in the North. (Personal interview, September 20, 2004)

Rowley's narrative traces the arc of his encounter with Zapatismo from resonance to a grounding and materialization in the form of Big Noise Tactical. Through this narrative the inspiration of Zapatismo is interwoven with the elements that account for its relevance to activists in contexts wildly different from Chiapas. In this way, the bases for and consequences of Zapatismo's resonance as a radical political imagination outside the borders of Zapatista territory become visible only if one attends to the lived significance of encounters such as these—a significance that only becomes visible if one takes seriously the ways in which those who have experienced this resonance render their own accounts of it. This is something that dominant trends within social movement studies have largely avoided taking up, choosing instead to advance successive paradigms (resource mobilization, new social movements, political opportunity structures, framing) that make sense of movement activity retroactively without ever asking the question of what makes these struggles and their attendant radical imaginations significant. Eric Selbin exhorts, "Along with the material or structural conditions which commonly guide our investigations, it is imperative to recognize the role played by stories, narratives of popular resistance, rebellion and revolution which have animated and emboldened generations of revolutionaries across time and cultures" (2003, 84).

Once the Zapatista struggle began to circulate transnationally through real and virtual (websites, listservs, digital media) networks in the weeks following the uprising, Zapatismo became a catalyst for the reinvigoration of the radical imaginations of others located far from the geographical space of the rebellion. Activist narratives such as the one offered by Rowley stand as a testament to the power of Zapatismo's transnationalization, but so too does the plethora of writing that has emerged from out of the ranks of the alter-globalization movement. This writing explicitly and self-consciously references the Zapatista uprising and Zapatismo as central to the rise of the "movement of movements" and to the political possibilities that have come after it (see, e.g., Callahan 2004; Juris 2008a; Kingsnorth 2003; Klein 2002; Midnight Notes 2001; Notes from Nowhere 2003; Solnit 2004). Jacquie Soohen's encounter with Zapatismo occurred differently. From a rural upbringing marked by economic insecurity in the Canadian prairies, Jacquie came to the challenge and inspiration offered by the Zapatista struggle through a set of life experiences that challenged the liberal conflict-resolution framework she had been socialized to invest in as a young person growing up in a "well-governed" country like Canada. Jacquie explained her encounter with Rick, Big Noise, and Zapatismo, as well as the consequences that flowed from it, during the course of our conversation:

> [When] I first met Rick and a few of the other people from Big Noise, they'd just come back from one shoot in Mexico. [I was just] amazed that you could take that inspiration, the idea of victory, the idea of standing up for something and fighting and winning and then also hearing it through stories—you knew that the demos didn't work, you knew that it had to be something else, and it had to be something about taking possession of a history that was both your own and expanded beyond your identity boundaries that were clearly marked for you inside a world of individualistic capitalism. I went down for the second half of that shoot. [I] hadn't even thought about making films but it was when we finally started screening [*Zapatista*] that [film] began to make sense as a weapon and became something that we decided to keep doing as long as it made sense, because you'd go places and you weren't talking to people who had, for the most part, even ever heard of Zapatismo, or for the most part they weren't politically active. It wasn't like they were audiences of activists, [but] people were so moved by it. We came to realize that it was our weapon that we could use

and something we could give over to a larger movement. (Personal interview, September 20, 2004)

The connections (interpersonal, conceptual, political) that Jacquie traces here are, in part, illustrations of what I refer to as the "Zapatista rhizome." Literally speaking, the rhizome is a plant stem capable of producing both roots and shoots. Conceptually, Gilles Deleuze and Félix Guattari (1987) explain that the rhizome is a way of understanding sociopolitical realities that shifts our attention from the fixedness of things (individuals, events, institutions, organizations) to the fluidity of movements. Rather than accepting the sociopolitical as constituted by discrete things that encounter one another on a relatively established terrain, the concept of the rhizome compels us instead to see the sociopolitical as a space defined only by the connections, encounters, and relations that occur within it. A rhizome has no essential form; it changes as the relations that compose it change. Counter-posed to the familiar sociological perspectives on social movements that have tended to privilege rationalist, cause-and-effect analytical and explanatory models, the concept of the rhizome encourages an explicit consideration of the way everything from institutions to social change movements to subjectivities are brought into being through a process that is intrinsically relational and has no meaning or direction outside of that relationality. In this regard, the rhizome as a conceptual and analytic tool is a metaphor through which to explore different dynamics and consequences of contemporary social movement activity.

AN ETHNOGRAPHY OF RADICAL IMAGINATION

The concept of the rhizome also allows for the appreciation of the non-linear paths through which political imaginations like Zapatismo travel on a transnational plane. The rhizome compels us to attend to the way radical politics is made and remade continually—just like the social order—not through a fixed structure, virtual networks, or institutions but through living, social relationships. Because of the unpredictable, dynamic paths the rhizome traces and the living, collective labor necessary to bring radical imaginations into being, ethnographically grounded approaches are uniquely situated to explore these phenomena, which has significant implications for the possibilities of and challenges to radical social struggles.

This is perhaps clearer when juxtaposed with an example of the dominant discourse about transnational contentious politics and Zapatismo. While social movement analysts such as Sidney Tarrow (2005) and Thomas Olesen (2005a) offer explanations for the transnationalization of the Zapatista struggle based on the explanatory tools of diffusion and framing theory, respectively, neither takes up the question of the significance of the transnationalization of Zapatismo for activists and their social change projects. While both of these accounts provide important insights, they are fundamentally teleological, offering explanations of Zapatismo's transnational resonance steeped in largely hegemonic assumptions about the nature of capitalist globalization viewed as technological innovation, the rise of new media, the development of transnational organizations, and economic integration—dynamics that elide the experience of capitalist globalization for the world's majority. These analyses also serve to reify processes, pathways, and practices while nearly erasing the presence and agency of living, sociopolitical subjects without whom none of this elaborate infrastructure would exist or have significance.

So how could this story of radical politics and transnational connections be understood differently? I turn once again to the reflections offered by one of my research partners on the subject of the radical significance of Zapatismo's transnational resonance. Patrick Reinsborough is an activist with and founding member of the *smart*Meme Strategy Training Project, a U.S.-based collective dedicated, according to its mission statement, to "build[ing] movements and amplify[ing] the impact of grassroots organizing with new strategy and training resources, values-based communications, collaborations, and meme campaigning. *Smart*Meme uses the power of narrative to advance a holistic vision of grassroots social change that connects struggles for democracy, peace, justice, and ecological sanity."[6] In the course of our conversation in 2004, Reinsborough offered a compelling insight into the relationship between the significance of Zapatismo's transnationalized political imagination and the mechanisms used to circulate it, which serves as a strong corrective to analytical visions predicated on the primacy of technological infrastructure or teleological assumptions about the nature of globalization:

> There's a very simple analysis [that some] people have developed
> [with respect to the resonance of Zapatismo] around technology
> and the rise of the Internet. Not to diminish the tools, but tools
> don't build a house, carpenters use tools to build a house. I think

that the beauty and the wit and the strategy with which the Zapatistas set the terms of their own conflict [allowed them to intervene] in something much deeper than state power in Mexico. They intervened in a global system in a way that was creating new spaces. [For] someone like myself, much of my political work is sort of tiny ripple effects of some of the amazing leaps of work that the Zapatistas created. Also [there's] the power of poetry, just these incredibly powerful poetic critiques [made by the Zapatistas] that were happening in a very systemic way. [The critiques] incorporate all the different pieces, whether you're talking about an economic critique or a political critique or an ecological critique, but also ground them in a commonsense emotional critique. I think that's something that I've been very attracted to in the struggle of the Zapatista movement and other similar resistance movements, and [I'm] trying to figure out how we translate some of that clarity of vision, how can we help the people that are right now comfortable and are caught up in the brainwashing apparatus of consumer culture. How can we help translate some of the experience [of] the communities who are being massacred and bulldozed and the places that are being destroyed to feed the insatiable appetite of global consumer society? In the face of what would seem like the most powerful destructive empire ever created, a global empire of corporate control, the Zapatistas were very effective in reminding us where our real power was. Those are the ripple effects that are being felt around the world. (Personal interview, March 9, 2004)

Reinsborough's comments speak to the reasons for why this political imagination resonated for so many in the United States and Canada. Indeed, many of my research partners engaged in a host of different social change projects would describe their own encounters with Zapatismo in such ways as: "real hope and also an understanding that there was still dignity" (Dave Bleakney, personal interview, March 25, 2004); in a world awash in neoliberal globalization, a "spark and an inspiration . . . [in] quite a dark time" (Eric Doherty, personal interview, March 12, 2004); and as "a tear in the fabric of the present," a crack through which radical political possibility seemed to reemerge (Rick Rowley, personal interview, September 20, 2004). Alberto Melucci once wrote of contemporary social movements: "The medium, the movement itself as a new medium, is the message. As prophets without enchantment, contemporary movements practice in the present the change they are struggling for: they redefine the meaning of social action for the whole society" (1985, 801). While Melucci's analysis of social movements tends toward a systems-privileging perspective that is perhaps overly invested in a postmaterialism with an essentially liberal identity politics focus, his characterization of the potentially revelatory and prefigurative elements of social movements is an important observation—one that speaks to Zapatismo as a transnationalized political imagination.

As a revelatory event that ruptured the defeatism that had sunk in for so many on the Left in the aftermath of the neoliberal declaration of the "end of history," the Zapatistas reignited hope in a politics of radical possibility. While it is possible to discern the most obvious signs of the circulation of radical imaginations on the fabric of contentious politics by mining the record for groups and events organized in explicit solidarity with different struggles, the indirect and often powerful effects of these imaginations will remain largely unconsidered. Even more problematically, while this kind of analysis can provide diagnostic insight into what has already happened, it cannot offer anything substantive in terms of understanding and engaging with the deep, potentially world-changing significance of social change struggles as they unfold. This is where ethnographically grounded insight offers its most robust contribution by taking seriously the fact that radical imaginations and radical politics do not enter the world as given; they are the product of activists' collective "power-to,"[7] collaborative labors of love situated at the intersection of the material (the real) and the immaterial (the more than real). What I have sought to provide here is a window to the terrain of the radical imagination. My research on the transnational resonance of Zapatismo raised for me as many questions as it modestly answered, and I have no definitive point to offer to bring closure to the relationship between new and radical challenges to the status quo and the imaginations that serve to inspire them. This is not a proscriptive analysis and the radical imagination is not a silver bullet through which to defeat the forces that have proved so formidable in preventing real, mass radical movements from realizing radical social change, particularly in the global North. But as I have sought to demonstrate, the radical imagination cannot be dismissed and if it is to be engaged, the ethnographic lens is essential to critical explorations of it.

NOTES

The research project that formed the basis of this chapter was made possible by funding from the Social Sciences and Humanities Research Council of Canada, the School of Graduate Studies at McMaster University, and the Institute on Globalization and the Human Condition, also housed at McMaster University. My sincere thanks and deep solidarity extends to all the activists who have and continue to share their thoughts, insights, commitments, and struggles with me during this project and those since. This chapter is dedicated to my partner, Candida, and our two sons, Indra and Eshan.

1   The corporate media has consistently used the term *antiglobalization* to refer to the diverse actors who have come together to disrupt meetings of transnational political and economic elites, protest corporate globalization, and challenge the making of a New World Order predicated on capital's mobility and people's exploitation via direct action. In a typically dismissive move, this term implies that the many and varied social change movements that came together to oppose capitalist globalization were simply marginal, poorly informed, and oppositional. In contrast to these dominant representations, many activists within this transnationalized "movement of movements" refer to it not as something against globalization but as a struggle for an *alternative* form of globalization; thus the term *alter-globalization*. While the specific content of this alternative form of globalization depends on the specific struggle, this alternative vision prioritizes social justice over the demands of capital and aims to put the technologies and processes of globalization at the service of struggles for justice, dignity, and freedom.

2   Francis Fukuyama declared "the end of history"—a reference to the end of ideological conflict and the global ascendance of capitalism and liberal democracy—in his book *The End of History and the Last Man* (1992), while U.S. President George H. W. Bush declared the birth of a "New World Order" on January 16, 1991, in a speech announcing the invasion of Iraq.

3   These collectives and organizations can, roughly speaking, be grouped into two camps. The first, more conventional one is constituted largely by groups and networks focused on issues of fair trade, human rights, educational campaigns, and public-awareness raising for the purpose of provoking political action. The second is composed of collectives and networks with an explicitly anticapitalist and antistatist orientation grounded in principles of grassroots, direct, and radically democratic political action.

4   In a communiqué issued in July 2003, Marcos (2004) referred to this dynamic as the "Cinderella Syndrome."

5   In the summer of 1990, a conflict erupted between the Mohawks of Kanesa-

take and settler Canadians from the town of Oka, Quebec. When a decision was made by the town to expand a golf course onto contested territory—some of which contained burial land sacred to the Mohawks—members of the Mohawk Nation, including the Warrior Society, erected barricades and engaged in direct action to prevent construction from proceeding. The local, provincial, and federal governments all chose the path of escalation, first sending in police and then the army to deal with the situation. The conflict lasted seventy-eight days with the Mohawks eventually putting down their weapons and ceding the barricades to the army while the mayor of Oka canceled the plans for the golf course expansion. The conflict became an iconic moment in the long history of indigenous struggles for sovereignty and land reclamation against the Canadian state.

6 See the "Vision" page of the *smart*Meme website, www.smartmeme.org (accessed June 21, 2012).

7 John Holloway, an autonomist Marxist theorist, asserts that "our capacity to do is always an interlacing of our activity with the previous or present activity of others." He further suggests that it is only when "the social flow of doing is fractured that power-to is transformed into its opposite, power-over," rendering the vast majority of people from *doers* (i.e., active subjects) "into the done-to, their activity transformed into passivity, their subjectivity into objectivity" (2002, 28–29).

3

The Possibilities and Perils for
Scholar-Activists and Activist-Scholars

Reflections on the Feminist Dialogues

MANISHA DESAI

Feminism, among other critical social movements, has a long, rich history of scholar activism (see Hewitt 2005). From bringing in women's voices to challenge hegemonic social theories to methodologies that are attentive to power differentials between researchers and their subjects, from scholarship that facilitates transformation of patriarchal institutions and practices to being active in movements, feminists have consolidated a dynamic relationship between the scholarly and political projects of feminisms. What is increasingly evident now, and less studied, is the ubiquity of activist-scholars, whose primary location is in social movements or NGOs but who also produce knowledge, are in dialogue with feminists in the academy as well as policy arenas, and who move easily between the academy and other sites. Hence, it is not an overstatement to note that we are all scholar-activists now, albeit differently located and resourced, engaging each other in virtual and physical spaces.

As with other hyphenated identities, that of scholar-activist is fraught with tensions depending on which part of the hyphen is privileged and who does the privileging. There are also different consequences for scholars in the academy and activists in social movements. I begin by reflecting on how I experienced these tensions in my early years as a scholar-activist, and how changes in the academy and in social movements have made this movement across borders easier. I then discuss some implications of this relationship for ethnography and for activist-scholars located in transnational movements by examining the Feminist Dialogues (FD) at the World Social Forum (WSF).

SCHOLAR ACTIVISM AND ITS DISCONTENTS

I came to graduate school in the United States in the early 1980s having learned the power of social movements in my training in social work school in India. I assumed the identity of a scholar-activist from the beginning of my graduate career. This identity was facilitated by changes in the U.S. academy at the time, in particular the institutionalization of feminist scholarship, which highlighted the intrinsic relationship between the intellectual and activist projects of feminism. It was understood that feminist scholars would have an activist commitment, which often was the focus of their research, and that this commitment would be reflected in their analysis and writing. This meant that ethnographic research methods, specifically participant observation and interviews, became common in feminist research.

At the same time, ethnography was undergoing its own transformations (see this volume's introduction), which resulted in rewriting the role of the ethnographer from an authoritative producer of knowledge to one of several interpreters in dialogue with each other. This was particularly the case for ethnographers of social movements, who, as movement participants along with other activists and advocates, sought to contribute to movements through their analysis. Yet, when I undertook my dissertation work on the origins of women's movements in western India, I unconsciously privileged on-the-ground activism in India. This was reinforced by my research experience. Friends and colleagues now saw me not as an insider but as a double outsider, first as an academic and secondly as an academic in the United States. This was evident in my exclusion from some feminist meetings in Bombay.[1] When I completed my dissertation, I sent copies of it to each of the women's groups with whom I had worked. But there was no engagement or dialogue with my analysis. In feminist methodology, power relations between the researcher and the subjects of research, and how the researcher can give back to the community, are important issues of discussion and debate (see Hesse-Biber 2007). In most cases, the assumption is that the researcher holds greater power. In my case, the activists of the women's movements were not only equally powerful but exercised power in ways that made me question the legitimacy of the scholar-activist role. Can one still be an activist if one is located in the academy, particularly halfway around the world?

Such tensions were diffused to some extent by two important factors, one related to the analysis of activism and the other to the increasing proliferation of transnational social movements. Social movement scholars, particularly of U.S. women's movements, began in the 1980s to address the vexing issue of what counts as activism (see B. Hess and Ferree 2001; Whittier 1995). Activism, they argued, happened in multiple sites and in diverse ways, including in the academy. Thus, using feminist methodology, praxis, and pedagogy in one's research, writing, and teaching; being guided in daily practice by feminist values of transparent and participatory decision making; and working to end women's invisibility on campus and in professional organizations were all considered legitimate forms of activism. This redefinition moved away from privileging one site of social transformation and recognizing the multiple structures, institutions, and everyday life as locations of change. This was a reflection of the multiple strategies and sites used by social movements, the increasing number of feminists in multiple sites who took their activism to those sites, and new social theories of the operation of power and oppression as a matrix of domination. This was true for other identity-based movements, such as those surrounding race, sexuality, and physical abilities. This did not mean that what you did in your workplace absolved you of activism on the ground, or in other sites, but this new conception of activism recognized the academy as an important site of struggle.

The second factor that destabilized the relationship between scholars and activists was the growth of transnational social movements, which shifted the "ground" of activism. Facilitated by the global economy and the emergence of information and communication technologies, social movements increasingly reached out across not only geographical borders but also identity- and institution-based borders. Activists connect with others around the world, teach in universities, and often publish in the same journals as scholars (see Casas-Cortés, Osterweil, and Powell, this volume). So although most activists are still located in specific places, many now function in multiple spaces. In other words, not only is there no single definition of what it means to be an activist but one can be active without being situated on the ground.

These shifts enabled me to move beyond my early doubts as a scholar-activist and to make interventions in transnational feminist movements. These shifts, however, have had important consequences. For scholars, they have pushed us to rethink not only our research methods and relations in the field but our role as knowledge producers. As Juris and Khasnabish note in the introduction, for ethnographers of social movements, such shifts have prodded us to theorize a militant ethnography in which research is an ethical and epistemological stance and where the scholar is one of many producers of social change-oriented knowledge. For their part, activists and social movements have had to deal with gaps between their burgeoning role as knowledge producers and their inability, in many cases, to generate lasting material changes. In what follows, I use the case of the FD to demonstrate and reflect on these consequences.

I have assumed various roles in relation to the FD, ranging from serving as a facilitator in Porto Alegre, Brazil, in 2005 to being a participant in Nairobi, Kenya, in 2007. As a facilitator I had more access to behind-the-scenes discussions and debates among organizers. As a participant in Nairobi I did not have the same degree of access but, given that several of the organizers were decades-long friends from India, I still had some sense of the dynamics. My analysis is based on participation observations, conversations with participants and members of the FD Coordinating Group, concept papers circulated by the FD, and the FD website. Based on my participation in and analysis of two Feminist Dialogues, I argue that although imagined as a dialogical space, this global gathering has, perhaps ironically, produced limited dialogue, and the dialogue that has ensued has primarily involved organizers rather than participants. At the same time, as dialogue became the primary goal of FD activists, their initial aims of making the WSF more feminist and energizing transnational feminist organizing were undermined.

THE WORLD SOCIAL FORUM, FEMINIST DIALOGUES, AND THE NEW CULTURAL LOGIC OF SOCIAL MOVEMENTS

Organized as an alternative to the World Economic Forum, where the elites of corporate globalization gather, the WSF was first organized in Brazil in 2001.[2] The WSF Charter of Principles defines the forum as "an open meeting place where social movements, networks, NGOs and other civil society organizations opposed to neo-liberalism and a world dominated by capital or by any form of imperialism come together to pursue their thinking, to debate ideas democratically, to formulate proposals, share their experiences freely and network for effective action. Since the first world encounter in 2001, it has taken the form of a permanent world process seeking and building alternatives to neo-liberal policies."[3] There is a rich body of literature on the WSF process written by both activists and academics (see Conway 2007; Eschle and Maiguashca 2010; Fisher and Ponniah 2003; Juris 2008a; Santos 2006; Sen and Waterman 2007; Jackie Smith et al. 2007). My intention here is not to review this body of literature, but to highlight some features common to most analyses.[4]

First and foremost, the WSF is seen as one of the most important expressions of the global justice or anticorporate globalization movements today. Second, most analysts differentiate between the global event that has taken place almost every year since 2001 and the many local, national, and regional forums that it has inspired, leading to what is often called the WSF process, involving social movements networking across their differences at multiple scales. Finally, the forums have also come to be seen as expressions of the new cultural logic of transnational movements (Juris 2008a).

What is this new logic? At its core, this logic is about a methodology and epistemology that values an open, democratic, nonhierarchical process; diversity and plurality of ideas and strategies about the matrix of domination; the network form for alliances with other movements; and an understanding of power that operates not just in macro structures and institutions but also at micro and meso levels, within and between movements. In short, this new cultural logic is about a new way of doing politics. Analysts have traced this logic to the socialist anarchists of the late nineteenth and early twentieth centuries, to the New Left of the 1960s, and most recently to the Zapatistas (see Juris 2008a). Of course, what is new about this logic today is its incorporation of feminist and indigenous concerns as well as the ways in which contemporary communication technologies make the network form viable in ways that could not have been imagined before.

Despite the commitment of the WSF to the elimination of gender oppression and even though the insights of feminist practices and processes were highlighted in the WSF Charter of Principles, the first three World

Social Forums, held in Porto Alegre, Brazil, from 2001 to 2003, did not reflect this commitment in the makeup of its International Council or the National Organizing Committee (the two bodies that plan the WSF), in the identity of keynote speakers, or in the sessions on gender. This is despite the large presence of women as participants in most of the movements present at the WSF. It was to challenge this marginality that feminists from seven feminist networks in Africa, Asia, Latin America, and the United States met,[5] "under a tree," during the 2003 WSF in Porto Alegre to organize a plan of action that would render the WSF more feminist. As an FD document explains,

> The Feminist Dialogues (FD) was first conceptualized at the Women's Strategy Meeting held in Porto Alegre, Brasil in January 2003. Over 50 women attended the Meeting—held under a tree, for lack of any other space! . . . The FD was initially seen as a strategy space to explore how to collectively make more feminist the WSF in Mumbai. Through subsequent discussions of the Coordinating Group, the FD's concept broadened to include objectives that would go beyond the WSF and strengthen feminist political organizing across borders. (Feminist Dialogues 2005, 1)

In the next section, I analyze how the FD engendered two kinds of transnational encounters among feminists: the first an ongoing transnational dialogue among fifteen or sixteen feminists from the networks that organized the FD, undertaken via the Internet and occasional face-to-face meetings, and the second a global gathering in conjunction with the WSF in which 150 to 300 women participated in order to dialogue and strategize. As we shall see, these different kinds of transnational encounters have different consequences for movement organizing.

FEMINIST DIALOGUES AS ACTIVIST SCHOLARSHIP

The first global gathering of the FD was held a few days before the 2004 WSF in Bombay. Since then it has been held twice, in 2005 in Porto Alegre and in 2007 in Nairobi, each time several days before the WSF. At the 2009 WSF in Bélem, Brazil, there was no FD but it organized sessions within the WSF. The three global gatherings were a result of months and eventually years of ongoing transnational dialogue among the seven networks, more specifically among the fifteen to sixteen activists from those networks.

After the first strategy meeting in Porto Alegre in 2003, Latin American and Asian feminists took the lead, articulating a transparent, participatory process through e-mail exchanges and chats to plan for the FD in Mumbai. A nine-member Coordinating Group (CG) was formed that was responsible for pursuing ways to make the WSF in India more feminist. These ongoing transnational dialogues had two aims. One was to negotiate with the planners of the WSF and the second was to dialogue among themselves to plan for the FD global gathering before the WSF. Because several CG members were Latin American feminists who had worked with the movements and groups involved in the International Organizing Committee, the negotiations with the WSF organizing committees were productive. This strategy clearly bore fruit as the Indian Organizing Committee and the International Council that planned the 2004 WSF in Bombay had a fairly high percentage of feminists and the WSF in Bombay was one of the most feminist WSFs to date. More than half of the sessions focused on gender, about half of the plenary speakers were women, and about half of the Indian Organizing Committee was composed of women activists. But the success of the Bombay WSF did not continue at the 2005 WSF in Porto Alegre or at the 2007 WSF in Nairobi and the 2009 WSF in Bélem, though feminists from the CG, particularly from India and Latin America, are still on the International Organizing Committee.

The second aim of the ongoing transnational dialogue was to prepare for the FDS, the global gathering in conjunction with the WSF. This second goal became the dominant concern of the continuing interaction among activists. In keeping with the CG's principle of autonomy, the FD was held not at the WSF but before it. Through Internet dialogues and face-to-face meetings, the CG focused on the process, the method, and the content of the FD. Initially, the ongoing transnational dialogues were taken up by logistical and financial decisions, but soon after, the focus shifted to the methodology and epistemology of the FD.[6]

Prior to each FD, the members circulated thematic papers that would form the concept papers given to the participants. For the first FD in India, the CG produced four thematic papers: "Women's Human Rights Tensions at the Intersection of Globalization and Fundamentalisms"; "Reclaiming Women's Bodies: The Struggle for Reproductive Rights"; "Challenging Sexual Borders and Frontiers: Affirming Sexual Rights"; and "Beyond the Local-Global Divide: Resistances in Current Geopolitics" (Feminist Dialogues 2005, 7). For the second FD, "the body" was seen as the lens through which to interrogate the relationship of women to globalization, militarization, and fundamentalism. For the last FD, the concept paper was titled "Transforming Democracy: Feminist Visions and Strategies." This paper was culled from five background papers circulated for the FD and included topics such as "feminist ways of working and articulation, fundamentalisms and body politics, neo-liberalism, democracy and militarism, and global feminist strategies, challenges and common approaches" (Feminist Dialogues 2007, 10).

It is impressive that activists from across multiple regions and networks were able to collectively produce such scholarship within a relatively short period of time. As their reports note, however, these were not easy endeavors as members had different political and theoretical positions, and while most shared a feminist analysis that highlighted women's multidimensional oppression and agency (hence the need for alliances), to come up with a concept paper that all could agree on required constant negotiation and revision. The CG's ability to produce a collective, scholarly product should serve as an inspiration to scholar-activists in the academy. The workshop organized by Jeffrey Juris that led to this volume (see the acknowledgments) is an important way to make our knowledge production more collective. Although, given our location in the academy, even when we engage in such a collective process the product is almost always individual in keeping with our concerns related to tenure and promotion.

The ongoing transnational dialogue among FD activists not only produced scholarship; it also successfully organized three global three-day FD gatherings, bringing together more than five hundred women in total. In addition to planning the logistics and methodology of the FD, the CG raised funds to support activists to travel to the FD. The decision to select a few activists from the many who had applied for the scholarship when the funds were limited was difficult and fraught with tensions. To accomplish this without an office or paid staff is in itself noteworthy. But to achieve this with a process that was self-reflective, participatory, and transparent speaks volumes about the feminists' commitment to the new cultural logic of social movements.

In its evaluation of the FD, the CG saw the effective collaboration between the seven networks as one of its most important accomplishments (Gandhi and Shah 2005). To build relationships of trust; overcome language, technology, and political tensions; and yet effectively produce ongoing dialogues and global gatherings over a period of three years is indeed a political success. But such ongoing transnational dialogues are successful only among a small number of activists and the focus of such dialogues is often behind-the-scenes negotiations, discussions of process, planning and organizing events, and production of analyses and concept papers. While all of these are important, Ruth Pearson (2003) cautions that feminist analysis is not the same thing as feminist politics. According to Pearson, it is this disproportionate focus among feminist activists on process and dialogues that explains the discrepancy between feminist visibility and lack of material change for a majority of women around the world. Hence, both activists and scholars need to be cautious about celebrating dialogue and global gatherings that do not translate into material social changes.

Beyond ongoing dialogues among the network activists, the CG also organized three global gatherings at the three WSFs. The rationale for holding the meeting before the WSF was "to achieve a two-way political exchange." As the FD explained: "Firstly, we hope to effectively intervene in the broader WSF process as feminists organizing for change, and to establish strategic and politically relevant links with other social movements. As a site of resistance, the WSF is one of the most dynamic spaces available to us as feminist activists and it is important to participate in it while at the same time retaining our autonomy within the FD" (Feminist Dialogues 2005, 5). Consequently, the two explicit aims of the FD were to intervene in the WSF and to establish strategic links with other social movements to reenergize the transnational feminist movement. Yet WSF organizers and activists from other social movements were not invited to participate in the FD. Moreover, each of the FDs was organized as a dialogic space, with several plenary sessions and then small-group discussions organized as workshops or buzz groups. The CG had established ambitious objectives for the FD which included the following: "To facilitate interaction between diverse global feminist organizations for strategizing on key issues; to plan an autonomous event around the WSF to raise feminist concerns within the WSF; to build up collective and transparent ways of functioning together as groups and networks; to deepen analysis regarding neo-liberal globalization, fundamentalisms, and militarism from a feminist lens; to learn from one another what feminists are doing; to explore dynamics, contradictions, and limitations within global feminism, such as issues of funding, race, class, [and] professionalization; and to highlight [the] diversity of approaches and strategies" (Feminist Dialogues 2005, 6). No one event can fulfill so many objectives, certainly not over two to three days when hundreds of women are involved. As I argue, some of these objectives were realized in the global gathering, but its main aims of intervening in the WSF, energizing the transnational feminist movement, and working with other movements were not.

The first FD in Mumbai was a two-day meeting involving 150 women. It was a closed gathering—participation was by invitation only among members of the seven networks involved as well as some donors and independent feminists. Several long panels led into workshops. Some participants were assigned as interlocutors. But since their roles were not well articulated, the workshops did not function as a means of encouraging dialogue among various transnational feminist networks. From logistical issues to participants not knowing what to expect, it would seem that the first FD did not meets its objectives. Yet, according to the organizers

> despite various shortcomings—particularly in methodology that made it difficult for the organizers to explore convergences and divergences—after the Mumbai FD, many groups showed keen interest in continuing with this process. In a three-day evaluation of the FD in Bangkok, Thailand[,] in May 2004, the CG critiqued and reflected upon the event, agreed to improve on its methodology and political impact, and made a general re-commitment to the Feminist Dialogue process up to 2007.[7]

In this sense, organizing the FD and doing it in a transparent and participatory manner became the main objectives rather than changing the WSF or making political alliances with other social movements to reenergize the feminist movement.

The second FD in Porto Alegre took into consideration the comments from participants as well as the CG's own critical evaluations. First, it became more open: one-third of the participants were selected based on an open call, and the remaining two-thirds were selected from FD member networks. Feminist media were invited to cover the event rather than keeping it closed. Second, a new structure—the Consultative Network Group (CNG)—was created to expand the organizing group to eighteen networks. Representatives from the new networks were invited to the FD but they were not given any specific charge. Finally, to address the surprising lack of dialogue in Mumbai, the second FD made some key changes to the format. A website was set up and participants were asked to indicate their interest in and expectations of the FD. Facilitators were also picked from among the participants to enhance discussion in the small groups and were given specific questions to guide the discussion. I served as one such facilitator.

Despite these changes, given the large numbers (250 participants), the structure of the three days, and the very broad questions for discussion during the breakout sessions, dialogue was again restricted.[8] For example, the first plenary in the Porto Alegre FD was on the history and methodology of the FD. At the end of this plenary, the tensions and contradictions were already evident. Several participants asked what the FD hoped to achieve. Would there be specific FD interventions at the WSF? The answers about dialogue and strategizing did not really satisfy the participants. This tension was furthered at the next plenary, called "Further Provocation: Moving Forward with Our Multi-dimensional Identities and Internal Diversities."[9] Most of the presenters and the interlocutors were academic feminists who laid out a critique of where we were in the present neoliberal conjuncture. In the discussion period following the presentations, many participants sought clarification of the academic concepts presented by the panelists, others expressed frustration at the general and abstract nature of the discussion, while still others urged the FD to make a statement against the war in Iraq. Some used the discussion period to outline the issues women face in different regions or to note confusion regarding the process and the goals of the FD. And despite the focus on dialogue, the structure of the event meant that discussion had to be cut short to move on to the buzz groups. During lunch and coffee breaks many of us noted our frustration with the contradiction between the goal of dialogue and the overly structured nature of the gathering that was not conducive to it. We all hoped that the smaller buzz groups would better facilitate dialogue.

As a facilitator of the buzz group I found that even the small groups did not result in dialogue for several reasons. First, as I mentioned earlier, we were given a fairly large list of questions to guide the discussion, which had to be reported back to the larger group. Second, participants came from different generations and different backgrounds, some from NGOs, others from movements and the academy, while for some this was their first global gathering. This diversity made the discussions both interesting and difficult as a common vocabulary had to be developed before we could converse. Finally, given the lack of translators for the small group discussions, groups were formed based on language competency—around English, French, Spanish, and Portuguese. This meant there was little cross-regional dialogue. As a result of this tension and frustration several subgroups began to emerge based on language, interest, and location. For example, the academics at the gathering met several times to share notes and discuss possible ways to connect the FD and the WSF. It was precisely here in such informal, impromptu groups that dialogue occurred and perhaps continued beyond the FD.

Throughout the three days participants were confused about what to expect and how the FD was going to intersect with the WSF. There were clear divides between feminists who saw the FD as a space for reflection and those who saw it as a space for political strategizing. The Latin American feminists wanted to use the space to come up with political strategies that could be carried out in the context of the WSF. Most of the Asian feminists were reluctant to do so. This was surprising given that all the FD materials emphasized that the FD was to be a strategy space to make the WSF more feminist. As a result, at the end of the second FD, there were no strategies to either ensure that the WSF was more feminist or to revitalize organizing among the feminist movements represented in the room.

The closing plenary in both the FDs that I attended consisted of presentations of reports from each of the buzz groups or small working groups. The purpose of the presentations was to enable all the participants to have a sense of the kinds of discussions that took place in the small groups. But given that each presenter had just a few minutes into which to condense three to four hours of discussion, the task was challenging to begin with. Furthermore, the presenter had to follow certain guidelines that made it difficult to capture the full dialogue. As a result, the uneven presentations did justice neither to the small-group processes nor to the goal of furthering dialogue. Moreover, the closing plenaries did not serve to plan for ongoing dialogue or to strategize with other movements at the WSF. Rather, they were a way to conclude the FD process. At the final plenary in Nairobi, for example, a PowerPoint presentation attempted to summarize conversations from the previous three days, outlining a few points made by various groups, announcing the FD organized sessions and marches at the WSF, and asking the dwindling number of participants to write in one sentence their feelings about the FD. As can be expected, most of the resulting "sound bite" comments were congratulatory and only a few were critical. Undoubtedly, many participants and subgroups used the FDs to build new networks and organize new campaigns, but without a follow-up process this is hard to know for sure.

Participant evaluations of the second FD noted that by the end of the event there was still a lack of clarity about the purpose of the FD. Several participants also noted the lack of grassroots women's organizations and activists in the CNG. Although the CNG was set up, there were no discussions between the CG and the CNG, so it was unclear what purpose the CNG was to serve (Feminist Dialogues 2005). In their own evaluation, CG members, while acknowledging the problems and tensions, highlighted the FD as an important political process within the transnational feminist movement.[10] Yet there was no sustained discussion about what makes it an important political process, or whether a political process should have concrete objectives that go beyond dialogue and deepening our understanding of the current conjuncture. The questions raised by the CG at the evaluation meeting are telling. For example, "What can an FD achieve? Is it enough to have an open space? Does FD have a link to the WSF? If so what are the links? Should it seek to intervene in the WSF process?" (Feminist Dialogues 2005, 30). Given that the FD emerged in response to the lack of attention to feminist issues in the WSF and that its stated objectives were to make it more feminist, the appearance of such questions two years into the process suggests that the FD event had lost its original purpose and that organizing the FD had become a political end in itself, "an experiment in collective feminist organizing" (Feminist Dialogues 2005, 5).

Such reflections did not stop the CG from organizing the third FD in Nairobi in 2007. More networks became part of the organizing, including Women in Development Europe, Akina Mama wa Africa, Tanzanian Gender Networking Programme, and Women Living under Muslim Laws. Despite the feedback from participants that the plenaries were not productive, the third FD was also organized around plenaries. In 2007, however, there was no debate about whether the FD was a space for dialogue or a strategy space to intervene in the WSF. It was seen as a global gathering of feminist organizations for reflection and to draw inspiration and energy from feminist movements around the world (Feminist Dialogues 2007).

The theme in 2007, drawing on the African Feminist Forum, was "Transforming Democracy: Feminist Visions and Strategies." Plenary speakers addressed the contradictions and limits of formal liberal democracy and the possibilities of liberal democracy through participatory methods such as gender budgets, but the presenters also highlighted the need for a radical democracy, which was defined as "a consciousness and a way of organizing social life in all dimensions in which we experience being human. Today's existing democratic systems (whether liberal or neo-liberal, or post-socialist) fail to engage in this all embracing way" (Feminist Dialogues 2007, 13). To enact this radical democracy, speakers focused on new notions of citizenship and sovereignty in the era of globalization evident in the struggles and mobilizations of feminist and other movements around the world. They emphasized the notion of shared authority instead of domination and subordination of the economic realm to the political and of markets to social interests. In the discussion period that followed, as in the plenary in Porto Alegre, the conversation was rather limited and participants were most animated when singing feminist songs from different countries at the beginning of the plenaries.

Following the plenaries, as in the other two FDs, there were small-group discussions, but with reporters instead of facilitators. Participants were asked to sign up for groups based on themes and to keep to those groups for the duration of the event. Needless to say, most of us did not keep to the same groups but circulated among various groupings based on our interest in particular themes or whom we happened to be seated with for lunch or during the plenary. The first set of discussions revolved around the challenges of redefining democracy, rights, and citizenships. Within this theme, groups could either discuss struggles for economic security and alternatives to neoliberalism or challenging exclusions, discriminations, and intolerances. Another set of discussions involved threats and challenges to democracy. Under this rubric we could address violence, war, and militarism; resurgent nationalism and the assertion of ethnic identity; or claiming spaces and leadership. The final theme for discussion was feminist organizing and feminist contributions.[11]

In my groups most participants did not specifically address the questions. Having used such discussion groups in our classes at universities, scholars are all too familiar with the pitfalls. Not everyone participates, even in small groups. Some participants are more familiar with this style of interaction and tend to dominate the discussion. And unless there are specific tasks to be completed, the small groups serve more to relieve the tedium of a lecture than for actual dialogue and learning. As there were no goals for the discussion besides reporting back, it often ended up as a free-flowing conversation. I do not mean to suggest that there is no room for discussion and dialogue that are not instrumental or goal oriented. But as a strategy for political change it seemed rather vague and ineffective.

Despite ambivalences and differences, each FD did intervene in the respective WSFS. At the 2004 and 2005 WSFS, this was done by organizing an intermovement dialogue between the feminist; gay, lesbian, and transgender; labor; and Dalit/antiracism movements. This session grew out of the CG's commitment to work with other movements, recognizing that transnational feminist movements have to make alliances with other movements to ensure true global justice for all. It was a way to take intersectional politics seriously. Most of the CG feminists had become autonomous from parties and other movements decades ago and were now seeking to build solidarities based on a position of strength and well-developed feminist perspectives.

The aim of the intermovement dialogue was to enable each movement to reconceive its vision and strategies by incorporating those of other movements. A representative from each had a chance to reflect on the ways in which they had succeeded and failed in addressing the issues of the other three movements. While all of the representatives stressed the need to build alliances, none of them specifically engaged the questions posed by the FD of the relationship of their movement to the other three movements. There was no effort to think through ongoing coalition building for redistributive efforts at local or regional levels.

If the intermovement dialogue sessions organized at the 2004 and 2005 WSFS were indicators of the FD's intervention in the WSF to make it more feminist and to build alliances, they were not very promising. The participants and most of the panelists were women. It was one session among hundreds that occurred simultaneously. The representatives of the other movements did not address how their movements had either rearticulated their visions to integrate other visions, reorganized their movements to include others, or reformulated strategies to address issues of inequalities, class, race, gender, and sexuality, among others. In fact, despite the ongoing networking among FD feminists and WSF organizers, the participants for the panel had to be confirmed at the last minute. Several panelists who had agreed withdrew. If the WSF was indeed the space to meet and exchange ideas with other movements, it was clearly not happening in the session organized by the FD. Yet the CG's evaluation notes that the intermovement dialogues have "begun transformation" of the debate in that arena. At the 2007 Nairobi WSF the FD discontinued this intermovement dialogue and instead organized a rally. The rally was well attended but again mostly by those who had participated in the FD. There were many other sessions on gender, feminist, and women's movements at the WSF that had no engagement with the FD and with which the FD did not coordinate. So the FD's attempts to ensure a feminist presence at the WSF were restricted to working with feminist networks that CG members belonged to rather than reaching out to other women's groups and movements. There was no FD at the 2009 WSF in Bélem, though the intermovement dialogue session did take place.

The CG's own evaluations recognized that they had not been successful in making feminist struggles visible at the WSF or in reaching out to other movements. The WSF is a difficult space to highlight specific struggles as there are so many movements, NGOs, and activists vying for visibility. To do so requires concerted work with the WSF committees to organize special large-scale events that are promoted actively throughout the spaces of the WSF. The indigenous movements succeeded in doing so at the 2009 WSF. They accomplished this by integrating their issues in the major theme of the WSF and by organizing major events such as concerts and plays, as well as having a special space in the WSF. Merely organizing sessions or even a rally that is not well publicized cannot make feminist struggles visible.

In the 2005 and 2007 WSFs, feminist activists who did not attend the FD were unaware of its existence. While the FD made no claims about representing anyone it still did not engage activists beyond its own networks. Hence, the issue of representation today is not who speaks *for* whom as much as who speaks *to* whom. While it is not silencing, it is not inclusive either. It is not easy to be inclusive at the transnational scale, yet it is important to build bridges within and across movements if the goal is to transform the WSF and transnational feminist organizing more generally.

SOME REFLECTIONS ON ACTIVIST SCHOLARSHIP
AND SCHOLAR ACTIVISM

My analysis of the FD is an intervention of a scholar-activist in the ongoing debates about scholar activism and activist scholarship in an age of transnational social movements. In this final section I highlight some of the implications of my analysis of the FD for both sides of the hyphen. The FD's transnational encounters consisted of an ongoing transnational dialogue among a relatively small group of feminists, and a global gathering over two to three days in which hundreds of feminists participated. The ongoing dialogues, while fraught with tensions, were a participatory way to accomplish collective knowledge production, organize large global gatherings, and, via behind-the-scenes negotiations, impact other global gatherings such as the WSF. As the experience of the FD suggests, such dialogues enable feminists to actively engage the new cultural logic of social movements.

But when dialogue operates as the primary political strategy, it shifts focus from other political goals and becomes an opportunity for disconnected interaction and organizing among activists who attend such gatherings. The FD organizers, whose aim was to intervene in the WSF and engage other social movements, became so focused on the methodology of dialogue that the FD's two original aims were undermined. The focus on dialogue was not the only reason for this, but it was a major one. This suggests that activist-scholars face different dilemmas than scholar-activists in the academy. When activist-scholars' commitment to process outweighs other concerns, particularly at relatively large, global gatherings, both process and specific aims are undermined. Dialogue as a goal and a process is more suited for smaller groups that meet on a regular basis. At larger gatherings, if there are concrete political projects, dialogue may hinder those goals. So activist-scholars outside the academy have to articulate other strategies to meet concrete political goals.

I also question some of the claims made by scholar-activists about engaged ethnography. While militant ethnographers no longer claim to be authoritative knowledge producers, and are often transparent about their commitments to the movements they study, how does their work contribute to social movements or social transformation? In the introduction, Jeffrey Juris and Alex Khasnabish state that one role for engaged ethnographers of social movements might be to contribute in more concrete ways to social movement theorizing and strategizing beyond analysis and critique. Can ethnography do more than provide critical analysis? To answer this, it is useful to revisit Alain Touraine's (1981) concept of sociological intervention, which he defined as a research methodology to identify new social actors and movements. Sociological intervention consisted of three stages: (1) sociologists form research groups through which they facilitate and provide critical analysis to a group of activists; (2) the groups interact with other social actors as interlocutors; and (3) groups analyze their experiences to shape both an understanding of the social relationships and conflicts as well as social action (Touraine 1981). There are many critiques of this methodology (see, e.g., McDonald 2002),[12] but for my discussion what is important is that even in this interventionist methodology in which social movements are central, Touraine saw the role of the sociologist as using his or her skills of social analysis to enable actors to define themselves socially and perceive the social conflicts and actions. In a similar sense, I would like to suggest that engaged ethnographies are perhaps most important to movements as a supportive interlocutor. This limited contribution to social movements does not in any way diminish the contribution of militant ethnography, either to social movements or to scholar activism. Indeed, militant ethnography has played a central role in rethinking knowledge production. Such engaged ethnographic work has questioned the theoretical and methodological foundations of our disciplines and also contributed to new pedagogies, resulting in more-engaged students. And the limited contribution of engaged ethnography does not restrict our contribution as activists. But the contribution of ethnography, however engaged, is going to be necessarily limited. And given the emergence of engaged ethnography in a context of widespread distrust and questioning of metanarratives, we should not be troubled by such limitations.

In memory of Bina Srinivasan; feminist, friend, and organizer of the Feminist Dialogues.

NOTES

1   In this chapter I use both *Bombay* and *Mumbai* to reflect people's usage in the city: Bombay when speaking in English and Mumbai when speaking in a regional language. Specifically, I use Bombay in my general writing and Mumbai in those contexts where it was used by activists and participants: WSF India, the Feminist Dialogues, and Mumbai Resistance. My usage of Bombay also reflects my opposition to Shiv Sena, the right-wing nativist party that changed the name of the city from Bombay to Mumbai.

2   The corporate elite, however, have now begun to include activists from the WSF in their deliberations.

3   See the "FAQ" page of the Charter of Principles section on the WSF website, www.forumsocialmundial.org.br, October 26, 2005 (accessed December 25, 2011).

4   There is also a small body of literature that sees the WSF as another example of neoliberal cooptation; such a critique is evident in some of the counter-summits organized in Canada, India, and Europe and addressed in this volume (see, e.g., Iqtidar 2004). See also the Mumbai Resistance website, www.ilps-news.com/central-info-bureau/events/mumbai-resistance-2004/ and www.countercurrents.org/chossudovsky260910.htm (both accessed December 25, 2011).

5   The seven networks were Development Alternatives with Women for a New Era, Women's International Coalition for Economic Justice, Articulacíon Feminista Mercosur (the Mercosur Feminist Alliance), National Network of Women's Autonomous Groups, African Women's Development and Communication Network, INFORM-Sri Lanka, and Isis International-Manila. Feminists from these networks had known each other over a decade of organizing at regional and transnational meetings. Akina Mama wa Africa, Latin American and Caribbean Committee for the Defense of Women's Rights, Latin American and Caribbean Youth Network for Sexual and Reproductive Rights, Network of Popular Education between Women, Women Living under Muslim Law, and Women in Development Europe became involved for the third FD in Nairobi.

6   The FDs were funded by donors such as the Global Fund for Women (U.S.) and Mama Cash (The Netherlands).

7   "Feminist Dialogues: Evaluation 2005" (pamphlet), in the author's possession.

8   Some of these questions were, "What dilemmas do we face as feminists? What are the sites of resistance? How do we interlink with other movements and why should we engage them? Where are you in relation to the present trends in the context of globalisation, militarisation, and fundamentalism? How would you express/understand these forces of globalisation, militarisation, and fundamentalism from the perspective of your Body?" (Program of the Second Feminist Dialogues, World Social Forum, Porto Alegre, Brazil, January 26–31, 2005).

9   Ibid.

10 Throughout the FD and the reports, the terms *transnational* and *global feminist movement* are used interchangeably.

11 Program of the Third Feminist Dialogues, World Social Forum, Nairobi, Kenya, January 18–19, 2007.

12 Among the main criticisms of Touraine are his focus on defining the main social-movement actor for each era (although that is no longer the case), his "over-rationalized" conception of social movements (Kivisto 1984), and his sense of missionary zeal or sociological Leninism (McDonald 2002).

4

From Local Ethnographies to Global Movement

Experience, Subjectivity, and Power among
Four Alter-globalization Actors

GEOFFREY PLEYERS

Fifteen hours into the August 2005 gathering of Zapatista *comandantes* (commanders), youths, and civil society in the remote Zapatista village of Juan Diego, speakers took their turns at the podium, one after another, exchanging ideas about their local experiences. At three in the morning, Tito, a young man from a working-class neighborhood of Mexico City, took the mic and explained, "I don't know how to speak well in public. Actually, there are only two things I know how to do well: graffiti and hip-hop. So I'm gonna sing one of my songs, a rebel Zapatista song." As he performed, the energy of the crowd began to peak and people rose to their feet. When the first song concluded the young singer took the opportunity to launch into a second tune "dedicated to Subcomandante Marcos." Despite the late hour, the dozen Zapatista comandantes all stayed to listen to the teenager, who expressed in his own way the difficulties of life in the poor suburbs, his disappointed hopes, and his desire for a better world. As Tito broke into a final song, a Trotskyist and long-time supporter of the Zapatista cause came over to me and began to fidget, before whispering, "This is all very well, but what use is it? What conclusions can be drawn from all of these speeches? What text will come out of them?"

From the point of view of institutional politics, such meetings and actions seem limited. Indeed, the many Zapatista mobilizations for constitutional reform in Mexico clearly failed at the politico-legal level. How might these songs in the middle of the night in the remote mountains of Chiapas have any influence or help to improve the rebel indigenous situation? Similar questions arise about expressive activism elsewhere. For example, what is the political impact of tagging billboards in the subways of Mexico City, London, or New York? Many would consider these kinds of actions counterproductive in that they impair the functioning of a vital public service. Or what about the convivial "critical wines" gatherings (alternative wine fairs) organized by Italian social centers (Toscano 2011)? How might these have any political or economic impact? These actions might be seen as symptoms of decreasing participation in the mechanisms of political life or social movement decline (Phelps-Brown 1990). At best, such activities can be viewed as indicative of an early phase in the cycle or development of a social movement when innovations proliferate, creating "relatively open spaces for new collective experiments" (Tilly 2004, 105).

In contrast, ethnographic field research has led social scientists to emphasize the energy and creativity of young activists, suggesting the emergence of distinct cultures of activism rather than a lack of maturity or social movement weakness (see Juris 2008a; McDonald 2006; Osterweil 2004b; Pleyers 2004; Ponniah 2006). The actors in the above-mentioned actions are not interested in taking their place as "challengers" in the political arena (Gamson 1990). On the contrary, they seek to escape the political sphere in order to develop a resistance to corporate globalization that centers on subjectivity, lived experience, and the development of concrete alternative practices. An ethnographic approach allows us to emphasize emerging elements that have been largely ignored by more-objectivist methods. This is particularly true with respect to subjectivity, local practices, and alternative visions of social change. Ethnographic research, through its close interaction with activists and its lengthy time commitment, facilitates an "adjustment between hypothesis and evidence, especially in the form of interrogating activists about what they think they are doing" (Jasper 2007, 97).

This chapter argues for the importance of an ethnographic approach for grasping the *expressive* and *global* dimensions of emerging forms of activism. Following the sociology of social movements proposed by Alain Touraine, my approach consists of isolating, for heuristic purposes, the main features of contemporary anticorporate globalization (or alter-globalization) activism in order to draw out, beyond the specificity and particularities of each case, the meanings and coherence underpinning similar actions in distinct local contexts.[1] I base my analysis on field data obtained in a wide range of settings in the global North and South related to both globalized and more-localized forms of action. I mainly draw on observations and analysis of four collective alter-globalization actors that have embodied this subjective or expressive current, serving as incubators of an emerging political culture: the autonomous process developed by Zapatista indigenous communities in southern Mexico; an alternative social and cultural center in Belgium; autonomous *piquetero* (picketer) groups organized by Argentine unemployed workers; and networks of young, highly individualized and cosmopolitan alter-activists.

The following two sections outline my epistemological approach and introduce the case studies. I then go on to explore four principal elements of the movements addressed here: the centrality of experience and subjectivity; the conception of alternatives emerging through concrete processes of experimentation; the idea of "spaces of experience"; and similar notions of learning and knowledge. I focus throughout on one of the logics of action within the wider alter-globalization movement. The latter also includes groups more oriented toward deliberative democracy, advocacy, and active citizenship, as well as political actors who place their hopes in progressive political parties and governments. Elsewhere I have shown how these different political cultures interact in the context of alter-globalization events such as the social forums (Pleyers 2011; see also Juris 2008a).

FROM MULTISITED LOCAL ETHNOGRAPHIES TO GLOBAL ACTION

Ethnographic observations provide an important counterweight and a complement to the data and insights regarding global issues gained from other methods, such as statistics, textual analysis, or interviews. If ethnography challenges the dominant conception of the global as distant, universal, and abstract, suggesting instead that the global is produced and consumed locally (see Abélès 2008; Burawoy 2000; Friedman 2004), the global challenges ethnography as a methodology that has traditionally been locally rooted. Global ethnography presents significant challenges with respect to cases that are embedded in specific local contexts.[2] How do we shift from local ethnographic observations to an analysis of movements that are global in scope?[3] From Porto Alegre to Mumbai and Dakar, from Seattle to Genoa, Hong Kong, and Pittsburgh, a series of discrete yet connected mobilizations have been viewed and experienced as phases in a singular alter-globalization movement. On what basis can we refer to a common, integrated movement unifying heterogeneous events and actors?

Multisited field research conducted in various countries and localities often presupposes a comparative approach that focuses on the similarities and differences between ethnographic sites, despite the intention of George Marcus (1995), the principal proponent of multisited research, to focus on linkages and flows rather than discrete cases. In terms of the alter-globalization movement, studies in this vein often conclude that although activists discursively refer to a common movement, the alter-globalization movement is distinct in each country due to the specificity of the national culture, the particular history of local civil society, or the structure of political opportunities (see Agrikoliansky, Fillieule, and Mayer 2005; Pleyers 2008). An alternative approach consists of focusing on the specific features of shared political cultural forms (Escobar 1992), constituting a coherent logic of action defined as a set of normative orientations, practices, and modes of organizing (Dubet 1994), as well as a way of relating to an adversary and a distinct approach to social change (Touraine 1981).

This perspective builds on field research data to reveal underlying commonalities beyond the variations among the concrete subjects that embody a movement in distinct local and national contexts. Such an approach does not seek to homogenize alter-globalization activists, networks, or organizations in various countries but rather to reflect on shared meanings and challenges that confront and are produced by these actors within the interlinked spaces of a locally rooted yet globalized movement. Political actors generate the movement and its underlying logic, but movement actors cannot be reduced to these logics. In this sense, the unity of a movement is not incompatible with the heterogeneity of a movement's constituent actors. As Touraine argues, "we sometimes forget, in speaking about *the* workers' movement, that it is embodied by unions, parties, cooperatives and mutual aid organizations" (1981, 124; emphasis in the original). The alter-globalization movement is similarly embodied by diverse and relatively autonomous actors and events. Moreover, the unity of this movement is not to be confused with the existence of a single organization encompassing its various components. Rather, the unity of the movement relies on social meanings shared by the actors who embody them (Melucci 1996; Touraine 1981), and on the major challenges these actors face. Following this approach, I propose a framework for understanding expressive action, one of the main political cultures and logics of action of the alter-globalization movement as embodied by a range of movement actors.

While a series of experiences, speeches, gatherings, and demands are associated with this historical alter-globalization actor, none of these precisely or completely corresponds with the historical subject of alter-globalization (Dubet and Wieviorka 1995, 9). However, it is at this level that the unity and coherence of the practices, events, and actors associated with alter-globalization can be grasped (see Touraine 1981, 2000). This epistemological move arises from an attempt to synthesize reality that borrows from the Weberian ideal type in the way it reduces complexity and selects facts (Coenen-Huther 2003), thereby effecting "a deliberate accentuation of certain features of the object under consideration" (M. Weber 1995, 91). As Max Weber notes, "the fact that none of these ideal types we have discussed are historically present in a 'pure' state cannot prevent a conceptual fixation as pure as possible" (1995, 290).

In this perspective, the focus of analysis will be less the social actors themselves and more a series of meanings and practices generated by these actors that can help us to understand the rationale, aims, and significance of their activism. The ethnographer's contribution is less to provide a panorama of the organizations than to trace the connections between networks that embody the alter-globalization movement. The aim is to develop an analytical perspective with respect to underlying logics of action defined as "heuristic devices which order a field of inquiry and identify the primary areas of consensus as well as contention" (Held and McGrew 2002, 3; see also M. Weber 1995). At the same time, such an analysis may uncover the impossibility of actors' aims by examining the structural contradictions, the distance between the achievements and espoused values of the movement, and how these particular actors distance themselves from the underlying meanings of the alter-globalization movement (see Pleyers 2011; Wieviorka 2003).

A modest contribution of ethnographic analysis to social movements thus consists of helping activists to grasp the implicit meanings of their action (Juris 2007, 165–66), as well as the main challenges raised by their practices, goals, and conceptions of social change. While meeting some of these challenges may require institutional solutions (e.g., democratic global institutions), responses are in no way limited to the institutional domain. Deeply embedded and participatory ethnographies can help us grasp the meaning of global activism beyond institutional arenas, generating reflections among activists and researchers regarding broader social goals and visions of society.

EMBEDDED ACTORS

While the Zapatista movement's resonance at the global level constitutes one of its major impacts (see Khasnabish 2008; Khasnabish, this volume), the movement's strength, its "essence," as the Zapatistas themselves refer to it (EZLN 1994, 133), lies in the local indigenous base communities. Outside the system of political parties and Mexican institutions, autonomous municipalities organize the lives of dozens of villages, implementing local autonomy in various spheres, including government, justice, education, and health. At the first "Gathering of the Zapatista Peoples with the Peoples of the World" held in Chiapas in January 2007 (see Pleyers 2008, 66–71, and this volume's introduction), a Zapatista comandante defined autonomy to me as a process that "allows people to decide how to live and how to organize themselves politically and economically." Another indigenous woman told me, "Autonomy is about governing ourselves as indigenous people, saying how we want our political authorities to work, no longer being subordinate to policies from above."

Barricade is an alternative social and cultural center that has been active since 1996 in a working-class neighborhood in the center of the Belgian town of Liege.[4] It hosts diverse activities, all of which create new forms of sociability and implement alternatives to consumer society and passive leisure activities: an activist bookshop, a social bar, a "Cyber-Center" that promotes free software and offers introductory computer courses to unemployed workers, a theater company, a choir, and a collective buyer's co-op. As a cultural center, Barricade sees itself primarily as a convivial space where it is possible to read or have a discussion about one of the many beers available at the collective's bar. This multifaceted project seeks to translate political demands and a general questioning of neoliberal policies into concrete activities inscribed in everyday life ("to act from our daily life," in the words of one member). In this sense, around twenty people meet each Monday to address agricultural and food problems through a collective purchasing co-op, ordering their food directly from politically committed local producers. One participant explained during a meeting in April 2003 that the project aims to demonstrate the possibility of "alternatives to the supermarket and to a productivist agricultural policy."

"Alter-activists" are a segment of young alter-globalization activists who put subjectivity and creativity at the center of their new forms of political commitment (Juris and Pleyers 2009; Pleyers 2004, 2006, 2011). Alter-activists converge in the context of alter-globalization protests and social forums, but they often do so by maintaining a critical attitude toward internal hierarchies and the lack of democracy within certain sectors of the movement. They seek to avoid the grammar of representational practices (see McDonald 2006), implementing instead practices based on the ideals of horizontal coordination, direct democracy, and flexible networks (despite multiple contradictions). Alter-activist cultural forms and practices, including direct action and self-managed protest camps, are characterized by expressive modes of action and an emphasis on process and experimentation. For example, youth camps at the World Social Forum (WSF) gathered 2,300 activists in 2002, 15,000 in 2003, and 30,000 in 2005. In June 2003, the Intergalactic Village during the mobilization against the G8 summit in Evian, France, involved more than 4,000 activists and had a deep impact on young French activists. The 2007 anti-G8 autonomous protest camps near Heiligendamm, Germany, hosted more than 10,000 activists. The organization of the camps, like the Occupy encampments in cities around the world in 2011–12, was participatory and surprisingly efficient, at once experimental and functional with respect to cooking, security, workshops, cleaning, and action trainings.

The Argentine piqueteros are part of the popular mobilizations of the unemployed that emerged following the Argentine government's adoption of neoliberal policies in the 1990s. The piqueteros were frontline actors in the mobilizations of 2001 and 2002, which led to the successive resignation of several Argentine presidents. During a visit to Buenos Aires in February 2003, my ethnographic research focused on the autonomous fringe of the piquetero mobilizations that was characterized by an extremely critical attitude toward government efforts to reorganize neighborhood life. In subsequent years the social policies of President Nestor Kirchner and the decision of many piquetero leaders to join the officialist camp marginalized this autonomous tendency.

In the contentious politics,[5] political process, and resource mobilization frameworks and other utilitarian paradigms, many actions undertaken by the activists considered here seem irrational and counterproductive. Tagging subway billboards drains resources available for public transport while breaking bank windows contributes to a negative image of the alter-globalization movement in the press and helps the movement's opponents sharpen the division between "good" and "bad" activists (Daro 2009a). However, such actions appear more coherent when considered in the context of their cultural politics (S. Alvarez, Dagnino, and Escobar 1998). These activists seek to construct themselves as actors not through political advocacy but by asserting their subjectivity, which I define as the affects, emotions, and thoughts generated by the will to think and act by oneself, to develop and express one's own creativity, and to construct one's own existence. According to John Holloway, activists believe that "the oppressed are not just a particular group of people, but rather a particular aspect of the personality of all of us; our self-confidence, our sexuality, our creativity" (2002, 157).[6] Touraine further explains, "We cannot oppose this invasion [of personal subjectivities] with universal principles but with the resistance of our unique experiences" (2002, 391). These activists want to defend the autonomy of their lived experience in the face of the influence of a globalized society and of economic powers over all aspects of life (see Habermas 1984; Illich 1973). Against the sway of the dominant ideology and markets, they seek to produce their own forms of cultural life and to transform and assert themselves through their own creativity, beyond the manipulations of the hegemonic culture industries. Their movements represent a call for personal and communitarian freedom against the logics of power, mass production, consumption, and the media. Subjectivity is at the core of these forms of struggle.

While indigenous communities have developed a collective and communitarian version of this activist culture by focusing on preserving their ways of life, their specificity, and their resistance to capitalist commodification, young alter-activists have adopted more individualized ways of opposing the hold of capitalist society (Juris and Pleyers 2009; McDonald 2006). They express their subjectivity and creativity through their many actions, from the subversion of advertising (ad busting) to songs, festive parades, and performances on the part of clown armies during blockades of global summits (see Daro, this volume; Routledge, this volume). Everywhere, it is a matter of "posing against the misery of power, the joy of being" (Hardt and Negri 2000, 496). For example, after the final march at an anti–World Trade Organization (WTO) demonstration in 2003 in Cancun, three thousand activists gathered at the fence protecting the resort area where the WTO meetings were being held. Young Mexican women and Korean trade unionists began opening holes in the fence, while others shouted slogans and sang. After an hour a hole finally opened, leaving protesters directly facing the police. As the tension rose and the observers were expecting a violent confrontation, protesters sat down for a moment of silence. This was followed by a few speeches. Then protesters burned an effigy representing the WTO and laid flowers before the police. Hundreds of activists then began dancing to Korean, Latin, and North American music to celebrate their symbolic victory against the WTO (see Juris and Pleyers 2009). Such theatrics aim to make events attractive and media worthy, to invite the public to reflect or simply have fun while protesting.

Moreover, the struggle does not only play out against an external adversary or system. Activists also situate their struggle with respect to the personality of each individual and each movement organization. As a young activist from the Anibal Verón piquetero network pointed out, "The struggle is just as strong against oneself as against the enemy. We must be conscious of and recognize the tendencies to pride and opportunism we all have, since we are all steeped in this system" (personal interview, February 2003; see also Holloway 2002). An activist at the "Beyond the ESF" gathering during the European Social Forum in London in October 2004 put it to me this way: it is "also a matter of transforming the self, including one's relation to others, which involves escaping the spirit of competition and consumerism promoted by neoliberalism."

EXPERIMENTATION

Another key element shared by the four alter-globalization actors considered here involves an approach to activism as a permanent process of experimentation. As the Zapatista comandante Brus Li stressed to me at the First Encounter of the Zapatista Communities with the Peoples of the World on January 1, 2008, "There are no guidelines for how to become autonomous." Youth protest camps emphasize a similar challenge: "We are feeling our way, seeking out concrete and emancipatory paths toward the transformation of social relations."[7] Alter-activists conceive of these camps not only as a base to prepare and lead actions against neoliberal institutions and to host workshops on alter-globalization issues, but also as spaces of experience, laboratories where alter-activists can experiment with new ideas, practices, and forms of social action. Alter-activist camps are opportunities for experimenting with different forms of participation and social interaction.

Everything starts with concrete, limited projects, which, when taken together, begin the process of creating a different society. Experience is central. As Holloway states, "the revolt must be practical; it must involve the construction of another way of doing, another sociability, another form of life" (2003). Activists seek to build another world from the starting point of their concrete practices and experiences: other ways of consuming, horizontal and participatory organization, and convivial neighborhood relationships. According to this perspective, change is not limited to the local level but resolutely unfolds from the bottom up, beginning with practical solutions. Activism starts in the context of interactions of daily social life. Building different kinds of social relations that are joyful and noncompetitive is of great importance. As a young Mexican activist explained to me during a Zapatista solidarity meeting at the anti-WTO protests in Cancun on September 11, 2003, "We can't change the world if we don't start with ourselves. Helping our neighbors, seeing how things are going in our neighborhood." Similarly, the "first revolution" of the Zapatistas is not the 1994 uprising but the promotion of egalitarian gender relations in their communities (EZLN 1994, 107–10).

Central to this process is the principle of consistency between means and ends, between practice and values. A leaflet from the 2003 European Social Forum in Paris quoted an alter-activist as stating: "We do not separate our practices and aims. We choose a horizontal, antisexist, self- and eco-managed way of operating."[8] An activist from Barricade had this to say: "Our manner of working has to reflect the values we are defending as part of our resistance" (personal interview, April 2003). Activists thus conceive of struggle as a process of creative experimentation in which the values of another world are put into practice within movement organizations and meetings (Grubacic 2003). Political engagement is thus performative: the objective does not precede action but is rather produced in the context of action. How alter-activists behave in their everyday lives and in their activism prefigures the better world they wish to build, reflecting the slogan on which Gandhi built his movement: "You must be the change you wish to see in the world." Alter-activists have seized upon and developed this idea. As a piquetero activist from the Movimiento de Liberación Territorial (Territorial Liberation Movement) explained, "It's not that tomorrow there will be change; change is visible today in the movement" (personal interview, February 2003). Consequently alter-activists devote a great deal of energy to organizing their networks in a democratic, horizontal, and participatory fashion, reflecting an innovative experiment in local/global democracy (see, e.g., M. Smith 2008; Teivainen 2008).

The forms of activism explored here are generally suspicious of overarching models, prefabricated social projects, or pre-established plans. In this sense, Zapatismo does not represent a model to be followed; it is more of an inspiration that needs to be adapted to local realities, specificities, and aims (see Khasnabish 2008; Khasnabish, this volume). As an activist explained during a meeting on Zapatismo at a social center in London in October 2007, "It's not a transportable, prebuilt model but a source of inspiration in order to rethink our democratic practices." Or, as a piquetero suggested to me, "Zapatismo is a model that has had particular success and from which everyone has a lot to learn. But it is in no sense a universally applicable model. Each place must find its own. The experiences of others can help, but importing a model wholesale can never work" (personal interview, February 2003). Indeed, as Miguel Benasayag and Diego Sztulwark explain, "There is no social model that represents the implementation of the desire for liberty and emancipation. . . . The only thing that exists are multiple acts of liberation" (2000, 29). Alter-globalization activists call on a multiplicity of alternatives in order to create "a world in which many worlds fit."[9]

SPACES OF EXPERIENCE AND ANTIPOWER

A similar ideal of autonomous spaces is implemented by different actors in distinct ways, but with similar meanings. Confronted with the invasion of life by the logic of the market, these actors all seek to build spaces of experience: places sufficiently autonomous and distant from capitalist society that permit actors to live according to their own principles, to knit different social relations, and to express their subjectivity (see Pleyers 2011, 37–48).

Indigenous communities, social centers, movement gatherings, pique-tero neighborhoods, and protest camps are places where alternative prac-tices are implemented and experienced as well as platforms from which struggles are organized against commodification, hostile states, and neo-liberal institutions. These spaces simultaneously constitute places of struggle and "antechambers of a new world" (EZLN 1995, 385; see also Ornelas 2004), allowing individuals and collectivities to construct them-selves as subjects, to become protagonists in their own lives, and to defend their right to be unique. Zapatista, Barricade, and youth camp activists place particular importance on nonhierarchical relations as they try to create spaces of experience "freed of power relations through the dissolu-tion of power-over" (Holloway 2002, 37),[10] and outside the domination of market ideology and communalism.[11]

While the spaces of experience developed in the movement contexts considered here share many similar aims and meanings, the forms they take may vary. Some spaces are created to allow participants to (re)con-struct their lives entirely. These include the Zapatista communities and their caracoles (good government councils; see, e.g., Speed 2007), pique-tero neighborhoods, occupied factories, neorural communities in Argen-tina (Mésini 2003), European squats, and Brazilian landless worker settle-ments. For example, the group of landless peasants I visited in 2002 in southern Brazil had established small individual farms on land they had appropriated, but there were also collective organic fields, a school ap-plying Freirean pedagogy, and a health center that practiced natural, tra-ditional, and alternative methods. Similarly, the main challenge of Zapa-tismo lies in the assertion of dignity as recovered self-esteem and the transformation of social relations within the communities themselves, whether relations of production, political decision making, or gender.

Other spaces of experience are more ephemeral. Many occupations last only a matter of days. During the one-week occupation of a school building in Liege, for example, activists set up L'École des Cybermandaïs with an independent radio, workshops, concerts, discussions, and party spaces, resulting in a temporary mode of community life that provided a respite from the principles and values of capitalism. Even more transient are the occupations and reappropriations of the streets, which generally only last a couple of hours. This type of action was highly valued by the Reclaim the Streets network at the end of the 1990s: "Whether we were re-claiming the road from cars, reclaiming buildings for squatters, reclaiming surplus food for the homeless, reclaiming campuses as a place for protest and theater, reclaiming our voices from the deep dark depths of corporate media, or reclaiming our visual environment from billboards, we were always reclaiming."[12]

Alter-activist protest camps and, more recently, climate justice, and Occupy camps are of particular interest. These are spaces of experience where alter-activist youths talk about and plan actions and experiment with alternatives in areas such as organizing social spaces, speaking, cleaning, and gender equality. Centered on the experiential and experimental dimension of social life, alter-activist camps allow for socializing, exchanging, celebrating, mixing private and public spheres, making friends and developing new commitments, and generating emotional attachments and collective solidarity (see Juris and Pleyers 2009). Within such youth camps, formal leadership is shunned, decisions are collective, and all residents are meant to participate in the building, organization, and management of the camps. While celebration and the pleasure of living an alternative experience are at the heart of these activist spaces, the will to encourage more participatory forms of organization demands considerable investment. Strolling around the 2005 WSF youth camp in the evening, for example, journalists and participants encountered festive images and sounds of samba. Just a few steps away, while many activists were unwinding in downtown bars and restaurants, youths from alter-activist spaces such as the Carácol were meeting to organize the following day's activities. Online meetings during the previous weeks had enabled activists from Europe and the Americas to establish certain principles and ground rules. However, to allow everyone to participate, decisions also had to be made on site: each person would speak and each idea would be discussed, even if it took all night. Nonetheless, like all social spaces and despite their commitment to egalitarian politics and interactions, alter-activist camps are spaces of power relations, conflict, and informal hierarchy (see Juris and Pleyers 2009; Pleyers 2006, 2011).

While movements centered around experience and self-transformation seek to contribute to social change, they also often involve what Hirschman (1970) refers to as an "exit option," retreating to the margins of society rather than challenging social relations from the inside. But does social withdrawal achieve the social transformations that activists aspire to? On the contrary, in some situations, withdrawing can help to reproduce systemic relations. If actors refrain from engagement in conflict in the arenas of politics and civil society, turning their backs on state institutions and power, do they not effectively abandon the field to their adversaries? Indeed, as Michael Hardt and Antonio Negri write, "Battles against the Empire cannot be won through subtraction or defection. This desertion does not have a place; it is the evacuation of the places of power" (2000, 265).

The logic of subtraction from political and economic power can represent an inability to shift from the local contexts of daily life to more global arenas of social, political, and economic struggle. The question of how to move from change at the individual and local level to broader transnational and global scales thus remains a blind spot for activists and theorists of antipower. Unanswered questions include: How do we move from the alternative organization of a few indigenous communities to global transformation that would guarantee indigenous rights? To what extent can small collective-purchasing co-ops really offer a global alternative to large-scale distribution? Can experiments with horizontal organization and alternative social relations within ephemeral camps or interstitial spaces have an impact on the future of society?

TO LEARN THROUGH EXPERIENCE AND EXPERIMENTATION: SHARING KNOWLEDGE AND ACKNOWLEDGING ONE'S NOT-KNOWING

The idea of learning by experience and trial and error in a process of experimentation is captured by the Zapatista expression "to learn by walking" (*aprender caminando*), which interviewees from the four movements considered here have expressed in diverse ways. A piquetero activist from the Organización Teresa in Buenos Aires put it this way, "We are learning with each step we take" (personal interview, February 2003). Or, as a member of Barricade suggested, learning by trial and error is a central aspect of our projects, which are constructed "by feeling around" (personal interview, March 2004). For activists in the alter-globalization movement, which arose in opposition to proclamations of the "end of history," permanent questioning and an awareness of the limits of knowledge and transformation are fundamental. As Holloway explains, "Our not-knowing is also the not-knowing of those who understand that not-knowing is part of the revolutionary process. We have lost all certainty, but the openness of uncertainty is central to revolution. We ask not only because we do not know the way (we do not), but also because asking the way is part of the revolutionary process itself" (2002, 215; see also Juris 2008a; Pleyers 2011; Shukaitis and Graeber 2007).

Aside from learning by personal experience, learning from the experiences, successes, and failures of other activists is also of great value. This is the purpose of international meetings, caravans, and many alter-globalization events. For example, world and regional social forums are moved by an "explicit attention to learning across times and places," encouraging activists to take ideas both from global events and from other local activists they meet back to their local settings (Jackie Smith and Reese 2008, 350; Jackie Smith, Juris, and the Social Forum Research Collective 2008, 386). Workshops in WSF alter-activist spaces are often, according to a Spanish activist at the 2002 WSF, about "talking through experiences of struggle." Similarly, before beginning the march on Mexico City in 2001, the Zapatista comandantes Susana and Yolanda emphasized the importance of meeting with women from other regions of the country: "We will learn something from you and you from us. In this way, we can help each other to struggle together."[13] For Barricade activists, a visit to food producers has much more to teach about the challenges of alternative agriculture than many books.

Without always avoiding them, activists call into question traditional structures of learning, particularly lectures in which speakers are placed on a pedestal in front of a passive audience. They prefer meetings based on an exchange of lived experiences. As an activist explained to me on May 1, 2003, during the opening of the temporary École des Cybermandaïs, the school rejects traditional pedagogies "where people think they know and don't want to learn anymore." Activists thus organized meetings and workshops centered on sharing their experiences of life and struggle.

The wish to learn from the experiences of others has also contributed to waves of alter-activist "tourism." Trips to Porto Alegre, for example, have allowed many activists to take part in neighborhood participatory budget meetings. A dozen foreigners were present during two of the three participatory budget meetings I observed in Porto Alegre in 2002, and the subject quickly spawned many activist books and writings. Similarly, foreign volunteers have been present as observers in the Zapatista villages since 1995, hoping to learn from the experience while contributing to it. In 2002 and 2003, it was Argentina's turn to receive waves of international activists, who came to meet with and learn from the pique-

teros, the neighborhood assemblies, and the workers at occupied factories. Later Venezuela and Bolivia played host to Western activists.[14] The
exchange is not one-way. In return, several groups asked foreign visitors
to share their experiences in their home countries and at global events.
The presence of alter-tourists also testifies to the transnational support
for local experiments;[15] representing not only a source of pride for local
activists but also protection against repression, which was particularly important for Zapatista villages. In Buenos Aires, the links established with
international visitors, foreign media, and other Argentine movements
greatly contributed to the reopening of Bruckman, the most prominent
of the Argentine factories that were occupied and run by their workers in
the aftermath of the economic crisis in 2001. Sometimes the connections
made through particular experiences lead to further visits and exchanges.
For example, in the anticapitalist village against the G8 summit at Evian
in 2003, a Mexican peasant recounted, with much emotion, her struggle
against the planned development of an airport on the lands of her village
in San Salvador Atenco. Returning home, alter-tourists share their experiences with other local activists, thereby contributing to the globalization
of the "grammar of experience" (McDonald 2006).

CONCLUSION

The desire to "change the world without taking power" (the title of John
Holloway's [2002] influential book on nonstate-oriented revolutionary
change) focuses on society as opposed to the realm of politics. As a Mexico
City–based student activist explained at a meeting in July 2005, "What we
want is for the people to make the changes, not the politicians." One of
the most important goals for these activists is to develop alternative subjectivities that move away from a politics of representation toward one of
direct participation. Donatella della Porta puts it this way, "To those who
accuse them of being 'anti-political,' the activists respond with a concept
of politics as an activity based on 'strong' forms of participation of all citizens rather than as delegation to a few professionals" (2005, 201).

Although emerging in distinct local contexts (urban versus rural, North
versus South, local versus global orientation), indigenous Zapatistas in
Mexico, piqueteros in Argentina, young alter-activists, and members of
alternative social centers share a set of emerging activist cultural forms and
practices based on the production of resistant subjectivities, experimenta-

tion with concrete alternatives and spaces of experience, and an openness to ongoing patterns of learning. However, these cultural forms are not coterminous with global gatherings, participation in transnational networks, or specific organizations. Rather, they rely on a set of shared values, meanings, imaginaries, logics, and scopes of action. Although each actor remains autonomous and rooted in local contexts and specific struggles, he or she may be inspired by other movements' actions that resonate with local struggles (see Khasnabish 2008; Khasnabish, this volume).

The multiplication of field research strategies rooted in distinct locales (Gille 2001), which Martin Albrow (2007) refers to as "globally conscious ethnographic research" are thus essential tools for going beyond dichotomies such as local-global, personal experience–global movement, or particular-universal. This allows us to bring together "the radical diversity of subjectivities in struggle and the explicit recognition of the irreducible significance of a multitude of struggles" (Khasnabish 2007, 520). At the same time, we can also appreciate that the stakes go far beyond the local level, encompassing a much wider global context. Perhaps more important, ethnographic research has led to increased attention to the subjective and expressive dimensions of alter-globalization activism, including a focus on significations and meanings (Holland, Fox, and Daro 2008), political imaginaries (Khasnabish 2008), personal experiences (McDonald 2006; Touraine 2002), and cultural practices (Juris 2008a). This provides a perspective that can enhance the critical reflexivity of activists (including critical reflection about and evaluation of the reach of one's actions; see Giddens 1991), and eventually contribute to their activism by helping them to reflect on and devise strategies for narrowing the gap between their practices and their aims. In many ways this kind of ethnography recalls Max Weber's (2004) view of the role of the social scientist, which is not to impose meaning on actors but to help reflect on the meanings, outcomes, and limitations of their practices.

NOTES

Some of the examples in this chapter are further developed in part II of my book *Alter-globalization*. I want to thank Jeffrey S. Juris and Alex Khasnabish for pushing me to further reflect on my underlying epistemological perspective and for their stimulating comments on previous versions of this chapter. I translated quotes from my fieldwork into English.

1   By *alter-globalization movement* I mean those social actors, movements, and forums that contest globalization in its neoliberal form and have developed new ways of becoming actors in the global age.

2   The use of the term *global* refers to the increasing importance of the global scale as articulated by Martin Albrow (1996). Several authors (see Beck 2000; Held 2010) also suggest that although the national scale remains important, it is not the central referent that it used to be in the twentieth century. Similarly, Kevin McDonald (2006), Alain Touraine (2002), John Urry (2003), and Michel Wieviorka (2005) argue that the conceptual tools we use to make sense of societies as bounded areas of social life corresponding to the territories of nation-states are less adequate to the task of "making sense of emerging forms of social life and conflict that are increasingly global and that increasingly take the form of flows" (McDonald 2006, 9). While the term *transnational movements* draws attention to forms of activism that cross national boundaries, the national remains the central point of reference (see Tarrow 2005). For a discussion of the critiques of the term *global* in the context of global civil society, see Kaldor (2003).

3   By *global movement* I refer to collective historical actors in different regions of the world that share a common adversary and a similar culture of politics and a concept of social change. Global movements are often connected by a loosely shared identity or are networked together, but this is not always the case. McDonald specifically defines global movements as "new kinds of networks and flows of communication, action, and experience" (2006, 3).

4   Uncited quotes are drawn from comments made by members of Barricade during meetings and interviews between February 2003 and February 2004.

5   *Contentious politics* has been defined as "episodic, public, collective interaction among makers of claims and their objects when (a) at least one government is a claimant, an object of claims, or a party to the claims and (b) the claims would, if realized, affect the interests of at least one of the claimants" (McAdam, Tarrow, and Tilly 2001, 5). The term aims primarily at crossing the borders between institutional and noninstitutional politics.

6   Holloway is an activist-sociologist and a proponent of Zapatismo. His book *How to Change the World without Taking Power* (2002) about revolutionary change from an Autonomist Marxist and nonstate-oriented perspective has become an important reference for activists with respect to political subjectivity.

7   Leaflet presenting an alter-activist youth space at the European Social Forum in Paris (2003).

8   Ibid.

9   This is a well-known Zapatista slogan (i.e., "un mundo donde quepan muchos mundos").

10 Here Holloway is building on the philosopher Baruch Spinoza's distinction between *potestas* (power-over), which refers to power as control or domination over another person or group, and *potentia* (power-to), which refers to one's own capacity to act. According to Holloway, these two forces are in antagonism: "power-to exists as power-over, but the power-to is subjected to and in rebellion against power-over, and power-over is nothing but, and therefore absolutely dependent upon, the metamorphosis of power-to" (2002: 36).

11 In the early 1970s, feminist theorists produced similar discourses. As Helen Wortis and Clara Rabinowitz suggest, "We cannot wait for the revolution before we change our lives, for surely changing our lives now is part of the revolutionary process" (1972, 129–30). In order to distinguish these practices from those aiming at countervailing power (Montesquieu's "counterpower"), I use the term *antipower* despite the fact that several theoreticians of this trend refer to the term *counterpower* (see Benasayag and Sztulwark 2000; Hardt and Negri 2000, 489; Holloway 2002).

12 E-mail from the Toronto chapter of Reclaim the Streets, which was quoted in Klein 2002, 486.

13 Guiomar Rovira, "Entrevista con las comandantas Susana y Yolanda" [Interview with commanders Susana and Yolanda], February 19, 2001, http://palabra.ezln.org.mx (accessed January 4, 2012).

14 Naomi Klein's *Fences and Windows* (2002) provides a good example of activist "tourism" that seeks to learn from the experiences of other movements.

15 The use of the neologism *alter-tourists* does not intend to dismiss these practices, which have allowed for important exchanges of experiences among alter-globalization activists throughout the world. It points, however, to the contrast between the sporadic, adventure-seeking character of the modes of activist travel on the part of many European and North American activists I met in Latin America and the well-organized tours developed by certain activist organizations in the global South, including the Brazilian Landless Workers' Movement, piquetero groups, and Zapatista communities.

DISCREPANT
PARADIGMS

5

The Global Indigenous Movement and Paradigm Wars

International Activism, Network Building, and Transformative Politics

SYLVIA ESCÁRCEGA

Chief Oren Lyons, the faithkeeper of the Onondaga Nation and a leader and pioneer of Indigenous activism in international arenas, recalled in a panel with James Cameron (the director of the film *Avatar*) during the 2010 United Nations Permanent Forum on Indigenous Issues (UNPFII), that when Indigenous leaders came to the UN in the 1970s to bring a message of peace and to alert the world of what was happening to Mother Earth,[1] they did not imagine that today there would be several UN bodies dedicated to the study and promotion of the human rights of Indigenous peoples.[2] They could not imagine that today Indigenous delegates from around the world would not only participate in large numbers in UN meetings but that they would also take part in decision-making processes. And Lyons added that they never imagined that mainstream media and entertainment industries would change the way they have historically engaged with Indigenous peoples.

Avatar resonated with Indigenous delegates at the UNPFII because the film echoed their struggles and visions with respect to alternative paradigms for relating to Mother Earth.[3] The film was not without controversy, however. After it was screened, the delegates saw the opportunity to establish a productive dialogue with Cameron—and by extension with the mainstream media—as representatives of Indigenous peoples worldwide.[4] They challenged Cameron in relation to the plot (the Na'vi being saved by the white man), the characters (the portrayal of Indigenous women as restricted to the role of spiritual guide or accompanying warrior), and the use of anthropological sources (they reminded him of the harmful effects that anthropology, as a disciplinary child of imperialism, has had on Indigenous peoples). But the delegates also saw the film and dialogue with Cameron as an opportunity for networking with mainstream media, potential allies in their struggles at the international level and supporters of Indigenous filmmakers and media specialists. Media can play a role beyond simply monitoring and providing information; they convey meanings and messages Indigenous peoples are seeking to use and shape to give voice to their own visions of humanity and nature.

These events illustrate Indigenous peoples' achievements at the international level,[5] along with their continued efforts to establish horizontal collaboration and networks to gain support for their causes by engaging in intercultural dialogues. One of these achievements is the creation and consolidation of the global Indigenous movement (GIM). Through this movement, and in various spaces of action, Indigenous activists are proposing new paradigms that challenge us to transform our understandings of humanity, the world, and nature. How have Indigenous organizing and diplomacy at the international level challenged the colonial narratives and Eurocentrism that categorize Indigenous peoples as subordinate Others with little jurisdiction and control over their own affairs and territories? How have Indigenous paradigms challenged dominant views that see cultural and biological diversity as something to control and domesticate? How have Indigenous activists challenged NGOs, social movements, the media, and individuals to rethink their relationship and duties to Mother Earth? How have Indigenous activists engaged in transnational networking and how has this helped empower new global political actors?

Since the 1970s, aided by increasing media attention, Indigenous activists, women and men, and their allies began to push the UN to recognize their distinct cultures; to study, protect, and promote Indigenous rights; to bring attention to the environmental damages in Indigenous territories; and to incorporate Indigenous peoples in decision-making structures at all levels. In so doing, new global political actors have emerged—Indigenous peoples, Indigenous women, Indigenous youths, and so on—who have been able to influence politics and law making and promote novel ways of thinking. The GIM has recently expanded into the realm of transnational social movements with the goal of building an alternative global consensus around economic, sociopolitical, cultural, environmental justice, and alternative Indigenous paradigms. Beyond the UN, the World Social Forum (WSF) and its satellite local and regional forums have provided new platforms for Indigenous activists to dialogue with representatives of diverse social movements, NGOs, and other advocacy groups.

One of the novel proposals Indigenous activists bring to the debates is a notion of how development from an Indigenous perspective could provide solutions to climate change. In their interactions at the UN and WSF processes, Indigenous activists have linked notions such as *buen vivir* (living well) as a model for/of "development with culture and identity" (Tauli-Corpuz 2010) with the concept of climate justice and the rights of Mother Earth. These notions challenge many Western narratives about who we are, how we live in society, and how we relate to nature. The GIM has thus become an important space (albeit not the only one) for the intercultural production and negotiation of Indigenous paradigms, which also find resonance among non-Indigenous activists.

In this chapter, I examine two case studies to illustrate how the GIM has become an important networked space of transnational encounter, how it empowers new global political actors, and how it serves as a space for the intercultural production, circulation, and negotiation of alternative paradigms. First, I consider Indigenous women's activism within the GIM to reveal how they have used networking strategies to articulate a variety of actors, discourses, and practices in order to form transnational spaces and communities of/for action. Indigenous women have challenged dominant and entrenched patriarchal notions that place women outside politics and decision making by creating autonomous spaces from where they can negotiate and enunciate their roles as contributors to emerging Indigenous paradigms and forms of diplomacy, other social movements, and the well-being of Mother Earth. Second, I examine how Indigenous activists are proposing their own paradigms as alternative solutions to global crises and how they are using the WSF process to network with other transnational social movements. The GIM can be viewed as a space of encounter among diverse discourses and practices. Although Indigenous paradigms are presented as radical alternatives, I argue that close examination reveals that they are contested from within and are infused with a Western human rights framework. Ultimately this interculturality allows for consensus building on the part of Indigenous activism and diplomacy.

I have undertaken my activist ethnographic research with Indigenous struggles at numerous international and local sites over the past fifteen years, including diverse UN- and WSF-related gatherings and events.[6] The ethnographic observations and conclusions I draw derive from my political commitment, accompaniment, solidarity, co/laboration, and learning from Indigenous struggles and the individual actors involved in those struggles.[7] Guillermo Delgado-P. claims that co/laborating, more than a research strategy, is a human agenda that promotes horizontality and co-working with political struggles (2002, 38). For Delgado-P., in co/laborating with academia, Indigenous movements challenge and delegitimize the modern dichotomy of "civilization" versus "barbarism." Consequently, this relationship becomes an important condition for a project of decolonization. I have argued elsewhere that working in co/laboration with Indigenous struggles is an ongoing intercultural exercise in the construction of knowledge (Escárcega 2009). I have referred to a research methodology and epistemological practice born of this co/laboration as *trabajar haciendo* (working in or by doing), following the terminology inspired by the Zapatista political philosophy used by Indigenous activists from the Americas. Trabajar haciendo is a way to engage with Indigenous movements on an everyday basis, aided by technologies such as the Internet, in the creation of activist communities that produce alternative knowledges, epistemes, and research practices. In the course of our work, Indigenous activism has profoundly challenged many of my own theoretical frameworks, methodologies, and politics. Such collaborative activist work has not only contributed to changing legal structures for the recognition of collective rights and the reframing of justice but it has also served to decolonize the academy by helping to legitimize Indigenous knowledges. In turn, Indigenous activists have made scholars and academic research important parts of their transnational network-building efforts and transformative politics.

UNDERSTANDING THE GLOBAL INDIGENOUS MOVEMENT

Three propositions guide my analysis of the GIM. First, while in past decades Indigenous struggles were driven by the goal of establishing nonintegrationist/nonassimilationist relationships with states via legal instruments, today Indigenous activists are also establishing new political alliances and networks with diverse transnational social movements that are enabling them to further a project of decolonization and to propose alternatives to global processes that affect Indigenous communities and prevent them from achieving justice. This has resulted in the emergence of new global political actors and in broadening the scope and goals of Indigenous struggles, which advocate for new paradigms of living, not only for Indigenous peoples but for all peoples. Second, to understand Indigenous activism, diplomacy, and network building, as well as the negotiation of discourses and paradigms in their full complexity, we have to look at the external and internal dynamics of the GIM in the context of intercultural dialogues. The GIM is the global expression of a multitude of highly diverse and networked Indigenous struggles, and those of their allies, occurring at various levels and in many geographic places, which makes the GIM an international and a transnational social movement with its own unique characteristics. Third, Indigenous paradigms have to be understood as the product of (1) Indigenous cosmovisions;[8] (2) contextualized and contested (temporally and spatially) notions of what it means to be Indigenous; (3) power dynamics among a variety of actors; and (4) ongoing intercultural dialogues within a human rights framework.

To address these dynamics, I draw on two analytic concepts. In rethinking how theorists have analyzed a variety of social movements in local and global contexts, Jeffrey Juris and Alex Khasnabish propose in this volume's introduction that many of the social movements we encounter today can be understood as "networked spaces of transnational encounter." As I conceive this concept, it evokes transnational social movements as spaces for (1) the articulation of people, resources, flows of information and meanings, strategies, and technology, and so on; (2) subjectification, where diverse meanings are created, coexist, and enter into conflict; (3) lived relationships by which dense networks at different scales emerge; (4) consciously constituted communities where many struggles come together; (5) action that is enacted in ephemeral (that is to say, made and remade) social spaces; and (6) and the production of knowledge and emergence of epistemologies that have the potential to radically transform sociocultural logics. In this sense, transnational social movements are dynamic and rhizomatic (connected horizontally through multiple nodes), continually constituted and becoming, self-reflexive, and embedded in transformative cultural politics. This concept specifically helps us to look at how the GIM articulates different actors, discourses, and practices, as well as how, through network building, the GIM has become a transnational community of and for action, and a site for the negotiation and enunciation of alternative paradigms and transformative politics.

The other concept is the notion of paradigm, which helps us see how Indigenous proposals can be examples of intercultural transformative politics. I understand *paradigm* (Kuhn 1970) as a set of assumptions, concepts, values, and practices that pertains to a specific yet unbounded worldview of an imagined community of actors (e.g., Indigenous peoples, Western civilization, neoliberal advocates). Paradigms are constructed and imagined, although they can have very real effects. The Kuhnian concept of paradigm allows us to understand how different worldviews judge and naturalize their own constructivist natures. It also enables us to appreciate how Indigenous paradigms are often discursively presented as radically alternative ways of being, knowing, acting, and living that are constructed in opposition to Western paradigms. Unlike the Kuhnian concept of paradigm, however, in practice many Indigenous activists see their proposed alternatives not as incommensurable with all Western logic but as incompatible with the specific logic of capital. Although, as I explain later, some Indigenous activists talk about a *civilizational crisis* that requires new paradigms, ultimately, GIM diplomacy based on consensus building suggests that all knowledges are capable of dialogically contributing to the construction of a more heteroglossic and transnational knowledge (Ribeiro and Escobar 2006). Indigenous knowledges are thus produced interculturally in multiple places and as part of ongoing struggles at multiple levels—local, national, regional, and international. These struggles have diverse political agendas and are situated in specific processes of production. This helps us to understand how and why Indigenous activists and diplomats talk about "paradigm wars" in networked spaces of transnational encounter and at the same time work within the same institutions that embody the dominant paradigms they oppose.

INDIGENOUS WOMEN: BUILDING AUTONOMOUS SPACES TO CHALLENGE PATRIARCHY AND COLONIALITY

Indigenous women as a group became a strong and respected voice within the GIM and the UN in the 1990s (Escárcega 2003b, 2011; Rivera Zea 1999). In that decade, through a variety of workshops and encounters in many parts of the world, Indigenous women began to develop their own ways of doing politics, challenging dominant patriarchal notions in their communities, the GIM, and the UN. Organizing in autonomous spaces and through transnational encounters was a key dimension of this process (see Gutiérrez and Palomo 2000; Pacari 2003; Sánchez Néstor 2005). The Global Indigenous Women's Caucus at the UNPFII, although part of the GIM, allows women to voice and address their own concerns. In their transnational encounters, Indigenous women continuously redefine what autonomy means from a gendered perspective with an ethnic lens, their role in Indigenous struggles, their participation in global politics, and the kinds of networks and alliances they want to build at the international level and with transnational social movements. This has enabled the emergence of the "Indigenous woman" as a new global political actor with a unique identity and consciousness that is an important part of, yet acts autonomously within, the GIM.

Indigenous women do not simply conceive of autonomy as the right of their peoples to organize socially, economically, culturally, and politically; they also include in their vision, based on their gendered and ethnic experiences, notions of a woman's place and the right over women's bodies and souls. Autonomy, as defined from a gendered and an ethnic perspective, is understood as having individual and collective elements, both of which are exercised within the community, organizations, and spaces of encounters in which they participate as Indigenous women (Gutiérrez and Palomo 2000). The autonomy demanded by Indigenous women has come to be more accepted within the GIM, yet it is still contested. Thus, Indigenous women constantly insist on the primacy of ethnic over gender struggle. However, they have been able to negotiate their demands for autonomy in various ways without jeopardizing their overall ethnic demands while challenging the political subordination of women.

In their autonomous spaces, Indigenous women link their demands for the recognition of Indigenous rights to the right to participate equally in political structures at all levels. At the parallel event Leadership Development Workshop during the 2010 UNPFII, Myrna Cunningham (Miskita) explained that Indigenous women practice *aprender haciendo* (learning in/by doing) to open up spaces "little by little" where their voices can be heard and where they can participate in decision making.[9] The IV World Conference on Women (1995) in Beijing marked a watershed for Indigenous women as they began to develop gender and ethnic perspectives on Indigenous and women's struggles. The resulting Beijing Declaration of Indigenous Women became the basis for subsequent demands at the global level (Rivera Zea 1999).

By the end of the 1990s, I witnessed how Indigenous women had decisively challenged entrenched racist and patriarchal notions that construct them as "victims," "apolitical," and "uneducated" in high-level politics. During the 1998 UN Working Group on Indigenous Populations, Indigenous women from the Latin American region had decided to stay in the room following the meeting of the Latin American Indigenous Caucus to talk about the ongoing establishment of international networks, the commercialization of arts and crafts, and intellectual property issues. As Indigenous men lingered in the room talking to each other, the presiding Indigenous woman told them that "No es para que se rían compañeros" (It is not a laughing matter) and that they could stay but to be quiet. The men left the room and the women proceeded with their meeting to talk about how to make their demands heard within the UN and their own organizations (Escárcega 2003b).

While their participation was still questioned by some, in the 1990s Indigenous women began to hold meetings all over the world to address how to access decision-making posts. At the same time, they were increasingly appointed to make statements to the UN on behalf of their organizations and delegations. Indigenous women have used the spaces provided in UN hallways and NGO quarters to sell their arts and crafts, engage each other, share information, and learn about other struggles, all of which is essential for networking. It is not uncommon to find high-level UN officials talking unofficially to Indigenous activists in such spaces. This has facilitated the strengthening of relationships among women, as well as the articulation of people, resources, flows of information, and strategies. At the same time, these unofficial conversations have facilitated the conformation of a consciously constituted community and a global political collective actor with a distinct consciousness as Indigenous women.

The declared focus of the Fifth Continental Meeting of Indigenous Women of the Americas in Kahnawake, Quebec, in 2007, which had the theme of "Restoring Our Balance," was to strengthen friendships and relationships among Indigenous and non-Indigenous women from various NGOs and academic settings as well as with Indigenous men. Indeed, Tarcila Rivera Zea (Quechua) explains that building personal relationships based on mutual recognition with different actors has been critical for Indigenous women's networking.[10] This is accomplished not only by sharing experiences but also through various cultural activities organized for the exchange of handicrafts, music, videos, and dances (1999, 11). These activities are an important part of the learning process among Indigenous women and, ultimately, part of the development of a global Indigenous consciousness (Escárcega 2003b).

After the showing of the film *Avatar* at the 2010 UNPFII, participants told Cameron his portrayal of Indigenous women had failed to take into consideration that they had been actively looking for ways to make connections to find solutions to the problems faced by Indigenous peoples, particularly given the suffering of women as a result of the problems in their communities. Cameron responded that in his film Indigenous women represent persistence and wisdom, and that they are simultaneously moral compasses and warriors who work for peace. For their part, Indigenous women responded by explaining that not only are their roles and actions critical to the cultural production and reproduction of their communities, but also that they have actively sought ways to access decision making, which media should recognize. As Nina Pacari (Quechua) has pointed out, the kind of power that Indigenous women are struggling for "implies a distinct power, a horizontal one, shared, more democratic, with space for decisions and the redistribution of resources on equitable terms on the level of gender and cultural participation" (2003, 202). This idea of power challenges patriarchal paradigms where certain "traditional" roles are assigned to Indigenous women that deny them access to decision making. At more recent UN meetings, this idea of power was frequently raised in reference to how power was traditionally shared, in a balanced manner, between the genders in Indigenous communities prior to colonization.

In their international struggles, Indigenous women have emphasized their roles as "guardians of culture" while challenging those cultural practices that deny them equal political participation, condone violence against them, or, as Margarita Gutiérrez (Hñähñu) and Nellys Palomo suggest, break the harmony in gender and power relations (2000, 56).[11] In the 1990s Indigenous women continuously referred to the effects of war and militarization on women and the daily life of their communities over the past decade, but now they have also begun to address in international arenas the effects of domestic violence as a result of colonization and dispossession and as a problem that affects both the individual and the collective. In several meetings I have attended where the issue of domestic violence has been discussed, collaboration with non-Indigenous women and institutions has been notable, contributing to solutions that are culturally appropriate to Indigenous communities.

Many of the women who spoke at the Leadership Development Workshop at the UNPFII explained that the consolidation of transnational networks, first among Indigenous women and then with other women and social movements, has been another key factor in their political organizing. In the early 1990s Indigenous women from the Americas realized the need to simultaneously weave local, national, regional, and international levels of action to formulate a global agenda. As they describe it, *el andar de las mujeres Indígenas* (the roads of Indigenous women) is the process by which they move from the local to the global, getting to know each other, exchanging, reflecting, learning from each other, and weaving experiences (see Blackwell 2006; Gutiérrez and Palomo 2000; J-A Juanena 2010a, 2010b; Rivera Zea 1999). In this *andar*, Indigenous women activists have constructed what Coro J-A Juanena (2010a, 2010b) refers to as a new global collective actor: Indigenous women. This new actor has crafted its own spaces of political action and consciousness in networked spaces of transnational encounter.

Indigenous women's global politics are based on crafting a place among other women and within transnational networks according to their Indigenous cosmovisions, and on finding ways to incorporate women's rights into Indigenous peoples' cultural patterns and everyday collective practices. It is in the autonomous spaces they have forged where Indigenous women have been able to conceptualize *autonomía con mirada de mujer* (autonomy with a woman's gaze) (Gutiérrez and Palomo 2000), bringing together gender and ethnic demands to fortify Indigenous struggles. Yet Indigenous women have had to iron out many differences with other women's movements. Reflecting on her participation in Beijing, Esther Cámac, of the Indigenous Women's Council of Costa Rica, gave voice to this struggle: "Even with the difficulties encountered, we feel we have opened a two-way street, toward the interior of our process as Indigenous peoples and toward the women's movement. We believe our task is not finished with this journey" (quoted in Rivera Zea 1999, 21).

Indeed, the task of establishing an equal and shared space for decision making is never complete. At the 2009 UN Climate Change Conference in Copenhagen (Conference of the Parties, COP 15—part of the UN Framework Convention on Climate Change, UNFCCC), for example, individual Indigenous and non-Indigenous women met and participated in discussions with the intention of exploring possibilities for a joint strategy between Indigenous peoples and Gender constituencies.[12] As a group, though, it was more difficult for Indigenous women to find a common platform with other women. One of the reasons was the misunderstanding of the ethnic dimension in their struggles and worldviews. The lack of recognition of Indigenous women's primary loyalty to the ethnic struggle and how they are challenging patriarchal notions from their particular positions has been a common problem and a source of misunderstanding in their interactions with non-Indigenous women (see Escárcega 2003b; Hernández Castillo 2008; Suárez Navaz and Hernández Castillo 2008). In the end, at COP 15, the Indigenous peoples' and Gender constituencies ended up working separately without building a common platform of action because some non-Indigenous women also questioned whether Indigenous peoples are truly close to Mother Earth.

Indigenous women who participate in the GIM are trained in global politics and Indigenous diplomacy as they create autonomous spaces of transnational encounter. These spaces articulate in different ways with other transnational social movements. This has allowed Indigenous women to relationally weave their own notions of indigeneity from a gender perspective, and their own notions of femininity from an ethnic perspective, resulting, as J-A Juanena maintains (2010a, 2010b), in the creation of a particular locus of enunciation in which Indigenous women have gone from being talked about to talking for and about themselves. In these spaces, patriarchal notions and practices are reworked as Indigenous women emphasize and exercise their right to politically participate in decision making. For example, they use the global view on indigeneity and the narrative of human rights to talk about themselves as political actors with inherent rights, who, by way of such rights, nurture communities, safeguard culture, maintain a harmonious relationship with Mother Earth, and embrace humanity.[13]

In 2006 Jerry Mander and Victoria Tauli-Corpuz (Igorot; she was also
the chair of the UN Permanent Forum on Indigenous Issues),[14] co-edited
Paradigm Wars: Indigenous Peoples' Resistance to Globalization. In this
book, the editors and authors explain how Indigenous peoples are suffering alarming attacks on their livelihood, survival, and culture due to
the dominant economic model of global corporate capitalism, which is
"dependent upon a never-ending resource supply to feed [economic]
growth" (Mander 2006, 3). At the same time, Indigenous peoples are resisting assaults on their lands and knowledge through local/global organizing, revitalizing Indigenous traditions, adopting technologies that
guarantee the well-being of their communities and Mother Earth, and
pursuing legal strategies at national and international levels. *Paradigm
Wars* was released as Indigenous activism began to move beyond international governmental organizations and into the realm of civil society and
social movements. The book was also published when climate change was
becoming the largest issue bringing together social movements from various contexts to fight the effects of neoliberal policies.

Paradigm wars are worked out interculturally in response, adaptation,
and resistance to colonialism, neoliberalism, globalization, and a world
dominated by international organizations. Yet the GIM has gone beyond a
simple reaction or resistance and has proposed alternative ways of living
that its participants view as a solution to the global crises that affect us
all. These alternatives and solutions are the outcome (always already contested) of the encounters, lobbying, networking, and forging of common
agendas with various social movements. Indigenous proposals for new
paradigms in spaces such as the WSF and its processes are examples of
transformative politics in that they seek to influence a radical shift in the
global consciousness regarding our relationship with Mother Earth and in
relation to how we view justice. This shift would redirect not only how we
have conceptualized development in Western paradigms but also what it
means to have economic and social justice without obliterating our obligations and duties to nature. In this section I explore how paradigm wars
have been waged within networked spaces of transnational encounter
through an analysis of the participation of Indigenous activists in the WSF
process. I focus on the Indigenous vision of *buen vivir* as a guiding model

for/of "development with culture and identity," and on the idea that the recognition of the inherent rights of Mother Earth is crucial for humanity.

Mander argues that the failure of development policies to increase the living standards and well-being of the world's poor, the increasing poverty linked to displacement, and the widespread lack of political representation are the new frontiers of struggle, physically and conceptually (2006, 10). For Indigenous peoples, these struggles include opposition to the pressure multinational corporations and other international organizations—such as the World Bank and International Monetary Fund—place on states with respect to opening up Indigenous lands to exploitation and appropriation, which is depicted by *Avatar* in a fictionalized way. The editors and authors of *Paradigm Wars* claim that addressing these injustices demands that the entire world rethink dominant paradigms by counterposing to the logic of capital different values and worldviews that can keep the earth alive for the generations to come. Tauli-Corpuz further claims that rethinking dominant paradigms means having to look at how "the legacy of colonialism, racism and discrimination which were perpetuated for centuries . . . relate to the contemporary problems we are tackling" (2010, 2). She links the current crises with historical injustices and the damage being done today to Mother Earth.

While leaders such as Tauli-Corpuz have worked for many years to integrate Indigenous concerns at the UN and at the national level, some Indigenous activists, especially young women and men, are now challenging the GIM to move beyond the political arenas dominated by states and international organizations and to incorporate in its agenda an active participation in civil society and social movement processes where crises and injustices can be addressed through different ways of doing politics. Some Indigenous activists have found that the WSF and its satellite forums are spaces of encounter with organizations from civil society where they can propose, debate, and negotiate new ideas and traditional visions to confront what they see as a worldwide civilizational crisis by building a global consensus. They have realized that while states might be slowly beginning to change their relationship to Indigenous peoples, to meaningfully change dominant mentalities and practices, they have to work with multiple transnational social movements.

While their proposed alternative solutions are by no means uniform and vary from one organization or network to another, causing tensions, many of the activists have reached consensus that only a holistic approach that addresses the structural root problems of this civilizational crisis will suffice. Indigenous activists call on scholars to look at how the existing ontological, epistemological, and pedagogical bases of the Western civilizational model have created not only the legacy of colonialism, racism, and discrimination but also the logic of capital and its destructive practices. Yet their alternative solutions are based on an explicit recognition of the necessity of a human rights framework and a view of justice that includes human and nonhuman beings and a project of decolonization.

Indigenous activists see *buen vivir* and the recognition of the rights of Mother Earth as steps toward decolonization and the formation of a new relationship with nature. *Buen vivir* is an Andean concept implicated in the search for new practices in relation to the environment. Since sustainable development is closely related to the maintenance of biodiversity, this Indigenous paradigm is seen as an alternative to the model of development advocated by the UN and the international financial system. *Buen vivir* conceptualizes the relationship between humans and nature as harmonious and balanced, guided by values such as reciprocity, equilibrium, and sharing, thereby helping to mitigate the effects of humans on nature. This idea was recently affirmed at the World Peoples Conference on Climate Change and the Rights of Mother Earth organized by Bolivia in response to the failures of the 2009 UNFCCC COP 15 meetings to reach a new global consensus on climate change that would meaningfully incorporate the voices of civil society and its social movements.

Buen vivir is recognized in Ecuador's 2008 constitution (known as *sumak kawsay*) as a right, and in Bolivia's 2009 constitution (known as *suma qamaña*) as one of the ethical and moral principles guiding a plural society. In the context of Latin America, the concept has been adopted as a banner by several Indigenous struggles because of the failure of existing development policies and the increasing inequalities and injustices due to neoliberal policies. However, Indigenous activism and diplomacy at the international level, and the consolidation of the GIM within the UN, have brought an emphasis on finding solutions within a human rights approach. Although they are presented as radical alternatives, Indigenous paradigms such as *buen vivir* have nevertheless been elaborated in an intercultural dialogue with Western values and worldviews such as human rights. Ultimately, I argue, this has facilitated network building as the proposed alternatives find resonance, understanding, and a common vocabulary with other social movements and at the UN.

Evo Morales, president of the Plurinational State of Bolivia, submitted to the UN a proposal on April 22, 2009, for a declaration of the rights of Mother Earth. A study undertaken by members of the UNPFII concludes that in Andean cosmovision, Pachamama, "Earth, fertile and productive Mother," has its laws and rights that humans have to comply with to live a full life in harmony with nature. Consequently, "the rights of Pachamama would be inherent in the rights of humankind, human rights" (see UN document E/C.19/2010/4). The reason why this idea resonates with other social movements is that in Western thought there has been an increasing recognition that human beings have a symbiotic *relationship*, and that we have to change our mode of *interaction*, with nature (the film *Avatar* is a manifestation of this shift). In the study mentioned above, the UN also recognizes that all life forms have intrinsic value irrespective of their value to humans. These paradigmatic shifts are not simply the result of new scientific evidence or of philosophical inquiry; they are the consequence of the rise of global Indigenous political actors, intercultural and transnational encounters, and intense activism through a variety of networks. UNFCCC COP meetings, for example, where Indigenous peoples are recognized as important voices, bring together many interest groups to find solutions to climate change.

Paradigm wars are specifically linked to decolonization projects from an Indigenous perspective. Indigenous decolonization as a paradigm shift means a deep criticism of the ontological, epistemological, and pedagogical bases of Eurocentrism and Western thought. It involves the challenging of "hegemonic narratives of modernity, history, nation, and cultural identity as these relate to the indigenous world" (del Valle Escalante 2009, 2), while "valuing, reclaiming, and foregrounding indigenous voices and epistemologies," and being always mindful of how the "endeavors might reify hegemonic power structures, thereby creating marginality" (Swadener and Mutua 2008: 31, 33). At the level of praxis, decolonization denotes, among other things, the recognition and active use of Indigenous cosmovisions, the redefinition of decision-making power structures, direct and horizontal consensus building, and the realization of autonomy. Yet, at the same time, Indigenous paradigms are not incommensurable with Western values and worldviews given that they are advocated using human rights language. This can be explained by the fact that the GIM was born through its engagement with the UN system. Furthermore, in certain instances, some Indigenous activists are proposing to work within the logic of capital to find viable solutions, which generates tensions inside the GIM. Decolonization is thus an ongoing project within and outside of the GIM.

In their engagement with the WSF and satellite forums, Indigenous activists have recognized that, beyond government, civil society has to be implicated in the remedies for the historical wrongdoing caused to Indigenous peoples, and ultimately in the decolonization projects that can bring solutions for current crises. Due to non-Indigenous social movements' persistent lack of knowledge of Indigenous peoples' circumstances, Indigenous activists often face many of the same problems they encountered when they first began to participate in UN processes. The conflict that erupted during the People's Movement Assembly on the last day of the U.S. Social Forum in Atlanta in 2007 (see Juris, this volume), for example, reflects the kinds of tensions caused by continuing misunderstandings of Indigenous "ways."

Further tensions arose between Indigenous activists and organizers during the 2009 WSF in Bélem, Brazil, where, despite their desire to participate fully, Indigenous activists had limited influence over the forum's organization. Elizabeth Smythe and Scott Byrd (2010) report that the International Council (composed of roughly 150 NGO and social movement representatives) had the intention of including and empowering Indigenous participation in WSF processes. However, although a local indigenous organizing committee was established, no Indigenous organizations were represented on the council itself (although delegates from the Indigenous Environmental Network participated through the Grassroots Global Justice coalition). As the activities unfolded, the most obvious conflicts I witnessed involved the Indigenous tent, the location of events, and the thematic axes, reflecting unequal participation in decision-making processes, disrespect for Indigenous protocols, and a lack of openness to criticism. Tellingly, during a meeting to address Indigenous peoples' complaints at the forum, a WSF cofounder and member of the International Council had this to say: "They are here participating, right? What else do they want?"[15]

Indigenous organizations at the 2009 WSF were divided about the need to denounce the exploitation of resources based on a model of consumerist production. For one group, this model had provoked a civilizational crisis that is leading to "planetary suicide" while, for the other, the problem is more one of racism and the exclusion of Indigenous peoples. The split also revolved around the relative importance of entirely rejecting capitalism and the Eurocentric development model or adapting to these while recognizing Indigenous rights. These debates are also occurring within the GIM. For example, at the 2008 UNPFII, participants were divided over the practice of carbon trading. At the 2009 Indigenous Peoples' Global Summit in Anchorage, differences of opinion were especially visible in relation to extractive industries (e.g., complete versus partial moratorium on oil and gas exploration). And at the 2010 UN Climate Change Conference in Cancun (UNFCCC COP 16), Indigenous activists had to negotiate differing views on market-driven solutions for climate change. However, inasmuch as there are conflicts, there is also an emerging consensus among Indigenous activists regarding the need to foreground the affirmation of inherent Indigenous collective rights (especially the right to self-determination), to work under a human rights framework, to demand respect for Indigenous cosmovisions as sites for the production of new paradigms, and to include Indigenous peoples in global political decision-making processes.

CONCLUSION

Indigenous activists have engaged the UN during the last four decades and in so doing have forged new global collective actors in world politics, including the GIM and Indigenous women. These actors have created important networked spaces of transnational encounter while engaging with other social movements and civil society activists. The proposals for new paradigms that Indigenous activists are bringing to the table closely relate to the development of Indigenous diplomacy at the UN. James Henderson (Mi'kmaw) explains that this was fueled by the refusal to accept the "colonial narrative" and the destruction of "Indigenous legal traditions and knowledge in the structuring of a global order" (2008, 10).[16] Yet, it was also fueled by Indigenous peoples' determination to preserve their cultural distinctiveness based on territorial claims. As a result, the GIM was consolidated internationally under a human rights framework, which has greatly influenced Indigenous discourses and practices not only at the UN but also in spaces such as the WSF. Acknowledging the Indigenous style of diplomacy—as resistance and as a project of decolonization, yet in continuous dialogue with dominant values and principles—is crucial for understanding Indigenous activism beyond UN arenas and Indigenous activists' participation in what they refer to as "paradigm wars." Due to the serious political issues that are at stake, activist ethnography is in a unique position to capture respectfully and in great detail how Indigenous diplomacy is able to maneuver with respect to global politics and social movements.

The key objectives of the GIM have been the generation of normative declarations that address Indigenous peoples' rights and the crafting of new relationships with nation-states and the international community, generating a global Indigenous consciousness. This was not an easy process. As Henderson explains: "We travelled to Europe to articulate our problems with Eurocentric colonization, only to discover cognitive imperialism surviving" (J. Henderson 2008, 42). This situation forced Indigenous activists to discover their shared interests, create a global voice, introduce their own diplomacy and concepts as part of negotiations, and coalesce as part of an "international Indigenous identity" (Niezen 2003, 46). The resulting global view on indigeneity resulted from what Guillermo Delgado-P. calls Indigenous peoples' "re/membering" of themselves as peoples with collective rights and a place among nations (2002, 38). Indigenous activists are drawing from their collective memories and consciousness to create new global Indigenous political actors. But this re/membering is constructed in interaction and in an intercultural dialogue with dominant narratives such as that of human rights and even the logic of capital.

I have examined Indigenous women's empowerment within the GIM and the UN because these paths illustrate and reflect how networking and familiarity with the human rights regime were key factors in the constitution of a global collective political actor. In their *andar* and in their re/membering, Indigenous women have recognized each other, shared information, and built common platforms of action, and they have also met and entered into dialogue with other transnational social movements. In the process they have carved autonomous networked spaces of transnational encounter where they can define who they are and what they are fighting for. From these spaces they have challenged entrenched colonial and patriarchal paradigms that place Indigenous women outside of politics and/or in subordinate positions.

My examination of the notion of paradigm wars reveals that as the environmental and economic global crises were being felt more acutely worldwide, Indigenous peoples' lifestyles became emblematic of a different relationship with nature. Indigenous activists have realized that engaging with the social forum process, where networking is paramount and where it is possible to imagine another reality outside of the logic of the nation-state, can be a fertile ground for advocating new paradigms based on Indigenous cosmovisions and for building an alternative global consensus that can potentially provide solutions for devastating crises that we all face. In many international and transnational meetings and encounters, Indigenous activists continually refer to how the eyes of humanity are upon them and how many are waiting for their guidance in helping to solve environmental problems. In fact, Indigenous activists and their issues are often put center stage in meetings and encounters, and yet, as I have shown, because of the legacy of colonialism, they are also marginalized and misunderstood.

Although Indigenous activism has privileged the UN as an international arena of struggle, it is increasingly engaging the WSF because many activists believe that through an intercultural dialogue with civil society and its social movements, it might be possible to come together as one mind, as Oren Lyons has frequently put it.[17] Lyons has claimed in many spaces that it is important to listen because we have not yet reached the point of no return in relation to the damage humans are causing to the environment. One example of how alternative paradigms advocated in social forums have influenced global politics is the fact that the UNPFII has recognized the need for integrating the Indigenous notion of *buen vivir* into the developmental agenda of the UN, arguing that it cannot be divorced from the aspirations declared in the United Nations Declaration on the Rights of Indigenous Peoples. Another example is the emergence of voices within women's movements that talk about women's special relationship with and obligations toward nature. In reference to misunderstandings at the U.S. Social Forum and the WSF, it is clear that the lessons learned after four decades of educating and sensitizing non-Indigenous government officials, diplomats, scholars, and NGOs in the context of the UN regarding the need to respect Indigenous peoples' histories, struggles, protocols, cosmovisions, and paradigms have to be repeated in the context of new interactions within a highly diverse global civil society.

Paradigm wars have thus been worked out interculturally as a project of decolonization in response, adaptation, and resistance to colonialism, patriarchy, neoliberalism, globalization, and a world dominated by international organizations. This is a project in which co/laboration with academia is crucial. Ethnographic research that is conducted in these settings is necessarily part of the activism that takes place there. The alternatives and solutions that emerge have to be understood as the outcome (always already contested) of the encounters, activism, networking, and forging of common agendas with various actors. Indigenous activists claim that the concerted solutions have to be sought and implemented under different economic, political, social, cultural, and ecological paradigms that include their own worldviews, but also a human rights framework as it is reflected in international law and standards. And as Indigenous women remind us, concerted solutions necessarily have to be worked out horizontally, in a shared way, and in equitable terms among all actors, respecting their cultural distinctiveness.

NOTES

1   See "The Haudenosaunee Message to the World" in Wilmer 1993 (204). The term *Mother Earth* is widely used by Indigenous activists from different parts of the world, especially from the Americas, in their discourses, official statements, and practices. The term has gained currency not only among Indigenous activists but also among state representatives and UN officials.

2   While it may not be conventional to do so, I capitalize "Indigenous" within this chapter as a sign of respect to the struggles and rights of Indigenous peoples. They argue that they are nations and should be given that status, including conceptually, and I concur with that.

3   James Cameron's film *Avatar* (2009) talks about the struggles of the Na'vi (a fantasy people) to defend their territory from a militarized corporation wanting to exploit their subsoil resources.

4   There is significant diversity within the category of "Indigenous peoples." They are not a homogenous group that speaks with one voice or has the same aspirations. However, Indigenous activists at the international level are acknowledged as a singular collectivity called "Indigenous peoples." Nevertheless, this representation is problematic and contested.

5   I use the words *international, transnational,* and *global*, depending on how they are used by Indigenous activists, international organizations, academics, social movements, and so on, in different contexts. Empirically, I talk about Indigenous struggles taking place at the international level because that is how GIM and other actors describe it. The label *international* also describes the motivation and goals of Indigenous activism and diplomacy, as Indigenous peoples claim nationhood as the basis for their collective rights, including self-determination. I am calling the GIM by the self-

ascribed name used by the movement. The word *global* refers to the fact that the movement intends to include Indigenous peoples from all over the world regardless of their sociopolitical organization. However, analytically, I talk about the GIM as an example of a transnational space because this theoretical concept is helpful for understanding some of its dynamics. Finally, Indigenous activism and diplomacy simultaneously weave various levels—local, national, regional, transnational, and international—of political action and cultural politics, and therein lies their potential for transformative politics.

6 Specific sites of my activist ethnographic research include the United Nations Working Group on Indigenous Populations from 1997 to 2006 in Geneva; the United Nations Permanent Forum on Indigenous Issues from 2006 to 2010 in New York; the 2007 World Social Forum in Nairobi; the 2007 U.S. Social Forum in Atlanta; the 2007 Fifth Continental Meeting of Indigenous Women of the Americas in Quebec; the 2008 Social Forum of the Americas in Guatemala City; the 2009 World Social Forum in Bélem; the 2009 United Nations Framework Convention on Climate Change Conference of the Parties 15 meeting in Copenhagen; and the 2010 United Nations Expert Mechanism on the Rights of Indigenous Peoples in Geneva. I have also collected information through various years of fieldwork in Mexico (Oaxaca, Mexico City, and Michoacán) since 1998; through video conferencing from the 2009 Indigenous Peoples' Global Summit in Anchorage and the 2010 United Nations Framework Convention on Climate Change Conference of the Parties 16 meeting in Cancún; and through a variety of archival documents made available online from various Indigenous conferences and encounters throughout the Americas.

7 For more information about the concept of *co/laboration*, see Guillermo Delgado-P. (1996).

8 Emilio del Valle Escalante argues that the concept of cosmovision in the context of Maya struggles is used "with the goal of rearticulating a political and epistemological locus of enunciation against anything that threatens the values and struggles of Indigenous peoples" (2009, 14–15). Some of those values, he explains, relate to Indigenous peoples' relationship with Mother Earth, the importance of community/collectivity, and the historical cohesion between past, present, and future. The concept of cosmovision can also be applied to the GIM as it helps to rearticulate and anchor discourses and paradigms of indigeneity, particularly in relation to regimes of human rights.

9 The Miskitos are an Indigenous people who reside along the Caribbean coast of Central America from Honduras to Nicaragua. In 2011, Myrna Cunningham was elected chair of the UN Permanent Forum on Indigenous Issues. She has an extensive record in the defense and promotion of Indigenous rights, gender issues, and interculturalism at the local, national, and international

levels (see www.un.org/apps/news/newsmakers.asp?NewsID=52, accessed December 25, 2011).

10   The Quechua people are a collection of indigenous groups in the Andean region of South America, including parts of Peru, Bolivia, Ecuador, Chile, Colombia, and Argentina, who speak a Quechua language.

11   Hñähñu is a frequent self-identification among the Mezquital Otomi, an Indigenous people from the Mezquital valley in the eastern part of the central Mexican state of Hidalgo.

12   During the meetings of the UNFCCC, NGOs representing a variety of interests—business and industry, environmental groups, farming and agriculture, Indigenous peoples, local governments and municipal authorities, research and academic institutes, labor unions, women and gender, and youth groups—form constituencies based on common interests. Representatives of these groups can be members of one or more constituencies.

13   The global view on indigeneity is not fixed; it is constantly contested, discursively and in practice, and it is flexible enough to include the interests and needs of several groups who self-identify as Indigenous and who participate in the GIM (for an ample discussion on indigeneity see Escárcega 2003a, 2003b, 2010; Muehlebach 2001; Niezen 2003).

14   The Igorot People are composed of a series of ethnic groups in the mountains of the northern Luzon region of the Philippines.

15   Among the 130,000 participants at the 2009 WSF, 1,900 were Indigenous, coming from 190 different groups, the majority of them from the Amazon region and South America (one of the goals of the WSF that year was to emphasize the consequences of the destruction and of neoliberal policies on the lives and cultures of Indigenous peoples). The Indigenous agenda in turn included, among other things, the rights to territory and self-determination, the concept of *buen vivir*, plurinational states, the decolonization of power and ways of knowing, and the search for common platforms and strategies for the Indigenous movement at the continental level.

16   The Mi'kmaq People (plural of Mi'kmaw) are a Native American Indigenous people that reside in northeastern New England and eastern Canada.

17   In many of his interventions at the United Nations that I have observed during fieldwork throughout the years, Oren Lyons has called on UN officials, diplomats, Indigenous peoples, civil society, and others to come together as one mind to bring peace and harmony, to find solutions to our common problems, and to change for the good of humanity. For one textual example of this idea, see Lyons 1994.

6

Local and Not-So-Local Exchanges

Alternative Economies, Ethnography, and Social Science

DAVID J. HESS

In a very autobiographical talk on June 26, 2004, Edgar Cahn (Cahn and Grey-Cahn 2004) described some of the life events that led to the creation of the type of alternative currency for which he is famous: time dollars. Time dollars are a way of logging volunteer time through a local exchange (sometimes called a time bank), in which people can "deposit" hours of volunteer work and make withdrawals based on the volunteer time of other members. Cahn noted that he was influenced by his late wife, the African American leader Jean Camper Cahn, who cofounded the national legal services program with him. He added that 70 percent of the time-bank members are women, and his twin sister calls time banks feminist economics. Because the use of time as a form of exchange levels the playing field of labor value, Cahn argued, time banks address social injustices created by the contemporary market economy. Whereas the market economy often fails to reward caring for children and elders, community service, efforts to promote democracy, and other forms of work, time banks provide a way to provide some compensation for such activities.

Cahn was just one of many speakers at the conference "Local Currencies in the Twenty-First Century," hosted by the E. F. Schumacher Society and held in the Hudson River Valley from June 25 to June 27, 2004. Among the networks and local experiments, time banks are most attuned to issues of inequality, but there are many other types of alternative currencies under discussion, and their purposes and politics vary considerably. For example, the alternative currencies that are most visible to the media and public are physical currencies such as Ithaca Hours, Burlington Bread, and Berkshares. Unlike time banks, these currencies address another type of inequality: the absence of policy support for the independent small business sector (see also Collom 2005; Maurer 2005; Seyfang 2003, 2004). By exchanging local currencies, the small-business sector can draw attention to its existence and unique contributions to a community. Another type of alternative currency is the scrip. In Great Barrington, Massachusetts, a restaurant that could not get bank financing for an expansion issued coupons that customers could purchase and later redeem at a premium with purchases of the store's products. The informal bonds, known as "deli dollars," enabled the business to expand without support from the banks. Much more numerous are local exchange trading systems (sometimes referred to as LETS), which are computer-based systems that do not require a currency and can carry debits. As Michael Linton (2004), the famed founder of the first LETS system (which he said originally meant "Let's," as in "Let's do something"), explained in another talk on June 26, 2004, at the E. F. Schumacher Society conference, the goal of the original LETS was to provide a source of alternative income and employment in an economically depressed community. For some young men with whom I had lunch, the LETS project they had developed was devoid of social change aspirations and was simply a temporary way for a group of friends to swap "stuff."

Although the conference organizers used the phrase *local currencies* in the title, there was no general agreement about what to call the diverse alternative currency projects: local, alternative, or community currencies; time banks; LETS; and so on. There was much exchange of information about the merits of different types of alternative currencies, and many of the sessions focused on the significant problems that advocates had faced after launching their local exchange systems. I certainly came away from the conference with a good awareness of pitfalls to avoid, the central features of successful systems, and the labor that would be required should I ever become involved in establishing such a project. Back home, when some members of the localist organization with which I am involved suggested starting a local currency, I cautioned them about the work and skill that would be needed in order to get one to operate effectively. Subsequently, an international research project was launched to catalogue and analyze the diverse projects across the world (Seyfang and Longhurst 2012).

Although there is a side of the alternative currencies movement that is, like the young men I had lunch with or stores that issue coupons, not very connected with social change aspirations, the more prominent sentiment was connected with a political critique and social change project. Frequently speakers stated that official fiat currencies were instruments of a system that enabled an unfair concentration of wealth. Most of the people who presented at the conference recognized the need for official fiat currencies, but the general aspiration was a populist one of returning financial power from the large banks, central government, and multinational corporations to the small business sector, local governments, and the "people." One speaker at the conference, David Boyle (2004) of the New Economics Foundation in the United Kingdom, drew clear parallels with the nineteenth-century populist tradition. Another speaker and leading figure, Thomas Greco (2004), articulated the relations between alternative currencies and a broader political project. Although he made such connections at the conference, he subsequently published a more detailed statement of his views in *The End of Money and the Future of Civilization*: "power and control need to be decentralized; wealth must be more fairly distributed; local economies must be nurtured; the commons, especially the credit commons, must be restored; monopolies must be eliminated or circumvented; the basic necessities of life—especially water, air, food, and energy—must be brought under popular control; and ecological restoration must be a high priority" (Greco 2009, 230). Achieving the goals is not possible, he argued, within the "present politicized global debt-money regime" (230). Such views are consistent with a wide range of social movements that have opposed a model of corporate-led globalization, which has increased environmental destruction and social inequality. Moreover, these views have become even more popular after the financial crisis of 2007 and the subsequent Great Recession, and have found their way into collective action such as the Occupy Wall Street movement and the Move Your Money campaign.

In this chapter I begin by making the argument that movements in support of alternative economies should be considered alongside protest-based movements as part of a broad family of antiglobalization movements. I then go on to consider the puzzle of how to theorize community-based antiglobalization and localist movements as both place based and transnational. Next, I step back to explore broader methodological and theoretical issues that have emerged in this volume and in my own research, specifically ethics in the ethnographic study of antiglobalization movements and the broader problems of ethnography understood as a humanistic product and as method for social science research.

ALTERNATIVE ECONOMIES AND ANTIGLOBALIZATION MOVEMENTS

The decision to call the networks of advocates of alternative currencies a movement is a matter of definition. Many of the participants used the term *movement* as a self-designation, but because the meanings of alternative currency advocacy can stretch from social change aspirations to business promotion to a hobby-like activity, I have tended to prefer the broader term *alternative pathway* (Hess 2009). Likewise, I prefer the term *reform movement* (in contrast with *social movement*) to describe collective social change action that does not use a protest repertoire. That this reform movement is transnational is obvious from the description of the conference just given; the alternative currencies movement is maintained through a global circulation of writing, knowledge, and people, punctuated by brief gatherings. Given the location of the conference, most of the attendees were from the United States and Canada, but there were also community currency advocates from Japan, Europe, Latin America, India, Australia, New Zealand, and other countries and regions. It was evident from the many references that people made to experiments around the world that knowledge about these heavily localized reform projects was circulating globally. As a result, the conference could be considered an example of the "networked space of transnational encounter" described in this volume's introduction.

The idea that locally based advocates and activists connected through transnational networks will occasionally gather for global events of collective effervescence, or at least nonlocal exchange, is hardly new or exciting. But the designation of the conference in terms of "local currencies" does imply something of more general interest in the study of transnational social movements: the question of the local in the world of transnational antiglobalization or alter-globalization movements. Although the conference and the local action that preceded and followed it were not the kinds of antiglobalization activity that entailed tangling with security forces in street protests against a global financial institution, it is fair to think about advocates of alternative currencies as part of a broad family of antiglobalization movements. Antiglobalization movements are highly diverse, but they share a common feature of opposition to a form of globalization that benefits large multinational corporations. Like many other social movements, antiglobalization movements embody both a politics of opposition—to a corporate-led, neoliberal vision of globalization—and a politics of alternatives in favor of more just and sustainable economies and policies. At least some local currency advocates share with antiglobalization activists a strong sense that the neoliberal model of corporate-led globalization needs to be changed, but they differ by emphasizing a pathway to change that leads through building organizational alternatives to multinational corporations, often via cooperatives, small businesses, and social enterprises. Whereas the antiglobalization protest mobilizations tend to fit more comfortably with the traditional analytical category of a social movement, alternative economies movements often operate as reform movements that take place more within institutional structures and appeal to a broader range of participants. The alternative currencies movement is closer to, and sometimes intertwined with, the social forum movement (see Jackie Smith et al. 2007 and several chapters in this volume).

The primary site of the alternative economies strand of antiglobalization movements tends to be local communities rather than global events. However, when people build local currencies or other types of local exchanges, it is usually not in isolation. Take the example of Berkshares, a local currency project launched by the E. F. Schumacher Society in Great Barrington, Massachusetts. I have been fortunate enough to have both Susan Witt and Sarah Hearn of the E. F. Schumacher Society, subsequently reorganized as the New Economics Institute, speak about local currencies in a lecture series that I ran on local social enterprises. My students have generally never heard of local currencies, and their imaginations are often lit as their hands hold the beautifully designed alternative currency notes. But as they learn about the local currency, they also realize that the Berkshares project is part of a much larger vision of building an alternative global economy to that of the large multinational corporation. The Berkshares project, its coordinators, and the New Economics Institute are networked with many similar organizations, both in their region and throughout the world.

A conceptual problem emerges. A transnational movement, which we might call the local currencies movement, can be viewed as part of the family of antiglobalization movements, which have been a focus of attention in the study of transnational social movements (see, e.g., della Porta 2007; della Porta et al. 2006; Juris 2008a). But when one follows the local currencies movement back home, it is embedded in an ecology of related reform efforts that do not have a global focus. I use the term *localism* to describe the wide range of efforts that rebuild or create local ownership, such as family farms, independent small businesses, local nonprofit organizations, community media, food cooperatives, credit unions, farmers' markets, community gardens, community financial institutions, and municipal electricity. Activists who build community currencies in a specific region are therefore not lone rangers; their work fits into an ecology of regional organizations and reform efforts that are also attempting to build regional alternative economy institutions. So how might one think of the relationship between localist movements and transnational antiglobalization movements? To answer that question, it is necessary to more deeply explore a localist scene that I know very well.

LOCALISM, SCALE, AND TRANSNATIONALISM

I became involved in a corner of the North American localist movement when I joined with people from the local credit union, the local food cooperative, and some other independent businesses to help form Capital District Local First in the region around New York's state capital. The primary goal of the organization is to promote the locally owned, independent business sector in the Albany area and to enroll the sector in a project of making the regional economy more fair, community oriented, and environmentally sustainable and to connect those efforts to others going on throughout the country and the world. The organization is locally oriented, but it is networked with efforts across the United States and Canada through the Business Alliance for Local Living Economies and some other organizations, such as the New Rules Project of the Institute for Local Self-Reliance.

As has been shown by some national studies, organizations like ours, with support from the alternative newsweeklies, are having a significant impact on consumer spending (Mitchell 2009a). There are many examples of communities and state governments that have responded to criticisms of policies that heavily favor the large corporate and retail service sector. Policy reforms include limitations on formula businesses, size-based zoning restrictions, legislation that requires community-impact reviews for big-box development projects, shifts in public-procurement policies to favor local businesses, Internet sales taxes, community renewable-energy initiatives, and decisions by state and local governments to move some of their money to local banks and credit unions. Although some of the people associated with Capital District Local First have occasionally talked about starting an alternative currency, and a few other people in the region have also talked about it, to date the project has not been launched, partly due to the awareness of the level of work required, which has flowed out of the experience of the transnational networks. Instead the closest projects are coupon books that serve local independent businesses and a range of community financial institutions that have flourished.

The impact of localist mobilizations is great enough that there are emergent corporate strategies to counter localism, such as efforts by Walmart to promote the sale (albeit limited) of local products and by Starbucks to offer debranded coffee houses that appear to be independently owned (Mitchell 2009b). Likewise, online retailers have made strong efforts to stop state governments from passing legislation that would establish Internet sales taxes. The model legislation in New York State was passed with strong support from the state's small business community, including one of the most active businesses within Capital District Local First. Although local-first activities generally are not openly hostile to big businesses (the idea is to encourage some shifting of patronage to small independent businesses from the region and around the world), there is a general sentiment that the global economy would be much fairer and democratically accountable if it were organized along alternative principles.

Although consistent with traditional Leftist politics on the issue of shared opposition to the corporatocracy, localist politics differ from the traditional Leftist strategy of advocating public ownership of the means of production by national governments or the social liberal ("social democratic" in Europe) strategy of strong antitrust and regulatory legislation. Instead, localists focus more on building democratically accountable economic organizations from the bottom up. Here I think there is an important general insight into the study of transnational social movements, especially those that oppose a vision of neoliberal globalization based on control of economies by large corporations. The issue of scale should be central to the theories of such movements. As I have seen in the day-to-day work with people in my region, at a local scale it is possible to mobilize people across traditional Left-Right political divisions when attention is focused on a shared identity with a place and a threat to that place posed by large multinational corporations. But the potential for building new kinds of political coalitions also creates tensions with the traditional socialist and social liberal visions of social change based on higher scale institutions, especially national governments and international organizations. The division within antiglobalization movements between opposition politics with repertoires of street protest and alternative politics with repertoires of alternative institution building is to some degree also a division in scale as a strategic site for action.

To movement leaders and social scientists who think in traditional socialist or social liberal terms, the emphasis on building alternative economic organizations may be suspect. One cause for suspicion is the idea that localist politics operate at the wrong level of scale and are therefore condemned to ineffectiveness. There is sometimes an underlying assumption that the best or most appropriate level of scale on which antiglobalization politics must be enacted is transnational. But if one accepts the proposition that antiglobalization movements, like many other social movements, are divided into opposition and alternative wings, then a range of strategies opens up: oppositional versus alternative politics, repertoires of protest versus institution building, as well as local and national versus transnational organizing.

The study of localism therefore may have some general value for the study of transnational social movements by broadening the study of scale from mechanisms and processes (della Porta and Tarrow 2004). The issue here is not a problem of the scale shift that accompanies mobilizational success but the variable politics and forms of social movement activity that occur at different levels of scale. For example, in localist politics, the more hands-on advocacy work occurs at the local and state government level, whereas at the continental and global level the work is more information sharing or establishing alternative trading networks such as fair trade.

The largely middle-class character of localist politics may also provoke some suspicion from traditional socialist and social liberal critics. Indeed, transnational social movements often highlight not only relations of global inequality between elites and the rest of us but also power differentials within movements (see Juris, this volume; Jackie Smith, Juris, and the Social Forum Research Collective 2008). Here scale is sometimes associated with power and privilege; those people within the movement who are able to circulate at a translocal scale tend to be from the more privileged strata of the movement. Furthermore, the result of their translocal circulation is access to greater knowledge, social networks, and other resources that enhance their positions of leadership within a movement. As a result, transnationalism may actually magnify differences of power and status between the cosmopolitan movement leaders and the locally anchored movement rank and file.

Returning to the conference on local currencies, such issues were very evident. The speakers and participants at the conference were largely male, well educated, and, aside from representatives from Asia, white. This reflects not a bias on the part of the organizers as much as the characteristics of the field. As I have moved through diverse alternative economies movements over the years, this network has been especially white and male. It contrasted with the alternative food movements, in which women are more heavily represented, and with community gardening (an alternative food movement), in which people of color, often with low incomes, are more prominent. However, it would also be a mistake to generalize that the alternative finance space is a zone of completely white, male, and privileged class position even within the broader field of alternative economies projects in North America and Europe.

In my region, the Capital District Community Loan Fund is one of the best examples of organizations that have a social address (and actually a physical address as well) in the low-income, African American and Latino neighborhood of Albany. Although the loan fund is affiliated with Capital District Local First and partners with it for some events, the demographic of the local-first organization is much more middle class, middle aged, and white (but with women in many of the prominent leadership positions). Based on my interaction with other local-first organizations and the national Business Alliance for Local Living Economies conferences, the demographic is widespread in this particular segment of the alternative economies movement. At the national level the Business Alliance for

Local Living Economies has developed an initiative to deepen connections in low-income communities. In other words, as in some of the other social movements, diversity is a shortcoming, an opportunity, and a goal.

The fact that local-first organizations are largely middle class and white (but gender mixed) may cause some activists and intellectuals to be suspicious, but again it may be valuable to use the social address as a point of departure for inspecting assumptions about the social address of antiglobalization politics. Just as those politics may not necessarily have as close a relationship with the transnational scale as might first be assumed, antiglobalization politics may not necessarily have the close relationship with the youths in rich countries and poor people in low-income countries that is sometimes assumed. Local-first organizations are about class injustice, but they are primarily about the plight of the petite bourgeoisie in the context of the predatory practices of corporate-led globalization. In the process of working with the Capital District Local First, I have come to see the need for better research and theory on the petite bourgeoisie as a source of radical politics (see Johnston 2003). For example, there are significant divisions within this class. There is an independent working class of small mom-and-pop shops that have somehow found a place to survive in the niches of industries dominated by chains, franchises, and large corporate retail and service enterprises; and there are larger enterprises that are locally owned, privately held, and loyal to the region but sometimes more identified with the policies and politics of the large corporate sector. In my experience, these two types tend to divide on some crucial issues, such as attitudes toward unions. Those divisions suggest both the potential for and limitations of possible cross-class coalitions.

Although it may seem contradictory to talk about localism in the context of the study of transnational social movements, there are some good reasons for doing so. The study of localist movements posed in the context of the study of transnational movements suggests a reflexive question about the particular valuation and devaluation of some levels of scale over others. Moreover, the study of localist movements also suggests the need to pay attention to possible assumptions about the social address of transnational antiglobalization movements. I suggest that there is a need to attend more to the trafficking of activists, ideas, politics, and strategies across levels of scale and social divisions, and to explore the particular kinds of politics that may be enabled by or constitutive of those different levels of scale and social address.

Issues of class, race, and gender within an organization and movement are always very delicate, and they raise the general problem of how a researcher should or should not write about those issues and other sensitive information (see chapters in this book by Juris, Conway, and Stinger). I have had two main roles with respect to the localist movement in my region. Within the university, I have taught a course on social entrepreneurship and sustainable communities. The title of the course was a compromise that enabled access to university entrepreneurship funding that supported a lecture series of local social entrepreneurs in the region (some of the speakers considered themselves to be activists and were surprised to find out that they were being redefined as social entrepreneurs, but they were happy to receive the honoraria). The money also allowed me to hire a graduate student to write case studies for use in teaching about alternative economies by exploring the life histories of leaders such as Edgar Cahn (time banks), Paul Rice (TransFair USA), Mary Houghton (Shorebank), Muhammed Yunas (Grameen Bank), Robert Swann (Community Land Trusts), and Amy Goodman (Democracy Now). My other role has been as a board member of the Capital District Local First. Within the organization, I ended up doing the legal work during the early phase, but as the organization evolved I tried to shift more into a role of making presentations to local groups, such as the chambers of commerce and business-improvement districts; serving as a liaison with similar organizations across New York State and the country; and doing some of the writing for the organization. Some members of the organization feel my talents would be best used in leading initiatives for policy reform.

There are at least two major ethical issues that emerge when one has separate roles as an organizational leader and as a researcher who writes about the broader social field in which the organization is positioned. Among some social scientists the coexistence of two roles or identities means that it is impossible to write with objectivity about the movement. Certainly a researcher with one foot in a movement is not likely to write highly critical treatises on it. But similar concerns arise for any kind of ethnographic research in which the researcher has established long-term relationships with people associated with a field site or sites. It seems that the proper way to handle possible conflicts is to disclose the relationships so that other researchers can weigh the potential conflict when evaluating

the research. As long as the position is disclosed, the research field benefits from the superior background knowledge of someone who has long-
term, real-life experience in the movement.

The second ethical issue concerns the obligations not of a researcher
to a research community but of an activist or advocate to an organization or movement. The ethical issues are more pressing the more deeply
one is involved. For example, at the conference on local currencies, I was
attending as an observer and taking notes on public talks and informal
corridor conversations. But as an insider and a leader of a localist organization, I have access to a high level of confidential information, and there
is a presumption that my primary role is one of community service, advocate, or activist. The role places restrictions on the use of the ethnographic
vignette in scholarly writing. Much as a court has rules for admissibility
of evidence, I have developed inclusion and exclusion rules for the admissibility of some forms of the ethnographic vignette in final, published
writing. To some degree the development of the rules is also informed by
my experience serving on the university's institutional review board for
human-subject research. After years of thinking through research ethics,
I have come up with two basic rules for ethnography when one has a role
that is different from that of a researcher.

A primary rule is as follows: when the ethnographic vignette reveals
nonpublic knowledge about an organization or individuals, it is off limits.
I treat the information obtained as a member of the organization the way
that journalists describe "deep background," that is, information that can
be used to inform general analyses but not in a way that provides a description of a specific event or person. An example is my discussion above
about the divisions in the petite bourgeoisie and attitudes toward unions.
I have access to some very colorful ethnographic vignettes, but rather than
capture that information as a vignette or group of vignettes, I watched
for more statements, and I gradually built up a pattern about the divisions in the petite bourgeoisie. This exclusion rule has implications for
the genre of writing. The second rule, the inclusion rule, is that if I want
to use specific information I have acquired in my service role, then I draw
on published statements or formal, recorded interviews with signed consent forms, where it is clear to the interviewee how I will use the material
and there is a right to be anonymous and to approve and edit quotations.
Otherwise, I use only general descriptions of public events, as reflected

in this chapter's opening paragraph, or summaries of highly anonymous conversations (see Hess 2010).[1]

The choices that I have made with respect to exclusion and inclusion rules in turn are related to a broader issue of what the term *ethnography* means. The term can refer to both a method of research (at its best, long-term fieldwork in which one gains an insider's knowledge of a social field) and a genre of writing (usually a descriptive and interpretive mode of writing based on a humanities style of alternating patterns of vignettes followed by exegesis). However, ethnography as method can be separated from ethnography as genre, and the separation is commonplace in sociology and some of the other social sciences. The difference raises deeper questions involving what might be called the "two cultures" problem of ethnographers. Because the problem is of great importance for an interdisciplinary volume on ethnography and transnational social movements, it is worth discussing in more detail.

TWO CULTURES OF ETHNOGRAPHY

The central question that this volume explores is apparently simple: can ethnography be of value for both the scholarly study of transnational social movements and the political strategizing of transnational movement activists and advocates? The immediate answer may be an obvious yes, but the question leads to some complex issues.

A first layer of issues involves the problem of writing for scholarly and nonscholarly readers in a single text. In publishing there is a term for this kind of project—the *crossover book* that can reach both a trade audience of educated lay readers and a scholarly audience—but in practice it is exceedingly difficult to write. For example, two books that I worked on during the 1990s as part of my research project on the alternative cancer-therapy movement in the United States were based on interviews with advocates, researchers, and clinicians (Hess 1998; Hess and Wooddell 1998). The books were influenced by the writing-culture critiques of the 1980s (see Clifford and Marcus 1986) and the idea that researchers should make room for the voices of the people with whom they work. The books carried the idea to the point that they essentially ended up as edited volumes with each chapter devoted to an interview. Although the books had moderate general circulation and press coverage, and both health-care professionals and patients found the books helpful, they produced almost no citations in the scholarly literature. I came to the conclusion that the crossover book was a myth for most fields, with the possible exception of feminist and popular media studies, where there does appear to be a general audience for academic work. Since then, most of what I have written with respect to knowledge, technology, and social movements is for scholarly audiences. However, I have also produced white papers and case studies for more general audiences. The divisions of genre are deeply ingrained in the reward system of academia and, with a few exceptions, fairly intractable to change (Woodhouse et al. 2002).

A second issue that is embedded in the question about the value of ethnography is the proposition that ethnography can have value for the scholarly study of transnational social movements. On one level, it is obvious that the method of ethnographic fieldwork has widespread value across a range of disciplines. On another level though, one can construct a more specific argument that a particular genre of writing up the results of ethnographic fieldwork, associated with an interpretivist strand that is prominent in North American cultural anthropology, has potential value for interdisciplinary social movement studies. As someone who was trained in that and other traditions of anthropological ethnography but also has circulated and published widely in interdisciplinary social science circles (mostly sociology, environmental studies, and policy studies), I have become acutely aware of some of the disciplinary differences and boundaries that can occur.

As a method and genre, "ethnography" is a socially contested field that stretches across a wide range of scholarly disciplines. Anthropologists may feel a particular ownership over ethnography, but the sense of ownership is not shared. Sociologists, for example, were writing urban ethnographies early in the twentieth century, even before the genre of the functionalist monograph became established in anthropology. Moreover, the *Handbook of Ethnography* shows that the practice of ethnography is deployed across a wide range of fields even beyond anthropology and sociology (Atkinson et al. 2001). At one extreme, I once attended a communications conference where two hours of classroom observation were called ethnography. In contrast, I had come to think of ethnography as requiring years of experience in one or more related field sites. Often ethnographers cannot see anything until they have known people and organizations for more than a decade and watched how they have changed.

In my chapter in the *Handbook of Ethnography*, I suggested some characteristics of "good" ethnography in the more extensive tradition and also discussed some issues related to intervention and activist-scholarship. In general, good ethnography as the result of long-term ethnographic fieldwork is a form of knowledge that approximates the competencies of one's informants but can interpret these competencies from broader theoretical frameworks (Hess 2001).

For anthropologists, as noted above, the term *ethnography* tends to include both the method, ethnographic fieldwork, and the final product, an "ethnography" or ethnographic monograph. There is generally a sentiment, at least in the United States since the 1970s, that the final product is an interpretivist one. There can be feminist, culturalist, critical, postcolonial, structuralist, poststructuralist, deconstructive, constructivist, and many other flavors, but the peace in the feud remains the shared project of interpretation, including a form of interpretation that might be considered critique. When used in this wide-tent sense, the term *interpretivism* is best defined negatively, as Clifford Geertz (1973) did, in opposition to an experimental science in search of laws. From this perspective, ethnography as an interpretivist product is something that varies greatly but might be likened to the work of a literary critic, cultural historian, journalistic commentator, or philosophical analyst. The project may articulate assumptions, draw connections, explore complexity, and chart tensions, but its primary goal is not social science in the sense of contributing generalizations to a body of knowledge.

Furthermore, anthropological ethnography has no inherent position of support or critique with respect to the people and communities described. It can be tilted in the direction of a project that is aligned with or against a movement. For example, there is a growing level of poking fun at and criticism of localist movements, often from journalists with a loyalty to an ideology of corporate-led globalization, who see the movements as anachronistic and romantic. There are also criticisms from those on the socialist or social liberal Left, who view localism with suspicion as either ineffective or implicitly market oriented. The ethnographic interpretation can be aligned with the critics of either the Right or the Left, or it can be turned on critics and marshal ethnographic knowledge to discredit the discreditors.

The ethnographer may also choose to explore some of the problems or tensions in the movement itself. At its worst, the writing can result in a snobby and elitist airing of the shortcomings of a movement's politics with a problematic use of the vignette. In the case of alternative currencies and more general localist and alternative economies movements, the project could involve the social address issue of the movements' locations in the middle class of progressive professionals and small-business owners. I have addressed the issue, but I do so by exploring it under the rubric of problems as well as potential for future development. In other words, I look for points where localist politics are in alignment with social justice and environmental sustainability problems. The analysis requires a balance between articulating a future vision and developing a critical analysis that can contribute to discrediting forces (see Conway, this volume).

Whatever stance the ethnographer ends up selecting with respect to the movement, there is little doubt that the ethnography as interpretivist genre can produce valuable insights. However, it also faces limitations as a scholarly project in an interdisciplinary social science field. Anthropological ethnography can serve as a corrective to overgeneralization in the social science literature (such as analyses that describe alternative economies as spaces of whiteness or as co-opted by neoliberal market politics), but it also tends to eschew another type of conversation with interdisciplinary social sciences. To understand this difference, it may be helpful to provide a typological comparison of the two cultures of ethnography.

Although both anthropologists and other social scientists have used fieldwork, even long-term fieldwork, for decades, there are differences, such as the greater attentiveness to cultural meaning among anthropologists and perhaps a greater attention to organizational dynamics and ecologies among sociologists, but those differences are not as significant as a larger one that involves a relationship between theory and empirical data. For anthropologists, theory tends to be something that is used to interpret the fieldwork experience; it tends to be in the background, even in the footnotes. The text may be arranged as a weaving in and out of "data" in the form of an ethnographic vignette and an interpretation. The goal is to understand the case (the field site, the novel, the movie, the historical event). Complexity, nuance, and the capacity to see nonapparent distinctions are characteristics of good ethnography in this tradition.

In the interdisciplinary social sciences, the relationship between theory and empirical material is inverted. Ethnography as a research method is separated from the research product. The goal of the social science project is some kind of generalization, and the "data" are selected often as cases to provide evidence for or qualifications of a theoretical proposition that advances a conversation in the literature. This type of project is consistent with theory-driven hypothesis testing in the quantitative social sciences, but in the qualitative social sciences the hypotheses may not be stated as explicitly as in quantitative research, and the data may be used to exemplify and explore propositions as much as to test explicit hypotheses. In either case, the genre of writing tends to be constructed differently from the text-exegesis format that is common in anthropological ethnography. A common form is the statement of the problem, a review of the literature, an argument about how the literature can be moved forward, an examination of empirical material that qualifies or exemplifies the argument, and a conclusion about general implications and future direction. This type of knowledge is more explicitly cumulative and engaged with other researchers; as a result the thought collectives of intellectual production are more dense, and (at least based on my own informal comparisons) the citation rates and the permeability (the accessibility of the literature to those in neighboring fields) are higher.

From the perspective of interdisciplinary social science, anthropological ethnography may appear to be loose, disorganized, and often without a main point. The work appears to invent new concepts that are quite similar to ones developed in other fields, but because there is generally an undeveloped literature review and no explicit statement about the theoretical arguments that are being advanced with respect to a referent literature, interdisciplinary social science readers may find it easy to dismiss the project as uninformed and the new concepts as pretentious jargon or stylistic wordplay that hide a failure to engage existing literature. In contrast, the social science method that carefully selects data for purposes of evaluating an argument may appear to those who write in the more humanistic mode of ethnography as forcing a template onto the complexities of a field site, lacking in nuance, positivistic, clunky, and unsophisticated.

One result of the two cultures of ethnography problem is that in order to publish in journals that have an approach that I am describing here as interdisciplinary social science, those who prefer to write in a more humanistic mode face a choice. They may adjust the writing convention toward the social science model, which is necessary in the higher prestige journals that will demand conformity to social science conventions in exchange for a venue that brings more visibility to one's work, or they may opt to publish their work in a location where the humanistic premises are understood and accepted (but that interdisciplinary social scientists will ignore) or in a journal where acceptance rates are high, the concerns with conventions less salient, and visibility is low.

My own writing has been mixed, drawing on both types of approaches. For example, I have explored some of the criticisms of localism from social scientists who have argued that it is in alignment with neoliberal policies of devolution and privatization. My argument is that there is a neoliberal current within the movement but that there are also other strands, such as the "local living economy" side, that are explicitly in opposition to the neoliberal model of globalization (Hess 2009). In other words, a more complex picture of the ideology of the movement emerges, and there is evidence for the picture in the texts and practices of the movement. Up to this point, I have tended to play the card of ethnographic particularism (or what might be called, less favorably, intellectual NIMBYism) against the hand of social science generalization: your generalizations do not apply in my backyard. However, I depart from this mode by also seeking to build some generalizations and to contribute to a generalizing current of theory in the literature. Specifically, I am most concerned with theories of neoliberalism and social liberalism that tend to conflate the state-versus-market dimension of the ideologies with the hegemonic-versus-redistributive-effects dimension. The alignments are especially prominent in the Marxist and post-Marxist theories of neoliberalism, which also tend to set up the distinctions as temporal regime changes. But rather than reject such work on the simplistic ground of overgeneralization, I have developed a method for analyzing political ideologies as a contested social field in which there are potentials for market-oriented policies to become aligned with redistributive politics, just as the state-centered politics of social liberalism can often be used for hegemonic projects, and that those changes involve shifts of scale (Hess 2011).

With respect to this tension in the field of ethnography and social science, it may be necessary to state the obvious: there are many gradations in between the ideal types, and some scholars possess a high-enough level of interdisciplinary knowledge to be able to understand and discount for the differences, much as one does after obtaining a level of familiarity with a foreign language and culture. Some can even write successfully in multiple genres. However, not everyone is attuned to the differences, and because the differences emerge in this volume, the schematic comparison offered here may be useful for developing an appreciation for different approaches to scholarship and for the volume's argument that ethnography both as method and genre may deserve a greater role in interdisciplinary social movement studies.

POSSIBILITIES

Within anthropology there is a comparativist, nomothetic, social science tradition, but in the dominant networks of cultural anthropology in the United States since 1973 that tradition was mostly rejected as dated, positivistic, and universalizing, if not masculine, white, and colonialist. In defining anthropological ethnography in opposition to an experimental science based on laws, Geertz skipped over the other, more salient alternative: a comparative social science in search of limited generalizations. Although the writing-culture studies of the 1980s were founded on a critical reading of Geertz (1973), they left as an area of agreement the formulation of ethnography as an interpretive, idiographic project. In some cases the views have extended to critical social theory traditions, such as a rejection of at least some versions of feminist and Marxist theory as universalizing. The intellectual histories of what was left on the cutting room floor when functionalism was in its death throes and successor paradigms were developed have not yet been written, nor have the connections with political events of the 1970s and 1980s (Harvey 2005). But certainly a generalizing social science based on the study of power differentials—class, race, gender, and colonialism—was erupting out of the scholarship of the 1960s and was an option for many social science fields. Although subsequent generations of scholarship seem to have superseded the postfunctionalist research programs of the 1970s and 1980s, there are also continuities that have not been adequately studied.

Skepticism of the value of publishing at least some of one's work in a mode of generalizing social science seems unfortunate, and this suspicion contributes to the involution of anthropology (or, to be more specific, the dominant networks of American cultural anthropology) with respect to the other social sciences. Certainly, the universal generalizations of older generations of anthropological theory are justifiably rejected, but Geertz and his followers and critics threw the baby of comparative social science generalization out with the bathwater of overgeneralization. I have tried to make the point in a visible way to anthropologists who study social movements (Hess 2007b), but so far the argument has not had much traction. The result is, in my view, a condition in which both cultural anthropology and the interdisciplinary social sciences are impoverished. The former needs the latter to maintain rigor, the latter needs the former to keep a check on runaway universalizing.

These metamethodological histories have implications for the relationship between scholarly and movement communities. Social movements certainly can benefit from both interpretive ethnography and ethnographically based social science. The latter is capable of producing valuable insights into issues of great strategic importance, such as how to generate backfire from repression, how to expand the scale of a movement, how movements become incorporated and transformed by elites, the conditions under which political opportunities may open and close, and so on. It would be interesting to empirically test which of the two cultures of ethnography is more valuable to activists by asking them to compare different genres of ethnographically based research. But the general point here is not to force a choice as much as to explore the grounds that would enable more fruitful conversations, both across scholarly fields and between scholarly work and the needs of activists and advocates. It is a tribute to the editors of this volume that they have allowed the uneasy tensions to be brought together.

NOTE

1   Also see the case studies archived on my website, www.davidjhess.org.

7

The Edge Effects of Alter-globalization Protests

*An Ethnographic Approach to Summit Hopping
in the Post-Seattle Period*

VINCI DARO

As the most visible and public of alter-globalization activities, protests during major summit meetings of global institutions such as the World Trade Organization (WTO) and the G8 became a widely recognized genre of resistance to neoliberalism over the course of the 1990s and 2000s.[1] This resistance was understood by many, inside and outside of the movements involved, to be global and networked (see Juris 2008a). This was due in part to actual transnational connections among different movements and to the kind of public attention generated by mass protests at global summits in that period. But as every activist knows, mass protests are excessive: they draw in more than—and other than—the core strands of movement activists that give struggles continuity and durability. While summit protests of this period were organized to publicly critique global institutions, they were also points of contact with actors beyond the dichotomy of activists and their targets, including people living and working in the cities that hosted the summit meetings. This chapter examines the protest events (excesses and all) that gave alter-globalization networks a public identity as a global actor during a period of high visibility. I focus, in particular, on summit protests as points of contact with local actors, and on how nodes and connections of movement networks—and the imaginaries of global resistance surrounding them—were loosened, twisted, and tangled at these points.

The following is based on multisited ethnographic research conducted at summit protests during the post-Seattle period of alter-globalization activity from 2000 to 2005.[2] As I was drawn into this project by the momentum of movement activity at that time, it became clear to me that the robust dynamism of summit mobilizations was at least partly due to interactions across distinct activist contingents. I was interested in encounters among different strands and tendencies of alter-globalization movements, but soon I also began to focus on encounters between activists and other kinds of actors: police, protest bystanders, local shop owners, local government officials, and others. My interest grew in what I call the "edge effects" of these encounters: the unpredictable, unintentional effects of interactions across social, political, and cultural boundaries, or edges, marked by different interpretive lenses and different relationships to global processes. I argue that shifts in the meanings and trajectories of activists' practices and alliances in edge zones—zones of interaction (often outside the scope of social movement studies) across distinct groups engaged in, or affected by, movement activity—are worth close ethnographic attention, particularly in terms of understanding the dynamics of transnational activism during the period of my research.

EDGE EFFECTS IN A TRANSNATIONAL MOVEMENT CONTEXT

Drawing from environmental ecology, photography, and statistics, an edge effect refers, respectively, to the enriched variety of life-forms at the interface between ecological communities (Odum 1971); the distortions at the edge of an image; and the indeterminacy of statistical information that can be caused by the limits of a measurement method or tool (El-Shaarawi and Piegorsch 2002, 628). I use this concept in the context of transnational activism to refer to three distinct phenomena. First, cross-fertilization among communities that results in an enriched variety of ideas, practices, and identities. Second, the distortions in representations—the images and imaginaries—of protest activism that happen through popular and activist media coverage, personal accounts, and policing practices. And, third, the indeterminacy of meanings inherent in processes of translation and interpretation, which are more active at the interfaces between distinct communities. These three edge effects—

cross-fertilization, distortion, and indeterminacy of meaning—were all active in encounters between activists and local hosts during the protest events I describe.

While the entire "assemblage" (De Landa 2006) of summit protesting took shape along the edges of global capitalism (as conducted through dominant international financial and political institutions),[3] and summit protests of this period included many interactions that blurred important edges (e.g., edges between legal and illegal activity or between movements and media), the edge effects I am focused on here resulted from encounters between distinctly positioned actors engaged together in the work of enacting and interpreting protest events. As in Anna Tsing's (2005) analysis of "friction,"[4] the edge effects of encounters between global activists and local hosts during this period of mass protest complicated and interrupted—but also propelled and redirected—the anticipated motions of global justice movements, and the imaginaries of global resistance in which these anticipations were rooted were tugged and tangled in the process.

THE IMAGINARY OF A GLOBAL MOVEMENT

By the late 1990s, raucous resistance to neoliberal capitalism had become a formidable presence at summit meetings around the world. With direct roots in a wide range of disparate struggles throughout the 1980s and 1990s, the antiglobalization movement became a recognized entity, a virtual subject (Massumi 2002), with a heightened capacity to shift the parameters of public debate.[5] At this historical juncture, policies and arrangements, developed within the institutional homes where neoliberal projects had been cultivated and elaborated, were brought into multiple arenas of intense public scrutiny, and by the mid-2000s, most of these institutions faced deep crises of legitimacy.[6] While I am not claiming a direct causal link between summit actions and the declining legitimacy of neoliberal institutions, I believe the disruptive capacity of protests is part of the story (see also Juris 2008a).

Protesters' capacity for interruption was a powerful *attractor* (see Chesters and Welsh 2006) for people who were already mobilized in global justice struggles and for those who were new to global justice activism. The articulation of new tactics together with preexisting analyses and critiques constituted a form of resistance that supported an imaginary of global resistance as well as an "imagined community" (B. Anderson 1991) of activists.[7] Indeed, the importance of imagination to the dynamics of transnational social movements is clear (see Khasnabish 2008, this volume). Summit protests were a primary site of actualization of this community, but even as summit hopping developed into a recognizable genre of resistance, it was always an inconsistent activity, with variations in emotional and media impact (Juris 2008a, 2008b), as well as disjointedness with respect to the global imaginaries that gave these protests significance.[8] My interest lies in the particularities of local protest settings without disregarding the global sensibility cultivated through the experience of summit hopping. After all, the ongoing struggles that converged during the protest events considered here did become globally connected in more ways than before, in part as a result of the imaginaries of global resistance cultivated in and through summit hopping.

Meanwhile, self-critique about the practice of summit hopping became a central feature of activists' own imaginaries of global resistance during this period. Summit hoppers themselves described it as a practice of the privileged—those who could afford to travel; to leave their jobs, families, and communities; and to expose themselves to the risk of arrest or injury—or as predictable, ineffective, or simply insufficient for producing "real" social change. Others criticized summit hopping as an unproductive waste of energy and resources, or, worse, as a practice undermining the "real work" of more durable campaigns and projects by jeopardizing their legitimacy or by monopolizing public attention with spectacular but politically insignificant clashes with police (see Juris 2008a, chapter 5). Still, summit meetings became increasingly "sticky engagements" (Tsing 2005, 6) during this period,[9] and the imaginaries that developed around protesters' capacity for interruption provoked a wide range of responses among local residents in cities hosting summit meetings. In what follows, I give an initial sense of the range of these responses and then present more ethnographic detail from two summit protests: the 2001 Free Trade Area of the Americas (FTAA) summit in Quebec City and the 2005 G8 meetings in Edinburgh. I suggest that the edge effects generated by the dynamics of encounter between incongruous but directly engaged and overlapping cultural worlds during these protests are best understood in relation to preexisting, locally made imaginaries of what global resistance is about.

While the imaginary of global resistance cultivated throughout the period of summit hopping was not initiated in Seattle, the dramatic images and narrative tropes of those protests played a major role in defining a new protest genre, particularly for popular understandings of subsequent summit protests (see Daro 2009b; Juris 2008a). Locals' perceptions of their global guests were partly shaped in response to security measures prepared ahead of summits, and by the careful public relations work carried out by law enforcement agencies, which routinely evoked the "Seattle tactics" supposedly used by activists during the WTO protests there (Graeber 2007). Responses to police and press warnings about the threat of violent protesters varied. For example, during the 2000 International Monetary Fund (IMF) and World Bank meetings in Prague, the Czech government provided strong incentives for residents to leave town on a recreational holiday and closed schools during the summit. Many people did leave, and many shops, restaurants, and banks closed for business (in many cases with plywood covering windows and doors), all of which became standard practice at summits thereafter.

But not all businesspeople sought to defend themselves and their property from protesters. Those who welcomed protesters as customers often did very well. For example, a kebob shop in Edinburgh was hopping with orders during the 2005 G8 summit while everything nearby was closed; the cheerful shopkeeper told me he was going to be sad when the summit was over because business would be slow again. A tourist gift shop in Quebec City even sold protest-specific paraphernalia, including T-shirts with "Fuck Le Sommet" printed across the front. In another example of protest entrepreneurship, a woman, also in Quebec City, set up a table and sold swim goggles as protection from tear gas. In perhaps the most optimistic of economic forecasts associated with summit protests, the tourist board of Edinburgh had hopes of attracting protesters who might want to combine their visit for the 2005 G8 summit with sightseeing activities as part of travel packages. In the end, when these efforts to capitalize on summit protests failed, and government officials refused to compensate businesses for financial losses due to slowed sales and property damage, estimated at £100 million,[10] the notion that summit hosting was both dangerous and bad for business was reinforced.

While the protests in Seattle were dangerous for many people involved and bad for many businesses—and set a kind of standard for what residents were to expect in hosting a summit meeting—the disruptiveness of those protests stemmed in part from local residents' *support* for demonstrators facing security efforts. Cross-fertilization between visiting activists and Seattle locals in anticipation of the summit was activated in part by a local political culture in which the claims and tactics of protesters were not only understood and well received, but coproduced.[11]

The following year, in Prague in September 2000, the dynamic between visiting activists and locals was very different. On the night the IMF and World Bank meetings were called to an early end, I talked at length at a bar with a Prague local who worked for HBO. He explained that "resistance to globalization" made no sense to him, and he talked excitedly about the opportunities presented by newly flourishing private enterprises in the media sector. Without directly mentioning the very visible patches of flags displaying hammers and sickles during the main march (S26) the day before, he and his friends argued vehemently that activists were misguided in criticizing something that is "at least better than what we had," and reminded us that they'd just overturned a decades-long Communist regime. Prominently displayed communist symbols, viewed through a certain lens of local history at least by some Prague residents, resulted in a distortion whereby the diversity and complexity of movement activity in the streets was reduced to a unitary, and misguided, critique of an economic system that many locals not only embraced but had struggled for. The indeterminacy in meaning of the protests had opened an interpretive field of competing understandings of what alter-globalization activism was about, understandings that were keyed to distinct imaginaries about what kinds of economic and political struggle are worthwhile.[12]

For ethnographic work in the context of transnational activism, the consequences of focusing on edge effects include broadening attention beyond central nodes of protest planning in order to follow the fragments of stories that trickle out from those nodes into the wider cultural worlds of people affected by or interested in those protests. Tracing how these bits of stories are woven and tied together with, or are pulled apart by, threads of other narratives (from police, in press coverage, and so on) requires an approach to understanding movement "outcomes" that is different from social movement scholarship, which focuses on the realization of movement goals (e.g., shifts in cultural, political, and economic power) (see Giugni, McAdam, and Tilly 1999; Tarrow 1998). Ethnographic attention to the edge effects of protest events reveals important, and often unanticipated, ways that the significance of movement activities can be distorted, displaced, hybridized, and/or multiplied.

For this project, I mainly conducted fieldwork in edge zones that were publicly accessible rather than within core activists' planning processes.[13] I also focused more on the experience of protest spaces than on political processes, social movement organizations, or frames. I argue that unlike the concerns of traditional social movement studies (e.g., movement goals, strategies, resources, and opportunities), activity at and along the edges of movements often involves such a mixture of forces, interests, and perspectives that intentions and structures are difficult to decipher. Ethnographic depictions from summit protests in Quebec City and Edinburgh show how activity at the edges of social movements was multiply "figured" (Holland et al. 1998) in the context of summit protests.[14]

GLOCAL LINKING, RELENTLESS POLICING: FTAA SUMMIT IN QUEBEC CITY

Experiences in Quebec City during the FTAA summit in April 2000 were shaped by a long history of regional political dynamics, including several different groups prepared to articulate their own locally particular claims and demands to the global resistance to free trade agreements: in the lead-up to the summit, it was clear that Quebecois sovereigntists would be a prominent part of the mobilizations against the FTAA.

The dominant political party in Quebec, the Parti Québécois (Quebec Party), emerged in the late 1960s from the Mouvement Souveraineté-Association (Movement for Sovereignty Association) and has maintained a focus on the struggle for Quebec's national sovereignty against the Canadian state through to the present. Many parties that have arisen to the left of the Parti Québécois have maintained, or intensified, the sovereigntist position, with some articulating explicit critiques of the neoliberal agenda. Coinciding with the summit, a new party emerged as Quebec's official *altermondialiste* (antiglobalization) party, the Union des Forces Progressistes (UFP, Union of Progressive Forces) which included rejection of free trade agreements as a central position together with support for Quebec sovereignty (Harden 2006). In a direct echo of the World Social Forum, the UFP's initial slogan was "Un autre Québec est possible" (Another Quebec is possible).[15] Following a related genealogy, the student union movement, L'Association pour une Solidarité Syndicale Étudiante (ASSÉ; Association for Student Union Solidarity), based in Montreal, was formed around the same time, and the FTAA protests were its first major demonstration (Christoff and Schoen 2008).

Compounding the antipathy within Quebec to the Canadian state, and to its participation in many global neoliberal projects, the premier of Quebec had no say in the decision to host the FTAA summit, and the heavy-handed security measures and policing behavior (especially the perimeter fence and the exorbitant amounts of tear gas discharged into central neighborhoods) further intensified local indignation and resentment toward Canadian authority (Doyle 2001). Direct resonance with Quebecois popular politics was expected to bring out a substantial local presence, particularly the labor unions and radical student groups. These explicit, and highly charged, overlapping antagonisms offered great promise to visitors from the global movement. Local sympathies for, and involvement in, planned marches and the People's Summit (an alternative counter-conference) were essentially guaranteed since much of the organizing for each was local, and the potential for a spectacular interruption of the neoliberal agenda being cultivated in the FTAA agreement was palpable as the summit approached. But students, unions, and sovereigntists were not the only sources of active local engagement in the transnational mobilization.

Although local support for visiting protesters was tremendous, getting to Quebec City turned out to be challenging. For activists traveling from the United States to Canada, tightened border security—meant to keep foreign demonstrators out of the country during the summit—presented a major difficulty. Activists' concerns about getting into Canada stemmed from rumors, past experience, and a growing list of people already being turned away at the border weeks ahead of the summit. One person I interviewed said that his father kept calling him, telling him to forget about going to the protests, saying, in my interviewee's words, "They're turning everyone back! I heard it on the radio. . . . They are turning *everybody* back!" Although my small affinity group did get across, it was not easy. We were detained for more than an hour at the border and questioned intensively, men separately from women, and we were threatened repeatedly about the consequences of giving misinformation. Afterward we all agreed that the interrogation technique was psychologically manipulative.

The Mohawk territory of Akwesasne straddles the border between the

United States and Canada across the St. Lawrence River, which divides the two countries, and in the context of difficulties getting into Canada, the Three Nations Crossing bridge over the St. Lawrence, on Akwesasne territory, became the centerpiece of a planned border crossing for activists traveling to Quebec over land from the United States. It was not clear to me at the time how the arrangement was initiated—for example, I did not know if plans began with an invitation from the Mohawk community to non-Native activists to use the bridge, or if the idea was first proposed by non-Native activists—but as the FTAA summit approached, talk of the border crossing on Mohawk territory became increasingly animated on activist listservs and websites.[16]

Excitement among activists about the involvement of Mohawk Nation members in the logistical planning grew tremendously as plans became more detailed. The plan I kept hearing about was this: there would be a caravan of cars, vans, and buses full of activists trailing behind a large contingent crossing on foot. Activists on the Canadian side were to swarm the border checkpoint on their side (or in other schemes, were to cross over to the U.S. side of the bridge and swarm that checkpoint), while the caravan assembled on the U.S. side and then traveled together to the border, crossing over Cornwall Island into the city of Cornwall in Canada. As these plans circulated, activists familiarized themselves with the history of the bridge as a site of Mohawk resistance to state regulatory power, including illegal alcohol trading during Prohibition and cigarette smuggling more recently (Bonaparte 2000).

For the Mohawk coordinators of the bridge-crossing action, resistance to the authority of the Canadian state was the dominant frame, but opposition to the free trade agenda fit well within this frame. One of the main Mohawk organizers explained his motivation for the action in this way: "My motivation is to assert and reinforce the sovereign integrity of Mohawk people within the Mohawk nation and to bring the organizing bodies together so we can stand and fight in preparation for the fall. . . . We will engage in attacks against the provincial economy, the provincial infrastructure. We will shut down highways, roadways, bridges until this government is brought to its knees."[17] He stated his opposition to free trade in more general terms: "Free trade does everything to help corporations, and absolutely shit to help people in poverty."[18] Motivations for non-Native activists to participate in the Akwesasne border crossing initially had to do with the practical need to get to Quebec City in the face of tightened border controls, but this motivation was layered with additional significance over time during the planning process. In particular, some activists began to focus more explicitly on the broader issues of border justice and state regulatory controls on the movement of people. The discourse developed through most of this organizing focused on the contradictions inherent in policies that open borders for capital and commodities but not people, a contradiction related directly to the project of the FTAA summit, but related as well—by "glocal" extension—to people engaged in struggles elsewhere and previously.[19]

Well before the FTAA summit began, cross-fertilization was an effect of the planning process: activists had mobilized a confluence of distinct imaginaries around the efforts to get to Quebec City for the protests, with multiple border justice actions and an indigenous-anarchist alliance. Finally, excitement about the action swelled further when a flurry of e-mails, listserv posts, and website updates announced that the caravan would be launched by a "family-friendly fish fry" on the Mohawk territory, adding a local detail to the global mobilization. Although the border crossing was logistically less successful than hoped, the action had an impact on activists preparing for the anti-FTAA protests in that even those of us who were not part of the caravan were very much tuned into the plans and felt some level of investment in it succeeding. Alliances cultivated in the planning process produced powerful narratives for making sense of the experience of being on the streets in Quebec City, including the shared experience of tearing down the security fence (see Graeber 2002).

Engagements between the global movement and preexisting indigenous, local, and provincial struggles in Canada and Quebec were significant in several ways. There was a natural link between resistance to trade agreements like the FTAA agreement and struggles for regional and indigenous political, economic, and cultural autonomy. The struggles of both Quebecois sovereigntists and the Mohawk Nation could be read as contemporary surfaces of historically deep struggles over territory, national sovereignty, and cultural autonomy: both were (and continue to be) struggles to preserve, or reclaim, independence and self-governance within the contingent geographies and histories of relations among hegemonic state powers (and both have been militant struggles at that). The deeply engaged local political culture in Quebec, and the strategic and symbolically rich alliance with the Mohawk traditionalists, suggested, in the lead-up to the summit, that momentum gathered ahead of the protests could produce a spectacular and unstoppable force of unity. But the interface with police proved to be another dynamic edge.

The state response to protesters was so overwhelming, and border security so tightened, that the force of connections between the global movements and local struggles was nowhere near enough to significantly disrupt the summit. What did disrupt the summit, however, at least for a few hours, was the tremendous amount of tear gas that made its way into the ventilation system of the building where the meetings were held. And indeed the tear gas together with the other features of the policing regime during the summit (the fence, water cannons, rubber bullets, and so on) had a powerful unifying effect not just among local, regional, and global social movement networks but also between activists and local residents.

Local residents' sympathies for protesters—already activated by hostilities to Canadian federal authority and by resentment about the top-down decision to host the FTAA summit—were intensified by their own exposure to the tear gas. I watched billows of gas waft directly into residents' windows and front doors, and the red teary eyes looking out from apartment windows spoke volumes about the compounded bitterness regarding the militarization of their neighborhoods.[20] Among the edge effects of the protest-police encounter in this context, therefore, was the effect of tear gas, which was a staple crowd control tool in protest-policing regimes of this period: tear gas is impossible to contain once airborne, and the indeterminacy in whom it hits results in indeterminacy in who is positioned as a police target.

The FTAA summit had an impact on local and regional political networks, insofar as several struggles followed active trajectories out from the protests. For example, since 2001, the student union ASSÉ became a major political force advocating for access to education in the context of a broader global social change agenda. One of the main organizers with ASSÉ, in reflecting on the origins of the union, commented on the importance for social movements to focus on a "broader analysis, beyond Québec [Province], looking at neo-liberalism and broader issues, while trying to build links with other social struggles in our society such as indigenous struggles at home, with social struggles internationally in Latin America, in the Middle East, in Europe and beyond" (quoted in Christoff and Schoen 2008). It is clear in comments like this that, as in Tsing's analysis of "friction" (2005), the global event of the summit protests added meaning to both the local struggles and global movements. The event had "glocalizing" effects in that triumphs and scars left by the experience were carried by many different activist communities, for years, in both local and global imaginaries of struggle.

Local and regional alliances were heavily prefigured, and the enormous work, energy, excitement, and intention that went into cultivating plans and relationships meant that cross-fertilization was a significant edge effect before and after the protests. But what became perhaps the most powerfully unifying force between visitors and locals was a shared encounter with an overwhelming display of state power, including the thick fog of gas that cloaked the entire city center indiscriminately and relentlessly. This shared experience of exclusion and criminalization added meaning and intensity to struggles against the neoliberal project for so many of us there.

THE MENACE OF PROTESTERS AND UNANTICIPATED AGGRESSION OF LOCALS: G8 SUMMIT IN GLENEAGLES

In the weeks leading up to the G8 summit in Gleneagles, Scotland, during July 2005, residents were bombarded with a flurry of news stories warning about violent anarchist outsiders coming to town. While initial reports about plans for the Make Poverty History march and Live 8 concert generated excitement about the influx of visitors coming to protest peacefully—and potentially giving a boost to the regional economy—these reports were overshadowed as the summit neared by warnings that anarchists were coming from all across Europe and elsewhere to create mayhem.[21] Two days before the summit was to begin, *The Express* (Glasgow) ran a story that exclaimed, "Hardcore anti-G8 anarchists from across the world, intent on causing as much violence and mayhem as possible[,] are already in Scotland."[22] On the same day, the *Daily Record* (Glasgow) had a story titled "Make Poverty History: Streets of Fear; Shopping Mecca Braced for Riots."[23] *The Daily Telegraph* (Scottish edition) published an article titled "Fortress Scotland Awaits Invasion of Protesters," which included this account:

> The alleged benefits associated with hosting the meeting of the world's most powerful men next week are becoming harder to discern. . . . Edinburgh is braced for an invasion that will bring it to a standstill, and Auchterarder, the small town nearest to the hotel, is

quaking in its sensible country shoes. . . . Though Central Scotland may support the aims of protests designed to win firm action on poverty and global warming, it wishes the summit was somewhere else. There have been dire warnings of violence, confrontations between police and protesters, and direct action against financial institutions. . . . Some businesses hope for a brisk trade, but have had plywood boards ready, just in case.[24]

With locals welcoming demonstrators coming to participate in the widely publicized Make Poverty History march, anticipatory anxiety about the simultaneous arrival of violent protesters mapped directly onto the divide constructed again and again throughout the post-Seattle period between peaceful (legitimate) activists and violent (illegitimate) activists.

Policing in Scotland was complicated by the involvement of law enforcement agencies from various parts of the United Kingdom, and it quickly became clear, at least in Edinburgh, that hostilities among many local Scottish residents toward the British police ran strong. This was especially obvious during the Carnival for Full Enjoyment (CFE), the most publicized "anarchist" event of the week. The CFE was framed in the local media as the most threatening of the planned protest events, despite its cheerful poster hung up around Edinburgh (fig. 7.1).

Activists and reporters both understood the event to be distinct in spirit from the Make Poverty History march and rally: it was horizontally organized, as opposed to the vertically structured Make Poverty History events (which had clear leaders, a stage and sound system, and a predetermined route and schedule). Also unlike the latter, the CFE did not have an official permit. These aspects created a more porous *event-space* (Massumi 2002) — open to intervention and recoding by people and purposes beyond the event's initial framing. As a result, the practice and imagery of theatrical anticapitalist street carnivals, made famous by Reclaim the Streets activists in the United Kingdom in the mid-1990s and cultivated globally ever since, was easily refigured by Scottish locals as a street fight with British police.

It was not difficult to distinguish protesters from the local residents who joined the event to fight with police. The locals whom I saw embroiled in street clashes were mostly (but not exclusively) male, white, aged twenty to forty, and dressed in brand-name sporting outfits. For example one man wore an Adidas jacket and light-blue jeans, another

wore a white Nike T-shirt, and many wore Nike shoes; several also wore new-looking light-colored billed sport caps. None of this apparel is common among alter-globalization activists, and the short-cropped (and in a few cases gelled) hair of the street-fighting locals made them even more conspicuous.[25] I saw them provoke police by throwing bottles, rocks, and verbal insults, and in one instance by directly attacking officers with their fists. Twice I watched as protesters from elsewhere looked on passively, with stunned expressions, as these locals took over the "frontlines."

Others corroborated these observations. One activist posted the following report of one of the street clashes to the local Indymedia wire: "There seemed to be no 'centre' of activity, and there were certainly no 'activists' left at this point. I cycled around a long way to get to the other side of the police line, where 4 or 5 people were being detained with plastic handcuffs in front of a boarded up mobile phone shop. They were definitely not pink, black, clown, or any other bloc. Just ordinary folk."[26] The pink, black, clown, and other blocs referred to were different activist groups—some well coordinated and some informal—that participated in the CFE. The U.K.-based Clandestine Insurgent Rebel Clown Army (CIRCA), in particular, had a central presence in the carnival (see also

Routledge, this volume), as did the U.S.-based Infernal Noise Brigade, a skilled activist marching band. Both of these groups engaged with police fairly directly, but never aggressively. One key distinction between activist collectives such as CIRCA and the Infernal Noise Brigade and other groups that engage the police in the streets is the significant degree of preparation, training, coordination, costuming, and artistic talent of the former. CIRCA clowns performed the acts and games they had trained for, including falling over each other into heaps in front of police vans as they attempted to depart; the Infernal Noise Brigade band members performed the music and marching formations they had trained for, including marching directly toward and alongside the temporary police "pens" containing activists (even after being contained themselves by police). In both cases, these groups intentionally and successfully created confusion and made police work difficult, but in a spirit of creative public performance rather than violent aggression.[27]

The post to the Indymedia wire also described how members of CIRCA even tried to intervene to protect police and deescalate the confrontation:

> The cops were getting nervous, and the crowd was telling them to fuck off (because most of the riot cops were English rather than local Police, it seemed). . . . A bagpiper blowing out traditional tunes seemed to be stirring the Scots into a bit of an anti-establishment fervor. It seemed as if this crowd had mostly just turned up after they saw what was happening on the news, and joined in the activities themselves. What happened next was bizarre and unprecedented. . . . Bottles were fired at them from close range, a dumpster was pushed straight at the line of shields, and a traffic cone and a bin were thrown at them when they charged their way back to the junction of the street. Four or five of the Clown Army showed up at this point, trying to stop people throwing stuff at the cops, and making faces and generally being silly right in front of the Police. One female clown was nearly hit in the head with the big traffic cone, and their attempts to calm the situation didn't really work at all, so they left fairly quickly.[28]

Demonstrations in the street during the G8 summit presented an opportunity for those engaged in the enduring Scottish nationalist struggle for autonomy from Britain, and the convergence of this struggle with a particular enactment of global anticapitalist struggle in the local setting of

Edinburgh made the contentiousness of the moment much more complex than street clashes during other summits.[29] I was curious about how local media would cover the event. The day after the carnival, local newsstands were filled with stories about the previous day's protest events. For the most part, these stories identified anarchists from elsewhere as the primary source of violence.[30] Many of the accompanying photos, however, did not quite match this storyline, as seen in the appearance—particularly the clothing and accessories—of the protesters clashing with police in the images from the *Edinburgh Evening News* (figs. 7.2 and 7.3).

In an article from the same issue of the *Edinburgh Evening News*, titled "They Came Looking for Trouble. . . . They Got Their Wish: Samba Fun and Dancing Give Way to Fear and Hate as Masked Anarchists Storm Police Blocking March," reporters focused on the "sinister presence of anarchists":

> The only ominous sign of things to come was the presence of a
> handful of anarchists dressed in black, members of the notorious
> Ya Basta movement, who tried to disrupt Saturday's Make Poverty
> History march. But the antics of hundreds of fancy-dressed revel-
> ers on Edinburgh's streets were overshadowed in one sudden mo-
> ment. At precisely 1pm, and with no warning, the all-in-black fig-
> ures, who had gradually grown in number, decided to storm the
> line of police preventing the protesters from continuing their noisy
> march. They didn't get very far, but the atmosphere of the day
> changed and the carnival spirit never really came back. An air of
> menace, rarely felt in the centre of the Capital, hung in the air for
> the rest of the day and into the night. . . . [A]s numbers swelled,
> the anarchists began a direct challenge against both riot police and
> mounted officers. Protesters blowing whistles stood on top of bus
> stops, while others flying flags and dressed in black cheered and
> clapped. The tension was briefly broken when a naked protester
> ran along Princes Street with two clowns in tow to the delight of
> bystanders. But the sinister presence of the anarchists, their faces
> covered with scarves, was clearly unnerving for all involved.[31]

There were certainly protesters dressed in black, along with other typically dressed activists from different contingents, and some were masked and stood on top of bus stops and other structures. But these were not the people I saw attacking police. Moreover, despite the reports, I never once felt personally at risk of being injured, even though I was pregnant at the

FIGURE 7.2.
Edinburgh Evening News, home edition, front page, July 5, 2005.

time; being shoved by police behind the gates of Princes Street Gardens along with hundreds of others in the crowd was the roughest moment of my day, and I felt far more at risk at other summit protests.

After the summit concluded, Edinburgh returned to its own rhythm. The legal proceedings for arrested activists, however, dragged on for months. In early November, the Lothian and Borders Police (the regional police force) issued a press release appealing to the public to help identify

FIGURE 7.3.
Edinburgh Evening News, home edition, page 5, July 5, 2005.

people involved in the CFE. Thirty-one photos of individuals were published in local papers along with the press release. The photos were stills from surveillance cameras used during the protests, and were accompanied by the following text:

> Some of the people featured in the photographs are very clear—we just need a name to put to the face. I would like to appeal to anybody who knows the identity of any of these people to contact the incident room. We hope issuing these images will prompt a positive response from the public who were rightly appalled at the scenes they witnessed in the city centre in July. This is not a case of police being vindictive but concentrating on those people whose criminal activity marred an otherwise peaceful week of legitimate demonstration.[32]

The use of local media to recruit local citizens to participate directly in police work demonstrated the extent to which criminalization had become part of how global justice activism was figured publicly.

The police strategy used in Scotland called on not only activists but also locals to answer the question "Which side are you on?" This question implied a clear boundary between legitimate and illegitimate forms of protest (see also Juris 2005c). However, related to the difficulty police had in isolating the "dangerous" from the "peaceful" protesters—and the "protesters" from the local residents—on the streets of Edinburgh, there was a tension in the attempt by Lothian police to enlist the public. While the press release addressed a public who was "rightly appalled" at the protests, the statement simultaneously addressed readers as people who might have been involved in the protests themselves. The press release continued: "If anyone recognizes themselves in these pictures released today we would urge you to make contact with us before we come knocking on your door. We believe the majority of these people live in the United Kingdom and I personally believe most will live in the Lothians and Scottish Borders area as a high percentage of those who have already been traced do."[33] This was an explicit admission that the protesters identified as most criminal may have indeed been part of the local population. Thus the public was doubly addressed—as both potential participant in, and potential target of, police efforts—as either "rightly appalled" or else guilty. The suggestion from the police that violence during the protests may have been perpetrated, at least in part, by locals *might* have succeeded in unsettling the dominant imaginary of the threat of visiting activists, but it did not.

The "discursive field of action" (S. Alvarez 1999, 184) prepared locally ahead of the G8 summit was so well inscribed by the dualism between violent anarchists from elsewhere and peaceful (legitimate) demonstrators in the Make Poverty History march that there was very little interpretive space for a third category (even one familiar to local residents). Aggressive Scottish locals played a major role in the event, yet the stories in the press about what happened were already prefilled (occupied) by a well-rehearsed narrative about other characters.[34] The violent clashes between Scottish locals and British police, unanticipated by many visiting activists, failed to interrupt or challenge dominant imaginaries of violent protesters from elsewhere; instead local media reinscribed the dualism between legitimate and illegitimate protesters, along with all of the distortions that dualism produces.

The experience of the protests was shot through with direct encounters between two distinctly figured worlds: one that was locally particular and one that was generated by a transnational activist network. Despite remaining entirely unacknowledged in popular press accounts, the edge between these worlds, animated for an afternoon in downtown Edinburgh, generated the most dramatic news stories (and photos) of the week's protest coverage. Militant locals recoded a global justice protest as part of their figured world of resistance to British authority, and then local media workers and residents coded their actions back into the local imaginary of visiting summit protesters as a dangerous threat. The police work after the protest then had to "correct" for these mistranslations, but still the complexity of the struggles activated that day was never sufficiently rendered in popular news coverage.

CONCLUSION

Edge effects generated by encounters among distinct groups during the summit protests I have examined included cross-fertilization (connections, alliances, extensions, and enriched diversity and adaptivity) that gave impetus to existing projects and seeded new projects; distortions (misinterpretations, misrepresentations, and "noise") that interfered with the clarity of boundaries around what counts as global justice activism; and indeterminacy in meanings (ambiguities, ambivalence, and outliers) that destabilized the identities of activist communities and widened possibilities for interpretation of their activity.

Combinations of these edge effects meant the local social, cultural, political, and historical circumstances of summit settings sometimes functioned as "strange attractors" that redirected the flow of global movements (Chesters and Welsh 2006), so that instead of dissipating when expected, connections and reactions moved through alternate circuits. The local attractors drew in/on elements of the global imaginaries selectively, and the pull of these attractors mattered (a lot) for what the global movement looked like—and felt like—in each place. The unique way that these elements were integrated into the assemblages of summit protests in each location fed directly into collective identity processes under way throughout this period: what the global movement was about, who the activists were, what they were up to, and the sense of global connectedness (in Alberto Melucci's [1996] terms, the construction of global "we-ness") were all at least partially tangled into the pull of local circumstances.

At the edges of activist communities, where this kind of external pull is often strongest, meanings are shifting and identities are unsettled and multiply figured as people try to make sense of events, slogans, and actions, with all of their inconsistencies in interpretation, in order to not only evaluate movement activity but also to identify as part of, or distinct from, this activity. Edges are often characterized by doubt and anxiety, but also excitement and possibility. I have argued that these edges are important zones of productive tension that signal expansion, contraction, and increasing complexity of movement activity. Organizing one's thinking around this framework can help to bring coherence to the kinds of decentralized, disparate fieldwork experiences that are so often part of transnational ethnographic research. Moreover, as I hope to have shown, an ethnographic approach is important for exploring the multiple and overlapping edges among distinct communities engaged in and by summit protest activities as zones of rich dialogic exchanges among different expectations, interests, struggles, and histories.

The kinds of edge effects I have described were part of the processes of "translation" (Tsing 2005; see Casas-Cortés, Osterweil, and Powell, this volume; and Juris, this volume) back and forth between actual events during each summit and the imaginaries of global resistance that evolved from summit to summit.[35] For activists and analysts of transnational movement networks, the disjointedness of these processes reveals the force and interplay of distinct imaginaries about what defines global resistance, and the multiple and distinct histories of struggle that can potentially, if sometimes problematically, be articulated to existing transnational social movement networks. While both cases described here emphasized the role of locally particular struggles for political, cultural, and economic autonomy, at other summit protests during this period potent edge effects involved other locally particular interpretive tendencies and possibilities for alignment and antagonism. In every case, though, the instabilities in the meaning of transnationally coordinated projects, for those inside and outside of them, are worth close ethnographic attention for understanding the dynamics of how global resistance is lived at different moments in different places.

NOTES

1   This movement has also been referred to as the antiglobalization movement, the anticorporate globalization movement, or the global justice movement. I prefer the term *alter-globalization* to emphasize the movement's promotion of forms of globalization based on social justice, autonomy, and democracy as alternatives to neoliberal capitalism.

2   This research included participant observation at summit protests during the IMF and World Bank meetings in Washington, D.C. (2000, 2002, 2005), IMF and World Bank meetings in Prague (2000), the FTAA summit in Quebec City (2001), WTO ministerial meetings in Cancún (2003), the FTAA summit in Miami (2003), the G8 summit in Gleneagles (2005), along with participant observation at dozens of other protest events, activist gatherings, conferences, *consultas* (consultations), workshops, planning meetings, and social forums.

3   Manuel De Landa's assemblage theory draws directly from Gilles Deleuze and Félix Guattari (1987) and focuses on the "relations of exteriority" between interacting components exercising different capacities in relation to each other rather than exhibiting essential properties (De Landa 2006, 10). Assemblage theory attends to the expressive and material role of components, e.g., their stabilizing (territorializing) and destabilizing (deterritorializing) role as well as their capacity for coding and decoding meanings. In this framework, summit protests would be better described as "summit protest assemblages." For more on the use of the concept of assemblages in anthropology, see Ong and Collier 2004.

4   Tsing (2005) examines the particularizing force of what she calls "friction" in local encounters with global projects of capitalism, including these projects' concomitant universalizing claims of liberal sovereignty. In her analysis, friction exposes the myth that global projects operate smoothly and consistently across places. I similarly explore the particularizing force of local circumstances on global summit-protest events.

5   See Turbulence Collective 2010 for multiple perspectives on this issue.

6   The Multilateral Agreement on Investments failed in 1998 (see Ellwood 2001, 65–67), the Free Trade Area of the Americas agreement has been stalled since 2005, the North American Free Trade Agreement is widely recognized as a massive failure (e.g., in popular political discourse during the 2008 U.S. presidential election), and the Doha round of trade negotiations, launched by the WTO in 2001, was suspended in 2006 after five years of failed attempts to reach an agreement.

7   "Imagined" is in Benedict Anderson's sense of being culturally produced and

cultivated largely through print, Internet, and other activist communication channels rather than face-to-face interaction (1991).

8   See Khasnabish 2008 for an excellent discussion of the significance of the imagination in transnational social movement processes and Appadurai 1996 for an analysis of imagination as a significant social practice in an age of global modernity.

9   During this period, many activists questioned the effectiveness of summit protests, even while participating in the protests; I was among them. Still, the growth in cost, intensity, transnational coordination, and technological and political sophistication of summit policing regimes during this period is but one indication of the threat of disruption, perceived or real, to summit meetings at that moment in neoliberalism's hegemonic struggle (for a range of analyses of security efforts for summits, see Daro 2009a; Elmer and Opel 2008; Fernandez 2008; and Klein 2002).

10   Mike Wilson, "Companies Lose Millions as G8 Benefits Fail to Show," *The Scotsman*, September 15, 2005; available at www.gipfelsoli.org (accessed December 25, 2011).

11   This coproduction included tactics that were directly informed by traditions of direct action used throughout the 1990s in the Pacific Northwest, but also included impromptu and coordinated support from locals during the protests. For example, taxi drivers went on strike in solidarity with the November 30 protests against the WTO in Seattle, with some providing free service for activists, and pizza makers decorated pizzas for activists with tomatoes and olives that spelled "No WTO." See Filastine 2003 for background on the taxi strike; see Daro 2009b for discussion of the pizzas.

12   It is worth noting that activists themselves were embattled over the visibility of communist symbols (displayed primarily by Turkish contingents).

13   By focusing away from core activist organizers, I was not exposed to a lot of specific information about plans that needed to be kept private for practical and legal reasons; this kind of information was not directly necessary for exploring the edge effects I was interested in, and remaining at the edge of these organizing processes meant that I did not present much of a risk to fellow activists' security by recording notes, conducting interviews, and producing ethnographic accounts of my observations and involvement. This is not to say that ethnographic work at the core of activist planning processes is not valuable and worthy of the risks presented in doing so (see Juris 2008a), it is just that I found much to explore away from central organizing nodes.

14   Dorothy Holland, William Lachicotte Jr., Debra Skinner, and Carole Cain's concept of a figured world is "a socially and culturally constructed realm of interpretation in which particular characters and actors are recognized, sig-

nificance is assigned to certain acts, and particular outcomes are valued over others" (1998, 52). Figured worlds provide contexts of meaning and activity in which social relationships and positions are lived, and individual and collective identities develop over time through continual participation in them (53, 60).

15 The close relationship between Quebec's altermondialiste movement and its much older nationalist movement has been analyzed by several writers (e.g., see Oscar Miklos, "Reshaping Federalism: Quebec's Future in Confederation," www.oscarmiklos.com; accessed December 25, 2011).

16 See Graeber 2009 for details on this protest and its planning.

17 Message posted to an international planning listserv to prepare for the protests against the FTAA in Quebec City in April 2001.

18 Ibid.

19 Note that this concern with border justice does not necessarily resonate with indigenous struggles generally, or for that matter indigenous struggles in the Canadian context specifically. Indeed, this is one issue that might be seen more critically through the lens of the disjuncture between the imaginaries of global resistance cultivated among non-Native activists and the legacies of indigenous struggles.

20 While some residents were surely angry with militant protesters (or all protesters) for causing mayhem in their neighborhoods, the residents I saw were very clearly furious at the police.

21 See Rosie and Gorringe 2009 for an examination of media coverage that anticipated violent G8 protests in Scotland, and Juris 2005c for a related analysis of representations of violence during the 2001 G8 protests in Genoa. See also Donson et al. 2004 for a more general discussion of media portrayals of anticapitalist protesters.

22 "We're Ready for Violent Protesters, Say Police," The Express, Scottish edition, July 1, 2005, 5.

23 Jack Mathieson, "Make Poverty History: Streets of Fear; Shopping Mecca Braced for Riots," The Daily Record, July 1, 2005, 6–7.

24 Auslan Cramb, "Fortress Scotland Awaits Invasion of Protesters, Host Country Is Apprehensive," The Daily Telegraph (London), July 1, 2005, news section, 10.

25 These locals were later described among activists as the "track suit gang" because of their athletic outfits and aggressive behavior.

26 Las Carnivalistas, "Carnival for Full Enjoyment—What Really Happened," Scotland Indymedia, July 23, 2005, www.indymediascotland.org (accessed December 25, 2011).

27 This is not to say that there were no alter-globalization activists who acted

aggressively toward police and property, as there were several major incidents, most notably during and after highway blockades on the outskirts of Gleneagles; however, the most aggressive acts toward police that I witnessed were carried out by Scottish locals who were relatively easily distinguished from visiting protesters.

28 Las Carnivalistas, "Carnival for Full Enjoyment."

29 See Dorothy Holland and Jean Lave's "history in person" approach for understanding the personal and collective identity processes at work in the local, and often contentious, enactment of these kinds of enduring historical struggles (2001).

30 See also Juris 2005c, 2008a, 2008b. The same storyline appeared outside Edinburgh. For example, the *Birmingham Evening Mail* ran the story "Live 8 2005: Anarchist Thugs Wreck Peace at G8," July 5, 2005, news section, 7.

31 Alan Roden and Linda Summerhayes, "They Came Looking for Trouble . . . They Got Their Wish," *Edinburgh Evening News*, home edition, July 5, 2005, 6.

32 See the Lothian and Borders Police website, www.lbp.police.uk (accessed December 25, 2011). For an example of the news articles that reported on the press release, see Louise Ward, "Can You Name G8 Riot Mob?" *The Mirror*, Scots edition, November 3, 2005, 33; and Brian Donnelly, "Wanted: Suspects in G8 Clashes Police Release Pictures in Hope of Identifying Alleged Rioters," *The Herald* (Glasgow), November 3, 2005, 3.

33 Ibid.

34 See also Holland et al. 2008 for further analysis of similar identity processes in other social movement contexts.

35 These edge effects were also, of course, integral to translation across distinct struggles and movements in a way that is more related to the sense of translation and possibility discussed by Boaventura de Sousa Santos (2004).

TRANSFORMATIONAL
KNOWLEDGES

8

Transformations in Engaged Ethnography

Knowledge, Networks, and Social Movements

MARIBEL CASAS-CORTÉS

MICHAL OSTERWEIL | DANA E. POWELL

In this chapter we situate ethnography as a political practice by combining insights from experimental ethnography with an emergent body of interdisciplinary work that recognizes social movements as knowledge producers. We argue for a shift in how we understand the aims and methods of both ethnography and political intervention and suggest that the role of ethnography should be understood not in terms of explanation or representation, but as translation and weaving, processes in which the ethnographer is one voice or participant in a *crowded field* of knowledge producers. Ethnographic translation enables the ethnographer's participation in the creation of new and different worlds and is a vital form of political intervention. While not unique to transnational movements or sites, the tasks of translation and weaving, as we elaborate them, are enhanced by the transnational dimension, in large part, because they become more visible when working in "placed but transnational" multisited translocales (see Conway 2004a).

We build upon implications from growing literatures on social movements as knowledge producers and practitioners (see Casas-Cortés 2009; Cobarrubias 2009; Conway 2005a; Escobar 2008; Eyerman and Jamison 1991; Osterweil 2010) and ethnographies of complex objects—also referred to as exemplary, experimental, or critical ethnography (see Marcus 2007). As a growing coterie of anthropologists and social theorists have noted, the nature of ethnographic projects in late or postmodernity has been radically changing: hospitals, scientists, environmental disasters, and professionals all form valid topics that require new, or at least different, notions of the how and why of ethnographic research. We believe the innovations and insights arising from current critical impulses and debates about ethnography and other models of engaged scholarship have the potential to improve the scholarship about, and with, social movements.[1] Likewise, these innovations and insights might also contribute to the efforts of many contemporary movements whose ongoing work is to generate the conditions of possibility for social change through the creation of new political imaginaries, narratives, and theories that support different ways of being and forms of knowing. Such ontological and epistemological contributions by movements are the subject of our respective research endeavors, as well as those reflected in many of the chapters in this volume.

This shift, which can also be seen as postrepresentational in so far as it depends on recognizing the ethnographer as contributing to, and not simply representing, reality,[2] bears on the methods and theories of politically engaged scholarship within anthropology in particular. But this shift also has relevance for other social science (trans)disciplines grappling with what it means to undertake research and produce knowledge in the crowded and networked fields in which academics find themselves with many other knowledge-producing actors. These fields tend to be translocal, often transnational, and are produced in large part by the ongoing exchange and circulation of stories, narratives, and political-theoretical analyses and concepts among myriad movements and other actors with whom movements engage. The circulation and dispersion of such stories, narratives, analyses, and concepts is a core practice in the pursuit of alternatives to the social, economic, ecological, and political crises we all face (see Juris 2008a).

This chapter is in many ways the continuation of a conversation and argument we developed in our previous collectively authored piece, "Blurring Boundaries: Recognizing Knowledge-Practices in the Study of Social Movements" (Casas-Cortés, Osterweil, and Powell 2008). The ideas therein were the outcome of more than six years of ongoing discussion with other colleagues, especially those affiliated with the Social

Movements Working Group (SMWG) at the University of North Carolina, Chapel Hill.[3] In that article, seeking to address what we saw as serious limitations in dominant approaches in social movement studies, we argued that it was crucial to recognize how collective action was engaged in a variety of knowledge practices:

> Knowledge-practices in our view range from things we are more classically trained to define as knowledge, such as practices that engage and run parallel to the knowledge of scientists or policy experts, to micro-political and cultural interventions that have more to do with "know-how" or the "cognitive praxis that informs all social activity" [Eyerman and Jamison 1991: 49] and which vie with the most basic social institutions that teach us how to be in the world. . . . [W]e claim that movements prolifically produce knowledge—a category often reserved for social and natural scientists, and other recognized "experts." (2008, 21)

With respect to our specific projects, these knowledge practices include Native American environmental justice activists engaging in debates about energy development and thus shaping debates within expert knowledge regimes (Powell); North American direct action activists developing new forms of democratic practice, therein participating in political theory production (Casas-Cortés); and Italian activists advocating critical and reflexive modes of thinking, thereby participating in meta-discussions about the nature of appropriate political knowledges and epistemologies (Osterweil). Our previous article points to several critical antecedents in various literatures that inform our argument about social movements as knowledge practitioners.[4] However, in that piece, as we elaborated upon the notion that antihegemonic collective action produces its own expertise and knowledge, we confronted additional dilemmas that we were unable to address. Most importantly, acknowledging the centrality of knowledge practices within social movements holds significant consequences for both the methods and aims of any ethnographic engagement on, or with, social movements.

Thus, in some sense, we are picking up where we left off. The present task is to address the methodological, epistemological, and political implications of recognizing social movements as knowledge producers and practitioners because we believe this recognition fundamentally shifts the nature, purpose, and politics of ethnographies of social movements. In this chapter, we begin by describing a discussion that took place in 2007 at the annual symposium of the University of North Carolina, Chapel Hill, SMWG, which pointed to an underdeveloped understanding of the implications of one of the central premises of the symposium and the entire working group: that social movements produce knowledge. This premise requires recognizing that social movements are complex, often translocal and transnational ethnographic objects, challenging the conception of a clear-cut ontology of the research object, and, therefore, traditional notions of research rooted in Cartesian realism. As a consequence, this premise further challenges the role of ethnographic knowledge itself. In the chapter's first section, we problematize the nature of engaged research vis-à-vis these complex objects. We then move on to discuss some of the emergent trends in ethnographic approaches that work with these kinds of reflexive and sophisticated objects in combination with trends in research on transnational social movements. In the second section we review some of the ethnographies of complex objects, examining how different modes of expertise, "writing machines," and networked objects have challenged ethnographers to question the nature and role of academic knowledge vis-à-vis other forms of authoritative knowledge.[5] These other forms include modes of knowledge production similar to those ethnographers might offer, such as the knowledges produced within the transnational, networked encounters of the alter-globalization movement.[6] In the final section, we interrogate the remaining role of ethnography if social movements (and others) are actively producing knowledge about themselves, even as they contend with expert knowledge regimes.

Confronted with a variety of ethnographic scenarios where these instances are common, we ask: what is the point of the ethnographer's work in transnational, increasingly populated research fields filled with a variety of knowledge producers? Understanding such scenarios as crowded fields, ethnographic experiences with indigenous energy politics in the U.S. Southwest help us to reflect on the dilemmas and possibilities of such encounters. By exploring the epistemological consequence of such crowded scenarios, we argue for a decentralized notion of expertise and the multiplication of authorized voices. Moreover, we suggest a mode of engaging with these actors without replicating conventional forms of objectifying representation. Based on experience with an alter-globalization journal, we argue that movements should be understood as situated sources rather than case studies or research objects. Finally, while analyzing transnational collaboration within a feminist collective in Spain involved in its own research on issues of precarity,[7] we discuss how such transnational ethnographic practices might be reconceived as a technology of translation or weaving. Such approaches imply a different vision of the political potential of transnational ethnographic work today.

REFRAMING DEBATES ON POLITICALLY ENGAGED RESEARCH

Our understanding of the complex, yet vital, relationship between what counts as politically engaged research and the ways that ethnography shifts when complex knowledge-producing objects are taken into account was strikingly reinforced during the 2007 annual symposium of the SMWG at the University of North Carolina, Chapel Hill, "Alternative Cartographies of Social Movements."[8] During the symposium's second day, with more than thirty people assembled, a debate arose over what constituted political engagement for academics or researchers, and in particular, for those working with and on social movements. The dynamic exchange became increasingly heated, despite the close political and intellectual affinities that had gathered us together. In question was the relationship of the researcher (ourselves) to the social movements we work with (our subjects—but also in some cases—ourselves). Or, more precisely, a problem emerged concerning how politically engaged our work as intellectuals could be, and through what forms and practices of activism we as academics might participate.

The discussion began to crystallize as a debate when one participant passionately implored those present to acknowledge that as politically aware and critical as we may all be there is a marked difference between the activism movements undertake and our own political engagements as academics or intellectuals. The point, the speaker emphasized, was not to suggest that in another facet of our lives we, as academics, could not be activists as well, but that we should not equate or conflate our intellectual and academic work with our activism, even if our professional academic work might have politically relevant or critical elements. These spheres of action should remain, she argued, separate and set apart from one another.

A frenetic surge of responses reverberated throughout the room. There were personal and political battles of identity, practice, and efficacy that were not easily assuaged. Despite the many more obvious commonalities among us in the room, there were numerous unarticulated differences. The kinds of movements the symposium participants worked with, and our relationships to those movements, were diverse. Some of us focused on community organizing initiatives in the southern United States, others of us worked with alter-globalization movements and World Social Forums, and still others of us had years of experience with indigenous rights groups in North and South America. Moreover, we came from different parts of the world: India, various countries in Latin America, culturally and historically distinct regions of the United States, as well as southern Europe and the Middle East. In addition, important vocational distinctions came into view, with some participants holding academic positions (and the associated hierarchical distinctions, from tenured professors to part-time adjunct employees), while others identified primarily as activists working in their home communities on pressing issues ranging from antiwar efforts to local food movements. And yet the debate's potency was not due only to the ways it touched on our biographies and identities; the intensity also derived from our shared belief that academics needed to be politically involved. Despite this shared belief, we had very different notions of what such political engagement might look like.

In the months following the symposium and through our more recent collaborative reflection, we have come to believe that what this heated disagreement made clear was that despite our collective articulation and agreement that social movements are knowledge practitioners (see Casas-Cortés 2008; Conway 2005a; Escobar 2004), as a group we fell short of defining what this might mean for our concrete practice. Nor were we clear about what political impacts, if any, such work might have. The speaker's sentiment—that our intellectual work, while critical, should not be thought of as our activist practice, per se—is not uncommon within Western and Northern social science. Given our location in the North American academy and our experience having done extended ethnographic fieldwork with diverse social movements, questions regarding the possibilities and limitations of activist scholarship are poignant concerns for each of us. However, we consider the manner in which engaged-scholarship practice is usually framed to be part of the problem.

Recently, this tension has been posited as one between *activist research* and *cultural critique* (see also this volume's introduction). In a pivotal piece, Charles Hale (2006) argues for the primacy of activist research over cultural critique. For Hale and others activist research refers quite explicitly to work on or with social movements,[9] whereas cultural critique, although sharing a political commitment to the historically marginalized and subordinated, refers to purely scholarly work where the research questions are not determined by one's informants or field site. Hale distinguishes between the two approaches primarily on methodological grounds:

> Scholars who practice activist research have dual loyalties—to academia and to a political struggle that often encompasses, but always reaches beyond, the university setting; proponents of cultural critique, by contrast, collapse these dual loyalties into one. Cultural critique strives for intellectual production uncompromised by the inevitable negotiations and contradictions that these broader political struggles entail. Activist research is compromised—but also enriched—by opting to position itself squarely amid the tension between utopian ideals and practical politics. (2006, 100–101)

While Hale's assessment of the differences between these research practices hits the mark in acknowledging an all-too-common divide in anthropology departments and the social sciences more broadly, we find this bifurcated frame limiting in terms of moving our ethnographic work toward more politically and intellectually effective interventions. We are sympathetic to the concern with academic work that lacks thoughtful political investment or fails to make clear its own underlying politics. Similarly, we are also frustrated with critiques of engaged academics as muddying their supposed "objective" position and point of view. However, it is precisely because of our affinity with Hale's (and others') aims that we believe this dichotomous way of framing the debate can actually perpetuate the problem of politically disengaged, underengaged, or, worse, irresponsible work. Thus, the dichotomy constrains our thinking not due to its intent but because the bifurcation is premised on epistemological and methodological assumptions that hinder rather than help us develop a better, more creative and effective theory and practice of engaged scholarship.

We see the opposition between researchers working with social movements "outside" the university and those engaged in critical deconstruction and analysis within the academy as overly rigid, imposing a choice between two predetermined, and therefore limited, spheres of practice instead of building effective and creative bridges between different spheres. There are three major flaws with this construction. First, such a bifurcation ignores the diverse complex forms of social movements as they emerge through contentious practice and enduring struggles (see Holland and Lave 2001). Second, it assumes a Cartesian, absolute divide between the world of the researcher and that of the movement. And third, it underestimates the political potencies and circulations of knowledge practices.

Many discussions of activist research, including Hale's, often begin by positing a particular ethical solidarity between a readily identifiable social movement and a concerned researcher as the requisite relationship for political engagement. However, in the changing conditions of fieldwork, social theory, and ethnographic research today, not to mention transformations in the political field, neither the parameters of what constitutes a social movement nor the relationship between the researcher and a movement is necessarily so obvious or predictable. The movements we work with in Europe, the U.S. Southwest, and Latin America are dispersed spatially and vocationally, composed of practices and actors that are themselves diverse, not only overlapping but often inclusive of the knowledge-production practices of experts and academics. The movements are more accurately perceived as networks, webs, or polycentric fields, composed of individuals, collectives, discourses, and so on, rather than as discretely bounded entities (see S. Alvarez 1999; Diani 2003; Escobar 2008; Juris 2004a, 2008a; Leyva-Solano 2001; Melucci 1996).

Even though we recognize that academia places many requirements and demands on scholars that are not necessarily or immediately commensurable with those of social movements (e.g., the production of theses, papers, grant applications, institutional advancement projects, teaching, advising, departmental service, and administration), this does not necessarily mean that those working in academia are less accountable politically. The perception that critical academics are only or primarily loyal to the rules of academia is premised on the notion that the academy and academic measures of value exist separately from the contemporary political world in which movements "move." Moreover, this perception assumes that academic institutions are secure worlds in themselves—"ivory towers"—rather than the often precarious, porous, even perilous sites of labor that they are increasingly becoming. This is especially the case when the researcher's findings challenge the collusion of institutional powers, such as between the university and the state (see Wing 2002). There are a number of other sites and issues that shape, or at least should shape, our work, including what kinds of research questions we ask and how we arrive at those questions, how we see the effects of our research and its distribution, and what concepts we choose to use, create, modify, and debunk (see Narotsky and Smith 2006).

The challenge is thus to address, head on, the fact that oftentimes the work and aims of a social movement and those of a researcher may occupy a common or overlapping political space, engaging or constituting similar if not identical problems—what we might call *problem spaces* (see Scott 2004). Said differently, we need to figure out how to address the way movements, academics, and a coterie of others—each with their particular location, powers, and, of course, partiality and limitations—together form a complex network of knowledge producers. We believe the fact that social movements are increasingly described as networks, by themselves as well as by researchers, is no coincidence.[10] Describing movements as networks opens up a better understanding of the complex, diffuse, and not easily delimitable nature of these movements. Others have defined social movements as polycentric, expansive "discursive fields of action" that regularly transgress the boundaries between movement and non-movement spaces (S. Alvarez 1999, 184). Such a redefinition involves the implicit recognition that social movements are not merely discrete entities but ensembles of actors, organizations, discourses, events, and practices. Incorporating the network concept is an important methodological and political step, leading to a shift not only in how we understand social movements—that is, being able to produce knowledge that recursively affects reality, the same realities inhabited and worked on by academics, and being organized in networked structures—but also in terms of our relation to movements. In the next section we discuss a series of trends in ethnographic practice that, in conjunction with the network turn in understandings of social movements, helps us move from ethnography as a purely scientific practice of representative explanation to an understanding of ethnographic practice as relational and creative.

ETHNOGRAPHIES OF THE COMPLEX: EMERGENT TRENDS
IN ETHNOGRAPHIC THEORY AND PRACTICE

While anthropology is not the only discipline in which ethnography is a vital tool, we believe that several debates within anthropology provide fertile ground for locating this discussion. In fact, a number of recent trends in the field recognize the need to develop new ethnographic practices in order to apprehend increasingly complex, dynamic, recursive, and knowledge-producing objects, or what we term *knowledge objects*.[11] Moreover, central to these "new" ethnographic objects is the fact that many knowledge producers generate products that are just as, if not more, sophisticated than the ethnographer's own.

However, our intent is not to reinforce disciplinary boundaries. In fact, we believe these discussions are not only pertinent to other fields where ethnographic practice is undertaken (such as education, public health, geography, sociology, cultural and performance studies, and folklore, among others), but that they depend on a series of theoretical and epistemological moves taking place in trans- and postdisciplinary terrains. In particular, the social-theoretical turn to relational and postconstructivist perspectives is informative (see Escobar 2009). Moreover, one of the crucial aspects of contemporary discussions in anthropology is that there are several concurrent conversations in which methodological innovations are understood to be intimately linked with conceptions of the political potentials of ethnography. This is particularly true of the field of science and technology studies as well as the closely related body of ethnographic work associated with emergence, assemblage, and complexity. When brought into orbit with conceptualizations of movements as networks, these literatures suggest possibilities for revisioning the nature of our ethnographic practices.

Science and technology studies, for example, has been crucial in challenging the kinds of objects considered appropriate for anthropological studies, and, along with poststructuralist and feminist theory, it has also been key in challenging the nature of the truth claims being made. We see these approaches as offering crucial methodological and epistemological insights into the nature of objects of inquiry, and of the role of social scientific inquiry more broadly. However, as of yet, these approaches have paid relatively little attention to power and the political implications and possibilities of their conceptualizations and methodologies. John Law has

argued that academics working on these complex objects have a responsibility to move beyond the dominant focus on science, technology, and
other privileged sites of truth making to lend our conceptual, theoretical,
and methodological tools to the study of other sites of knowledge production, lest we risk colluding with or reinforcing current power/knowledge
hierarchies (Law 2004, 8).

We are compelled by this call to take other sites of knowledge production seriously. In particular, when we add this to moves to understand
social movements as knowledge producers, Law's critique of *collusion* becomes an opportunity for intervention. Given the inextricable connection between the dominant knowledge systems of modernity and current
political impasses (what we might describe as the crisis of representation
in politics and epistemology) (see Osterweil 2010; Tormey 2005), enabling
other ways of knowing and being is absolutely critical for any project of
social-ecological transformation.

In another vein of literature, George Marcus (1999a) advocates for
a mode of engagement that is premised on recognizing the complexity
and possible affinities with new ethnographic objects. "Objects," as "producers of powerful and sometimes authoritative representations" (24–25)
of the world, complicate a neat distinction between the role of the anthropologist or social scientist and other objects of study and constitute what
Marcus terms *writing machines*.[12] Although social movements were not
in Marcus's list of instances of complex systems, we feel his conceptualization easily extends to include movements as the complex, unpredictable entities we understand them to be. Over the course of our respective
research and personal involvement with various social movements, we
have found an explicit turn by many social movements toward practices
of developing analyses, writing, and publishing, making them exemplary
of the complex objects and writing machines that Marcus proposes as a
new focus for anthropology.

In fact the very architectures, spaces, and practices of many activists
and other actors working for social change are thoroughly textual and
analytic. Many activists employ and produce an abundance of written material to be posted and circulated via the Internet, publishing independent news sites, creating and running independent publishing houses and
other endeavors, and, of course, keeping their own documentation. This is
particularly evident in strands of the alter-globalization movement, with
the increasingly diffuse practice of *encuentros* (gatherings), social forums,

and counter-summits. These gatherings, at times of hundreds of thousands of people from all over the world, are designed to develop better understandings of contemporary economic, social, and political systems and their problems, and to cultivate alternatives to these systems. These global gatherings are marked by events and relationships: workshops, large rallies, speakers, teach-ins, panels, direct actions, and other encounters in which literature and information are shared and out of which many publications are created.

Many workshops held in these spaces include discussions of texts and theoretical concepts that are remarkably similar to debates in seminars commonly offered in our universities. For example, during the second European Social Forum in Paris in November 2003, Osterweil attended the Radical Theory Forum workshop. In attendance were participants from around Europe, many self-identified as anarchists. Notably, the European Social Forum, part of the larger World Social Forum process,[13] was a thoroughly transnational site physically situated in Paris but constituted by actors and discourses from throughout Europe and the Americas, as well as other members of the alter-globalization movement. At this particular panel attendees discussed the rise of what they referred to as "poststructuralist anarchism" as a new theoretical framework for the movements that had emerged around the protest against the World Trade Organization (WTO) in Seattle in November 1999, and the Zapatista uprising in 1994 in Chiapas, Mexico. It was clear that the coming together of these actors was the product of the work and convergence of numerous translocal networks, compelled in large part by the very act of sharing stories and experiences in what some have termed a *new politics*, which can be understood to centrally involve underlying logics of networking and theoretical production.[14] Moreover, the nature of the discussions at this workshop, as well as at many others, was as sophisticated (if not more so) than any academic seminar on social theory.

Related to this, and in marked contrast to forms of theorizing in past Leftist movements, these networking logics and the kinds of analyses being produced tended to be partial, situated, and based on a critique of universalizing narratives or solutions, in large part because relationships with other networks and actors from various localities challenge any pretensions to universality. In fact, the critique of universalism did not preclude the interchange of stories, concepts, and ideas from various locales throughout the globe, nor the desire to investigate and share diverse local experiences, but allowed for a different place-based ethic of translation and storytelling, similar in many ways to the conceptions of ethnographic practice we are developing here. As Jeffrey Juris explains, "Transnational activist networking always already involves a form of militant ethnography, while militant ethnography among contemporary local/global movements necessarily requires the practice of transnational networking" (2008a, 23). In line with this, there seems to be a sense of this affinity between the nature of ethnography and contemporary activist practice. At the Radical Theory Forum workshop, a Scandinavian activist suggested that the kinds of practices emerging from social forums, and the alterglobalization movement more broadly, bore a striking resemblance to ethnography; he even joked that "anthropology was the discipline of the movement."

More than one hundred people attended the European Social Forum, and by its end at least fifty people showed their interest in starting a new movement journal for theoretical elaborations. While the actual constitution of the journal changed, this initial meeting during the 2003 European Social Forum can be seen as an important foundational moment for the journal-cum-newspaper *Turbulence: Ideas for Movement*,[15] itself a complex object that crosses between, therefore blurring and even working in collaboration with, academic and activist spaces.[16] As we discuss below, *Turbulence* and the European Social Forum are examples of the translation and networking logics of knowledge creation, circulation, and coproduction that alter our very notion of what ethnographic engagement can be. Given the changing conditions of fieldwork today, we propose that social movements be included among the complex objects that anthropologists use to rethink the nature and goals of our work. In the highly self-reflexive environment of activist groups with which we each have conducted research—namely antiprecarity activist research groups in Spain, translocal alter-globalist networks in Italy, and indigenous environmental activists in the U.S. Southwest—participants have highly refined practices of self-representation and are conducting tasks that are similar to those that a traditional researcher might carry out (e.g., interviewing, observing, and taking notes on what is happening for subsequent reflection and analysis). Although both careful observation and detailed note taking are clearly emblematic of ethnographic practice, such analytical writing tasks are not exclusive to the ethnographer, especially when dealing with populations engaged in explicit practices of analytical production and self-reflection.

For example, Casas-Cortés, while researching transformations in cultures of labor and structures of care work in the European Union, encountered an important civil society initiative, the members of which practiced a form of inquiry they called "activist militant research." When referring to the resulting doctoral research experience, however, it has been difficult to use conventional ethnographic terms such as informants, or field, or even participant observation. This was in large part due to the explicit knowledge production practices enacted by these social actors, in this case antiprecarity and activist research movements engaged in practices ordinarily associated with "experts." These forms of do-it-yourself science include conducting empirical research projects, arranging a series of theory seminars, organizing research laboratories, participating in conferences, engaging in translations and publications, and producing teaching institutions, such as alternative universities. From the very process of engagement with these actors, numerous instances arose where the fundamental division between subject and object—so cherished and presumed by the traditional social sciences—was complicated and blurred. At times the typical roles of the ethnographic field scenario were completely inverted, fracturing the conventional epistemological rules. The following account evokes this fracturing of expertise and the associated rearticulation of ethnographic practice:

> I was excited to participate in an activist conference on "Precarity, New Rights and Crisis of the Welfare State." The workshops were held at a squatted historic building in downtown Sevilla and my goal was to examine the discourses of a group of pan-European networks working on issues of precarity and care work in Europe. As I vigorously took notes relevant to my doctoral dissertation project in anthropology, a participant sitting next to me—a potential "informant" in the conventional research framework—asked me to polish my notes as a conference report to be published in the e-journal *Transform*, a hybrid cultural studies and activist publication based in Austria. When the draft was ready, before the publication was out, the text was already circulating via pan-European precarity network listservs. Another "informant," this time from

Italy, who was actually part of my list of potential interviewees, unexpectedly responded with several corrections. That same text was posted on a blog where I regularly posted my research notes, a blog shared with other members of my activist collective back in the United States. (Casas-Cortés fieldnotes, April 2007)

Without providing any further detail, this apparently simple translocal itinerary of a text evokes the multiple uses of ethnographic material, the blurring of the roles of researcher and researched, and the messiness of the ethnographic process. Originally written for a doctoral dissertation but also requested for inclusion in an academic-activist publication and distributed via antiprecarity network listservs, the text was corrected by one of the informants and posted in Casas-Cortés's research collective's blog and was later used as course material by a university professor involved in precarity struggles. In this fluid itinerary, where is the neat division between object of study and subject of research? In this spontaneous cotinkering of a text, who is the knowledge producer? Such blurring is becoming increasingly common when ethnographers encounter complex objects like social movements. While such behind-the-scenes intricacies of the research process are usually ignored or taken for granted, they are an important impetus to reflecting on a series of transformations in ethnographic practice, including the epistemological, methodological, and political consequences of recognizing social movements, and their diverse constituents, as knowledge producers (see Casas-Cortés and Cobarrubias 2008).

The shift to recognizing movements as complex objects and knowledge producers also corresponds and returns us to the notion of movements as networks and polycentric fields emerging in diverse scholarly disciplines, as well as beyond the academy (see Diani 2003; Escobar 2008; Juris 2004a, 2008a; Keck and Sikkink 1998; Levya-Solano 2001; Melucci 1996; and Notes from Nowhere 2003). In other words, thinking in terms of networks better conceptualizes the complex objects and actors under consideration as well as the patterns of interaction they produce. The concepts of networks and fields are crucial in rethinking not only the nature of movements, but also our relationships with, in, and to them. However, for the most part, researchers have deployed these two terms as a way to rethink the subject of their study—but not to rethink their own location and practice. In other words, many researchers' use of theories of networks and fields in social movement studies have not fully imagined, analyzed, or articulated scholars' own relation to the network or field, failing to recognize that they are often deeply connected to, and at times even constitutive of, the very networks and fields they study.[17]

In the example of the activist conference, the texts and research generated about precarity did not belong exclusively to the world of precarity groups or to the world of the researcher. Instead, each sphere played different yet important roles in a network of meaning making to increase knowledge and practices in light of the growing prevalence of precarious work conditions in both Europe and the United States. Throughout our research we have encountered difficulty in discerning when we are learning about "our object" or when we *and* our objects are interrogating and producing knowledge about a particular problem or conjuncture, situating all of us in a common political field or problem space. In the case of *Turbulence*, all of the journal's issues have involved inviting and engaging diverse contributors, many of whom Osterweil first met during fieldwork. In addition, Osterweil's essay in the first issue of *Turbulence*, "'Becoming-Woman?' In Theory or in Practice?" (June 2007),[18] directly engaged the political problem of the absence of women's voices, something she writes about as a political problem she herself is dealing with, building on her personal experiences as activist and researcher. That text was published and circulated in many of the spaces about which she was "researching." There was no clear distinction between the world of researchers and that of activists. While more fully recounting the complex intermingling of moments and relationships between and in these new complex research sites is beyond the scope this chapter, this discussion begins to move us toward a networked vision of ethnography.

METHODS AND POLITICS: IMPLICATIONS OF KNOWLEDGE AND COMPLEXITY

If the role of the ethnographer is not to explain, in the traditionally scientific, representational sense, then what is it?[19] If social movements (and potentially other knowledge objects) are themselves producing a great deal of knowledge and analysis, including about themselves (and perhaps even about the role of research), what does the ethnographer contribute? The answer to these questions requires rethinking the ethnographic encounter. First, instead of being studied as cases, movements' practices become situated sources of analyses and concepts that in turn shape our understanding of the problem, and potentially the solutions we are exploring. This in turn requires that we recognize that social movement activists are often engaging the very same or similar contemporary problems confronted by researchers. The fields within which movements move are in fact quite crowded. The key thus becomes articulating the potential benefit or specific contribution of the ethnographic perspective and its products.

For Powell, this realization that we increasingly inhabit crowded fields of common problems crystallized during an early morning propeller aircraft flight over the region surrounding Farmington, New Mexico, including the northeastern edges of the Navajo Nation. Far below, stitched together like the pieces of a quilt, the patchwork landscape held together disparate populations—urban and rural, Navajo and non-Navajo, ranchers and energy workers—each transformed by decades of intensive oil, gas, and coal extraction. A diverse group of grassroots leaders, governmental and nongovernmental organizations, and overlapping jurisdictional zones (tribal, state, and federal) currently engage these contentious energy issues, turning them into vibrant arenas of knowledge production and contestation.[20] Many of these actors move between the poles of resisting fossil fuel extraction and pursuing it, spanning political and ecological geographies, traversing overlapping jurisdictional and cultural boundaries as they engage allies and adversaries involved in transnational energy debates.

Pressed into the tiny six-seater Cessna airplane, I adjusted my bulky headset as the ground receded quickly beneath us, revealing the whole borderland below: the sprawling town of Farmington giving way to a strip of verdant farms flanked by oil well pads, buildings, highways, and sandstone outcroppings running along the wide San Juan River. The pilot, the environmental policy specialist, the activist, the reporter and photographer from the *Los Angeles Times*, and I, the anthropologist, were off early this morning for an aerial view of the river basin, its tributaries, and the energy infrastructures nearby. Each individual in the airplane embodies a numerous set of actors deeply invested in the controversies over energy development on the Navajo Nation. The pilot stands in for others with mechanical and technical expertise: renewable energy entrepreneurs, engineers, economists, and creative businessmen like himself, having started an "eco-flight" company to show these geographies to reporters, researchers, and policy-makers. The environmental policy specialist is a leading activist in the region and an ally to Navajo tribal members fighting the pro-posed power plant, but also represents a cadre of professional en-vironmentalists from Flagstaff to Washington, D.C., involved in the debate. The activist, herself Navajo, represents one group in par-ticular, but also hundreds of other tribal members involved in the dispute, whether through nonprofit organizations, tribal agencies, or grassroots campaigns. Her group has recently begun research on a technical and cultural document to outlay energy alternatives for tribal economic development. The reporter and photographer were two of hundreds of reporters following the controversy, creating a media maelstrom of interest in the issue. And I, the silent observer in the plane, stood in for other researchers, students, and allies interested in the debate and its broader effects. (Powell fieldnotes, August 20, 2007)

The aerial view and company on the plane made visible the very crowded field of action and knowledge production surrounding energy politics in the Navajo Nation. Here the ethnographer is but one interested and in-vested actor in a teeming arena of experts, who in many cases possessed and produced more critical, emplaced, and historical knowledge. In this instance, those experts have become Powell's collaborators, in processes of research and writing (Powell and Curley 2009; Powell and Long 2010).

As in many ethnographies today, not only are we joined by others with shared interests or pursuits in our research location, but we may find ourselves in direct competition to prove the relevance of an ethnographic perspective vis-à-vis the more seemingly pragmatic offerings made by re-porters (who offer the hope of getting the movement's story into national or international news), policy analysts (who offer the hope of affecting local, state, and federal policies), attorneys (who offer the hope of litiga-tion as a means to effect lasting change), aid workers (local or imported), and long-term, regional activists (who offer the hope of raising funds and awareness at the grassroots level). The sheer number of other producers of knowledge and action means that ethnographers have to work much harder to articulate the "what for" of our methodology and the unique contribution to these shared matters of concern (e.g., labor issues, energy development, regional violence, environmental degradation, sexism, and failing economies), particularly when our critical perspective is not always welcomed by others in the crowd.

Once again, the Malinowskian trope of the lone ethnographer in the field haunts and increasingly fails the ethnographer, perhaps especially in ethnographies of contemporary, complex issues, which garner interest from many other types of so-called experts. And yet, perhaps increasingly, ethnographers can see this as hopeful. They can realize they are not alone in the field—or alone in their concerns and analyses. They are instead among a broader network of people working on a shared problematic, with their various tools, disciplinary trainings, audiences, agendas, and alliances. In this way, the crowded field may be more of a norm in fieldwork today, a norm that pushes anthropologists toward sharper articulations of their unique contributions to collective analyses and courses of action. For us, this has to do with recognizing a shift toward conducting anthropologies of common problems, as well as new aims toward translation, rather than explanation.

One of the reasons we need new conceptualizations and designs of the fieldwork endeavor is because we are part of a coterie of anthropologists trying to move from doing ethnographies of a people (the classic area studies approach) to doing ethnographies of a problem (see Dombrowski 2001). The politics of this shift implies a relational reconstruction: we are shifting from seeing our informants as the subjects of our research to collaborating on common problems. Such a relational reconstruction also allows for the translocal nature of ethnography today; problems can no longer, if they ever could, be understood as purely localized phenomena. The ethnographer often travels with collaborators, following them to other sites of knowledge practice and action. This shift from a people to a problem further reimagines the way relationships are conceived in ethnographic practice.

However, joining others in crowded fields of knowledge production does not foreclose the possibility of critiquing (theirs and the author's own) practices and positions. Nor does it mean that the interest in knowledge production and development issues always converge with local actors' most urgent concerns. Working in a crowded field on commonly defined problems frequently involves difficult negotiations with the researcher's own perspectives (and biases of disciplinary training) and those of activists with whom the researcher is collaborating. The products of such alliances—themselves rarely smooth—are never predictable and cannot be taken for granted. However this does not negate the importance of such attempts. By setting the research compass on understanding a problem, we, as researchers, relate with people across multiple markers of difference, finding common ground where understanding is not predicated on homogeneity. This relational (re)orientation has the potential to refresh and rewrite the practice of ethnography both in and with indigenous communities, in particular, where the history of anthropology is fraught with malpractice, as well as in other communities and countries where our differences as researchers may be based on other distinctions than ethnic or political ones.

Recognizing such power dynamics is nothing new to critical anthropology, although the field continues to struggle to find productive ways to negotiate these historically fraught relations. As many feminist anthropologists have argued, epistemology is intimately linked with practice and never is outside relations of power (see, e.g., Behar and Gordon 1995; Visweswaran 1997). What we can know is related to how we go about knowing, and no knowledge production is free of historically particular power dynamics. Others such as Humberto Maturana and Francisco Varela link practice, epistemology, and ontology in claiming that "every act of knowing brings forth a world" (1992, 26). That is, how we go about knowing is constitutive of the worlds we seek to know and seek to create. This triad of doing, knowing, and being in research practice does not require complete homogeneity and erasure of all markers of historical difference among actors. Thus, uniting doing, knowing, and being while still accounting for historical relations of difference and power in research relations may offer the more honest and productive means of (re)building relationships as part of the still underestimated value of research interactions. In other words, the relational reconstruction we are arguing for goes beyond shifting from a people to a problem to also including a shift from a product to a process. If producing the article (or the dissertation, the report, the book, the data itself) is subordinated to cultivating a process of meaningful, intersubjective human (and nonhuman) relations, then the very practice and quality of relationality in research methods may be transformed. As such, this shift is an intellectual one but, moreover, it is a shift in our politics of engagement, and in some sense the nature of political engagement in translocal sites where knowledge circulates and is produced.

These examples demonstrate how our research practices—and their effects—are transformed through the recognition of movements as complex, knowledge-producing objects. We understand that movements are complex in the ontological and epistemological work they do: being able to produce knowledge that recursively affects reality—the same realities inhabited and worked on by academics—and organizationally operating through networked relations and fields.

BEYOND ETHNOGRAPHY AS REPRESENTATION: ETHNOGRAPHY AS TRANSLATION, AS WEAVING

Thus far we have addressed an epistemological shift in the research framework, emphasizing the proliferation of knowledge producers where the traditional "objects" become authoritative voices. We have also introduced the notion of a more relational understanding of research founded in a networked notion of reality. That is a reality composed of crowded fields, common problems, myriad nodes, relationships, and interconnections rather than separate compartments filled with delimitable objects and stable, expert positions. At this moment, the conventional research task of piecing together a chaotic jigsaw puzzle of data to explain what the natives/locals are saying is no longer valid. Not only are the natives/locals able to speak—and often quite eloquently—by and for themselves, the notion of a stable reality out there waiting to be explained has been definitively superseded. It has been done away with and replaced by a notion of reality transformed and affected by the very knowledges and stories being produced by that reality. This introduces yet another layer of dynamism and recursivity into the ethnographic project, which moves from representation and explanation supported by grand theories of the aims of science to the tinkering and more artisanal task of translation.

We are well familiar with Gayatri Spivak's (1994) famous query as to whether the subaltern can speak. How does this change if we recognize a field composed of interrelated knowledge producers actively making worlds? If we answer her question in the affirmative, we raise the question of the nature of what the subaltern (or movement) might be saying and the role of the ethnographer vis-à-vis this actor who holds epistemic authority in her or his own right. The researcher then cannot be the spokesperson for people considered to lack audibility or voice. Rather, as a member of Precarias a la Deriva (the Precariat Adrift, an activist research group based in Spain) suggested: "Researching is not about dubbing, but providing accurate subtitles for unique films" (Casas-Cortés, personal interview, January 20, 2008).

Rather than speaking for, we are interested in the careful, though still difficult, task of crafting appropriate subtitles to enable the content to travel to other terrains and audiences. In this specific regard, the ethnographer's role is more akin to a translator, a sorter, or a relayer (Latour 1993) — and to a connector among situated knowledges (Haraway 1991) — than to a scientist seeking to represent or explain a truth from one distant land to another. Similarly, Arturo Escobar suggests that his book *Territories of Difference* is an attempt "to build on ethnographic research in order to identify the knowledge produced by activists and to use this knowledge and analyses to conduct [his] own analyses about related topics . . . to build bridges between political-intellectual conversations" (2008, 25). The task of translation is not just about reproducing what others are saying; it is rather a practice of careful listening akin to what Romand Coles calls the "political arts of listening" (2005). These are skills of attuning oneself to others' utterances and modes of living, and putting what others are saying into another code (in this case the code of Anglo-American social sciences). Through that process, the ethnographer is also adding his or her own experiential and intellectual background, including anthropological knowledge and training. It is then a process of reappropriation and tinkering from which novel analyses might emerge.

In this scenario, and using terms from anthropological traditions, we need not understand the role of ethnographer in the crowded field as *ventriloquia* (Bretón Solo de Zaldívar 2008), in the sense of speaking for, but rather see our work as *translation* (Asad 1986; Tsing 2005). The notion of translation evokes one of the principal ethnographic transformations we are envisioning. We situate our argument within the orbit of social theorists working with this provocative metaphor as an intellectual practice attuned to the recognition of multiplicity, furthering a more relational mode of engagement among different knowledge producers. Boaventura de Sousa Santos discusses translation as a political alternative: "To my mind, the alternative to a general theory is the work of translation. Translation is the procedure that allows for mutual intelligibility among the experiences [and knowledges] of the world without jeopardizing their identity and autonomy, without, in other words, reducing them to homogenous entities" (2006, 132; see also Juris, this volume). In this formulation, ethnographic work as translation involves processes of cross-articulation among knowledges, rather than representation or explanation. While we do not eschew explanation altogether, our intent is to contribute to theoretical insights and action-oriented problem solving on the part of transnational networks of activists and academics by advancing the work of ethnographic description in multiple points of contact. By using the concept of translation we do not seek a perfect scientific correspondence from one language to another, but an effort at communication and ongoing conversation. This implies recognizing (with Gayatri Spivak and Bruno Latour), that translation, despite the best intentions, can never achieve a complete one-to-one correspondence of meaning. Something is always lost, but much can also be gained and added. Translation then can be understood as constituted by engaging with knowledges advanced from particular and transnationalized locations to put them into other codes of knowledge produced elsewhere without erasing the fact that there is a difference in every site and process of translation. This relational and more networked, or horizontal,[21] approach contrasts with the historical role of the researcher, who is granted an aura of cognitive superiority.

In anthropology, this assumed authority was historically used to confer upon the ethnographer the role of interpreting for those who made no sense, or speaking on behalf of the voiceless. The debates on the politics of representation tried to address this problematic position. The discipline of anthropology was crucial in the advancement of a new awareness with regard to the question of representation (Behar and Gordon 1995; Clifford 1988; Clifford and Marcus 1986; Marcus 1999a). Reflexivity was one of the solutions to this dilemma, although many contend that being reflexive is not sufficient to address the asymmetries of the established epistemological order (Probyn 1993). Building on these efforts, and together with other authors, we propose thinking of ethnography as translation as an epistemological alternative to the geopolitics of knowledge inscribed in conventional scientific research.

In addition to addressing this epistemological problem, translations are creative and productive, seizing upon the moments that transnational connections make available. They generate encounters across difference; they introduce new figures to determined circles of thought; they put debates that were hitherto unconnected in contact with one another; and they bring disparate and distant locales into orbit with one another through the subjects that travel and translate across borders. Overall, translations facilitate transnational processes of relation making and exchange.

Translation is also a critical step of putting distinct spheres of knowledge into conversation. By this we mean engaging the knowledge practices of the movements we are working with, putting them in relation to other sources, and at times putting them into other words. In this spirit, Casas-Cortés tried to compile and reflect on the findings advanced by a feminist activist research project on precarity, treating Precarias a la Deriva as a situated source on topics related to the EU, globalization, and transformations of labor. She related their analyses and concepts to other traditions, coming mainly from anthropology and other fields. Putting these analyses into dialogue with one another provided a solid basis for a richer understanding of current problematics, in particular transformations and efforts at social change in the EU. These "results" were then useful to both the author and the activist group with which she was working.

> *Precarias a la Deriva* brings the question of care work to the debates on labor transformations in post-fordist economies and knowledge society. My ethnographic engagement with their texts and broader set of research activities generated a genealogy of the social movements' concept of precarity and a glossary of *Precarias a la Deriva's* own terms related to care. . . . The concept of care is simultaneously emerging in different disciplinary fields and spheres of knowledge: from ecology, to feminist economics, and even liberation theology. By engaging the different literatures on care, I was able to identify what was distinct about Precarias' contribution: it was especially the site and format of enunciation. Coming from a location of struggle, their theory of care is presented as something in the making, more in search of a common lexicon of conflict than a coherent and fixed series of answers. (Casas-Cortés 2009, 423)[22]

Those heterodox sources about the EU are put in tandem with other literatures on the question of care work and labor changes, mainly feminist economics and anthropology of the EU, connecting those further and fostering a web of critical knowledge producers on those shared matters. These webs of critical knowledges are themselves multifaceted and dynamic, interpolating and involving others in various locales, including in other movements and the academy. In fact, at times our own positions and relations to spaces where information is shared put different people and networks into contact—this was certainly the case with precarity work and university struggles taking place in Europe and North America in 2008 and 2009.

The work of translation also has the goal of spreading, sharing, and building connections among transnational nodes of engaged knowledge producers, a practice akin to weaving. Recognizing ethnography as a technology of weaving begets recognizing that we move within a social reality that is constituted by networks.[23] Embracing the relational, networked dimension of the social implies a series of ontological and epistemological consequences for our research. A relational approach to ethnography would transform both researcher and researched into distinct nodes, knit threads, or rootstocks, each rooted in particular "territories of difference" (Escobar 2008). In this way the relationship would be flattened, or dehierarchized, although not made equivalent, and opened to mutual influences and explicit contagions. Ethnographic materials traveling among those networks facilitate these productive contagions, making ethnographic practice a weaving technology, of sorts.

The shift from representation and explanation to weaving and translation as the goals and effects of ethnography opens up possibilities for renovating the ethnographic endeavor. Within this framework it is possible to envision a new role for the ethnographer acting as a connective node knitting broader nets of engaged knowledge producers. Within this net, ethnographers are neither totally outside the arena of inquiry, in the sense of maintaining a necessary position for critical distance or signaling the neutral "god-trick" that Donna Haraway (1991) warns us against, nor are they completely inside, positioned as what some might describe as "going native." Instead, seeing the ethnographer as a translator as well as weaver or knitter in the midst of a crowded field entails accepting the fact that one—intentionally or not—becomes woven into denser and denser webs through the labor and politics of ethnography. In other words, the ethnographer goes networked (or, perhaps, "knitworked"). The embracing of networks as sites of enunciation and practice helps to advance the practice of ethnography as a more relational methodology. The ontological foundation of this approach is one of a different realism, which is based on the blurring and flattening of reductionist binaries, including the subject/object divide, a foundational part of the modern scientific tradition. This new realism involves the breakdown of the rigid border between self and others (see Escobar 2008). Rather than discrete, we can see entities as weblike: webs of interrelationships in which learning from each other, including sharing intellectual antecedents and political affinities, is a true possibility, and a political necessity.

The nature of the ethnographic approach—sustained inquiry, careful observation and participation, immersion in a place, and the ability to work translocally—makes ethnography a uniquely positioned research practice for much more than recognizing counter-hegemonic and subaltern knowledges. The ethnographic sensibility and its concrete research procedures are well positioned to see resonant forms emerging among various sites of knowledge production, drawing together literatures in innovative ways and seeing patterns of theory and practice across various sites of action.

Under the premise of social movements as situated sources and knowledge producers, ethnography, more than an interpretative or explanatory mechanism, becomes a process of translation and weaving, articulating distinct, often unrelated and widely dispersed knowledges in novel ways. In that process, the position of the ethnographer is not one of being totally "in" or completely "out." In this ambiguous position, the ethnographer is woven into the relational web that constitutes his or her own research topic intermeshed with her or his life trajectory. Still, the blurring does not entail equating researcher and researched. Going networked allows for the awareness and the openness toward unexpected multiple affinities, shared experiences, and common notions among the various parties involved. Moreover, such a strategy is premised on recognizing the relationships and networks crisscrossing the reality of academics, researchers, and the Others with whom the ethnographer engages. Indeed, these research practices are somehow intended to coconstruct a broader archive with the movement; this is why we talk about the possibilities of a post-representational notion of ethnography. In that sense, these techniques are not only about redrawing or even doing away with the subject/object divide but are also about generating research methods that are appropriate for a new politics of research.

Ultimately, we suggest that rather than remaining with such a stark distinction between political practice and academic ethnography, we would do well to consider what special strengths our practices as ethnographers contribute to the day-to-day and longer-term work of movements. While at times this means speaking as an expert on a court case for land rights explicitly for a social movement, at other times it might mean creating, defining, or generating concepts; destabilizing the hegemony or seeming solidity of expert knowledges; helping to make the case for different ways of knowing; or being the knitworker who builds conversations within conversations, broadening participation and deepening understanding. Transnational movements may find themselves working with ethnographers to generate and co-author the discourses, imaginaries, and plans for organizing things differently—based either on our work in nonhierarchical societies (something anthropologists might have a special sensibility for; see Graeber 2004, 2009) or simply on the fact that we have engaged, observed, recorded, and looked after their (or our own) practices ethnographically.[24]

In conclusion, studying movements as complex objects and networks that are prolifically producing knowledges, often across a broad geography of locales, poses a series of methodological challenges and possibilities. These challenges are raised to previous approaches in research on social movements, particularly within the subfield or discipline known as social movement studies, as well as to commonsense notions of the goals and purpose of research. When the researcher recognizes that she or he is dealing with objects and actors who are themselves producing analyses, data, and reflections, which in turn inform and even produce new realities for the actors involved, the act of research changes drastically. Rather than digging into social movements' own documents to justify extant theories or otherwise produce definitive representations of a social phenomenon "out there," ethnographers encounter authorities in their own right who are generating particular knowledges and stories, some that, at times, challenge the role and epistemic authority of the ethnographer. This not only shifts conventional notions of the ethnographic endeavor but also expands the traditional social scientific mandate of interpretation and representation toward unforeseen political possibilities.

NOTES

1 See Holland et al. 2010 for a discussion of some prominent models of engaged scholarship as recognized by university-based practitioners.
2 The term *postrepresentational* refers to an epistemological and political move that can be seen to be taking place both within social scientific disciplines and in the realm of politics (see Tormey 2005). In relation to the discipline of

anthropology and the methodology of ethnography, the term refers to a shift away from a conception of ethnographic analysis and writing as accurate and objective representations of reality to recognizing that ethnographic analysis is always involved in creating and producing that reality (see Clifford and Marcus 1986).

3　We have in mind, in particular, the voices of Arturo Escobar, Dorothy Holland, Charlie Kurzman, Don Nonini, Charles Price, John Pickles, Wendy Wolford, Juan Ricardo Aparicio, Mario Blaser, Elena Yehia, Gretchen Fox, Sebastian Cobarubias, Ana Araujo, Carrie Little Hersh, Georgina Drew, Vinci Daro, EuyRyung Jun, Joe Wiltberger, Alice Brooke Wilson, and others at the University of North Carolina, Chapel Hill, as well as colleagues elsewhere who have participated in SMWG's discussions: Xochitl Leyva-Solano, Marisol de la Cadena, David Hess, Sonia Alvarez, Orin Starn, Janet Conway, Gustavo Esteva, and Jeffrey Juris, among others. We find it no coincidence that several of the contributors to this volume have been part of the SMWG conversations since its inception in 2003.

4　These antecedents include feminist epistemology, traditions of popular education and participatory action research, as well as some recent trends, such as the decoloniality paradigm together with certain voices within science and technology studies. Moreover, we argue that among some working on and with social movements there is a recognizable "knowledge turn."

5　*Ethnographies of complex objects* is a term we use to refer to a trend in ethnographic work in the discipline of anthropology, closely related to science and technology studies and associated with the work of Kim Fortun (2001), George Marcus (2007), and numerous others, as well as some sociologists, including Karin Knorr Cetina (1997).

6　The alter-globalization movement is also known as the antiglobalization movement, the counter-globalization movement, and the global justice and solidarity movement, among other names. It is the movement most often associated with the spectacular counter-summits against the WTO, International Monetary Fund (IMF), World Bank, and other multinational institutions enforcing neoliberal corporate-driven globalization. Whether it is in fact a movement, or can be more accurately understood as a movement of movements, or even a network, is debated in academic and activist circles alike (see, e.g., Daro 2009a; Juris 2008a; Routledge and Cumbers 2009).

7　Coined by social movements in Italy and now widely diffused, the term *precarity*, perhaps better put as precariousness, refers to labor conditions associated with increasingly intermittent and short-term work. The term also refers at some level to the precarity of living conditions in post-Fordist capitalism overall and the knowledge economy in particular. While the word sounds rather awkward in English, it is a perfect example of the kinds of translations being done in transnational movement networks. For more on precarity and the transnational networks involved in organizing around the term, see Casas-Cortés 2009.

8 A longer version of this argument, based on the same episode, can be found in Osterweil 2008.

9 Hale writes: "By activist research, I mean a method through which we affirm a political alignment with an organized group of people in struggle and allow dialogue with them to shape each phase of the process, from conception of the research topic to data collection to verification and dissemination of the results" (2006, 97).

10 Juris (2008a) does a thorough job of describing not only the network-like nature of movements but also the networking logic that underlies and even drives them. Moreover, Escobar (2008) provides very useful reviews of the various social-theoretical and political implications of the notion of networks when applied to social movements, in particular transnational ones.

11 "Knowledge Objects: Finding the Political in Ethnographies of the Complex" is the title of the panel we co-organized for the American Anthropological Association annual meeting in Philadelphia in 2009.

12 Similarly, Michael Fischer astutely argues for recognizing that anthropology is increasingly acting in a series of "third spaces," sites for the "emergence" of "new forms of life" in late- or postmodernities (2005, 5). This in turn offers another idea of the political force of both knowledge production and movements that produce knowledge.

13 The World Social Forum is a critical part of the alter-globalization movement. For more on the World Social Forum, see Conway 2012; Fisher and Ponniah 2003; Juris 2008a; Santos 2006; Sen and Waterman 2007; Jackie Smith et al. 2007.

14 For more on these underlying cultural logics and theoretical practices, see Juris 2008a; Osterweil 2004a, 2010.

15 See *Turbulence*'s website, www.turbulence.org.uk (accessed December 23, 2011).

16 Osterweil is also on the editorial board of the newspaper.

17 This applies in particular to theories of networks in social movement studies, e.g., Diani 2003 and Keck and Sikkink 1998, as well as traditional social network analysis in sociology.

18 http://turbulence.org.uk/ (accessed December 28, 2012).

19 We do not want to suggest that there is not some form of cognition, or sense and meaning making, going on here, but rather that the notion of explanation, which tends to be thought of as univocal and correspondent to a sin-

gular, objective truth, is not appropriate. In this sense we are working very much in the vein of Charles Taylor (see, e.g., Taylor 1971) and others who recognize the difference between interpretive sciences and the explanatory and representational ones (see Rabinow and Sullivan 1979).

20 See Powell and Long 2010 and Powell 2010 for further discussion of the politics of knowledge production in relation to controversies surrounding energy development on Native territories.

21 For us horizontality does not mean complete equivalence or equality, and we are in fact critical of positions that see no difference between ethnographers/researchers and other actors.

22 Precarias a la Deriva's unique contribution stems from its innovative politicization of the care-precarity complex. The current work of the group centers around fighting back the emergent "care crisis," exploring the possibility of "care struggles" via the articulation of alliances between different care givers and care receivers, and posing innovative political proposals such as a care strike, care citizenship, and new care rights. These conceptual developments are not always at ease with the traditional analysis and politics of the Left.

23 Concepts of weaving and translation are not only related to the social theoretical turn to networks, they are also relevant to the stitching together of new assemblages associated with late modernity. Social movements can and should be understood precisely as the kinds of entities that are (re)assembling the social (Latour 2005), and positing new ethical and practical plateaus for emergent forms of life (Fischer 2003). The key is to recognize that the notions of emergence and assemblage are themselves premised on a vision of reality that is distinct from traditional positivist (Cartesian, modern) conceptions of the real.

24 Some have made the claim that one notable aspect of many contemporary movements is the ethnographic nature of activists' own research practice (see Juris 2004b, 2008a).

9

Transformative Ethnography and
the World Social Forum
Theories and Practices of Transformation

GIUSEPPE CARUSO

In this chapter I discuss the concept and practice of transformative ethnography as developed through and applied to engagement within a networked space of transnational encounter, the World Social Forum (WSF). Transformative ethnography seeks to contribute to the debate on engaged ethnography as a practice of change (see Hale 2006, 2008; Juris 2007, 2008a; Lassiter 2005, 2008; Low and Merry 2010; Scheper-Hughes 1995) through the theoretical and practical insights of transformative mediation (see Bush and Folger 2005). It also resonates with the values and practices of the WSF as enshrined in its Charter of Principles, and as experienced in my own engagement with the forum (see Caruso 2012).

While transformative ethnography is appropriate for daily ethnographic work, it provides its most compelling contribution when acting in, reporting about, and reflecting on situations of conflict. These are situations in which emotions run high and political and personal stakes are conflated by the unsettling dynamics of conflict generating communicational patterns that tend to exasperate and obliterate difference. Transformative ethnography is a communicative practice for engaging the field and our research collaborators in moments of crisis. Familiarity and comfort with conflict (gained through training and experience) can provide ethnographers with helpful resources to guide their practices as both activists and researchers. A sound theoretical understanding of conflict dynamics and a practical approach to communication in conflict can assist ethnographers' academic and activist work, shaping perceptions of conflicts and their dynamics, effects, and implications, as well as wider debates on society and social change.

Transformative ethnography addresses the constitutive tension between theory and practice. It eschews the abstraction of absolute knowledge from the lives of agents and rejects extractive investigative practices generally. Instead, transformative ethnography emphasizes the embodied nature of consciousness and the contextual uniqueness of human knowledge relationships (see Damasio 1994; Dewey 1922, 1925; Edelman 2006; Lakoff and Johnson 1999; Merleau-Ponty 1962; Varela, Thompson, and Rosch 1992). It contributes to nonprescriptive and nondirective knowledge that is collaboratively generated as a process of recognition, adaptation, and transformation by focusing on relational attitudes in collaborative work, ethnographic reporting, and collaborative theorizing. Ethnographers can contribute to knowledge making and deliberation toward transformative action within transnational activist networks, the academic community, and society by highlighting recurring relational patterns as matters of practical and theoretical concern emerging out of the friction produced by cultural, social, and political differences (Latour 2005). They can enact such practical and epistemological commitments by experimenting with the communicative practices developed in the field of transformative mediation and applying them in interactions with activists, academic colleagues, and wider publics.

Transformative ethnography complements the current debate on engagement in ethnographic fieldwork. This is not the place to review the debates on applied, engaged, public, and/or collaborative ethnographies (see this volume's introduction); instead I want to suggest that transformative ethnography, through practical and epistemological engagement with communicative practices developed in the field of mediation, can shed further light on the practical implications of engagement in the field, in this case with WSF activists, in academia, and in society. In particular, the communicative methods of transformative mediation and its theoretical underpinning can further ground engaged ethnographies and provide ethnographers with additional resources and field methods that are particularly useful in critical moments of conflict. The transformative ethnographer does not necessarily mediate conflict. Rather I am arguing that the theoretical and practical tools of transformative mediation can assist ethnographers in making sense of and highlighting matters of concern for further debate among activists, academics, and the wider public. Moreover, the resulting ethnographic description can also help activists become aware of and think through critical issues underlying conflict in order to develop future-oriented strategies for resolving subsequent conflicts and thereby engaging in more effective organizing.

The WSF mobilizes hundreds of thousands of activists in world, regional, and local events. It is not a conventional social movement in that it does not produce agendas for action or set goals for activists; nor is it based on a unitary ideology or a formal structure of governance. Instead the WSF has a transformational vision grounded in a culture of politics rooted in the value of difference and supported by an innovative organizational formula: "open space," which is defined in its charter as a "meeting place for reflective thinking, democratic debate of ideas, formulation of proposals, free exchange of experiences and interlinking for effective action."[1] The WSF convenes activists engaged in processes of intentional transformation to share experiences and set coordinated projects at local, regional, and transnational scales. Unlike traditional social movements, encounters at social forums fulfill the WSF's mission of sparking non-directed processes of change (Whitaker 2005). Transformation, it is believed by advocates of open space, ensues as a result of the recognition of, respect for, and adaptation to different worldviews. Such transformation can inspire action-facilitating processes of institutional and social change.

How can transformative ethnography generate knowledge with, for, and about transnational processes of transformation such as the WSF? Transformative ethnography, I argue, is particularly useful for engaging phenomena like the WSF. It can also contribute to the design and development of field research methods that engage critiques raised by scholars and activists who wonder why "in order to stay true to hopes for a more livable earth, one must turn away from scholarly theory" (Tsing 2005, 266–67). By allowing us to interact with, mediate, and account for the multiplicity of worldviews and social practices in the WSF, transformative ethnography complements and reflects the cultural politics of open space, contributing to struggles for epistemological emancipation from the hegemonic naturalization of historical and contextual worldviews such as neoliberalism (Santos 2004). At its best, transformative ethnography can help contribute to the imagination of alternative, emancipatory forms of knowledge and subjectivity, while helping to create, perform, and share knowledge regarding globalization and global transformation. Moreover, the collaborative work between ethnographers and activists can help transcend the perceived radical divides between theory and practice, action and speculation, permanence and change, and understanding and transforming.

TRANSFORMATIVE ETHNOGRAPHY IN/OF TRANSNATIONAL ACTIVISTS NETWORKS

Since the explosion of the most recent global crisis in 2008, WSF activists have expansively debated the crisis's origins, the multiscalar resistances to it, and possible alternatives beyond it. As I discuss in detail elsewhere (Caruso 2010a, 2010b), the debate around the global economic crisis and what to do about it is a highly contentious one at the forum and within the WSF International Council (IC). Such tensions generate anxiety about the ability of the WSF to provide a space for the elaboration of alternatives to the current crisis. Such was the level of anxiety that in several meetings of the WSF, IC members claimed that the global Left and the WSF itself were in crisis. How does transformative ethnography report about such discourses of crisis? How does a transformative activist act in such moments? How can ethnographic methods be combined with mediation practice and proactively relate to the transformative vision of a networked space of transnational encounter such as the WSF?

The WSF crisis has been debated in plenary and group sessions in IC meetings and informal discussions where terms such as *frustration, depression, disappointment,* and *disillusion* were often used by activists to describe their moods and their emotional and material investments in the WSF (Caruso 2010a). An IC member told me on July 25, 2010, that the upcoming forum in Dakar was "the last chance for the WSF." Other recurring expressions of the depth of the WSF crisis conveyed the inability to fully make sense of its nature or find alternative paths beyond it. At the October 2009 IC meeting in Montreal one IC member expressed the pervasive feelings of depression in the following terms: "We do not trust each other, people do not trust anyone in the forum" (Caruso 2010a). Similar dynamics can be found in the research and practice of conflict mediation;

engaging with such dynamics is at the core of both transformative mediation and transformative ethnography (see A. Beck 1999; Bush and Folger 2005; della Noce 1999; Mayer 2004).

At the height of the IC crisis a particularly significant conflict involved the tension between those who thought the WSF should become a more organized political movement and others who wanted to reconfirm it as a space for deliberation and transformation (see Juris 2005b, 2008a, this volume; Teivainen 2004). The awareness of the dynamics and relationships involved in such conflicts is crucial given that behavior such as providing (conscious or unconscious) support to one or another position, and perceived attempts to manipulate, can generate very different outcomes. Such behaviors can contribute to the transformation or the escalation of a conflict. Factional conflicts escalate because those involved demand (using a variety of argumentative strategies that range from righteous to ideological or scientific) that others take sides. Refusing this logic and maintaining a relatively impartial posture can prevent the escalation of conflict, while an intervention that exposes this behavior may help transform conflict. In the context of the WSF, rarely is behavior made the object of deliberate attention, and rarely are the complex dynamics of conflict and crisis engaged.

Transformative ethnographers' specific contributions are twofold. While sharing their insights on knowledge performance and conflictual relationships, they can contribute to the transformation of conflicts. During the IC meeting in Dakar in July 2010, for instance, I was warmly thanked by some participants for the way in which I reported to the plenary the diverging opinions expressed by the participants of a working group on methodology and strategy, in one member's words, "without giving prominence to my view," which I had clearly expressed during the debate. Summarizing, reflecting, and paraphrasing are communicative practices that I learned during my training as a transformative mediator. I am always ready to share my exploration of theories and practices of conflict with my collaborators, and I often discuss these theories and practices with them to raise issues for further reflection regarding how conflict is engaged in the WSF. However, it is not my claim that transformative ethnographers should position themselves outside the conflicts in the activist space in order to play the institutional role of the mediator. Such a role is already played regularly, if informally or unconsciously, in the IC by its members. It was this realization and the observation of successful strategies of conflict negotiation during my fieldwork with the WSF India that inspired me to develop the notion of transformative ethnography.

The Indian WSF took place in 2004 in a context of extraordinary cultural and political conflict. Indeed, India is a huge country with an extremely diverse, conflict-ridden civil society. I experienced the resulting complexities from the moment I entered the office of the WSF in Mumbai. Negotiating such frictions was my main concern in my daily engagement with the WSF India. These conflicts and my relation to them took the center stage in my research and my work with the WSF. However, it was only after my fieldwork was over and I returned to London to write that I started to engage the literature on conflict mediation. It was from that encounter and my training as a transformative mediator that I developed the theoretical and practical framework of transformative ethnography I present here, and which consequently facilitated the adaptation of my actions in the WSF. There are two components of this approach: ethnography and transformative mediation.

Ethnographic knowledge is contextual (performed in place[s]), relational (the outcome of selective and adaptive interactions), and potentially transformational (it can generate shifts in the perceptions and behaviors of those involved); in other words, it is knowledge *about* and *with*. The transformative approach to knowledge refuses the dualism implicit in the opposition between theory and practice, resonating with the WSF's transformative vision. One caution, however: my inspiration by the premises and principles of transformative mediation does not imply that I think ethnographers should act as mediators in the field (at least not any more than their activist colleagues). Ethnographers can of course play such a role if fully qualified and asked to do so, but in this capacity they would be transformative mediators rather than ethnographers. Using the principles of transformative mediation in ethnography can contribute to the transformation of conflicts but not necessarily to their formal mediation. Most crucially for our purposes is that the understanding of conflict dynamics through the framework of transformative mediation can guide ethnographers when (directly or indirectly) they are in the grip of conflict by both directing their actions and shaping their observations of particular dynamics, the analysis of and reporting of which can be useful to activists in terms of negotiating subsequent conflicts. In this sense, although

I am a qualified mediator, during my engagement with the WSF I never acted as formal conflict mediator.

Transformative mediation was developed by Robert Baruch Bush and Joseph Folger in the late 1980s. It is not possible here to recount the complex theoretical foundations and methods of transformative mediation (see Bush and Folger 2005), or to position it within the debates on conflict mediation over the past three decades (see Alexander 2006, 2008; Brigg 2003). Instead I highlight those aspects of transformative mediation that contribute most directly to my development of the concept of transformative ethnography. The transformative framework, grounded in relational approaches to society (McNamee and Gergen 1999), and influenced by feminist scholars such as Carol Gilligan (1982) and Daryl Koehn (1998), stresses the role of dialogue in the formation and transformation of self and society. For transformative mediation, conflict is the creative force of society and conflict escalation is a recursive, personally and socially damaging pattern of interaction between relatively self-absorbed individuals leading to crisis (Bush and Folger 2005). Transformative mediation thus aims to contribute to the establishment of liberating communication centered on two pillars: the recognition of the other position and its underlying humanity and the empowerment of all individuals involved. This can help overcome the perceived impossibility of understanding and taking appropriate actions to resolve conflict (see A. Beck 1999; Bush and Folger 2005; della Noce 1999). The role of the mediator is not directive and managerial as in other mediation frameworks where mediators indicate possible avenues out of the conflict and offer suggestions for settlement (Bush and Folger 2005, 9–18; see also Bush 2004). The transformative mediator does not presume to know more about the conflict or the possible solutions than the actors involved. The mediator's role is to facilitate communication by verbally recognizing the actors' insights and highlighting opportunities for mutual recognition and empowerment. Research has proven that such a nondirective and supportive approach can establish virtuous cycles of recognition and empowerment (see A. Beck 1999).

Transformative mediation's goals are not necessarily to directly transform society, but the transformation of conflicts may generate processes of relational change that can lead to wider institutional and social impacts (Bush and Folger 2005, 18). This attitude informs the ethics of the WSF's open spaces, which are centered on an understanding of change as a nego-tiated transformation rather than a directive hegemonic process led by a traditional social movement or a vanguard. As far as the values underlying transformative mediation are concerned, these eschew radical individu-alism and competition as the foundations of human societies. According to Bush and Folger, "although the individualist ethic of modern Western culture was a great advance over the preceding social order, it is now pos-sible and necessary to go further still and to achieve a full integration of individual freedom and social conscience, in a relational social order en-acted through new forms of social processes and institutions" (2005, 24). Similar values and goals are expressed in the WSF Charter of Principles: "The World Social Forum is . . . committed to building a planetary society directed towards fruitful relationships among Humankind and between it and the Earth."[2] Values and practices of transformative mediation are thus congruent with those of the WSF and the notion of transformative ethnography.

The web of relations and ever-changing configurations of difference and conflict that characterize the WSF pose several challenges to the eth-nographer, including positioning in and adapting to the surrounding en-virons; understanding the social dynamics across the meshed spaces of contention defined by multiple cultural, social, and political configura-tions; and producing a relatively even-handed account of those experi-ences. The ethnographer must confront these challenges while remaining committed to overcoming inequality and injustice. I began to develop the notion of transformative ethnography as I encountered such complexities during my fieldwork with the WSF India.

As far as the first challenge, positioning, was concerned, my liminal position in the Mumbai WSF between Indians and non-Indians, young people at the Intercontinental Youth Camp (IYC) and adults in the orga-nizing committee, and activists and scholars shaped the "constitutive hy-bridity" of my identity (Fardon 1995). The following incidents illustrate the point. At a program meeting for the IYC, some of the participants ex-pressed their frustration about how "they" (Europeans and Brazilians) were telling "us," the Indians (he was probably, in the heat of the conver-sation, forgetting my presence among them and that of many other non-Indians in the Mumbai office) how to organize "our" camp. The argument escalated to intolerance. Suddenly, someone imposed their authority and asked participants to "at least" respect "our brother Giuseppe" who might not feel comfortable with what was said about "his people." A similar dynamic occurred when several non-Indians complained about the supposed inability of the Indians to get any work done. Someone else warned them that this might upset me since my partner was Indian. The political and personal implications of such positioning greatly influenced my subjectivity and played a crucial role in defining the horizons of my research.

As far as the second challenge is concerned, in order to understand the social dynamics across spaces defined by multiple cultural, social, and political configurations, transformative ethnographers work to break down the opposition between theory and practice, operating across the two domains to offer themselves as actors in the processes shaping knowledge as relationships between individuals and between themselves and their social and natural environments (see Edelman 2006; Lakoff and Johnson 1999). Transformative research is based on the premise that knowledge production is an adaptive practice that affects the subjectivities of all involved. In my work with the WSF, my actions cause, directly and indirectly, decisions to be taken, things to be changed, and perceptions and understandings informing action to be negotiated (see Ingold 1996; Moore 1999). These negotiations contribute to transforming the relationships that are engaged in the fields of research and activism. This transformation can contribute to transcending the radical opposition between action and speculation, judgment and knowledge, and practice and theory.

Transformative ethnography confronts the third challenge—striving to produce an impartial or even-handed account—by working against managerial and directive approaches to engagement and representation.[3] In the conflict between different representational and organizational practices, transformative ethnographers apply nondirective communicative approaches, such as reflection, summary, and paraphrasing, to converse with collaborators, while attempting to remain as impartial as possible in reporting the nature of the differences and conflicts confronted. The actors in conversation are thus made aware of specific matters of concern, which become stepping-stones for reflection and action that ignite the transformative process (see Kezar 2003; Latour 2005). Regular ethnographic reporting of the meetings and activities in which transformative ethnographers take part can also contribute to internal debates among activists. By highlighting recurring patterns, the ethnographer can contribute to theory making and political deliberation that generate affective action as understood by transformative mediators and enshrined in the WSF Charter of Principles. Such patterns arise out of interactions mediated by cultural, social, and political differences and the conflicting perceptions and narratives they generate. In my case, the tradition of fragmentation and mistrust in Indian civil society reproduced social boundaries on the basis of preexisting divides across class, religion, gender, caste, and political belief. The ethnographic method can grasp the subtleties of such patterns in their performative aspects as reflected in the multiple daily interactions in the field. But ethnographic awareness is not unique to ethnographers. It should be understood as a way to approach Otherness shared by a great number of activists.

Transformative ethnography contributes to knowledge that is nonprescriptive and nondirective, involving a process of recognition and adaptation between multiple actors. To illustrate this point, consider the discussion regarding the crisis of the WSF. Rather than extracting objective knowledge from a densely networked space of conflicting relationships, the ethnographer recognizes and reflects on the complexities and divergences as expressed by the actors involved (instead of directing the attention of the readers to "what is really at play"), helping to contribute to a virtuous cycle of recognition—what I refer to as adaptive responses. This prevents the escalation of the conflict and promotes the full expression of the creativity of those involved. As discussed above and widely recognized in the field of mediation, such mutual recognition can ignite transformative processes (see A. Beck 1999; Bush and Folger 2005). Whereas transformation may or may not take place in the case of the debate on the WSF crisis, the mediation process aims to expose how factional approaches to the crisis (taking a position) may indeed contribute to its escalation. Whereas the full expression of political, ideological, and cultural differences is crucial to their negotiation and to the development of common political strategies, it is also the case that in moments of conflict and crisis the radicalization of these positions may exacerbate conflict rather than contribute to the complex process of negotiating differences. The transformative ethnographer is acutely aware of the communicative patterns in conflict and aims to help prevent their escalation and consequent radicalization.

The implications of this approach are humbling for those of us who recognize the lack of a foundation for abstract knowledge beyond that produced in human interaction. Transformative ethnographers will thus restrain as much as possible from extractive and potentially exploitative activity disguised as "data collection." Such a methodology seems particularly appropriate to the wsf's own methodology of open space and its emancipatory pedagogy (Freire 2000).

ENGAGING THE WORLD SOCIAL FORUM

How do these ideas relate to and how are they generated by the everyday activities of the transformative ethnographer? I referred to the differences expressed in the wsf, to its conflictual nature, and to the increasing tendency toward self-absorption among the actors in conflict—including the ethnographer. Conflict is so central to the discourse and practices of the wsf that at the ic meeting in Rabat, Morocco, in 2009, a member advocated the creation of special spaces where conflict could be openly engaged. Transformative ethnographers can contribute to processes of engagement and conflict negotiation both in the daily practices of the networks they engage and through their ethnographies of the social dynamics in which they are involved (see Bush and Folger 2005; Caruso 2004). These ideas can be illustrated through my experience in the wsf office in Mumbai by keeping in mind the three challenges: positioning and adaptation; social dynamics and multiple cultural, social, and political configurations; and the striving for impartial accounts.

I moved to Mumbai in October 2003 to volunteer in the wsf office responsible for the logistics of the forum to be held in January 2004 and to begin research for my dissertation. I had been invited by Ranjit,[4] a member of the Indian Organizing Committee involved in the coordination of the Mumbai office whom I had met in London in the spring of 2003, and by the volunteers of the ΙΥΟ who had received my contact information from the Brazilian organizers with whom I had worked the previous year. When I landed in Mumbai, I took on the task, among others, of connecting past and current organizers to ensure a degree of institutional knowledge transfer. The atmosphere of the office was welcoming and I soon felt part of the team, but I also sensed that some of the office coordinators felt a certain hesitation toward me. I quickly found myself enmeshed in the challenges of conducting an engaged ethnography of the forum. I was often asked about my political allegiances and my supposed other agenda, giving me the chance to discuss my trajectory within the wsf and my goal of an academic career. My association with Ranjit, a controversial character in the office, provoked some concern. Moreover, when Ranjit realized that I would refuse to take sides in the office conflicts, he became resentful. Later, as I was on the threshold of becoming an insider in the office space, Ranjit intimated that I should not attend a meeting of the Mumbai Organizing Committee for which I had been preparing. The rumor spread that I was not an ally of Ranjit after all, and this repositioned me in the political geography of the office. However, I became fully aware of this repositioning only through later conversations. At the same time, the work I was doing to establish a consistent interaction between the English-speaking Indian process and the Spanish- and Portuguese-speaking organizers of previous editions of the IYC helped me establish a degree of trust.

My academic interests also generated interesting exchanges. During conversations with senior organizers of the WSF India, for example, my questions about historical background and cultural and social context were sometimes met with injunctions to avoid "hair splitting" and "investigative research" and to concentrate instead on "real work." At other times I received responses referring to differences, rifts, and conflicts too obvious or trivial to be discussed.[5] This directed me toward some of the busy crossroads at which the idiosyncrasies of the Indian process intersected with the wider vision and political dynamics of the WSF. For instance, issues related to the tension between deliberation and action (or theory versus practice) were central in the political and theoretical debates within the global WSF process with respect to the divide between those who advocated for the WSF as an open space and others who claimed the WSF should evolve toward a full-fledged political movement with common declarations and calls for action. While these snapshots illustrate my complex positioning in the Mumbai office, they also recall some of the conditions of transformative ethnography: the striving for impartiality on the part of the ethnographer, the need to negotiate complexities and tensions with respect to the researcher's identity, and the difficulty of engaging in relationships based on trust due to ongoing conflicts in the office.

I soon came to realize that the atmosphere of the office and the mood of the organizers were shaped by a series of conflicts, the nuances of which I was initially unaware but was starting to experience directly. One day I asked a member of the Youth Organizing Committee about the tension I perceived, and she told me, smiling, that it was only "normal"—this was the nature of relations between activists in India. While making sure not to overstate the background questions—against which I had already been warned—I was able to elicit stories regarding the history and origin of the conflicts I was observing. These were further complemented by my reading of books, journal articles, reports, newspapers, and Internet resources (websites, online forums, and listservs). Despite reflecting a diversity of viewpoints, these multiple sources converged on a few basic points.

Foremost among these was the incommunicability and outright confrontation that had shaped the recent history of Indian civil society. This cleavage was particularly present along the almost impermeable divides between its three main sectors: the "new social movements," which are identity movements such as the Dalit (formerly Untouchables) and Adivasi (indigenous peoples), as well as issue-based movements such as the environmental and gay and lesbian movements; the NGOs; and the mass organizations linked to Communist parties (e.g., unions, peasant, and women's organizations). I experienced some of the consequences of these conflicts in the elusive answers to my questions. At the same time, I found this situation extremely interesting as a researcher. The most frequently recurring explanation of the conflicts within the WSF India referred to the tension between the traditional Left of the Communist parties (and the organizations linked to those parties) and the new social movements and internationally funded NGOs (NGOs are frequently perceived as tools of Western imperialism). According to more militant activists, speculation and endless deliberation by new social movement and NGO activists, coupled with the liberal ideology of human rights, contributed to the perpetuation of the causes of domination and exploitation of the majority of the Indian population. These militants advocated instead for radical struggle against the class oppressor.

The conflicts traversing the WSF India seemed to flow from four main sources: ideological disposition, political positioning, past experiences, and personal incompatibilities. These struggles exploded around several objects of contention, including the office's information technology (IT) system and the contentious experiments with free software (see Caruso 2005b; Juris, Caruso, Couture, and Mosca, this volume). These conflicts had multiple and complex consequences for the WSF process in Mumbai, including for my own and everyone else's daily work, for my dissertation research, and for Indian civil society leaders who were involved in the WSF process. Negotiating the complex configurations of political, cultural, social, and personal frictions became the central feature of my daily engagement with the WSF, and it seemed only natural to make this the primary subject of my research. I discussed these ideas with friends, colleagues, and members of the Organizing Committee, and it seemed that reflecting on conflicts and ways to engage them would constitute a legitimate dissertation topic and a valuable contribution to the WSF. These conversations sparked the process that led to the development of the notion of transformative ethnography.

I engaged the question of how to faithfully report on the WSF process to contribute to both the work of WSF activists and to the academic debates on social movements and global transformation in the context of three intersecting movements. First, I was becoming increasingly aware of the implications of my positioning, as I perceived it and the way it was projected on me by those with whom I worked. Second, my research into and discussions about the nature and history of the relationships that surrounded me also continued. Third, I was beginning to think about the foundations of transformative ethnography as a mode of research. The following discussion of the challenges of reporting the outcome of my fieldwork in the Mumbai office has to be situated in this context.

CENTRAL AND PERIPHERAL CONFLICTS

When I arrived in Mumbai I asked about the tense atmosphere of the office. I was told that it was due to IT system failures that set those who advocated a technical solution (reverting to Microsoft Office) against those who supported free software for political reasons (see Juris, Caruso, Couture, and Mosca, this volume). The conflict was often attributed to a clash of personalities. But when the clashes became harsher, allegations of corruption ensued. It became clear that the issues at stake were much larger than the idiosyncrasy of interpersonal relationships or the kind of software used. The conflict soon escalated. Not only was the daily work of the office affected, but other issues that could have been opportunities for creative engagement were suppressed, stifled, and "managed." As pointed out above, conflicts have the tendency to make involved parties so self-absorbed that they are unable to adapt to their surroundings and they tend to create a hierarchy based on differential social, political, and cultural capital where one conflict rises above and denies reality to the others. These two features became central in my selection and reporting of the fieldwork material.

Once I decided that conflict would be a focus of my research, I began to ask myself and my coworkers how to make sense of the conflicts I encountered. The impression I shared with most of those I spoke with was that the cause of all the troubles, or at least most of them, was the confrontation between mass movements and NGO activists. Although the conflict was widely attributed to a simple clash of personalities, this seemed to be a communicative strategy to avoid the diffusion of conflict. Given the circumstances, it seemed to me that I should concentrate on the issues that attracted the most attention in both formal and informal conversations.

However, I soon realized that giving the most attention to the most apparent conflicts can severely misrepresent the dynamics at play. It can also contribute to the escalation of such conflicts, because focusing increasing attention on a singular aspect of a clash can make it less and less intelligible, blowing it out of proportion. By generating a dualistic discourse of good and evil, right and wrong, and, consequently, a polarized political discourse of "you are with us or against us," dynamics of alienation and marginalization are produced that further complicate efforts to resolve the conflict. I do not have sufficient space to detail all the conflicts I observed, but a few snapshots illustrate the difficulty of making sense of and reporting the conflicts without silencing those involved or privileging any specific interpretation of the matters of concern that are raised in a given social space.

Shortly after my arrival, I went with a member of the Youth Organizing Committee on a bus ride to the office of one of the organizations involved in the WSF process to discuss issues of urgency. After a seemingly successful meeting, my female companion let out a huge sigh and blurted out to me, "We do everything; without women this thing would not even happen." I nodded and waited for the response. In the next forty minutes she told me how she felt: that in the WSF men made decisions and women implemented them. But what seemed to upset her most was the fact that this was not recognized and efforts to address the situation often led to condescending responses. Indeed, male domination in the WSF process has been regularly denounced by activists and scholars (see Vargas 2003, 2005). Toward the end of the process a European staff member told me that in dealing with her daily tasks she had to ask male colleagues to engage in certain negotiations when she felt she was not paid any attention. I observed that she seemed very frustrated, and she responded that this had been going on since the very beginning and that it was not only the case with outsiders but also with Indian members of the WSF process. More-over, she said that she felt she was further discriminated against due to her being European.

Another activist, a Dalit, denounced the fact that almost all of those involved in the Youth Organizing Committee were upper-caste Hindus or Christians. Furthermore, they belonged to a few organizations subsumed under the same organizational structure and political ideology, namely internationally funded NGOs. In the same period, a conflict erupted between WSF organizers and a Muslim activist who protested that the WSF reinforced existing structures of caste, class, and religious marginalization that plagued Indian society. These are merely a few snapshots of some of the recurring frustrations that reflect the lack of acknowledgment of the role and work of women, youths, and volunteers; of the reproduction of systemic structures of marginalization; and of cultural, social, and religious differences whose creative potential was not taken advantage of and was even stifled for the sake of short-term organizational demands.

For its part, the conflict around the IT system attracted significant amounts of WSF activists' energy for two principal reasons. First, it was considered to be the crucial conflict tearing apart the WSF process. Second, it was considered the key conflict between NGOs and social movements of the Left that, once resolved, would produce a coherent movement that would ripple throughout India and generate an irresistible wave of institutional and social transformation. This provides the context for one final vignette. With the WSF event approaching and the IT system showing increasing instability, a set of major reconfigurations of the forum's technological architecture was implemented. New volunteers joined and disruptions decreased, but new complaints soon arose against the IT technicians who were considered incapable, arrogant, and unhelp-ful, leading to an atmosphere of increasing tension in the office.

One day, the office staff members were having lunch together while the system was down. Some suggested that they would have to go to an Inter-net café to complete their work. One of the new volunteers in charge of the IT system remarked, trying to lighten the situation so we would not com-plain too much, that now we were getting paid for doing nothing. Some-one mumbled that this was not the ethos of the WSF and definitely not the reason why we were here. However, another commented that maybe we should question the ethos of the WSF itself if the accusations of corrup-tion and unethical behavior that were circulating were even marginally true. Perhaps the techies were right; maybe we were the only ones who cared while "the bosses" spent their time bickering about personal and political rivalries. The evolution of this conflict illustrates the tendency of unattended (or mishandled) conflicts to escalate. In this case a political and ideological, and perhaps also a personal, conflict between members of the Indian Organizing Committee, office staff and volunteers, and free software activists escalated to the point where the ethics of the entire wsf process were questioned.

In response, informal mediation strategies were mobilized by all of those involved in the conflict. The most frequent strategies were "rants" (as we called them) through which we would take turns relieving our frustration. I took note of which of those strategies was most successful, under which conditions, and with whom. It was clear that a rant would be successful when it was not interrupted, when active and deep listening were constant, when the speaker was not challenged with counterarguments, and when the speaker was not offered prepackaged solutions. Other factors were relevant in the successful mediation of a critical situation, including gender relations, age, power balance, caste, ethnicity, social background, as well as personal beliefs and prejudices.

One of my most complex fieldwork situations took place shortly before the forum. In early January, an intense confrontation arose between two camps of staff and volunteers. Some non-Indian volunteers had joined the process to deal with an issue of vital importance to the overall wsf event, and they felt that insufficient support was provided to them from either the office coordination or the office staff. The confrontation escalated to the point that the non-Indian volunteers protested by throwing office furniture out of a window. This story was conveyed to me by Indians who were outraged by the behavior of "Europeans" (as the Indians referred to them with contempt) trying to teach the Indians how to do their job, demonstrating a lack of humility and inability to understand that "here" things were done differently. When the non-Indian volunteers had initially arrived they were full of hope and excitement, whereas those who had been worn out by the months of tensions were struggling to work at least ten hours a day. Cultural and political misunderstandings between the two camps contributed to the inevitable and devastating implosion.

While I was trying to make sense of the often intolerant words hurled from all sides, I asked myself what would have happened had the wsf India process given more proactive support to the parties in conflict rather than underplaying the conflicts (e.g., by blaming them on personal clashes), or trying to stifle them (by avoiding mention of the reasons for the conflict and emphasizing instead that "we were all allies"), or attempting to manage them in the best interests of the collective (as perceived by authoritative and at times even authoritarian leaders). Such a lack of institutional awareness of conflict dynamics contributed to the incidents I have reported and cultivated a sense of disillusionment and disappointment in most of those who began reflecting on the outcome of the overall process. In all this I was not immune to stress, exhaustion, and uneasy personal feelings about those tensions and the actors involved. How was I to make sense of these conflicts? How was I to make sense of the WSF as a catalyst of a new culture of transformative politics?

In the field transformative ethnographers aim to overcome the limitations in the prevailing practices of conflict management. They refrain from explaining the reasons for conflict or second-guessing the actors involved out of awareness that rational interpretations do not always (if ever) apply to profoundly emotional interactions. Ethnographers refrain from interpreting motivations, implications, and behaviors; they eschew problem-solving approaches that provide their collaborators with pre-packaged solutions. Further they try to be impartial or at least aware of the implications of taking political and personal sides in the conflict and the wider social networks in which the conflict is situated. Ethnographers also consider the personal and political implications of attempting, or siding with, hegemonic approaches to managing differences and conflicts.

Subsequently, in reporting, theorizing, and writing about differences, conflicts, and broader social, cultural, and political issues, ethnographers carefully refer to these issues as matters of concern, treating them as contributions to the collaborative design of theoretical maps without imposing theoretical decisions with respect to controversial issues. Indeed, conflicts are, after all, conflicts among people who mobilize rational and emotional dynamics, worldviews, moral values, and social, cultural, and political relations. Moreover, the sensibility to conflict and its hidden dynamics, which are gained through the insights of transformative mediation, contribute to generating an ethnographic report of conflicts and dynamics that are not immediately evident in a given activist network. This gives voice to a multiplicity of actors who might otherwise be silenced by the roaring thunder of hegemonic conflicts, while simultaneously contributing to public debates around issues that might otherwise be obscured.

CONCLUSION

When I entered the Mumbai office my research methods were those I had developed in a completely different context during fieldwork in the Peruvian Amazon among the Shipibo-Conibo (Caruso 2005a). These were informed by a few basic suggestions given to me by a professor as he shook my hand and wished me good luck before departing Rome for the Amazonian rainforest. These went something like this: never interrupt a speaker, and when they stop, wait and then wait some more before following up on what they are saying; do not ask irrelevant questions from a questionnaire; note down all you see, and if you cannot note it down immediately tell it to yourself so that you can be aware of what you are observing; and during an interview, the person you are conversing with and the setting are the only things that matter. Later I found that the assumptions and values on which those suggestions were based were consistent with the values and vision of the wsf, and with the transformative framework developed by Bush and Folger (2005).

The tensions in the Mumbai wsf office created an atmosphere of volatility, sapping energy and contributing to escalating conflict, frustration, and, ultimately, disaffection with the wsf, colleagues, and fellow volunteers. These difficulties generated, and were generated by, communication breakdowns between activists. They were influenced by the political configuration and incommunicability that characterized Indian civil society (Caruso 2004), but they were also caused by the unique individual histories and political and ideological dispositions represented in the wsf office. A sophisticated and facilitated process of internal communication could have enhanced democratic practices in the wider wsf as well as participation and ownership on the part of activists not directly engaged in the wsf's organization. Moreover, democratic practices based on participation and ownership rather than representation and delegation are crucial to the wsf vision.

However, these conflicts also generated creative tensions within the office as well as camaraderie among office volunteers and employees. We spent long hours interacting in the office and comingling in "intercontinental" parties during many evenings. In moments of particular stress, mainly due to IT system breakdowns, we would come back to the office at night where technicians would work on the system while the rest of us would sing, share our life stories, and eventually fall asleep on the tables, couches, or the floor. The emotional intensity of the human relationships that developed (Goodwin, Jasper, and Polletta 2001), particularly given the significance of the WSF and the stress related to organizing such an important event, was crucial for negotiating the new alliances that the WSF promised to facilitate. The WSF was taking shape through a dynamic of conflict. The model of transformative ethnography outlined here was specifically shaped by the direct and indirect effects that such conflicts had on me and the space I inhabited. Engaging these conflicts on a daily basis, working in such a vibrant environment, and writing about my experiences was difficult at times. However, my commitment to the WSF, my engagement with its complexities, and my theoretical and personal disposition toward transformative practices, together with my experience with other social movements and other ethnographic field sites, influenced the nature of my fieldwork in Mumbai and helped me to develop my posture as what I now refer to as a transformative ethnographer within the WSF.

The tensions in the WSF between knowledge performance and social transformation, between theory and practice, and between activism and research suggest incommensurable positions based on dualistic conceptions of the world. Contextualizing knowledge relations through (transformative) ethnographic presence and writing might allow for the construction of a more satisfying theory of human organization and transformation. Direct engagement in activist networks provides an opportunity to address feelings, emotions, rationalizations, and experiences of knowledge and transformation as well as the conflicts they involve. Direct engagement also has political implications related to exposing the hegemonic processes that take place in activist spaces and are hidden behind conflicts as well as contributing to the potential shifting of attention and reformulation of political formations. An extractive "god's-eye-view" approach to data collection and computation in order to generate overarching social theory has proven to be fundamentally disconnected from the world it wishes to order and explain. I have advanced a proposal for a collaborative transformative ethnography that complements practices of investigation and transformation by engaging with them at the intersection of converging networks of values, relationships, and intentional practices of change.

Transformative ethnography's principles and communicative techniques are not the exclusive domain of either transformative mediators or transformative ethnographers. Other widely acknowledged arenas where such models and practices are common include therapy, counseling, and teaching, and they resonate with the fieldwork and interview methods of qualitative researchers more generally. Transformative ethnographers, by allowing their interlocutors to talk about themselves, can help them shed further light on their thoughts and reflections regarding issues of personal concern. In the process, transformative ethnographers can also make sense of the dynamics, motivations, and rationales involved in the fostering of a truly collaborative mode of transformative research and activism. This kind of ethnographic description and analysis can also help activists become aware of and think through issues underlying conflicts. In so doing, transformative ethnographers can contribute to the timely engagement and resolution of conflicts and, consequently, to more effective organizing. Transformative practices, in ethnography and in the WSF, built on the premises I have discussed, might specifically contribute to the epistemological struggle engaged by and within the WSF by contributing to new forms of critical pedagogy that generate inclusive, critical, and dialogical theories and practices of the global and, in so doing, have a role in shaping a truly emancipatory cosmopolitan society built on recognition, equality, and justice (see Santos 2004). Transformative ethnography, by contributing to debates both among transnational activists and in other public spheres, can be an instrument of social transformation by positioning itself in the midst of multiple networks of relations that shape processes of social transformation.

NOTES

1 WSF, Charter of Principles, August 6, 2002, www.forumsocialmundial.org.br (accessed December 25, 2011).
2 Ibid.
3 In this context *impartiality* is not the same thing as *objectivity* (meaning truth deriving from standing above or suppressing subjective positioning). Rather, impartiality seeks to maximize the possibility for all actors involved to object to what is said about them and to extend the debate to those with stakes in the matters of concern engaged by the ethnographer (see Latour 2000; Mosse 2005).
4 All names are pseudonyms unless otherwise indicated.
5 I had several close friends who were activists in different sectors of Indian civil society and who knew all the stories I was expected to know. Long conversations with them were crucial to my learning the idiom of Indian activism.

10

Activist Ethnography and Translocal Solidarity

PAUL ROUTLEDGE

For the past sixteen years I have been engaged in forms of ethnography that blur the boundaries between academia and activism, enacting a "third space" of critical collaborative engagement with resisting others (Routledge 1996b).[1] Such an approach is located within, and inspired by, a broader field of collaborative, activist approaches to research within the social sciences, not least those inspired by feminism (see Escobar 2008; Kobayashi 1994; Lamphere 2004; Lassiter 2005; Mohanty 2003; Naples 2003; Nast 1994; Riles 2000; Sanford and Angel-Ajani 2006; Scheper-Hughes 1995). For example, I have participated in direct action against motorway construction in Glasgow, Scotland (Routledge 1997); conducted workshops with, and collected information for, environmental activists in Goa, India (Routledge 2002); participated in antidam resistance camps along the Narmada River in India (Routledge 2003c); and facilitated activist meetings and organized activist conferences and workshops in various localities in Bangladesh, Nepal, Sri Lanka, and Thailand (Routledge 2008). Recently I have chosen to enact such strategies within "global justice networks" (Routledge and Cumbers 2009), and have conducted ongoing solidarity work with activists in various parts of the United Kingdom, South Asia, and Southeast Asia.

My approach is similar to Jeffrey Juris's notion of "militant ethnography," a research strategy that involves politically engaged and committed research that is practice-based and conducted in horizontal collaboration with social movements (Juris 2007, 2008a). An activist approach to ethnography implies an immersion in the field—in the various sites of research or places of encounter—and an immersion in the practices one is researching (Plows 2008). This necessitates critical engagement with resisting others in specific places that constitute embodied "terrains of resistance" (Routledge 1993). As I will argue, activist ethnography implies a concern with action, reflection, and empowerment (of oneself and others) in order to challenge oppressive power relations. It is about forging solidarity with resisting others through critical collaboration. An activist ethnography entails making certain active political commitments to a moral and political philosophy of social, political-economic, and environmental justice. Research is directed toward conforming to that commitment and toward helping to realize the values that lie at its root (Chatterton, Fuller, and Routledge 2008; Routledge 2009). In what follows, I discuss a range of engagements with activist ethnography involving the forging of solidarities with activist others in diverse geographical settings around multiple justice issues.[2] I first develop an analysis of processes of solidarity creation before going on to discuss their grounding in various places of encounter with resisting others.

FORGING SOLIDARITIES

I consider solidarity to be a practice and process of working together with proximate and distant others engaged in struggles for social, political, economic, and environmental justice. Solidarity is considered less altruistic (i.e., based on the worthiness of and sympathy toward the suffering of others) than reciprocal (i.e., when activists in different groups draw connections between the suffering of others and their own plights or claims). It is also based on shared dreams and desires, as well as threats or harm suffered, as a consequence of common identities between activists, where identity is dynamic, contingent, contested, and socially constructed and coconstituted with capitalism (Reitan 2007, 20–21).

Solidarities are forged out of the collective articulations of different place-based struggles and are constituted as the varied interconnections, relations, and practices between participants (Featherstone 2005). They are part of the ongoing connections, social and material relations, articulations, and negotiations between places and place-based struggles.

In particular, what requires negotiation is the politics of extension and translation of place-based interests and experiences in order for common ground (e.g., shared antagonisms) and productive connections to be generated between different place-based communities and organizations (Katz 2001; see also Featherstone 2003, 2008).

Certainly, shared notions of (in)justice can inform the practice of solidarity, potentially creating a common ground that enables different themes to be interconnected, and different political actors from different struggles and cultural contexts to join together in common struggle (della Porta et al. 2006). However, this must negotiate the problem of how place-based concerns transcend their locality to form common ground on which solidarities can be constructed. An initial requirement for the construction of such solidarities has been the forging of *convergence spaces* (Cumbers, Routledge, and Nativel 2008; Routledge 2003a). In convergence spaces groups can meet one another, exchange experiences, and plan collective strategies, such as the alternative conferences and global days of action during international summit meetings.

Places of (activist-ethnographic) encounter generate connections, however momentary, that serve as a basis for the construction of solidarities. Connections open us to myriad potential ways of being and feeling. They open our capacities to be affected through our engagements with, and work alongside of, others. This in turn requires thinking about power relations across space, adopting a relational perspective (Massey 1994). Indeed, the theorizing of ethnography has been enriched through implicit and explicit engagements with geographical notions of (relational) space and place (Burawoy et al. 2000; Gupta and Ferguson 1997b; Marcus 1998). This scholarship conceives of space and place as embodied practices and processes of production that are simultaneously material and discursive. Places are understood as always formed through relations with wider processes and other places, and their particularities arise through interrelations between objects, events, places, and identities (Massey 1994). Because ethnographic research can critically analyze these connections and interrelations between places and people, it helps to contribute to new perspectives on the possibilities and challenges of social change and the forging of solidarities.

Doreen Massey (2004, 2005) has recast the politics of place by considering how political intervention on the local scale might develop against global processes such as neoliberalism. She uses the phrase *geographies of responsibility* to make the point that, because places are relational and social relations flow through them, connecting us up increasingly to distant others in complex ways, we should think more about the political impacts, both positive and negative, of our own actions and interventions locally, wherever "local" happens to be (Massey 2004). Therefore, I am concerned with the roles that activist ethnography can play in the forging of translocal solidarities.

I use the term *translocal solidarity* to refer to the connections, relations, and campaigns between different placed-based (but not place-restricted) social movements and other grassroots actors. This is in preference to the term *transnational solidarity*, which elides the specificity of the particular places in, and from, which collective action emerges and operates. The practice of activist ethnography opens up potentials and problems for the forging of solidarities: it can facilitate social transformation; it can nurture a politics of affinity; it must negotiate power relations; it engages with emotions; and it can contribute to the development of relational ethics (see Chatterton, Fuller, and Routledge 2008; Routledge 2009). In what follows, I ground these arguments with reference to selected placed engagements with social movements and activist collectives with whom I have worked during the past decade. As noted in the introduction, such engagements are networked in the sense that they are sensitive to the complex meanings, flows, and dynamics that attend place-based encounters.

ACTIVIST ETHNOGRAPHIES

The first potential of activist ethnography is concerned with the development of practices aimed at social transformation rather than merely the production of knowledge or the solving of local problems. This recognizes that social movements are self-reflexive, producing their own knowledges (see Casas-Cortés, Osterweil, and Powell, this volume; Juris 2008a; Melucci 1989), and that an important element of ethnographic engagement is to move beyond the acquisition, cataloguing, ordering, and publishing of information and toward jointly producing knowledge with resisting others to yield critical interpretations and readings of the world that are accessible, understandable to all those involved, and actionable (Chatterton, Fuller, and Routledge 2008; Kelty 2008).

For example, since 2009 I have been involved (as a participant) in a translocal initiative concerning climate justice called So We Stand,[3] whose members include environmental justice activists, popular educators, community organizers, artists, and academics located in Glasgow, Edinburgh, and London. So We Stand uses popular education methods to support communities and workers who are concerned with, and are organizing around, issues of poverty and environmental justice. So We Stand is also concerned with taking direct action on environmental justice issues alongside such groups. In particular, So We Stand has been concerned with the social and environmental effects of transport infrastructure (such as airports) and extractive industries (such as open-cast coal mining); investigating climate change mitigation as an extension of existing environmental justice struggles; and focusing its efforts on those communities marginalized through class and racial injustices.

One of the ways I have worked with So We Stand to effect social transformation has been through popular education. Popular education practice adopts a politically explicit stance on the side of the poor, developing a knowledge base from, and out of, people's struggles. It actively uses Paolo Freire's (2000) work, mobilizing dialogic action in order to engage with the everyday lives and knowledges of the poor in order to coproduce understandings of the realities they face.[4]

On a cold, wet Saturday in Linnvale, Glasgow, on November 29, 2009, a group of thirty antipoverty activists from the Clydebank and Easterhouse communities met for a day-long workshop called the "Gathering under the Flightpath." The event had been organized by So We Stand to begin to address the lives of people in working-class communities who live in Linnvale and Clydebank, and who are affected by the noise and air pollution caused by their proximity to Glasgow's airport. A variety of games were used at the workshop to (1) draw connections between climate change and poverty; (2) address people's fears and concerns concerning the health effects of pollution and poverty; (3) highlight gaps in people's knowledges about one another's lives and struggles; and (4) search for common alternatives to the problems faced by the different activist constituencies. A key element of the workshop was the generation of a code.

We sat in a circle and discussed a photograph that the workshop facilitator had presented to us of a typical urban street scene in the United Kingdom. The image was of a street scene. In the background was a supermarket. Several women there were carrying full shopping bags, but had grim faces. To the left, a young man sat on the ground with an upturned hat on the floor in front of him. In the left-hand corner of the image a man was speaking into a mobile phone. At one point we began talking about how we thought the people in the photograph felt, which led to a conversation about our own feelings and explanations with regard to the rampant consumerism, poverty, unhappiness, and lack of fulfillment in society. Ultimately we began to envision what we as a group could do to change such a reality. The photograph—and the discussion it generated—was an example of a popular education tool called the "code." A code can be a photograph, diagram, film, theater performance, or other artifact that deals with a concrete situation that a particular community is familiar with and has strong feelings about. Codes are tools that attempt to make the familiar world unfamiliar to people and thereby generate thought, analysis, and action. A code contains opposing elements, is neither too explicit nor too mysterious, avoids sloganeering, and is designed to stimulate activists' thoughts and feelings. Dialogue about the particular issues that the code evokes in people works from the common ground established between activists and by their ability to learn from the differences of experience, knowledge, and so on embodied in So We Stand. The code is an example of a decolonizing method of ethnographic practice, and the workshop served as the beginning of a process to jointly produce understandings of climate change and its relation to poverty and social marginalization between the different constituencies of climate justice and antipoverty activists.

A second potential of activist ethnography is that it can nurture a politics of affinity with others. There is, of course, a rich lineage to this kind of approach in the social sciences. Inspired by politics rooted in anarchism, Marxism, feminism, and other critical movements, academics from the 1960s onward have attempted to facilitate the direct involvement of social scientists in the solving of social problems (Bunge 1971; Burawoy et al. 2000; Farrow, Moss, and Shaw 1995; hooks 1991; Mohanty 2003; Nast 1994).

The connections and affinities forged with resisting others form a key part of activist ethnographic research, implying a common identification of problems and desires among groups or individuals committed to social change, as well as a desire to work together to confront and reverse a set of issues that have a common effect on all the people concerned (Chatterton, Fuller, and Routledge 2008). Practically, affinity consists of a group of people who share common ground and who can provide supportive, sympathetic spaces for its members to articulate, listen to one another, and share concerns, emotions, hopes, and fears. The politics of affinity enables people to provide support and solidarity for one another. Ideally, such a politics of research should be built on consensus decision making, which is nonhierarchical and participatory and embodies flexible and fluid modes of action. The common values and beliefs articulated through a politics of affinity constitute a "structure of feeling" (Williams 1977), resting on collective experiences and interpretations that are cooperative rather than competitive and predicated on taking political action. The development of such affinities is an important element in the practice of mutual solidarity, that is, constructing the grievances and aspirations of geographically and culturally different people as always interlinked (Olesen 2005a).

Mutual solidarity enables connections to be drawn that extend beyond the local and particular by recognizing and respecting differences between people while also recognizing similarities (e.g., people's aspirations). Mutual solidarity is also about imagining global subjectivities through similarities of experience, recognizing the shared opportunities and techniques of struggle (see Cunningham 1999; Starr 2005). Putting mutual solidarity into practice means coproducing contextually relevant knowledges that are useful and accessible to groups in their struggles, and which may be more readily used and understood by the general public.

For example, in May 2004, while working as a facilitator for and ethnographer of Peoples' Global Action Asia, the alter-globalization network of Asian social movements,[5] I helped to organize with others a week-long activist conference in Dhaka, Bangladesh. The conference saw the convergence of 150 delegates from Bangladesh, India, Nepal, Thailand, Malaysia, Philippines, and Vietnam representing forty-six grassroots peasant movements (of farmers, fisherfolk, indigenous people, women, and laborers). Activists presented testimonies of their movements' struggles; workshops and plenaries were held on a variety of issues to facilitate discussion and generate usable knowledge for activists;[6] activists exchanged information and devoted time to formulating a range of possible issue-based campaigns; and language-based group discussions were held on the operational processes and strategic coordination within the network.

The purpose of the conference was to generate deeper interpersonal ties and commonalities between different activists from different cultural spaces and struggles, and in so doing, provide supportive sympathetic spaces for activists to articulate grievances and hopes, and develop soli-

darity and the mobilization of collective resources between different social movements in Asia. Some months after the conference, I undertook
ethnographic research in Asia with those activists who had attended. My
purpose was to listen to activists' views and experiences of the conference
in order to examine its efficacy in terms of its goals and to feed this back
into the network for discussion in the hope of improving future network
practices (see Routledge 2008).

What became clear was that the experience had been (largely) a positive one for activists. Communication between different people from different struggles and cultural realities had enabled the creation of common
ground among activists, which was a necessary precursor to the development of mutual solidarity, as explained by a Nepali participant: "Dhaka
provided a forum to share our work and experiences with others in different parts of Asia, others who have similar problems to us. We were able to
share political views and to identify our common ground. The local and
the national are not enough because globalization has intensified the exploitation process across the world. We need to develop global solidarity"
(personal interview, September 23, 2004). Moreover, activists' positionality in relation to others could be reassessed, as a participating Thai activist noted: "There was a real chance for exchange between activists. When
we meet face-to-face it breaks down the borders between us, and generates collective strength to make change" (personal interview, October 15,
2004).

The connections made between peoples (such as through the learning about others' struggles and testimonies) also helped to amplify
people's feelings and emotions (e.g., of anger, passion, and empathy) into
a sense of collective solidarity (see Jasper 1998; Juris 2008b; Mansbridge
and Morris 2001; Polletta 2002). Such solidarities can potentially form a
"chain of equivalence" or new "common sense" through shared identities and shared senses of threat, suffering, and hope (Laclau and Mouffe
1985; Reitan 2007). Creating common ground with resisting others can
highlight and ground differences (in language, ethnicity, power, access to
resources, etc.) in particular ways, potentially uniting differences in solidarity against shared enemies and addressing mutual concerns while also
providing material meeting points of constructed equivalence between
the diverse multiplicities that make up different movements. The building
of such equivalences is a process of ongoing negotiation, an engagement
of political practices and imaginations in which ground is sought where

struggles can construct common cause (Massey 2005). Nevertheless, any consideration of affinity and solidarity requires an examination of the power relations that exist between collaborators, often revealed through the ethnographic encounter.

A third consideration for activist-ethnographers is that they must be attentive to and negotiate problematic power relations that exist between (research) collaborators. It is crucial to theorize and negotiate both the differences in power between collaborators and the connections forged through such collaboration, and it is important to note that these differences in power are almost always diverse and entangled. For example, many of the networking tasks in Peoples' Global Action Asia devolved to a small number of key actors or *imagineers*, such as myself, who sustained the network through our interaction and personal communication (see Cumbers, Routledge, and Navitel 2008; Routledge and Cumbers 2009; Routledge, Cumbers, and Navitel 2007; see also Juris 2008a). Imagineers conducted much of the routine (international) organizational work of networks, helping to organize conferences, mobilize resources, and facilitate communication and information flows between movements and between movement offices and grassroots communities. We also attempted to ground the concept or imaginary of the network (what it was, how it worked, what it was attempting to achieve) within the grassroots communities who comprised the membership of the participant movements. Because of our structural positions, communication skills, and experience in activism and meeting facilitation, we tended to wield disproportionate power and influence within the network. For instance, there was an overreliance on the imagineers to instigate events and raise funds (Routledge and Cumbers 2009).

While solidarities are forged to challenge unequal power relations (manifested locally, nationally, and globally), in practice the operational processes of the network frequently involved significant power differences—due to differences in resource access among activists (see Eschle and Maiguashca 2007; Rai 2003). As one of the imagineers in the network, I had more capacity to direct the course of network relations than the majority of grassroots activists. As an activist ethnographer from a Scottish university, I had the time and resources to travel outside my home country, unlike the majority of poor peasants who comprised the membership of the social movements who participated in the network. I also possessed the cultural capital of higher education and the social capital inherent in my transnational connections and access to resources and knowledge (see Juris 2008a; Missingham 2003).

Such power inequalities created a sense of dependency within the network on imagineers and impaired the full involvement of grassroots communities within the network. A Thai activist in the Assembly of the Poor (a participant in Peoples' Global Action Asia) noted, "Activists in the North have more skills, knowledge, and higher levels of education and therefore they tend to dominate the process. They guide the process, often with goodwill, but they have the advantages of resources, power, and strategy. I have worked with Focus on the Global South, Via Campesina, the World Social Forum, the Asia Social Forum, trade unions, women's groups, and NGOs. It is the same everywhere. The Northern activists provide the analysis and control the process; the Southern activists provide the testimony" (personal interview, November 3, 2004). Hence, collaborations between activist ethnographers and others are neither relationships of difference articulated through an objectifying distance, nor relationships of sameness based on entirely commensurate backgrounds, interests, and ambitions. As Gillian Rose argues, "situating knowledge through [hypothetical] transparent reflexivity gives no space to understanding across difference" (1997, 313). Rather than map distance and difference between distinctly separate agents, activist-ethnographers ask how difference, regarding power relations, for instance, is constituted, tracing its destabilizing emergence during the research process itself.

Ultimately, the negotiation of unequal power relations means working with groups to uncover structures of power to empower people to take control of their own lives. While the inequalities that accrued to the existence of the imagineers, though acknowledged, were never satisfactorily addressed, other power inequalities were. For example, during the conference in Dhaka, I helped to organize and facilitate workshops on gender inequality and discrimination during which differences between participants generated antagonisms that could be addressed as part of the ongoing constitution of the Peoples' Global Action Asia network.

Moreover, in the collaborative politics of affinity, power accrues to different people at different times, depending on the context. Activist ethnographers are frequently in a position of power by virtue of their ability to name the categories, control information about the research agenda, define interventions, and indeed to come and go as so-called research scientists. Yet, because power circulates in relations of empowerment and disempowerment, there are still certain powers that accrue to research subjects within the research process, ones that might empower as well as disempower the activist-ethnographer.

For example, I have recently been working on issues of climate change and food sovereignty with one of the participants in the Peoples' Global Action Asia network, the Bangladesh Krishok Federation, the largest rural-based peasant movement in the country, with seven hundred thousand members, which has been involved for the past twenty years in land-occupation struggles. The conducting of activist ethnography here is in part dependent on information, research contacts, advice, and the good graces of my collaborators, who have significant influence within the collaboration process. Acknowledging this entails a shift of power from the ethnographer to his or her collaborators. While ethnography usually entails at least some intentional disruption of people's lives brought about by the ethnographer's intrusion into others' lifeworlds (see England 1994), it is important to remember that activists are fully capable of locating the activity of intellectuals in their broader strategies and agendas. Hence my work in Bangladesh (and subsequently in the United Kingdom) has been in part directed toward longer-term movement goals, such as organizing a caravan through the country on the issue of land rights, food sovereignty, and climate change that took place in 2011.

Some of my Bangladeshi collaborators are also empowered in other contexts. They are educated, middle class, and come from the more privileged sectors of their society. They too have their own material advantages within Bangladeshi society (e.g., access to computers, resources, the courts, contacts in media, the ability to travel), which they use to facilitate their activist work. Just as "we need to listen, contextualize, and admit to the power we bring to bear as multiply-positioned authors in the research process" (Nast 1994, 59), we also need to be attentive to the power that our collaborators bring to the research process.

A fourth consideration of activist ethnography is the engagement with emotion, not least because transformative encounters based on solidarity often emerge from our deep emotional responses to the world, as feminists, among others, have argued (see, e.g., Bosco 2006, 2007; Ettlinger 2004; Ettlinger and Bosco 2004; Goodwin, Jasper, and Polletta 2001; Jasper 1998; Juris 2008b; Mansbridge and Morris 2001; Taylor and Rupp 2002). Politically, emotions, which are intimately bound up with relations and affinity, are a means of initiating action. We become politically active because we feel something profoundly, such as social injustice or ecological destruction. This emotion triggers changes in us that motivate us to engage in politics, and it is our ability to transform our feelings about the world into actions that inspires us to participate in political action (see Chatterton, Fuller, and Routledge 2008; Routledge 2009). As feminist geographers and others have argued, collaborative association with (activist) others necessitates interaction with others, through the doing of particular actions and the experiencing of personal and collective emotions, through creativity and imagination, and through embodied, relational practices that produce political effects (see Anderson and Smith 2001; Bennett 2004; Bosco 2007; Pulido 2003).

Thus, emotions are both reactive (directed toward outsiders and external events) and reciprocal (concerning people's feelings toward each other). Shared emotions of activism create shared collective identities and are mobilized strategically (e.g., to generate motivation, commitment, and sustained participation). Activists create shared emotional templates in order to find common cause, and to generate common narratives and solidarities (see Bosco 2006, 2007; Juris 2008b). For example, during the protests against the G8 at Gleneagles, Scotland, in 2005 (see Daro, this volume), I participated as an activist-ethnographer in the Clandestine Insurgent Rebel Clown Army (CIRCA), a translocal initiative involving affinity groups from various parts of the United Kingdom, Ireland, and mainland Europe, to combine nonviolent direct action with the techniques of clowning (see Routledge 2005, 2010, 2012; see also Daro, this volume). As Juris (2008b) argues, protests operate by transforming emotions: they amplify an initiating emotion such as anger and channel or transmit it into a sense of collective solidarity (see, e.g., Henderson 2008).

CIRCA consisted of an army of clowns, replete with clown makeup, deconstructed military uniforms, and a range of learned clowning repertoires, games, and maneuvers that were deployed during the G8 protests. The purpose was to introduce a disruptive emotional intervention in order to communicate messages of opposition to the G8 and to alter the emotional dynamic of protests. The main target of protestors is a public that can potentially be mobilized rather than decision makers (Doherty, Plows, and Wall 2007). As a result, CIRCA's strategy was to acknowledge the vulnerability of activists as well as people's fear and concerns during protest events and in the climate of tension generated by the war on terror. Part of this strategy was also to transform fear through laughter, play, and ridicule.

Instead of battling the police and security at the G8 meeting—the by now familiar choreography of global days of action protests—rebel clowns actively sought to undermine and ridicule the intimidation and provocation of security forces at demonstrations. Rebel clowns blew kisses to riot cops behind shields and followed the evidence-gathering teams around, preventing them from conducting their surveillance by both idolizing police gear (e.g., uniforms) and hogging the lenses of police cameras, particularly when the police were attempting to film other protesters. When the police lined the streets to pen in the demonstrators, rebel clowns would intersperse themselves between the police officers and mimic and exaggerate their behavior. In order to mock the stop-and-search so-called antiterrorist laws, which have regularly been used to intimidate protesters, CIRCA "clownbatants" filled their pockets with deliberately ridiculous objects, such as strings of sausages, feather dusters, underwear, rubber ducks, and sex toys. In the event of a stop and search by the police, such items had to be laid out on the street and documented by the police. The emotional work of the rebel clowns was relational, exceeding the individual, creating emotional resonance between rebel clowns, between the clowns and other activists, and between the clowns and the public.

Playful confrontation exaggerated and inverted the social order, recontextualizing it in order to reveal its absurdity and invite others (such as the public) to reconsider it. By changing the context of policed protest spaces, intimidatory spaces get temporarily transformed through the laugh of recognition, creating empathic bonds between protestors. For example, some activists at the G8 protests commented after the event that the presence of CIRCA had helped diffuse tense situations at certain times and in certain places. Speaking about the demonstration to close down the nuclear submarine base in Faslane, Scotland, one activist noted to us,

> There had been a real sense of intimidation and threat from the
> police at the base during the early part of the morning. This all
> changed when you clowns turned up. The police didn't know how
> to respond to you. There was that hilarious moment when a group
> of clowns crept up behind a police chief and started following him
> around copying his movements. Every time he turned around they

would all freeze until he turned back and continued walking. We were all cracking up laughing. You really changed the atmosphere at the base. (Personal communication, July 4, 2005)

However, an activist ethnography also must provide critical interpretations of such emotional dynamics in order to generate political practices that can be more effective. Emotions such as anger can be a prime motivator for some activists (not least because it is a dominant emotional response to perceived economic and environmental injustices, and one that is also present and expressed at many protests, not least those against the G8) (Henderson 2008). Certainly, CIRCA's politics of ridicule and play generated deep emotional bonds between rebel clown activists, and the many rebel clown activists with whom I interacted viewed their interventions at the G8 protests largely positively. However, the absence of displays of anger by rebel clown activists was read by some protestors as a contravention of the "appropriate" emotional behavior at such an event and a breach of collective solidarity. Moreover, key elements of rebel clowning such as the deconstructed uniforms, clown faces, and clowning maneuvers set the clowns apart from everyone else at the protest. The emotional response from some activists toward CIRCA was one of annoyance and even anger. Under such circumstances, an activist-ethnographic sensibility provided important critical perspectives on the activities of CIRCA by paying particular attention to the embodied practices and emotions of working with others, in terms of both the performative character of activist subjectivities and the content and affect of activists' public performances.

A final consideration of activist ethnography is that of working with a relational ethics. Ethical considerations raise crucial questions concerning the role concepts of social (in)justice play in ethnographic research, and the extent to which ethical conduct is desirable, definable, and/or enforceable in the practice of ethnography (Scheper-Hughes 1995). For example, during 1999 and 2000, I conducted ethnographic research in collaboration with the Narmada Bachao Andolan (Save the Narmada Movement, NBA), a peasant-based social movement that had been conducting resistance against the construction of dams along the Narmada River in India since 1985 (Routledge 2003a). The NBA had a history of welcoming academics to its struggle from both India and the rest of the world as a way to educate others about the plight of its members, enabling a further circulation of action and solidarity.

While visiting the Narmada valley, I was asked by one of the movement leaders to draw up a set of ethical protocols to be applied to future visiting academics who wished to conduct research on, or with, the movement. The request came about because activists in the movement believed that certain academic publications had been critical of the NBA's structure, organization, and gender relations. The movement felt betrayed and undermined by those whom they had considered collaborators. This was accentuated by the movement's self-perception as underdogs against very powerful state and capitalist institutions. To prevent this from happening again, movement activists decided to apply a set of rules to visiting academics.

I complied with the request, seeing it as an opportunity to use some of my intellectual training to contribute to the movement and to improve the research practices conducted with activists. The protocols I drew up were neither particularly controversial nor original, and stated that (1) researchers should send their previous work to the movement when asking for permission to do research with them; (2) researchers should collaborate with the NBA on the types of research to be conducted once in the field; (3) researchers should engage in some form of collaboration with the NBA while in the field in addition to their personal research; and (4) all research concerning the NBA should be shared with the movement before being submitted for publication. These protocols seemed ethically sound to me. However, the NBA activist who had asked me to prepare the protocols saw them as a means of censoring future academic work with which the movement disagreed. My (unwitting) participation in potential academic censorship raised ethical questions concerning criticality and collaborative research with resisting others (Routledge 2003b).

In this volume's introduction Jeffrey Juris and Alex Khasnabish note that engaged ethnography can provide important critical understandings to help activists overcome obstacles to effective organizing. For example, activist ethnography can serve as a form of vigilance against the emergence of internal hierarchies, the silencing of dissent, peer pressure, and even violence within social movements. Activist ethnography can also demonstrate how various forces of hegemony are internalized, reproduced, echoed, and traced. Ideally, an activist ethnography would enter into dialogue with social movement collaborators about these issues, mindful of the balance between constructive criticism of social movements and how those critiques might be used by social movements' opponents. Consequently, academic critiques of the NBA (e.g., concerning gender relations within the movement) were seen by the movement as undermining its struggle and providing its opponents (such as government officials) with arguments to use against it.

Laura Pulido (2003) argues that there are benefits to cultivating a dialogue about ethics in political activism. First, we cultivate relations of honesty, truth, and interpersonal acknowledgment, so it is important for activist-ethnographers to be open about their dual positionalities when collaborating with others. Second, cultivating a dialogue helps scholars become more fully conscious human beings, in that, while political consciousness is distinguished by its focus on structures, practices, and social relations of societal and global power, self-consciousness refers to self-knowledge, including the understanding of one's past and present; one's motivations, desires, fears, and needs; and one's relationship to the larger world—hence nurturing a politics of both affinity and relationality.

The ethics of activist ethnography are relational and contextual, a product of reciprocity between collaborators, and negotiated in practice. Relational-ethical positionalities are required for dignity, self-determination, and empowerment, acknowledging that any collaborative "we" constitutes the performance of multiple lived worlds and an entangled web of power relationships. This contrasts with Habermasian notions of consensus reached through dialogue that is decided by the most persuasive argument, because a relational ethics acknowledges the plurality of voices and positionalities that comprise political collaborations.

Collaboration enables what J. K. Gibson-Graham (1994) termed a "partial identification" between ourselves and resisting others, as well as an articulation of a temporary common ground wherein relations of difference and power (e.g., concerning gender, age, ethnicity, class, and sexuality) are negotiated across distances of culture, space, and positionality in the search for mutual understanding. A relational ethics is based on the notion of difference in relation, constituted in an intersubjective manner where difference is not denied, essentialized, or exoticized but rather engaged with in an enabling and potentially transformative way.

At its root, a relational ethics necessitates the construction of trust relationships between the activist ethnographer and his or her research collaborators. This in turn necessitates research reflexivity: being explicit about the personal-political character of the research and the production of accountable knowledge (Plows 2008), getting used to not being the expert, and nurturing solidarity through the process of mutual discovery and knowing one another. A relational ethics is attentive to the social context of collaboration and the ethnographer's situatedness with respect to that context, and such an ethics is enacted in a material, embodied way (e.g., through relations of friendship, solidarity, and empathy). Activist ethnographies seek to embrace a politics of recognition that identifies and defends only those differences that can be coherently combined with social and environmental justice.

SOLIDARITY AND ACTIVIST ETHNOGRAPHY

Solidarities are forged out of the collective articulations of different place-based struggles and constituted as (often messy, problematic, and always negotiated) interconnections that mediate between the participants (Featherstone 2005, 2008). Solidarities are part of the ongoing connections, social and material relations, and articulations between places. Sustainable solidarities involve understanding the way that the local is enmeshed in wider spatial relations, as well as how particular struggles participate in making (and acting from, on, and in space in) their everyday realities. This is because solidarities can only flourish as a consequence of capacity built at the local level. Translocal communication and coordination is only possible to the extent that there are active place-based struggles from which resistance tactics and strategies are developed. Translocal solidarities manifested in networks and convergences can reinforce place-based movements and campaigns (Nunes 2009).

Indeed, a relational understanding of activism that stresses connection and negotiation between diverse (activist, ethnographic, and lay) communities is required to enable what Paul Chatterton terms "learning, acting, and talking together on uncommon ground" (2006, 277). Thus, solidarities across diversity will require "imaginative geographies of connection, composed of sympathies and affinities" (Featherstone, Phillips, and Waters 2007, 388), and require not so much a reactive, defensive, or parochial politics but rather a politics of hope (see Solnit 2004), and shared notions of (social, political-economic, environmental) justice embodied in proactive, positive interventions and initiatives that produce what Matt Sparke (2007) terms *geographies of repossession* of those resources and spaces colonized by capitalism.

In a time of resource depletion and resource conflicts, exacerbated by changing climates, it behooves activist-ethnographers to embrace militancy and to acknowledge and act on the common ground and hope that lives in all of us, that fuels our anger, inspires our passion and love, and nurtures our pursuit of economic, political, and environmental justice. As a minimal requirement, activist ethnographies must always stress the inseparability of knowledge and action, which impel them to be self-consciously interventionist in approach. For a critical ethnography to be fully critical, the researcher must be deeply engaged in some way with those others with whom he or she is conducting research. Drawing on some of my recent activist-ethnographic engagements with So We Stand in Scotland, Peoples' Global Action Asia, the Bangladesh Krishok Federation, and the NBA in India, I have argued that the practice of activist ethnography can open up both potentials and problems. While it can facilitate social transformation and nurture a politics of affinity, it must also negotiate power relations, engage with emotions, and develop a relational ethics. Such an approach grants no special privileges to ethnographers and acknowledges that their understanding of the world as it is and their actions to achieve a world as it "ought" to be are inseparable. Through such a broad approach, and through a variety of possible engagements, ethnographies can be made relevant to real-world concerns.

NOTES

1 The term *resisting others* means communities, groups, social movements, or nongovernmental organizations that are challenging various practices of dominating power. *Dominating power* refers to power that attempts to control or coerce others, impose its will on others, or manipulate the consent of others. These circumstances may involve domination, exploitation, and subjection at the material, symbolic, or psychological levels. This dominating power can be located within the realms of the state, the economy, and civil society, and articulated within social, economic, political, and cultural relations and institutions. Patriarchy, racism, and homophobia are all faces of dominating power that attempt to discipline, silence, prohibit, or repress difference or dissent. Dominating power engenders inequality, and asserts the interests of a particular class, caste, race, or political configuration at the expense of others, for example through particular development projects associated with neoliberal capitalism.

2 A substantial academic literature exists concerning issues of justice (e.g.,

Burczak 2006; Fraser 1997; Heynen 2006; Pickerill and Chatterton 2006; Young 1990); the scope and content of justice in the context of anthropogenic climate change (e.g., Beckerman and Pasek 2001; Beckman and Page 2008; Dobson 1998; Page 2006; Roberts and Parks 2006); and environmental justice (e.g., Agyeman, Bulkeley, and Nochur 2007; Schlosberg 2004, 2007; Walker 2009; Wolch 2007).

3   The So We Stand website is http://sowestand.com (accessed December 27, 2011). So We Stand was originally called the DIY (do-it-yourself) Collective.

4   Freire believed that it is through the process of dialogue with others that we create and re-create ourselves (2000). According to Freire, educators should create the conditions for dialogue that encourage the epistemological curiosity of the learner in order to promote free and critical learning. Dialogic action to promote communication enhances understanding, cultural creation, and liberation.

5   *Alter-globalization* refers to alternative forms of globalization, in particular the struggles for inclusive, democratic forms of globalization by using the communicative tools of the global system (e.g., the Internet). Alter-globalization emerged during the past decade in opposition to neoliberal globalization.

6   These were gender, privatization, and exploitation of resources; labor conditions and migration in Asia; indigenous rights, peasant rights, and food sovereignty; war and militarism; and biodiversity, sustainability, and biopiracy.

11

Ethnographic Approaches to
the World Social Forum

JANET CONWAY

Initiated in 2001, the World Social Forum (wsF) is an expression and innovation of the antiglobalization movement. The wsF, a mammoth episodic event that occurs in varying locations in the global South, is simultaneously a place-specific *plateau* event and a geographically dispersed, de-centered, and *rhizomatic* phenomenon (Chesters and Welsh 2006). Since 2002, the wsF has been expanding rhizomatically, as "networks of heterogeneous elements . . . grow in unplanned directions, following the real life situations they encounter" (Escobar 2004, 352). What Peter Funke (2010) calls the "Global Social Forum Rhizome" is composed of multiple place-based processes, emerging at varying scales and unfolding according to differing temporalities that produce events organized as open spaces in which a wide variety of movements and groups of civil society converge.

As a global project in process and a multiply situated rhizomatic phenomenon that is punctuated by plateau events, the social forum is evolving, mutating, and recombining constantly as it is taken up by groups in different geographical locations, in different historical contexts, and at various scales. Specificities flow from place and scale, the historical-geographic conjuncture in which any iteration of the social forum and the discourses, practices, preoccupations, and strategies of its constitutive social movements occur. The WSF is emergent: its contours, sites, and relationships cannot be known in advance. As a focus and terrain of study, it is mobile, mutating, and multiply situated.

Given these complexities, how might we approach the WSF ethnographically? What kinds of ethnographic knowledges can we hope to produce about the WSF and how might these contribute to a more adequate understanding of this transnational phenomenon? Other ethnographers have confronted such challenges by charting particular events, organizing processes, and problematics (see, e.g., Caruso 2004, 2007; Juris 2005b, 2008a; Osterweil 2004a). There is no one right way to approach the WSF, ethnographically or otherwise. The WSF is such a mammoth, complex, and emergent phenomenon that we need multiple studies produced from different places and perspectives that experiment with diverse methodologies. However, reflexivity about one's positionality, with its attendant limitations and possibilities, along with the weight and effects of one's methodological choices, remains an underlying imperative.

This chapter narrates and reflects on a seven-year process of fieldwork on the WSF in changing sites and at shifting scales through which I have sought to understand the WSF both as a rhizomatic global phenomenon and as a series of sui generis plateau events (see Juris 2012). My study of the WSF is one of "political transnationalism" in that I am preoccupied with the political practices of activists in a transnational social field in the larger context of a globalized struggle for other possible worlds (Jackie Smith 2008, 14).

I begin by exploring the challenges of adequately conceptualizing and representing the WSF. Then I discuss my "entry into the field," who I was in 2002 attending my first WSF, how my analytical engagement shifted and re-focused over time in relation to the historical and geographical dynamics of the forum, and why this matters for doing ethnography. I then consider how I constructed the WSF as a field for ethnographic study. Over time through a process of concrete engagement, four methodological decisions crystallized. As a way of demonstrating this approach concretely, I offer a reading of the 2009 WSF in Belém. In conclusion, I distill from this story the particular contributions of ethnography to the study of transnational social movement fields.

Originally conceived as an alternative to the World Economic Forum held annually in Davos, Switzerland, the first WSF was convened at the height of the antiglobalization mobilizations in 2001 to gather groups and movements of insurgent civil society from around the world.[1] The vision of the Brazilian founders was an open forum for the free and horizontal exchange of ideas, experiences, and strategies to generate and enact alternatives to neoliberalism (Whitaker 2007a). The gathering would be thoroughly international but anchored geographically and experientially in the global South. The first WSF, held in Porto Alegre, Brazil, in January 2001, attracted fifteen thousand participants. This astounding success led organizers to commit to the WSF as a permanent process. Each January since then, in varying modalities,[2] the event has taken place and expanded in size, diversity, complexity, and importance.

After three years in Porto Alegre, Brazil, the WSF moved to Mumbai, India, in 2004 and to Nairobi, Kenya, in 2007. Brazil remains the homeplace of the WSF, returning to Porto Alegre in 2005 and taking place in Belém in the Amazon in 2009, but there is now a widespread commitment to moving the world event to other regions in the global South. This is a strategy for expanding the forum and deepening its intercontinental and cross-cultural character. In a related move, at the second WSF in Porto Alegre in 2002, organizers called on participants to organize similar processes in their own places that would be defined by participants' own priorities and conducted at whatever scale made sense. Social forums have proliferated, inspired by the WSF and organized in accordance with its Charter of Principles, with regional scale processes emerging with particular vigor and importance. The civil society entities present at the WSF vary considerably depending on the location of the event but are in every case amazingly diverse in their demographic makeups, organizational forms, cultural expressions, geographic roots, and reach, strategies, tactics, and discourses.[3] In any analytical discussion about the WSF, it is critical to maintain a distinction between the forum and its constituent social movements and networks.

The development of the WSF, understood as an annual event, is central to most discussions, but it is critical to recognize that the WSF is more amply represented as an amorphous worldwide, movement-based, multiscale, and multisited cultural process. The world event, along with the organizing processes in which it is embedded and through which it is produced, is significantly re-created when it is taken up by groups in different parts of the world, changing what follows, locally and globally, although not in any mechanistic or predictable way. It is in this sense that the social forum can be described as a rhizome, characterized by connectivity, multiplicity, and heterogeneity.[4]

The WSF also embodied a political project in its ethical commitment to the creation and preservation of open space. The WSF is both a regular mammoth global event and a proliferating series of autonomous local processes, constituting what some commentators refer to as a social forum movement (see, e.g., Chesters and Welsh 2006).[5] Notwithstanding the naturalistic metaphor of the rhizome, the WSF, like all actor networks, is "shot through with political determinations, contested social relations, and power inequalities" (Routledge 2008, 201; see also Juris 2005b, 2008a; Desai, this volume; Juris, this volume).

The annual, now becoming biennial, global gathering is a critical node in a network or plateau in a rhizome that is particular in space and time. The global WSF event helps to consolidate and articulate the social forum process on a world scale, but this process cannot be reduced to the global WSF event. As a global process and multifaceted phenomenon, the social forum is evolving and mutating constantly. It is characterized by great ongoing creativity and dynamism and some degree of shape shifting, which present problems of representation and analysis. Indeed, it is becoming increasingly untenable to refer to the WSF, as event or process, in the singular (Conway 2008b).

It is the dispersed, rhizomatic, and multiscale character of the global process that makes the WSF phenomenon so impressive, intriguing, and powerful. These same qualities also make it elusive to analysts, especially ethnographers. While it is not possible to "know" the Global Social Forum Rhizome in any comprehensive or authoritative way, I have nevertheless found that its expanding diversity and globality are especially compelling qualities and worthy of analytic attention in their own right—despite the risks of overreach inherent in such an approach.[6]

I did not set out to study the WSF. I went to the WSF for the first time in 2002 as a Toronto-based activist demoralized in the months after 9/11 and searching for signs of hope that the movement for global justice was, somewhere in the world, still stirring. In Porto Alegre in January 2002, along with sixty thousand others, I was enraptured by the WSF. The energy and creativity; the spirit of rebellion and the search for alternative ways of living; the throngs dancing, marching, and singing; the internationalism; the diversity of movements, bodies, discourses, languages, and modes of struggle; and the Partido dos Trabalhadores (Workers' Party) on the verge of electing Lula, the former head of the metal workers' union, as president of Brazil, made for a heady antidote to despair. Another world was not only possible; in some sense, in the communion of these forces for life, it was already present, pulsating, and powerful.

As an activist, I entered the WSF in some respects as an insider, an active collaborator committed to the antiglobalization movement, familiar with the dynamics of coalition politics, and grounded in significant movement histories and cultures of my own region. At the time of this first encounter with the WSF, I had been a longtime feminist with fifteen years of accumulated experience in national-scale women's and anti-poverty movements in Canada. Prior to the eruption of the antiglobalization mobilizations, I had been organizing in an urban cross-sectoral social justice coalition in Toronto for a decade.

In other important ways, I was decidedly an outsider to the WSF. Although I had been to Latin America several times as a student and solidarity visitor, and had been deeply influenced by liberation theology and popular movements of the region, I had never been to Brazil. My Spanish was rudimentary and my Portuguese nonexistent. And I had not been active in the circuits of international activism, either around the UN conferences or in any antiglobalization convergences outside my own region. The cues through which I situated the people and movements I encountered were based on my political experience and my academic study of social movements, neither of which I felt were altogether reliable in navigating and interpreting this new transnational and transcultural encounter.

I was a traveler entering into a transnational and transcultural space— as were all others present, but to vastly differing degrees. Whether from the host city or from another continent, we were all visitors to this temporary "networked space of transnational encounter" that was the social forum (see this volume's introduction). We, the participants, groups, and movements, constituted the social forum, yet it was also already beyond us, more than the sum of its parts and bigger than any one of its iterations. Even at this early stage in the forum's history, some were already more inside the process, particularly through their involvements in emergent structures of governance like the Brazil-based International Secretariat or the International Council. Participants from the host region and activists in its major movements were more on the inside with respect to particular forums in terms of knowing the issues, discourses, actors, and organizations as they were localized. However, several years on, my experiences at multiple social forums on several continents and as an organizer of one in Toronto made me more of an insider to the process as it was unfolding globally. Despite my accumulating history, being in social forum spaces in various places and at different scales continued to feel both familiar and foreign to me, although the mix of familiarity and otherness would be different every time. My own social and political location as an insider-outsider shifted continually in relation to the changing times and spaces of the WSF and to the differently located persons and movements I encountered within each event.

I also entered the WSF having just completed a Ph.D. in political science. My central interest was in the knowledge arising from activist practice and the significance of that knowledge for generating postneoliberal alternatives and reimagining democratic politics. I eventually settled on ethnography to best describe my methodological orientation. My turn to ethnography has, from the outset, been transdisciplinary, relying on ethnographic work and debates about ethnographic practices in anthropology, sociology, and geography even as I remain driven by problematics that are essentially about "the political."

Under pressure from activist networks in Canada to report on my experience at the 2002 WSF, I quickly began to speak and write about the forum and immediately experienced the difficulties of describing it and communicating my nascent sense of its significance to those who had no experience of it. Within a year, I was in Porto Alegre at the WSF again, this time also as a researcher, driven in no small part by reaction to the political commentaries that were in wide circulation on the Internet and that were shaping activists' opinions worldwide, and thus shaping the future possibilities of the WSF. Many of these opinions were politically reductionist and argumentative, and they reproduced worn debates on the Left, reducing the WSF to the terms of such debates: should the WSF be revolutionary or reformist, should it include or exclude parties of the Left, should it constitute a fifth International, and so on. Commentators gravitated to the spectacular and the scandalous, the contentious and the conventionally political. They frequently misrepresented the forum by equating the statements of its alleged leaders or the positions of particular groups within the forum with the declarations or beliefs of the forum itself. Further, such commentators missed most of what was going on and what, to my eye, was most arresting about the WSF. The new, radical, innovative, and alternative were taking shape everywhere in the interstices of the forum, enacted through the interplay of activist practices and knowledges across issues and identities from around the world.[7]

Reductionist discourses about the WSF, which continue to abound, reinforced my earlier scholarly convictions about ethnography: the injunction, first and foremost, to observe; to look, listen, and perceive through bodily presence; to describe as fully and as thickly as possible the actual practices; and to ask questions such as: Who is present? What are they saying and doing? If so many are here, why are they here? What do they think is the significance of the WSF? What does the open space of the WSF enable? Who is not present in the open space? Who is present but marginal and why?

ORGANIZING THE ETHNOGRAPHIC GAZE

My broad and abiding interest in the social forum has been its power to attract into its orbit a stunning array of critical movements worldwide. I have been fascinated by the WSF as a new political form, the forum's praxis of open space, and by what this praxis was enabling culturally and politically in specific local places and at regional and global scales. I have also been interested in the possible meaning of the forum for the struggle for alternative futures. In continuity with my earlier work, I was interested in tracking and theorizing this praxis as a new form of knowledge arising from social movements and as prefigurative contributions to postneoliberal worlds and alternative forms of democratic political life. In light of this, I made four early and medium-term decisions that oriented my fieldwork.

First, I sought *to apprehend plateau events in all of their diversity*, while knowing that I was like the blind one touching the elephant. No one could apprehend a WSF of one hundred thousand people in any comprehensive way. Nevertheless, I would be as attentive as possible to the demographics of those present, the array of issues being discussed, and the range of ways in which people were being political. How were different movements using the space and assessing its usefulness? Is the open space favoring some at the expense of others? What constituencies, issues, and struggles are marginal and why?

I sought to better represent each event at whatever scale (and with it the expanding social forum phenomenon) by being more conscious of its internal dynamism and heterogeneity while also remaining cognizant of the particularity of my own immediate experience and angle of vision. The massive opening and closing ceremonies of each world event attracted tens of thousands of people with flags, banners, signs, and slogans. Each print program indicated who was organizing with whom and around what issues. Information tables and displays provided other clues. As with every activist gathering, people handed out pamphlets incessantly, promoting their events and their perspectives. All the world events have also produced a daily newspaper that chronicles major controversies, star speakers, and the streetscapes of the forums. After some years, statistics on registrants and their national origins became available. Researchers began to do surveys. The program went online and became searchable. I also relied on the eyes and ears of student assistants, friends, and fellow travelers, and, of course, the aforementioned voluminous commentary that each forum provoked. All these sources supplemented my own planned journeys and chance encounters in forum spaces.

In the lead-up to each major social forum, there inevitably emerged some key conjunctural problematics that shaped my research agenda at that event. For instance, the impending war in Iraq cast a long shadow over the 2003 event in Porto Alegre; the massacre of Muslims in Gujarat and the specter of Hindu communalism were critical in understanding the politics of the WSF in Mumbai in 2004; Hugo Chávez, the Bolivarian revolution, and the relationship between the forum and so-called friendly governments were obvious problematics in Caracas in 2006; and the preponderance of churches and NGOs in Nairobi in 2007 provoked questions about the historical composition of insurgent civil society in different world regions and conflicting conceptions of the movement working within the WSF.

As I followed the continually expanding process(es) across time, space, and scale, these mostly holistic but inevitably partial readings of particular social forum events remained sui generis, but they were increasingly informed by comparison and by my attempts to situate the events in the local, regional, and global histories of the social forum process—to produce both local genealogies and comparative archaeologies of the phenomenon I was attempting to understand (Comaroff and Comaroff 2003, 172).

The second major choice I made early on was *to focus on the everyday goings-on in the spaces* of social forum events rather than the debates under way in the organizing and governing bodies. In order to understand the Global Social Forum Rhizome, it is critical to maintain distinctions between (1) any one plateau event; (2) the dispersed, decentered social forum phenomenon as it is instantiated in a variety of place-specific ways through particular social forum events at a variety of scales; (3) the multiscale organizing processes that produce each event; and (4) the international governing and organizing bodies and their ongoing processes beyond particular events. Many commentaries continue to collapse these differences, attributing to the social forum event under discussion the character of its organizing committee or, even more problematically, attributing to the WSF as a global phenomenon the putative shortcomings of the International Council.[8] While the deliberations of the International Council are an important pole in shaping the global process, and the decisions of organizing committees indelibly shape specific events, each social forum event takes on a dynamic of its own and many of the most interesting developments were neither authored nor anticipated by the organizers.

Scholarly works, including ethnographic accounts, on various organizing bodies and processes, are essential to understanding what is producing the social forum, its genius, its internal conflicts and power struggles, its limitations, and its specificities. Works by José Corrêa Leite (2005), Boaventura de Sousa Santos (2006), Teivo Teivainen (2002, 2004), and Francisco Whitaker (2007a) give us some important windows into these worlds, and thus into the social forum as a transnational political project in process, by men at the center of the organizing or who have had intimate access through membership on the International Council. Works by researchers with one foot in specific organizing processes have also provided invaluable insights (see, e.g., Caruso 2004, 2007, and this volume).

These accounts have provided important sources for me in addition to the interviews I have conducted with organizers of social forums in different parts of the world, whose perspectives are an essential pole of interpretation. However, these are not the ethnographies that I have chosen to produce. Aside from the problem of access to these committees, especially in my early years of research, I have been consistently drawn to the dynamics on the ground, the everyday worlds of the WSF in those days when the social forum opens its big tent in a particular place and invites movements around the globe to perform for one another. I have been persistently interested in what the open space was enabling within and among the participating movements, before, during, and after the forum. Each event has been of great significance to me as a way to view the particular movements and their attempts to connect and to grow beyond the sum of their particularities. The events have provided a terrain on which emergent movement practices have been enacted—which are regularly outside and beyond the discourses of the WSF organizers. I therefore continually resist reducing the social forum to the preoccupations of its governance bodies. As significant as these concerns are, the social forum as a phenomenon enacted in its plateau events has consistently exceeded the (contesting) visions and terms of debates of its facilitators.

At the world level, organizing processes in Brazil remain opaque, where the leading personalities insist that the point of the WSF is the facilitation of the open space, not the process of organizing it. More has been said or written publicly about other processes, particularly in Mumbai and Nairobi, where the processes themselves have been more politicized and contested than in Brazil. Historicized ethnographic accounts of all these processes, but particularly those in Brazil, remain to be written and would invaluably add to the studies I have undertaken.

The third orientation, which became clearer and more pressing after the 2004 WSF in Mumbai, was my growing attention to *multiplicity, difference, and inequality* within the WSF. One key aspect of this was attention to place-based difference—the difference that place made for who organized and populated the social forum, what discourses were most audible, and what political and intellectual traditions were most prominent. Closely related to this is the positionality of the place (and the social movements of the place) in the modern colonial world system, including in the political geography of the WSF.

Attention to place-based difference and relations of inequality and coloniality, especially across vast regions of the global South, also provoked a host of new problematics. Moving the WSF geographically and making it more accessible to subaltern movements, as occurred in India, raised questions of intercivilizational dialogue, (in)communicability, and cross-cultural translation that were not so apparent in the more cosmopolitan WSFs of the early years in Porto Alegre.[9]

My growing attention to difference was also a political response to the hegemonic representations of the WSF. In both activist and scholarly commentary, discussions of the WSF continue to be overwhelmingly centered on Brazil. The WSFs in Mumbai and Nairobi hardly figure analytically or politically. Politically inflected analyses too often revolve around the preoccupations of conventional Leftist politics, particularly in Latin America, and in terms set by the events in Porto Alegre: discourses of capitalist crisis, imperialist war, relations between movements and political parties, twenty-first-century socialism, the Bolivarian revolution, and the "pink tide" of antineoliberal governments in Latin America. These discourses, ranging from social democratic to socialist, privilege statist projects and modernist politics and do not seem to see politics under way in other terms—even as diverse activisms proliferate in the space of the forums.

In such representations of the WSF, the incredible plurality and ferment on the ground during the forum disappears. Political struggles over gender, race, caste, sexuality, coloniality, and the environment—all of them interpolated in opposition to neoliberalism—are systematically erased. Although the WSF is a phenomenon putatively without a political center, political hegemonies are evident, both in the production of the events and in struggles over their meaning. They are difficult to specify and analyze but they are there.

Finally, flowing immediately from the third development, the fourth orientation was *to focus on some politically significant, consistently present, but systematically marginalized movements* to uncover their histories of engagement and their discourses in relation to the social forum. This allowed me to precisely study the dynamics of hegemony and marginality, and the resulting contestation over the forum. In this regard, I looked to feminist and indigenous movements. In each case, I identified several distinct entities representing different strands of praxis and politics and tracked them through several WSFs, observing selected events and pursuing their leading activists as key informants.

As stated at the outset, it is critical to analytically distinguish the WSF from its participating social movements, including those that help constitute single events and those that have been present from the beginning and are active in sustained ways and at multiple levels in producing the WSF. To maintain this distinction, and move beyond an analysis of difference and marginality, it is useful to focus on particular movements in an ethnography of the WSF for additional reasons. First, it can help get at the persistent and thorny question of the political outcomes of the social forum. A major, if not the only, way to address this is through the social forum's effects on the participating social movements, throughout and after the processes in which they partake. Further, focusing on particular movements helps us see how such movements actively use the space created by the social forum, the effects this participation creates within and beyond the event, and the transforming effects the movements undergo as a result. These effects, which often transcend the hopes of the organizers and managers of the social forum, reinforce the importance of a focus on the everyday goings-on in social forum spaces. Examining particular movements also foregrounds movement-specific practices and perspectives that are a constitutive part of the social forum but rarely get noted or taken account of in more-global or more-holistic approaches. Moreover, studying specific movements also highlights many actors that often go unstudied, including feminists, Dalits, indigenous and queer activists, and subalterns more generally. Finally, focusing on specific movements also helps us to distinguish between localized and cosmopolitan discourses, for example, by seeking out movements in the host region and in events conducted in the local language, and then situating these movements vis-à-vis wider global movement contexts and the forum as a whole.[10] The next section provides an example of the kind of analysis the foregoing ethnographic approach has yielded as I attempted to apprehend the breadth and diversity of the 2009 WSF.

READING BELÉM: INDIGENIZING THE GLOBAL AT THE 2009 WORLD SOCIAL FORUM?

The 2009 WSF took place from January 27 to February 1 in the equatorial city of Belém. It was the fifth time the event took place in Brazil, but it was the first time outside the southern city of Porto Alegre, the birthplace of the WSF. As with the earlier events, Belém attracted hordes of participants—130,000 of them from 142 countries, but well over 90 percent were from Brazil, many of them from Pará and neighboring states in the Brazilian north. The local newspaper reported participation by 1,900 indigenous persons from 120 ethnic groups and 1,400 Afro-descendants. Although these numbers represent breakthroughs by the WSF's historical standards in Brazil, the forum remained an overwhelmingly light-skinned, young, urban, Brazilian, Portuguese-speaking space—in these respects, disappointingly parochial. Paradoxically, it was this forum's novel and clear-eyed focus on the host locality that prompted its most significant political advances. While the global financial meltdown had displaced all other discussions among the cosmopolitan Left within and beyond the WSF, a wide diversity of issues and debates marked the forum. Climate change, resource extraction, and the plight of indigenous peoples were particularly prominent. As always, there was no one standpoint from which to see it all. My focus during this forum was the question of indigenous participation.

Belém is a city of 1.4 million inhabitants and is best known as the gateway to the Amazon. It is located at the confluence of three major rivers as they meet the Atlantic Ocean. In late January, temperatures regularly climb to 45 degrees Celsius with 98 percent humidity and daily torrential rains. The forum was held on two university campuses, contiguous but vastly different in their built environments. The Universidade Federal Rural da Amazônia (Federal Rural University of the Amazon; UFRA) is a sprawling site, with huge green spaces of varying kinds of vegetation and a few small scattered buildings. Fenced areas of dense brush warned of poisonous plants and animals and discouraged wandering off the beaten path. The ribbon of blacktop that wound through the site became, for the days of the forum, a river of humanity with currents diverging and converging toward one or another of the 2,600 events. At the UFRA, the forty-five-minute walk from end to end in blistering heat or tropical downpour could be eased by perching on the back of one of the numerous bicycles that careened through the crowd.

Indigenous peoples, forest peoples, Afro-descendants, stateless peoples, the international human rights movement, and peoples of the pan-Amazonian region were among those housed in thematic tents with their own rosters of movement-specific activities that ran alongside the more than two thousand self-organized activities planned by participants in general. The UFRA also hosted the Intercontinental Youth Camp, a sea of pup tents and clotheslines, fifteen thousand young bodies hanging out, playing music, selling T-shirts and jewelry, and reveling in a time outside of time and shared hope in another possible world. The youth culture in Belém prominently included espousal of vegetarianism, sexual pleasure, and experimentation and marijuana use, none of which had been such visible elements of the camp's politics in the past.

The Universidade Federal do Pará (Federal University of Pará; UFPA) offered quite a different scene, with a much more urban feel. Dense clusters of buildings were laid out along roads open to traffic. For reasons known only to the organizers, there appeared to be a division of political labor between the two sites. With most of "the movements" occupying the tents and green spaces of the UFRA and the talking heads assigned to the classrooms of the UFPA, each site had its distinct political culture. Given the difficulty and time involved in moving across the two sites, there was too little opportunity to partake in events at both, resulting in de facto segregation of different political actors, problematics, and modalities. Interestingly, among the few movement spaces assigned to the UFPA was the World of Work tent where trade unionists from around the world congregated in close and convenient proximity to those debating the global financial meltdown.[11]

One of the significant features of the Belém forum was its unabashed focus on the host locality's global importance. In the lead-up, this WSF was billed as a pan-Amazonian event, recognizing the global environmental significance of the river and the rain forest and the transnational political character of a bioregion (see Escobar 2008) that traverses the frontiers of Brazil, Ecuador, Peru, Bolivia, Colombia, Venezuela, Guyana, French Guiana, and Suriname. This WSF built on a pan-Amazonian process that had seen four social forums organized in the region between 2002 and 2005. The first day of programming was dedicated to the Amazon and its peoples and the threats represented by climate change, megaprojects, and extractive industries. This explicit and intentional political attention to a specific place was a novel development for the WSF, especially in its Brazilian enactments, which have regularly been more cosmopolitan in their aspirations and internationalist in the discourses and practices of the organizers.

Perhaps because of these orientations, the WSF in Brazil has been historically weak on environmental questions. The forum in Belém offered some important correctives to this through its focused attention to place and the global significance of place-based struggles. Expressions of this ranged from the spectacular to the mundane, the precious to the problematic: Amazon Watch, a Northern-based international environmental NGO, orchestrated an aerial photo of a thousand Amazonian indigenous people spelling out "Save the Amazon" with their bodies; a "fuck for the forest" campaign was promoted in the youth camp; drum-beating, flag-waving vegetarians invaded the food courts; and the Brazilian minister of justice arrived with a police escort and helicopters hovering overhead to hear Amazonian indigenous leaders' protests about land invasions by settlers and multinationals despite constitutional protections. Whatever one's reactions were to any one of these occurrences, and they were heated and varied among participants, that hundreds of less spectacular events wove a novel politics of environmental justice through the WSF program in Belém was indisputable and noteworthy.

The choice of Belém as a site helped propel the appearance of these discourses among entities that had not previously attended to questions of climate change, resource extraction, or indigenous peoples. Belém's selection also promoted international environmental NGOs such as Amigos de la Tierra (Friends of the Earth) and Amazon Watch, indigenous peoples in general and indigenous groups of the Brazilian Amazon in particular, and indigenous-environmental coalitions like Alianza Amazonica (Amazon Alliance) to a new prominence within the social forum. It is interesting to note that in the lead-up to the forum, the official rationales for the choice of Belém made no mention of indigenous peoples beyond vague references to the biodiversity and cultural diversity of the region. By the time of the forum, however, local indigenous groups had assumed a highly visible, although not unambiguous, role in the constitution of the WSF.

Historically, indigenous peoples and their perspectives have been exceedingly marginal at the WSFs in Brazil. Demographically, there are fewer than 350,000 indigenous peoples in Brazil, about 0.1 percent of the national population. In the early years in Porto Alegre, they were most visible selling crafts or performing in cultural spectacles, a role that has been decried as merely folkloric by indigenous and nonindigenous participants alike. The Indian organizers of the WSF in Mumbai in 2004 were far more intentional and successful in politically incorporating mass movements of tribal peoples. Powerful discourses of indigenous land rights and critiques of development emerged during the Mumbai forum but were not sustained in Porto Alegre the following year. In the Americas, hemispheric social forums in Quito, Ecuador, in 2004 and Guatemala City in 2008 were deeply informed by the presence and political perspectives of indigenous movements of the host countries. During the WSFS in Brazil, however, despite a serious effort to organize a space for indigenous peoples at the 2005 forum in Porto Alegre, indigenous perspectives have been barely audible. This is changing though, assisted both by the choice of Belém as a forum site and developments within the indigenous movements.

Fueled by events over the last decade in Ecuador and Bolivia in which indigenous peoples have been central protagonists, there is a continental indigenous movement in formation, with strong leadership emanating from the Andean region. The Coordinadora Andina de Organizaciones Indígenas (the Andean Coordination of Indigenous Organizations), in partnership with Amazonian and Guatemalan entities, assumed major responsibility for orchestrating the historically unprecedented indigenous presence in Belém. The indigenous peoples' tent was the site of vibrant and diverse discussions, prominent among them a series of events on "civilizational crises." What was extraordinary in the context of the forum, and perhaps more generally, was the assertiveness with which indigenous leaders articulated alternatives central to imagining other possible worlds: concepts of plurinationality and *buen vivir* (living well— not better; see Escárcega, this volume), indigenous knowledge of climate change and sustainable interaction with natural environments, radical perspectives on postdevelopment, and direct action in defense of indigenous lands and for survival as peoples against developmentalist governments, land-hungry settlers, and rapacious corporations.

Disparities and tensions were apparent between indigenous entities from regions that are differently positioned at home and internationally. This was especially evident between the Brazilian Amazonians and those from outside the region, from countries with sizable indigenous populations with longer histories of collaboration with one another, which has resulted in cross-fertilization of discourses and perspectives. The most advanced dialogues appeared to be under way among indigenous women, who listened carefully and respectfully to those from contexts different from their own and supported other voices, especially with respect to men in their communities. Indigenous women had been preparing for the first continental encounter of indigenous women, which took place in

Puno, Peru, in late May 2012 in advance of the fourth *cumbre* (summit) of indigenous peoples and nationalities of Abya Yala (the Americas). The cumbre process has enabled this intellectual and political efflorescence of indigenous peoples, and indigenous entities are using the social forum process in the Americas to advance their movement's consolidation and expansion of their international reach.

For the Amazonian indigenous peoples of Brazil the forum in Belém was a watershed event in terms of their sheer numerical strength and visibility. They numbered well over one thousand—mostly men, and highly visible in their distinctiveness, with painted bodies, feathered headdresses, and handcrafted weapons. They often entered the indigenous peoples' tent in groups, singing and dancing, and they were subsequently identified according to the Brazilian state they hailed from. In one extraordinary moment, a highly respected older man was invited to come to the dais. The moderator publicly recognized him as a leader of national stature. His community, standing and chanting, sent him off from his place in the bleachers, and two dancing warriors escorted him to the stage.

Another powerful moment occurred in the opening march through downtown Belém. The march, like the forum, was overwhelmingly peopled by young, light-skinned Brazilians from the host region. From where I was for most of the event, surveying the first two-thirds of the massive parade, there was no indigenous presence of any kind. Following a large, raucous, and diverse indigenous peoples' assembly at the UFRA that same morning their absence was startling. Had they decided not to participate in the march? Was it conceivable that they were at the end of the march—which in Canada would have been an insult?

Suddenly, a group of perhaps thirty Amazonian indigenous youths appeared singing and dancing, moving as a bloc up through the stream of demonstrators and stopping periodically to chant and bop before surging ahead. And in their wake came a line of indigenous leaders, all men, stretched the width of the march, arms locked and moving fast, opening a path through the crowd through the sheer force of their collective presence and momentum. What was this about? Was this a political statement? Was this a normal mode of being in a mass demonstration that I had never before seen? Was it a way of moving to the front of a march where, in Brazil, as in many places, the front lines are colonized by political parties of the Left with their flags, banners, and chants? Its ambiguity

FIGURE 11.1.
Amazonian indigenous youths dance in welcome at the opening ceremonies in Belém, January 27, 2009. *Photo by Dominique Caouette.*

intensified when, upon arriving at the march's destination, it became apparent that these same indigenous leaders were the central actors in the
opening ceremonies.

The opening ceremonies were noteworthy in their remarkable departure from past practice. Unlike the highly professionalized and thoroughly internationalized extravaganzas of music, song, dance, and political speeches in Porto Alegre, Mumbai, and Nairobi, the opening in Belém
was thoroughly indigenous—vastly different in tone, mode, and personnel. Although the Andeans made an appearance, it was an event almost
exclusively expressive of indigenous groups from the Brazilian Amazon.
Indigenous delegations were identified and invited to move through the
crowd to the stage, which they did often by linking arms and snaking
fluidly as groups through the throngs of people. Group after group enacted greetings to the crowd through their communal songs, dances, and
poetry, and very occasionally in a speech. What to make of this—in terms
of indigenous positionality in the Belém forum, in Brazilian movement
politics, or in the wsf process more generally—remains an open question.

FIGURE 11.2.
Indigenous women leaders from across Latin America organize toward the
first Continental Summit of Indigenous Women, January 30, 2009.
Photo by Andréa Browning Gill.

As with any WSF, the forum in Belém eludes definitive analysis. It continues to provoke awe, critique, comparison, and bafflement. No one account can do justice to the vast array and richness of the processes under way in any one iteration of the social forum, much less in terms of its mutations and accumulations across time and space. The fourth day of the forum was "alliances day," an innovation of the 2007 forum in Nairobi and expressed in Belém through sectoral assemblies, all of which produced declarations. The indigenous peoples gathered at the WSF in Belem issued a call for a global day of action on October 12 of that year, the anniversary of Columbus's arrival in the Americas, in defense of Mother Earth and against the commodification of life, and for a thematic social forum in 2010 on the crisis of civilization—notably including but not limited to the financial meltdown. Indigenous peoples are not standing still and neither is the WSF.

FIGURE 11.3.

Indigenous women activists close a session at the indigenous peoples' tent during the WSF in Belém, January 27, 2009. *Photo by Dominique Caouette.*

CONCLUSION

My ethnographic practice vis-à-vis the WSF has involved sustained participant observation in social forum spaces, involving multiple sites and scales over almost a decade. My research has yielded an appreciation of the place-based character of each instantiation of a complexifying transnational process. I have been following the WSF on routes that could not have been predicted in a research design. They are not the only possible routes that could have been taken nor are they adequate in and of themselves. The WSF deserves many ethnographies. Many have been written, others remain to be written, and most, no doubt, will remain unwritten. The focus of my ethnographic interest, while consistent in the general terms I have outlined, sharpened, blurred, shifted, and refocused numerous times in response to historical developments in the process, changes in geographic context, issues raised at particular events, and my own evolving thinking about this increasingly complex, historically dynamic, multifaceted, and mutating phenomenon.

FIGURE 11.4.
Amazonian indigenous leaders present on the WSF's main stage on
Pan-Amazon Day, January 28, 2009. *Photo by Marc Becker.*

By way of conclusion, I want to distill the following claims arising from this account about the particular contributions and limitations of ethnography to the study of transnational social movement fields.

First, *ethnographic approaches promise to root transnationalism, or more precisely, the production of particular transnationalisms, in concrete practices and geographic places.* It is these place-based practices and the relations among them—mediated by travel and information and communication technologies—that constitute transnational networks. Ethnography calls for deep, extended, repeated interactive local encounters and thus grounds our understandings of the transnational in everyday practices—in this case, activist practices.

Second, this persistent focus on localized, historically embedded practices and discourses *privileges the agents of those practices and discourses as subjects and knowers, as producers of the transnational and of transnational social movements.* However partially, and never unproblematically, ethnographic sensibilities prioritize representing these agents, first and foremost, in their own terms and from within their own worlds.

Third, epistemological and ethical debates about the practice of ethnography have been intensifying over the last decade. Particularly in anthropology but also by feminists across disciplines, *the presence, role, and power of the ethnographer have been profoundly problematized* (see Behar 1996; Visweswaran 1994). Especially given anthropology's historical imbrication with European colonialism, the contemporary practice of ethnography is fraught with concerns about reflexivity, voice, and representation, especially across (post)colonial divides. Many ethnographers have become acutely conscious of their own positionality in geopolitical and other relations of power and have problematized translation across difference, cultural and otherwise.

These debates have not resolved themselves in the production of formulas or blueprints for pursuing ethnographic research. Their value is in problematizing and politicizing the production of knowledge about Others, a contribution that is underrated in many social scientific fields but that, in my view, is centrally important—especially vis-à-vis the study of social movements that we support, and for me as a white, Northern-based researcher studying the wsf, a phenomenon primarily of and about subaltern movements of the global South.

Fourth, ethnographic attention to the local and the embedded enables *social heterogeneity to come more fully into view* (see Burdick 1998; Juris 2008a). The fine-grained resolution of the ethnographic gaze on concrete practices makes visible their infinite multiplicity and constant mutation. In terms of transnational social movements, ethnographic attention to difference interrogates the easy cosmopolitanism of many discourses of the transnational, including of transnational social movements and of the wsf. Such an ethnographic gaze uncovers the plural local worlds that constitute any transnational social phenomenon and the panoply of difference within and across those worlds that produce the flows and hybridities, indeed the newness, associated with the transnational. An ethnographic orientation can thus help us counter both Eurocentrism and positivism (Gupta and Ferguson 1997a, 5).

Fifth, ethnography is not and never has been analytically self-sufficient. Because of its attention to embedded specificity—the very source of its rich and unique knowledge making, ethnography needs history and theory to make sense of what only it can see. My account of the 2009 wsf in Belém provides a textured description of the event from an embedded point of view. The story gestures to the significance of larger histories and translocal flows in understanding the practices described. It is analytically suggestive. It is rife with theoretical possibility. But in this account, these are nascent potentialities. Unavoidably, ethnography "is engaged in a dialogue with other ways of making sense of the present" (Comaroff and Comaroff 2003, 156). This epistemological humility has the added virtue of reminding us that emergent phenomena like the wsf, which appear as "a focal point at which the preoccupations of the period ha[ve] taken tangible shape," continue to elude our grasp (156).

NOTES

1   I use the term *insurgent civil society* to highlight the politicized, rebellious, surging, and movement-oriented character of the social forces assembled by the wsf, which departs from conventional understandings of civil society.

2   The 2006 wsf was organized as a polycentric process, with the "world" event taking place in three sites: Bamako, Mali; Caracas, Venezuela; and Karachi, Pakistan, each organized with a high degree of autonomy and regional specificity. In 2008, the world event was a global day of action dispersed over hundreds of sites and finding expression on every continent.

3   The wsf is open to any group anywhere in the world that professes opposition to neoliberalism, that is not a political party, and that is not engaged in armed struggle. See wsf, Charter of Principles, August 22, 2002, www .forumsocialmundial.org.br (accessed December 25, 2011).

4   Funke (2010) cites Arturo Escobar, who in turn is following Gilles Deleuze and Félix Guattari (1987): "the metaphor of rhizomes suggests networks of heterogeneous elements that grow in unplanned directions, following the real life situations they encounter" (Escobar 2004, 352).

5   This sociological observation is not to be confused with the "space vs. actor" debate that pits the social forum as open, nondeliberative space against the social forum as a unified movement that takes positions and embarks on actions. See Teivainen 2004 and Whitaker 2004 for the two classic statements of these opposing positions.

6   For a similar observation about any single wsf event, see Anand 2004.

7   There is a sizable literature of this nature circulating on the Internet. For an exchange that gets at some of the issues at stake, see my article and contributions by Peter Marcuse in the *International Journal of Urban and Regional Research* (Conway 2005b; Marcuse 2005a, 2005b).

8   This is very characteristic of Teivo Teivainen's work (2002, 2004, 2007, 2008). It is also common among those authors who stress the importance of continuity between means and ends. A recent example is Jeffrey Juris's analy-

sis of the 2007 USSF in this volume. He concludes that organizers created a "space of intentionality" through their favoring of mass-based organizations of working-class people of color in organizing the USSF, yet deemphasized openness and horizontality in the organizing process. However, the important point for my purposes is that the space of the event itself remained open to the self-organizing efforts of whichever group wanted to participate.

9 I use the term *cosmopolitan* to describe the more modern, urbanized, and mobile elements, often multilingual in the colonial languages and Western educated, coming from anywhere in the world but disproportionately from the West and North. I am counter-posing it to the term *subaltern*, which describes the movements of the poor and marginalized, who are much more confined to the local place and scale. In describing the events in Porto Alegre as more cosmopolitan, I am commenting on the absence of large numbers of subalterns of any kind, as well as the absence of indigenous or Afro-descendants with different civilizational discourses than the modernist Left. See Conway 2008b for an extended treatment of the growing claims of subaltern movements on the WSF.

10 For further discussion of this point with respect to feminist movements in the WSF, see Conway 2010.

11 See Juris 2005b and 2008a and Osterweil 2004a for ethnographic depictions of how diverse political-cultural spaces played out at previous WSFs in Porto Alegre.

SUBVERSIVE
TECHNOLOGIES

12

The Transnational Struggle for Information Freedom

M. K. STERPKA

What if we were to accept that the goal of theory is not to extend knowledge by confirming what we already know, that the world is a place of economic domination, conflict and oppression? What if we asked theory instead to help us see openings, to enable us to find happiness, to provide a space of freedom and possibility?

Julie-Katherine Gibson-Graham, A Post-Capitalist Politics *(7)*

In the last few decades there has been an upending in the natural sciences that has entailed a reassessment of the role of complexity in the composition of ordinary things. Foremost among these revisionings is an understanding of the importance of small things. Edward Lorenz observed as much when he formulated a model that became known as the butterfly experiment (1969). *Butterfly* in this sense referred to the fractal shape of his model that was composed of a multidimensional set of overlapping curves that evolved to become more dynamic over time. The model revealed how small, local changes evolve into larger transformations. Consequently, there has been a reevaluation of the thinking surrounding complexity and the nature of composition. In the physical sciences, this has involved the study of self-organized, dynamic systems—called "emergent" for their potential to initiate dramatic effects (see Barabasi 1999, 2003; Mandelbrot 1983; Prigogine 1997; Watts and Strogatz 1998). In the social sciences, the effort has been geared toward examining social constitution in terms of complexity and networks (see Bale 1995; De Landa 2006; Deleuze and Guattari 1987; Pool 1984; Eglash 1999; Escobar 2008; Juris 2008a; Lansing 2006; Marston, Jones, and Woodward 2005; Milgram 1967).

In this chapter, I employ the language of *complexity* to describe the evolution of transnational networking as a complex historical process. I draw upon historical ethnographic material from an initial process of transnational networking surrounding the New International Information Order and the development of a pre-Internet civil society network. Ultimately, I outline the prospect for a provisional network ethnography that takes into account the small and hidden history of technological collaboration among transnational networkers. More deliberately, I seek to represent history in a way that reflects the aspirations of the activists in the ongoing struggle for information freedom in the hopes of lending weight to such labors.

REPRESENTING COMPLEXITY

The task of representation is necessarily the art of defining structures. Anthropologists use observation as an instrument for recording social transactions. However, observations of people and places contain expectations about behavior, even as they reflect cues about possibility, utility, and nonutility. In this sense, the ethnographic lens is an instrument for grasping reality, but it is also a projection of a reality. The word *projection* is instructive because it reveals the purposefulness of the looking. The act of projecting also betrays the unexamined intents of representation. While projection is an exhibition of one's ontological reality, there is a simultaneous projection of unconscious attributes, thoughts, and emotions that are ascribed to the observed world. For some time, ethnographers have been aware of the connection between the subject under observation and the ramifications of negative projections. This awareness is an offshoot of reflexivity and a consideration of the power in the gaze of the observer (see Asad 1973; Bourdieu 1984; Ruby and Myerhoff 1982).

Yet, often there has been difficulty incorporating the flip side of the representational dynamic when it comes to characterizing human behavior without resorting to categorical projections of difference. At issue is the concept of an "incommensurability of difference." A central premise underlying the concept of incommensurability is that particular cultural formations are so intrinsically separate and different as to be unintelligible to one another. Moreover, such difference is further quantified into hierarchical notions of inside and outside, or above and below. The tendency to lump behavior into social hierarchies is an outgrowth of the comparative method. From its inception, the methodology set up a double bind for the discipline. During the nineteenth century, the comparative method ordained a set of general laws about human nature, thus laying the groundwork for exclusion based on differences, which were further ascribed to notions of dominant and subordinate culture (see Santos 2006; Yngvesson 1992). Even though current ethnographic convention affords that individual identity may be socially constructed, one's associations are somehow rendered internally consistent. Thus, the tendency remains to attribute to social organization what cannot be assigned to identity.

This tendency may be recognized in the portrayal of good and bad transnationals. The process of valuation reveals the preference for distinct categories of activism: the socialist over anarchist, indigenous over union, social movement over NGO. These distinctions often have more to do with the signature of academic specialization than the breakdown of cultural practices in space and time. The technique perpetuates an overemphasis on the preeminence of diversity as culturally intrinsic while linking such observations to the categorical ordering of embraceable and unembraceable differences.

Often cultural differences are assigned to place-based contexts—for instance, the informal sector, the periphery, or the least developed. In this sense, activity is subject to the representational scales that characterize social life in terms of tenuousness, insignificance, and divisibility against an adversarial force depicted as unified and global. The Zapatistas were aware of this insider-outsider dynamic when they proposed "One no, many yeses" (see Khasnabish, this volume). This slogan was a call not for multiculturalism but for an alternative representational strategy. In academic language, one could call it a methodology.

People and places do not occur in isolation. Every place is defined in relation to another. Yet, through the process of comparison, the specter of division emerges. The distinction is most evident when invoking location. The rootedness of local life seems evident, just as the verticality, and thus dominance, of global life appears equally apparent (Dirlik 1998). It is within the duality of this global-local distinction that people and places fall subject to the laws of scales and ordering. The challenge, then, remains to develop an ethnographic project that is sensitive to difference without fetishizing it, and that is able to envision diversity as part of a longer transformative process rather than segmenting difference from social context. Moreover, the task remains to represent events and practices without succumbing to a narrative that reifies the winners and losers of history.

The current globalizing impetus is but one of a series of discourses that aim to capture the "pure" identity, "pure" place, or "pure" body, in effect to isolate the discrete attributes of culture as captured, articulated, and subdivided within the truth of representation (Foucault 1975). The power of such an impulse has been reflected in the inability to conjure counter-proposals to the dominant narratives of our time. In their project to deconstruct capitalism, Julie Gibson and Katherine Graham, writing together under the name J. K. Gibson-Graham, insisted that discourses about the economy—as an essential, global capitalist system—represented deliberate attempts to project capitalism as the central organizing force in social experience. This included an understanding that politics, culture, and subjectivity categorically reinforce each other. In this sense, place, biology, and life are subsumed under a narrative that essentializes any uniqueness while simultaneously projecting their subordinate status. Gibson-Graham's research revealed that the majority of economic activity, even in the United States, has been noncapitalist. Yet while social life is incredibly diverse, the discourse regarding the economy has remained hegemonic (Gibson-Graham 1996). In this sense, the power of the ideology behind neoliberalism has been a closed system: "an end of history" (Fukuyama 1992).

It does not take a great leap of imagination to surmise that behind such spatial references stand "enormous omissions, absences, and social invisibilities" (Delgado Díaz 2004, 53). Boaventura de Sousa Santos (2006) detailed such negation when describing the "sociology of absences" to contrast the epistemic systems of the Northern and Southern Hemispheres. He associated the ontological commitments of the North with capitalism as spun from the long history of colonialism and European rationality. The Northern ontology remains devoted to fundamental principles. This is reflected in a monoculture of knowledge that produces linear time, the naturalization of difference, hierarchical scale, productive efficiency, and the globalizing language of universal truth. In this view, the epistemology of the North has been a vast engine driving what is plural into conformity. Santos compares the Northern framework to the potential of a Southern ontology that is inclusive of an ecology of knowledges, the recognition of differences, trans-scales, multiple productivities, and biodiversity (2006, 15–34). While there is an implied dichotomy between North and South in Santos's framework, it remains possible to imagine that the promise of such imagery derives from its ability to project difference without recourse to hierarchy.

When it comes to describing complexity in terms of networks, it is difficult to fix the essence of representation according to scale. Most networks are of a relatively transient nature. They exist in a continual state of formation. This distinction was identified by Bruno Latour when drawing attention to the performance of networks. Many mechanical networks are thought of as singular devices. For instance, an automobile with a disabled engine causes the driver to become aware of the vehicle's constitution as a network of parts (Latour 1996). For a social example, one may consider the World Trade Organization (WTO) as an assembly of actors who habitually perform their roles so as not to dissolve the structure of the trade network. When subject to scrutiny, the performance may become rigid to mask internal tensions, or it may dissolve. The unfixed nature of performance in this case conveys some of the complexity of human relations. This observation about performance reveals how relationships are fluidly constituted. As Sallie A. Marston, John Paul Jones, and Keith Woodward (2005) suggest, networks do not automatically assign individuals a position that fixes their subjectivity within force relations. At the same time, the nature of openness does not necessarily become trapped within the language of "absolute flows," which often dominates the conceptualization of networks. Networks are neither totally fixed nor free flowing. From actor-network theory we gain a sense of both the materiality and contingency of networks as they draw resources and energy and are assembled from human and nonhuman elements. This allows us to appreciate connections. It offers the possibility of projecting a nonessentialized representation of social organization coupled with a nonessentialized version of events.

HISTORY AS A NETWORK

History may be thought of in a networked framework as the organization of events and activities in the complexity of daily life. Behavior in these terms is unbounded, creative, and multiple—subject to ordering and dis-ordering—while spatial relations are continually composed and decomposed through human activity. In this framework, history becomes plural. The emphasis is on openness. A vast majority of human activity transpires at the smallest levels of social action. The word *grassroots* is the embodiment of such a distinction. Grassroots invokes the imagery of the earth at the surface of soil. It implies a groundswell of practices and events, a history teeming with social activity.

Networks incorporate out of diversity to assemble and form part of a larger trajectory. The history of social struggle is similarly diverse and borrowed from preceding movements, fashioned from the cherished heir-looms of resistance and spun out of a cross-fertilization of activities, ideas, and strategies. Today's social struggles are part of a legacy bequeathed by generations of activists and scholars. Even much of the terminology has been borrowed. The World Social Forum slogan "Another World Is Possible" follows a genealogy derived from the Zapatista imaginary of "another world," itself claimed from the "Another World Development" of civil society organizing in the postcolonial language of the last century.[1]

FIRST-WAVE TRANSNATIONAL NETWORKING

Transnational organizing refers to a conscious form of activism across borders, fostered by the use of communication networks. This first wave of transnational networking took place predominantly among advocates of decolonization, often emerging in the context of negotiations at the UN. The main protagonists were political intellectuals from the global South who had been educated in the Western political tradition. Civil society groups began participating earnestly in such discussions during the 1970s and these two groups formed a transnational network of advocacy focused on environmental and global justice issues. The movement was animated by postwar cosmopolitan aspirations. However, the increasingly sophisticated use of communication systems caused the coalition to diverge, tending toward self-organized and autonomous distributions of activity. Such activities commingled with the technological features of the computer networks themselves. Transnational activists built an early computer network to aid their organizing efforts that was designed to be open, adaptable, and alive. More specifically, the technology was created as part of a mutually interactive political scheme that came to influence behavior even as the architects built the system to facilitate their actions that were already in process.[2]

One of the most important transnational gatherings in this early stage of transnational networking was the Asia-Africa Conference held in Bandung, Indonesia, in 1955 (see Amin 1990, 1–37; Carter and O'Meara 1985, 31–44). In this meeting, Third Worldism was a cause for unity among decolonized countries and represented the germ of "another development" that was neither completely capitalist nor communist. This initial wave of transnational networking also drew momentum from the rise of the nonstate sector, a phenomenon stirred in part by the formation of multilateral agencies, such as the Bretton Woods institutions and the growth of the UN system. In particular, transnational activism grew apace with a number of multilateral environmental negotiations. The expansion of the UN contributed to the emergence of new modalities of citizenship, even as a unified trade system cohered around the idea of a coordinated global economy (see Appadurai 2002; Chabbott 1999; Ribeiro 1998). The rise of multilateralism and the cacophony of activism surrounding such proceedings comprised two ends of the same rope, each legitimating the other at the expense of the state while contributing to transnational modes of identification.

The 1972 Stockholm Conference on the Human Environment represented a major change in international diplomacy. Prior to the conference, international proceedings were monopolized by states. During the conference in Stockholm, civil society groups were allowed to interact with delegates, obtain information, and lobby for their causes. Alliances were formed between postcolonial delegates and civil society groups. For the first time, both sets of groups had firsthand information to share, allowing for an expansion of the deliberations with the possibility of radical participation (Selin 2003, 1–15). The environmental meeting formed a significant point of divergence. In the following years, a number of civil society groups turned their attention away from national campaigns to focus on the international arena, which was seen as more receptive to their environmental goals.

The circulation of extragovernmental discourses concerned with the environment, development, trade, and human rights within the UN became an undercurrent facilitating the idea of nonstate governance (see Chabbott 1999; Ribeiro 1998; Selin 2003). Arun Agrawal (2005) refers to this phenomenon as *environmentality* to highlight the union of the environment with Foucauldian ideas of governance, specifically the way in which new forms of knowledge, institutions, power, and identity form in the context of global reorganization. While much of this transformation may be viewed as part of the process of state disinvestment (regarding subcontracting services to the private sector), the shift also fueled the practice of horizontal politics and direct modes of political access.

The process of networking tended to foster modalities of governance based on self-organization and self-representation. Though globally oriented, many groups began articulating their claims on the basis of situated politics, by identification with a location, culture, or ethnic affiliation. While not completely divorced from notions of liberal individualism, such categories also transcended their designation by way of shared group practices that favored cooperative arrangements and collaborative struggles for autonomy bolstered by the collective use of communication systems.

Arjun Appadurai has written that "one of the many paradoxes of democracy is that it is organized to function within the borders of the nation-state—through such organs as legislatures, judiciaries, and elected governments" (2002, 45). The project is premised on a view of the common good as administered through the practices of voting and representative politics. Representative democracy is founded on the utility of government by proxy, whereby elected officials maintain the authority to act for "the people." This vision stands opposed to direct democracy or anarchist forms of self-representation, in which no one can speak for another. Everyone has a voice. Direct and representative democracy exist as somewhat idealized constructions because each has been theorized within the context of the nation-state. The logic of democracy, however, only makes sense if it is universalized because the pretense of access is global in aspiration, particularly when regarding discourses surrounding the freedom of information and universal human rights.

First-wave activists built the mechanism for an informational transnationalism when they constructed the architectural commons for global communication. They constructed the system on the premise of a global democracy they foresaw as imminent. The initial network contained the purposes, protocols, and tactics for expanding the "another development" paradigm. Through repeated use, the early techniques for cyber activism became more deeply embedded in the ethos of activist practice. The urge to network, therefore, grew out of the transnational orientation that remained part of the postcolonial discussions of "another development," followed by a second wave of networking facilitated by electronic communication.[3]

SECOND-WAVE TRANSNATIONAL NETWORKING

Such networking activities were already under way in 1972 when the UN Educational, Scientific, and Cultural Organization (UNESCO) held its first deliberations, titled "The Use of Satellite Broadcasting for the Free Flow of Information, the Spread of Education and Greater Cultural Exchange." This conversation continued during the 1973 Summit Conference of Nonaligned Countries in Algiers, as leaders called for action to "reorganize the existing communication channels which are a legacy of the colonial past and have hampered free, direct, and fast communication between them" ("Moving" 1976, 8). In July 1976, the ministers of information for nonaligned countries met in New Delhi and reached a critical agreement for the establishment of a network of press agencies from which to pool their resources and share information. Follow-up conferences occurred in different developing countries from 1974 until 1980 (8–11).

An influential conference in this regard was the 1975 Dag Hammarskjöld Foundation "Third World Journalists' Seminar," held in conjunction with a UN special session. The seminar proceedings were made widely available to a number of parties, including reporters, intellectuals, members of civil society, and various agencies for public education and information (see Da Costa 1976; Raghavan 1976; Somavia 1976). During the seminar the attendees devised their own vision of information empowerment that they named the New International Information Order (NIIO), calling for a coming era of information freedom:

Citizens have a right to inform and be informed about the facts of development, its inherent conflicts and the changes it will bring about, locally and internationally.

Under present conditions, information and education are only too often monopolized by the power structure, which manipulates public opinion to its own ends and tends to perpetuate preconceived ideas, ignorance and alienation.

A global effort should be made to give the new international relations their human dimension and to promote the establishment of genuine cooperation between peoples on the basis of equality and recognition of their cultural, political, social and economic diversity. The image of the Other should reach each of us, stripped of the prevailing ethnocentric prejudices, which are the characteristic feature of most of the messages currently transmitted.

Such an effort should be concerned both with information and with education in the broadest sense of the word; it should be directed towards "conscientization" of citizens to ensure their full participation in the decision-making process. (Dag Hammarskjöld Foundation 1975, 17–18)

This consensus statement was notable for the way it predicted the coming digital age, broadening the concept of development to encompass the public right to information awareness. In the declaration, local control over information was articulated as the key to broadening public participation in the political process. The participants called for the NIIO—an idea predicated on the faith that widespread economic change and alternative development would be readily adopted through the UN system.[4] The participants referred to "information dependence" exemplified by the unequal relations between the Third World and the companies controlling the information for the benefit of wealthy nations (Raghavan 1976). The NIIO became a movement to dislodge the corporate hold on news and information based on the recognition that four transnational companies (United Press International, Associated Press, Reuters, and Agence France Press) dominated world news distribution leading to a structural dependence that reinforced power relations between North and South.

The authors of the NIIO criticized the transnational news system on three grounds. First, it was recognized that transnational news agencies carried a political-military-intelligence dimension; sometimes, the relationship was covert, as when Western journalists doubled as agents for their home countries. More often, the relationship had to do with promoting certain kinds of asymmetrical relations between North and South whereby developing countries were often portrayed as open for specific forms of military intervention and political interference. Second, the dominant press agencies were denounced for promoting economic and industrial trade policies that were unfavorable toward the South. The Bretton Woods institutions were named as specific instruments for engendering the unequal division of power and wealth in the world. More significantly, such trade bodies were seen as integral to the creation of "mimetic development models," which specified a uniform path for development at the expense of another development vision (Somavia 1976, 17). Finally, transnational news agencies were accused of promoting a consumer culture seen as alien and corrosive to many of the values of the newly independent nations. Principally, such a worldview was seen as affording "the control of that key instrument of contemporary society: information. It is the vehicle for transmitting values and life styles to Third World countries which stimulate the type of consumption and the type of society necessary to the transnational system as a whole" (Somavia 1976, 17).

The NIIO declaration was marked by the language of the day and contained vague references to "the system" and "power structures" ("Moving" 1976, 8). But the recommendations were notable for the emphasis on a diversity of opinion and the insistence upon information as crucial for political equality. Throughout the 1970s, the NIIO remained part of a growing movement for accessing and controlling information in developing nations (8). Such advocacy was based on an ad hoc coalition that arose in the space that opened in the political arena. The movement allowed for a tentative transnational alliance to emerge. A party to the discussions characterized the times in terms of its pervasive hopefulness:

[There was] a lot of the new thinking around the world; the new economy happened in those days. I think that was like a central body of hope where the Third World got together and that's where all the new ideas were developed. At that time, all of civil society clustered around the UN. There was really a momentum to make use of the United Nations to actually try to establish a more just world order. In that space there was something like a move in civil society to take over the United Nations. Afterward, you could perhaps call it a bit naïve, but there was a lot of effort to make sure that the United Nations was representing another development that was more equal and more just. There was a lot of input on the part of NGOs, going to the FAO [Food and Agriculture Organization] meetings and manifestations in front of the building. In the aftermath, a lot of NGOs were formed, new groups to actually bring the debate forward. It was a sign of the times that the UN opened up. (Personal interview, March 16, 1999)

The participants involved in the Third World Journalists' Seminar were astute in assessing that the control over information was integral to achieving political and economic clout in the world. Additionally, the group predicted that information would only grow more critical in the coming years. However, they were not in a position to anticipate the extent of the coming information revolution. Their prescriptions for achieving the NIIO mostly centered around establishing a network of journalists from developing countries to access and share information. Such networks were based on traditional broadcast and print journalism. Yet by the early 1980s, the commercial Internet was expanding and alternative communication systems were also being envisioned.

The collaboration that emerged among information activists would not have materialized except for the linkages obtained in the transnational field of postcolonial discussions. This field engendered a set of specific social relationships that encouraged transnational ways of thinking and behaving that became more entangled over time, even as the capacity to network deepened.

ANOTHER WAVE OF TRANSNATIONAL NETWORKING

The urge to communicate internationally began as a deliberate attempt to construct a communications medium to facilitate transnational activism. Building on the successes of the NIIO, activists began to seek ways to use emerging computer technologies for social purposes. In 1980, the Canadian media activist Christopher Pinney was heading a number of organizations, including the International Coalition for Development Action in Brussels and the International Development Education Research Association in Vancouver. Part of his job also required him to sit on the board of the Canadian Council for International Cooperation. Merging the three organizational perspectives, he summarized the interest in information:

The constant issue that came up in meetings with our Southern partners was the issue of how do we have regular ongoing communication aside from coming together at a conference every once and a while. From that basis, I took a systematic interest in establishing and setting up an NGO computer network. As we looked around at educational resources, educating people with information about the Third World, transferring information back to the Third World, the whole issue became one of technology—a technology transfer mechanism for information. Doing an analysis of development made you realize that in fact the North was the primary repository of information about the South . . . and most of that information was inaccessible other than to academics. So it was looking at that whole perspective, of "how do we get information back to the South, how do we actually start to have a communication around development with ourselves and partners," that led to my interest in setting up a development communication center. It was in that context I started looking at computer database systems that could manage information, store information, and then secondarily distribute that information across Canada and with our partners in the South. (Quoted in Murphy 2000, 166)

At the same time, a UN-affiliated organization based in Rome called the International Documentation Center was created to assist civil society with documentation and training in information science. The International Documentation Center supported the NIIO by aiding developing countries with their information needs, including the creation of a manual indexing system meant for computer systems that they termed "freetext."

Starting in late 1981, the International Documentation Center sponsored a series of conferences for international civil society groups that were experimenting with communications in Valletri, Italy, to strategize ways to create a prototype of computer networking. Such a system would need to function using affordable and homemade computer systems, as well as operate over low-grade phone lines. Pinney collaborated with David Balsam of the International Development Research Center, Canada, to research the possibility of using computers and phone lines for information storage and retrieval. A decision was made to establish initial networking experiments in collaboration with civil society groups in Brazil, Chile, and Hong Kong.

Ongoing planning among the collaborators took place over a period of three years. These collaborations grew, forming their own centers of communication as regional nodes in a network of expanding operations. In October 1984, the collaborators met to evaluate their experiments. Partners from the three participating countries had managed to install and operate computer communications, demonstrating that sharing databases, e-mail, and conferencing were possible (Murphy 2000, 169). During the meeting, they made an agreement to formalize the development of the computer network and to set up further collaborations between North and South. They also established a new coalition (Interdoc) that would assist activists in the operation of computer networking. At the conclusion of the meeting, the participants signed the Valletri Agreement, agreeing to share information while formalizing a commitment to make computer networking open:

> The well-being of an individual and community depends on their access to and ability to apply information. Information is thus central in the development process in all societies. Recent rapid developments in information technology have opened up new possibilities for NGOs to communicate and share information. Such a global network only has a valid role to play in development if it is created by, linked to and at the service of local activities. It must be stressed that the management of information is not a goal in itself, but is simply an essential element in action for concrete and sustainable results and improvements in people's lives. Information management and related practices of networking must be geared to the mobilization of information, not its immobilization. (Quoted in Murphy 2000, 26)

Interdoc facilitated an international outreach program to teach activists how to use the computer system. A user's manual was prepared, titled "Communication for Progress: A Guide to International E-mail." Brian Murphy (2000) refers to this document as a manifesto for the operation of "The First Social Movement Cyberspace." The orientation of the guide specified that its mission was to deliver technology to the grassroots for liberation purposes and to facilitate the appropriation of information in order to better serve the people. The guide was clear about becoming not "one big network" but "an informal network of networks" (2000, 171).

Interdoc continued to expand internationally, linking together with other geographically dispersed civil society networks. In 1990, Interdoc activists collaborated with the Institute for Global Communications in

San Francisco to build a global network for use exclusively by civil society. The groups joined together to create a new computer network, the Association for Progressive Communications (APC). By the early 1990s, the APC was a fully functioning polycentric network servicing more than fifty nodes, including many in underserved areas of Africa, Asia, and Eastern Europe (see Slater 1998).[5]

Almost simultaneously, the UN began actively posting on the APC's conference boards to prepare for the Rio Earth Summit. UN representatives participated in online conferences, disseminated official documents, and posted policy briefings as well as logistical and agenda information. The APC staff provided computer communications and technical support during Summit Preparatory Committee meetings. These meetings were held in different countries to facilitate regional coordination for the upcoming event and were heavily populated by activist groups. In this way, the conversations that took place were slanted toward civil society concerns.

When the 1992 Rio Earth Summit eventually took place, many of the transnational discussions revolved around themes and issues that were already part of a conversation in process. Days before the summit, however, a decision was made to exclude most civil society representatives from the formal sessions. Hastily, a parallel counter-conference was convened by the rejected parties. This convergence space became a model of self-organized activity, because it was assembled with direct participatory collaboration among the network of global activist groups.

The Rio Earth Summit was meant to usher in a new era of sustainable development. The summit produced a number of noteworthy outcomes, including the Climate Change Convention and Kyoto Protocol, a position on indigenous territorial sovereignty, and the Convention on Biological Diversity. Civil society rallied around the Agenda 21 document, which specified the need to achieve just and sustainable goals by the next century. Throughout the summit, the APC operated through its Brazilian affiliate, Alternex. The network specialists set up on-site technical facilities for both the UN and the civil society convergence. They also established local area networks that linked to other APC sites, as well as connecting numerous e-mail addresses. Computers and printers were available for document preparation, while training and technical support were provided free of charge. In Rio, daily features in English, French, Portuguese, and Spanish were delivered through the APC message board to forty-seven civil society groups and multiple nodes in the different countries (O'Brien 2004).[6]

Even though activists were excluded from the proceedings, they gained their autonomy by assembling into a separate convergence and advocating their positions directly to the world media. The parallel civil society convergence became a networked site of transnational encounter while also opening a space for widespread engagement and collaboration. The value of the alternative space was not the influence it generated within the official Rio proceedings, but rather the effect it had on activism overall.

The run up to the summit process forced activists to mobilize for a chance to have input in environmental and development decision making. Even though the promised access never materialized, the mobilization led to subsequent networking activities. While the outcome of the Rio Earth Summit could barely be called a success, the civil society groups were hardly responsible for the failure—excluded as they were from the decision making. But what was more relevant was the way the summit affected civil society groups by accelerating their growth and transnational association with one another (Princen and Finger 1994, 209). The summit in Rio strengthened the transnational orientation of such groups who learned to network and strategize like never before. In the meantime it provided them a vehicle to do so. The effort created linkages and helped many organizations transcend their national focus. It helped to create a model of participation based on technological organizing and the building of a counter-convergence space. In other words, the transnational networking of activists prepared the way for the establishment of autonomous, self-organized zones of political activity characterized by transnational networking. Mobilized and networked, activists continued to build momentum. The Rio Earth Summit raised expectations about the environment and development. It led activists to believe that another world—inclusive, sustainable, and just—might arise.

SELF-ORGANIZATION

The civil society cyberspace possessed the capacity to self-organize. This was evidenced on January 1, 1994, when the APC network broadcasted that an indigenous movement calling itself the Zapatista National Liberation Army had captured seven towns in the Los Altos region of Chiapas, Mexico. The Zapatistas displayed a brilliant use of the APC network in a farsighted strategy to contain the Mexican military while mobilizing a vast, unseen reservoir of civil society to aid in their objectives.[7] The defense strategists John Arquilla and David Ronfeldt characterized the Zapatista struggle as the first full-scale information warfare (see, e.g., Ronfeldt et al. 1999).

In their struggle, the Zapatistas were able to count on the self-organization of a multitude of civil society groups acting as a protective wedge between themselves and the state. The wedge was physical, as with the human rights observers who stationed themselves within Zapatista territory to safeguard their sovereignty (Cleaver 1995). But the wedge was also virtual—residing in the nodes, connections, and innumerable eyes watching the situation. These eyes formed a plane of observation that constrained the actions of the Mexican state and amplified the means available to the rebellion. In many ways, the Zapatista struggle was well situated to carry out both virtual and on-the-ground resistance. This was due to the history of popular action in the region and the labor expended by local organizations and NGOs that set up the technical infrastructure for an electronic communications system a decade earlier.[8]

The Zapatista struggle produced a bandwagon effect. Out of the subsequent Zapatista *encuentros* (gatherings) arose the Peoples' Global Action (PGA), a transnational anticapitalist network of coordination and communication, which organized a number of protests against the Bretton Woods institutions by using the networked capability of affinity groups and new information technologies. These Peoples' Global Action–inspired processes would help give rise to and ultimately become superseded by the World Social Forum, an even broader networked space of transnational encounter (Juris 2008a). While not seamless, it was this grassroots history of transnational networking that allowed the idea of "another world" to carry forward from one era to the next.

POLYCENTRIC EMERGENCE

In his formulation of actor-network theory, Bruno Latour (1993) proposed that the power of a network derives from the sum of ever longer and denser network chains. Although they may be envisioned as corporate hierarchies, powerful networks are geographically dispersed and horizontally organized. The key to deconstructing a powerful network is to analytically grasp how it is constituted and how it monopolizes assets, and the resources it mobilizes to maintain control. This technique allows us to recognize the occurrence of monopoly networks and their inevitable weaknesses, as well as the networks of resistance to them.

For an illustration of such contingency, one need only examine the composition of the demonstration against the WTO in Seattle in 1999. The organizing effort for Seattle took the better part of a year and required money, resources, venues, food, housing, and other necessities. The coordination occurred on multiple interacting planes. With the help of the Internet, the event self-organized a seemingly illogical coalition of individuals and groups working to provide the necessary inputs (see Daro, this volume; Juris 2008a). The event was punctuated by a number of bizarre juxtapositions: a fifteen-foot skeleton on stilts wearing a sash reading "WTO under siege" near a group of butterflies carrying a wide net labeled "Global Civil Society Network"; black-masked protesters arguing about neoliberalism with members of a German trade delegation; demonstrators locked together with PVC pipes and bottle fed water by uniformed airline pilots; a group of children dressed as sea turtles asking directions from police in riot gear; diplomats from Qatar shaking their heads while dancers leapt around a giant Mother Earth puppet; white-robed delegates from the global South strategizing with Northern NGOs; Young Republicans trading insights with ACT UP activists; union members in motorcycle gear dancing to a Brazilian drum band; and a group of nuns in full habit standing in front of a fifty-foot green condom with the name "safe trade."

The convergence was a hodgepodge of demands and desires. Simultaneously, the event opened a portal into the horizontality of difference. Seattle was an encuentro, in the Zapatista use of the word. Moreover, it would be a mistake to represent the formal practices of the trade meeting as distinct from the street activities, as each interpenetrated the other. One of the boldest moves involved the trade minister for Ethiopia who led the majority of indebted nations out of the talks to join the carnival against capital in the streets. A participant familiar with the behind-the-scenes WTO deliberations framed the activities in this way:

> *Protest* is too narrow a term for what happened; participation, agitation—definitely. All government officials were tremendously impacted by what went on in Seattle. You have to understand what happened in Seattle was an example of what I call an inside-outside

process. It wasn't only the protests that did it. It was the fact that the protests lined up on many points with the positions of delegates who were parties to the WTO. And maybe a lot of the protesters didn't have any idea of that, which I don't think they did. They don't understand that there are politics within the WTO. The WTO is not a monolithic kind of thing. It was the Third World minus the three Latin American countries that were part of the Plan Miami, minus Mexico, which supported the Millennial Round. What finally came to be called the Compromise Group, which everybody that wasn't part of anything else was thrown into, those were the ones who walked out. That's a huge group. It's enormous. It represents maybe three quarters of the world's population and maybe 85 percent of the world's biodiversity. (Personal interview, April 28, 2003)

Seattle revealed the underlying divergence that foments momentum. Viewed from a network perspective, the event was derived from a polymorphic combination of social actions, resources, technologies, and environments that interacted on many simultaneous planes of activity. Such diversity does not lend networks an a priori progressive nature; there are well-established military and corporate networks that operate in the same space as their liberatory counterparts. The constitution of a network, however, seems to confer advantages to grassroots emancipatory politics because networking favors modes of sharing and collectivity that complement the social activity often absent from reactionary politics. The challenge confronting ethnography is to account for such points of contact, hybridity, and migration of cultural activities that constitute the complexity of a network.

TOWARD A NETWORK ETHNOGRAPHY

As chroniclers of human geography, ethnographers were among the first to engage transnationally. From its inception, ethnography has involved multiple voyages and crossings between cultures. Anthropology has embraced the translation of languages and worlds. The horizontal encounters I have recounted reflect earlier waves of transnational networking that stemmed from a desire for political access. Such interactions involved direct collaboration beyond the constraints of state politics. In the case of transnational networking, what led to the horizontality and self-organization was the kind of labor involved. This labor unleashed enormous creativity when deployed by activists to create their own communications systems. Such creativity operated on a positive-feedback loop, generating a predisposition toward the politics of autonomy. The spirit of the politics was built into the spirit of the technology in a mutually reinforcing fashion (see, e.g., Juris 2008a). While in subsequent years transnational organizing has undergone periods of dormancy and activation, the desire for another world has remained remarkably consistent. It is in acknowledgment of such continuity that the proposed idea for a network ethnography emerges (see also Casas-Cortés, Osterweil, and Powell, this volume; Escobar 2008; Juris 2008a).

In order for a network ethnography to become more than a suggestive methodology, the technique needs to focus on human organization from a different ontological vantage point. That is to say, rather than describing human activity in terms of discrete individual associations, a network ethnography would examine the multiple entanglements of human behavior across established boundaries and categories. History in this method becomes significant for its continuity as opposed to its rupture into discrete units of time. The emphasis is on the relationships under construction, including all of the accumulated activity that occurs at ground level. Such a technique would recognize the transnational, and therefore geographic, dimensions of networks.

For a number of geographers, networks have inspired a rethinking of sociality in terms of flat or horizontal relationships (Gibson-Graham 1996; Marston, Jones, and Woodward 2005). A network ethnography would render human geographic interactions in terms of their lateral character. Such an undertaking would aim to describe the materiality of surface features: the landscape and its division into continents, countries, climates, plants, inhabitants, and industries. Networks provide a means for portraying mutual relations writ large upon the planet. They depict a sense of space through the use of geometric planes, as a plane is a surface that conveys activity. Planes contain lines that adjoin points along a flat or even surface. They are horizontal in that they provide a surface for describing interrelations. In this conceptualization, horizontality is not a one-dimensional layer. Rather, a plane is a surface that is able to accommodate features and shapes not possible in three-dimensional space. A horizontal plane represents multidimensionality.

The idea of horizontality suggests that the Earth's surface is the preeminent plane that encompasses all others. Horizontality conjures the continuousness of this surface as it weaves together the substance of life; the world's biodiversity, human diversity, and technical diversity are rendered in terms of fecundity and frailty. This concept imagines sociality existing along planes of intersecting activity that are flat and accessible. In this sense, a network ethnography uses the concept of horizontality as a theoretical tool for leveling.

In the geographic description of surfaces, the concept of networks is harmonious with observations in the physical sciences, thus presenting an opportunity to merge such findings with ethnographic techniques. The prospect of a network ethnography takes complexity seriously as a means for overcoming some of the limitations of representation. The technique is open to the materiality of both human and nonhuman circulations. It is not site specific but rather premised on movement. Envisioning sociality through networks allows for the possibility of representing multiple interacting planes of activity. To one degree or another, such activities become accessible for inspection. Such accessibility does not erase the existence of constellations of power. Nevertheless, examining power through the dynamics of networks exposes the links of associations, multiple access points, and physical weaknesses, much the way Latour proposed that power in a network is a function of longer, denser chains. Notwithstanding, the result of thinking in these terms is to speak of ethnography as a technique for recovering the surface accumulation of details. The task involves rendering what is usually small or unseen into accessibility.

At the same time, the technique entails a redeployment of the measurements and registers used to describe what is socially "given." The effort entails a readjustment of the lens of representation. As an engaged methodology, a network ethnography defines the research stance not merely in terms of what one chooses to research but also how and what is written. The task requires an ontological shift. It may involve entering into the still relatively uncharted territory of studying up (Nader 1972). Foremost, it means adopting complexity as the principle of research in the first instance, while drawing on the rich interdisciplinary language used to describe such processes. The language itself goes a long way toward repositioning the observational tools for envisioning sociality as complex, diverse, and multiplying. In some measure it involves adopting the language of fecundity, speaking in the many tongues of affirmation that replicate the Earth's processes for social and biological reproduction. This includes registering human and nonhuman complexity in all its bottom-up contradictory fertility. The technique remains faithful to the definition of emergence—out of one (provisional) order erupts an entirely new order.

As cultural habits become ever more horizontal, cross-pollinated, and expansive, the ethnographer becomes an extension of such political aspirations by virtue of situating him- or herself in the thick of social desire. Networks level the theoretical obstructions that distinguish between inside and outside, up and down. By way of commitment, a network ethnography rejects the false dichotomy between theory and action, recognizing that engaged ethnography is born of a knowledge forged in the fires of action. Such an acknowledgment accepts that critical theory is not the mother of social action; it is the other way around. We know what we know because we are in the midst of it.

NOTES

1   While it is difficult to pinpoint the exact origin of the phrase, the use of *another* to signify that diverse alternatives to capitalism have existed since at least the early 1970s when it was employed in the "another development" paradigm, under the sponsorship of the Dag Hammarskjöld Foundation and other agencies. Participants in those meetings went on to engage with the Zapatista encuentros. The same sponsoring organizations also contributed financial and technical support to the subsequent World Social Forums.

2   The idea of civil society has a long history. The use of the term in this text follows the lead of interviewees who employed the designation to refer to attitudes, practices, and modes of identification compatible with their transnational activism. In this case, the term is used in a Gramscian sense as something of an open container that reflects the intermediacy of perceived sectors and social activities.

3   "Another development" was a local-centric model of development promoted in the UN throughout the 1970s with support from Southern countries, civil society groups, and northern European countries. The technical support for the initiative was undertaken with assistance from the Dag Hammarskjöld Foundation. The movement lost financial and political momentum during the Reagan-Thatcher years.

4   The NIIO was an initiative that grew out of the New International Economic Order, a global economic-reorganization movement among postcolonial countries, civil society, and some northern European nations during the 1970s. The NIIO was theorized as a component of the New International Eco-

nomic Order, because information was viewed as crucial to the economy and thus necessary for grassroots empowerment.

5   I only provide a very brief account of the activities contributing to what Brian Murphy calls the "Prehistory of the Internet." For a more detailed account, see Murphy 2000; O'Brien 2004; and Sterpka 2006, 2008.

6   See the "History" page of the APC website, www.apc.org/en/about/history (accessed December 25, 2011).

7   See Information Habitat, "NGO Alternative Treaties: 2—Rio de Janeiro Declaration," habitat.igc.org/treaties/at-02.htm (accessed December 27, 2011).

8   The Institute for Global Communications (reformulated later to become IGC-APC) is one example. Previously, a local organization had set up an Internet connection in Mexico in 1989. After completing the various legal requirements, it formed PaxMex with the governmental telecom in Mexico and a connecting node in San Francisco. The connection lasted until 1993 when local civil society, including church, social, and human rights groups and NGOs collaborated to fund a communication alternative. Maria Elena Martinez-Torres (2001) claims that a key role was played by the women's group Mujer a Mujer (Women to Women) and Red Interinstitucional (Agency Network) and Servicios Informativos Procesados (Processed Information Services), who invited twenty-five organizations to donate money for a telephone line to establish the local network La Neta. La Neta was itself an NGO. With a grant from the local Catholic organization Fundacion de Apoyo a la Comunidad (Foundation for Community Support), they acquired a local server to set up their own node. PaxMex merged into La Neta and joined APC through PeaceNet. Throughout the early part of the decade this served as the primary Zapatista connection.

13

This Is What Democracy Looked Like

TISH STRINGER

In this chapter, I take a look back at Indymedia, a radical media collective and an early adapter to the Internet as we now know and experience it. Interactive and full of first-person multimedia reporting, Indymedia grew from a one-off experiment to report on a single demonstration into a transnational network—a full-fledged experiment in democracy from below. Indymedia was concurrently inventing similar tools and practices as Silicon Valley (such as photo and video sharing, open publishing, and peer-to-peer networks), but it did so with an orientation toward social justice rather than short-term profits. Indymedia began as a way for social movements to tell their own stories, but it inadvertently served as a training ground for a new generation of journalists who bring a radical vision to their work.

My research from 1999 to 2006 with Indymedia, a networked space (and community) of transnational encounter in which I was an active participant and a vocational observer, led to a practice of liminality. I spent a lot of time in-between: between locations, between roles, and between languages, media, and ethics. Networked spaces of transnational encounter are not fixed, rigid, or bounded locations for anyone involved. Add to that the dual roles of the activist-ethnographer and the hyphen separating them becomes home. In response, in this chapter I focus on the apparent dichotomies of such in-between places that characterize this field: citizen and reporter, producer and consumer, open and closed, activist and anthropologist. I offer three concepts to speak to these in-between places: the first is the mask, which mediates between Indymedia's commitment to openness and need to protect privacy; the second is the hybrid, a way to rethink the compartmentalized selves of academics who are participants in their field sites; and the third is the snitch, a problematizing figure for academics circulating among and writing about political activists.

BE THE MEDIA

At the close of the twentieth century, a new social movement took the public by surprise during the Ministerial Conference of the World Trade Organization (WTO) in 1999. Activists appeared on the streets of Seattle and caused people the world over to ask, "The World Trade Who?" Along with the antiglobalization street-protest movement, Seattle was also the birthplace of a new alternative media network called the Independent Media Center (IMC), or Indymedia (see fig. 13.1). Conjured by Zapatista dreams from the Lacandon Jungle and the brainchild of several alternative media groups,[1] Indymedia was set up in a Seattle storefront to provide grassroots firsthand coverage of those now historic events.

Organizers of the Seattle protest were tired of seeing their stories told through a corporate news lens from behind police lines. To avoid being dismissed, once again, by corporately owned media as uniformed rabble, they set plans in motion after a grassroots media conference in Austin, Texas, to open a media center that would facilitate the coverage being produced by a network of grassroots journalists in Seattle and around the world. A storefront media center, a couple of studios, and a central open publishing website were to become the production and distribution nodes of the fledgling independent media center. My excerpt from the notes distributed following the conference sessions in Austin show how planning was devoted to the technological infrastructure of multimedia coverage and how distribution was made possible through a mix of traditional and new digital-media forms:

Technically, the news of actions coming out of the [IMC] in Seattle will be abstractly converted into print, audio, video, graphics, and photography. The available methods for distributing these media

FIGURE 13.1.
Seattle Independent Media Center, 1999.
Photo by Paul Riismandel.

include web, email, listserv, RealAudio, RealVideo, MP3, satellite, audio and videotape, disk, paper, mail, phone, fax, events and
gatherings, and word of mouth. . . . A one-stop-shopping website,
to be mirrored on decentralized URLs and servers, was proposed
to connect people outside of Seattle with the available news. The
site would allow media activists on the ground in Seattle to upload
their particular offerings through a web-based interface, and also
allow any community or media group outside of Seattle to down-
load whatever they would like to pass on.[2]

With a populist "be the media" approach and belief that "everyone is a reporter," Indymedia urged all to participate and encouraged people to tell
their own stories in their own voices. Errol Maitland of *Democracy Now*, a
popular Left-wing radio program, described this practice in an interview
with Indymedia's own *Blind Spot* newspaper: "Let the voice of the people
be heard. If it's in a different language, get a translator. If they stutter

and stammer, let them speak. If they have a foreign accent and they talk 'funny,' let them speak."[3]

The IMC straddled the local-global divide by providing localized news via print and low-power radio for people in Seattle, as well as video programs and Internet content for national and international audiences. Some of the IMC media projects produced in Seattle during the WTO protests were five daily half-hour video programs called *Showdown in Seattle*, produced and aired on Deep Dish TV via satellite;[4] six daily editions of the *Blind Spot*, a broadsheet newspaper made of 11 x 17-inch folded photocopies and distributed on the streets;[5] *Studio X*, a twenty-four-hour-a-day radio program streaming online and on low-power FM; and Indymedia .org, the website, which received more than one million hits on November 30, 1999, alone. The very first posting to Indymedia.org boldly declared the intention of the IMC and foreshadowed how Indymedia would become an early adapter to contemporary online media practices: "The resistance is global . . . [,] a trans-pacific collaboration has brought this website into existence. The web dramatically alters the balance between multinational and activist media. With just a bit of coding and some cheap equipment, we can set up a live automated website that rivals the corporates. Prepare to be swamped by the tide of activist media makers on the ground in Seattle and around the world, telling the real story behind the World Trade Agreement."[6]

In the late 1990s, a constellation of factors produced an environment ripe for the successful launch of an international network of alternative media at the service of social movements—a "collective of collectives": the rise of the Zapatistas, the networking of groups fighting corporate globalization and free trade, Internet-based progressive media groups, the widespread availability of consumer-grade digital-media technology, the open-source and free software movement, and a particular piece of software called Active, which made open publishing possible.[7]

Indymedia traces its roots to the Zapatista *encuentros* (gatherings) in Chiapas, Mexico. There are three main reasons for this. First, the Zapatistas, by pioneering the rapid diffusion of news and ideology through Internet-based e-mail listservs, bulletin boards, and activist websites, were able to build a transnational solidarity network and could sound the alarm and mobilize international assistance rapidly when they encountered state repression (Arquilla and Ronfeldt 1996; Cleaver 1999;

Khasnabish 2008). Second, the global justice movement identified with the Zapatistas' struggle, a central pillar of which was resistance to neo-liberal capitalism. Third, and perhaps most important, the Zapatistas envisioned an international activist communications network as an alternative to a corporate-dominated media landscape. They communicated this directly to the very activists who would go on to form the first IMC in Seattle through a videotaped message from the Zapatista spokesperson Subcomandante Marcos at the Freeing the Media Teach-in in 1997:

> We have a choice: we can have a cynical attitude in the face of the media, to say that nothing can be done about the dollar power that creates itself in images, words, digital communication, and computer systems that invades not just with an invasion of power, but with a way of seeing that world, of how they think the world should look. We could say, well, "That's the way it is" and do nothing. Or we can simply assume incredulity: we can say that any communication by the media monopolies is a total lie. We can ignore it and go about our lives. But there is a third option that is neither conformity, nor skepticism, nor distrust: that is to construct a different way—to show the world what is really happening—to have a critical world view and to become interested in the truth of what happens to the people who inhabit every corner of this world.[8]

Originally conceived as a one-time experiment, the up-to-the-minute rich multimedia coverage provided by Indymedia at the protests in Seattle was wildly successful, and participants wondered whether this model could be repeated in other cities. As the video activist Jill Friedberg explained, "We've also started talking about using this model and trying to go elsewhere around the country and the world and help people set up similar centers so that there really could be an alternative media network."[9]

Indymedia continued to grow following the first day of transmissions during the WTO protests in Seattle, following the trajectory of mass global justice mobilizations at meetings of institutions of global finance and trade, such as the World Bank, International Monetary Fund, and the G8. Quickly adding new sites and new cities to the growing list of collectives, Indymedia was rapidly becoming the largest experiment in transnationally coordinated, volunteer-based media making ever. As explained on the Indymedia website: "The independent media center is a network of collectively run media outlets for the creation of radical, accurate, and passionate tellings of the truth. We work out of a love and inspiration for people who continue to work for a better world, despite corporate media's distortions and unwillingness to cover the efforts to free humanity."[10]

All local IMCs agreed to a shared set of working principles that defined Indymedia as a grassroots, independent, noncorporate media network that would function as a decentralized, leaderless organization informed by concepts of consensus and participation. The ability of everyone to become the media by uploading content to open-publishing websites was successful in terms of news coverage and distribution, but this also became a communications strategy for an emergent global social movement (Juris 2008a). Sheri Herndon, a founding member of Indymedia Seattle, described the network in 2003, after a period of sustained growth:

> So what is Indymedia? Indymedia is many things to many people; it is no ONE thing. [It is:]
>
> An international news organization;
> A participatory media production and distribution platform;
> A decentralized social and digital network;
> A people's CNN;
> An activist communications network;
> An experiment in global democracy;
> A social phenomenon;
> An advocacy network;
> A bulletin board;
> An organizing tool;
> A chat room;
> A laboratory for social and technological innovation;
> An incredible experiment in self-governance; and
> A pioneer in the communication landscape.[11]

Indymedia continued to grow, rapidly and steadily, hand in hand with a rise in social movement action around the globe. Five years after it was created, Indymedia had grown from one website and collective in Seattle to nearly two hundred local IMCs whose participatory websites provided news production, distribution, and commentary in eighteen languages and across six continents. Indymedia had become a full-fledged, global network—quickly becoming a radical household name.

COLLABORATIVE MODE OF PRODUCTION

This chapter's title refers to the film *This Is What Democracy Looks Like*, coproduced by the Seattle IMC and Big Noise Films (see also Khasnabish, this volume), which is about the demonstrations that shut down the Ministerial Conference of the WTO in Seattle (the film title is taken from a chant that is popular with street activists and asserts that public, political activism is an expression of democracy in action).[12] The film was made from over 350 hours of footage captured by more than a hundred video activists who worked with the IMC. Its official description quotes Rick Rowley, the codirector, as explaining: "We had more cameras in the street than any corporate news agency could possibly mobilize. This amazing collection of activist video footage gives the film a scope and intimacy that the corporate media could never achieve."[13] The film documented a watershed event in contemporary politics and purported to evidence a new kind of democracy afoot in the United States. But the film also heralded a new kind of democracy in media making, one that allowed multiple insiders to share their perspectives without a corporate filter, to weave their voices together collectively.

In his book *An Accented Cinema*, Hamid Naficy (2001) differentiates between mainstream and alternative cinemas by highlighting the differences between them with respect to content as well as the means of production, distribution, and reception. Naficy follows Walter Benjamin in arguing that it is not sufficient to have oppositional politics or content; in order for cinema to be considered "accented," oppositional production practices are also necessary. The work of film collectives (groups of people, such as Indymedia, working together on common projects with common aims and goals) is accented not only because of their alternate distribution and screening practices, but also because the production process itself differentiates it from a studio-oriented production model. Naficy characterizes this "collective mode of production" as "working collectively and considering filmmaking to be a type of 'collective enunciation' in which filmmakers and audiences are conjoined by their membership in communities of address. . . . [I]f the postindustrial mode tends to situate the directors as manufacturers and the spectators as consumers, the accented mode's collective enunciation and reception potentially blur the line that separates producers from consumers" (2001, 45).

Corporate media attempts to dehistoricize and depoliticize its production and distribution processes. It presents itself as an impartial professional observer by concealing its political and economic location. This posture of distance and objectivity is the aesthetic counterpart to a centralized and hierarchical corporate production process. Against this model, Indymedia is conscious of its involvement in the political moments it documents. It imagines its production, distribution, style, and content to be extensions of broader movements for cultural, political, and economic democratization. Indymedia video production is built around massively parallel collaborative storytelling that usually involves hundreds of loosely coordinated, autonomous camerapersons and dozens of editors sharing directorial decisions. Unlike the corporate news media, IMC cameras are not positioned as impartial outside observers; they are passionate participants in the events they document and their perspectives are intimate and engaged rather than distant and objective. In place of the monotone voice of corporate news, collaborative editing produces polyvocal videos that employ many different styles, ideological shades, and forms of address.

By using collective modes of production to make media, Indymedia is able to critique the mainstream media's production process by "inserting politics at the point of origination" through the very modalities used to create the films (Naficy 2001, 45). A collective mode of production is a social practice of openness; it opens the boundaries between fixed roles: directors, camerapersons, and reporters, and even between producers and consumers. This is not just media for media's sake; it is a political intervention in the fight against global capitalism in all its forms. Rowley defines this type of filmmaking as explicit political action: "Sometimes we fight with our bodies in the street, sometimes with pixels on a screen, but we are not making works of art, we are making a new world."[14] Participants in Indymedia consciously build their network and make media based on shared principles of participatory democracy, horizontality, and cooperation. In doing so, Indymedia is much more than the content it produces or a political critique or an intervention; it is a transnational social experiment in building alternatives, a concrete example of globalization from below.

OPEN AND CLOSE

As I have discussed, Indymedia is committed to radical openness. It was precisely the focus on openness that allowed Indymedia to experience the rapid growth that it did. Openness in Indymedia extends deep into its structure as horizontality and leaderlessness are negotiated using consensus-based decision-making practices and mechanisms of transparency. Not restricted to structure or to collective modes of production and consensus, however, openness is also expressed through technical practices (see also Juris, Caruso, Couture, and Mosca, this volume). The collaboration between the media makers and open-source software techies who helped launch Indymedia made openness a practice at work at every level of organization, down to the code.[15]

The software that powers Indymedia websites (such as the original Active) was designed so producers could publish news stories and multimedia themselves from their own Internet browsers and have the content appear immediately on the website with no editorial intervention (see Halleck 2002; Juris 2005a, 2008a; Kidd 2003; Meikle 2002; Noguera 2002; Pavis 2002; Uzelman 2002). But open publishing is more than just the simple, yet crucial, difference in the way news is distributed. Matthew Arnison, who was one of the programmers behind Active, broadly defined open publishing in a widely circulated and influential document in 2001: "Open publishing means that the process of creating news is transparent to the readers. They can contribute a story and see it instantly appear in the pool of stories publicly available. Those stories are filtered as little as possible to help the readers find the stories they want. Readers can see editorial decisions being made by others. They can see how to get involved and help make editorial decisions. If they can think of a better way for the software to help shape editorial decisions, they can copy the software because it is free and change it and start their own site. If they want to redistribute the news, they can, preferably on an open publishing site."[16]

All IMC websites run similar open-source software, a technical manifestation of democracy at the level of the code. Jay, an Indymedia volunteer, described the internal structure of the IMC as well as the manifestation of that structure in the software used to run websites as "fitting this movement like a glove" (personal interview, March 25, 2001). Indymedia flourished in large part because of the commitment to participatory democracy embodied in these social and technical practices of openness, which reflected the goals of the movement. But total openness is an ideal, and as such must be constantly renegotiated and rearticulated. Gal Beckerman's essay, "Edging Away from Anarchy" uses the New York City Indymedia's newspaper collective's chaotic meetings to illustrate some of the contradictions associated with the open model. She writes, "Like all

things at the center, the process has been precarious, democracy teeter-
ing on the edge of anarchy. There are some rules—people raise their hand
to speak—but the collective believes everyone should have his or her say.
An open, representative form of media may be a worthy ideal, but in
reality is often a messy thing" (2003, 27). Indymedia is inseparable from
the movements in which it exists. It is inside of, because of, and for these
movements. Indymedia's reporters are not simply journalists with a day
job—they are political activists using media production as their weapon.

Political activists are very familiar with the historical use of surveillance
and infiltration to provoke and divide political movements. In the United
States, this history includes the Pinkertons (founded in 1850 and known
best for union-busting work), the Red Scares (1917 to 1920), McCarthy-
ism (late 1940s through mid-1950s), and the FBI's notorious counter-
intelligence program COINTELPRO (1956 to 1971). Released documents
and personal histories show how government and private agencies kept
tabs and files on activists—from Martin Luther King Jr. to Quaker peace
groups—and continue to do so. Recent court cases have revealed that the
use of provocateurs and undercover agents continues to be a commonplace occurrence against contemporary political movements, including
Indymedia.[17]

Indymedia centers have encountered many facets of repression, including grand jury subpoenas, requests for IP logs and media evidence,
server seizures, corporate lawsuits, state censorship, monitoring of IMC
sites by law enforcement agencies, police intimidation and raids at large-
scale Indymedia centers, and even horrific police brutality. Indymedia
developed technical and social practices to adapt to this environment,
which can produce high degrees of suspicion and what George Marcus
has termed *paranoia within reason* (1999b)—a rationality that makes
sense within the discourse of the group and operates as a type of native
discourse. The practices of openness I have previously described are examples of these adaptations when considered together as a "we have nothing to hide" position, but other responses center on concealment instead.

Indymedia and the movements it operates within use a set of social
and technical practices to protect the identity of participants. Concealment practices can be summed up by the concept of security culture, a
collectively practiced behavior-oriented plan that gives peace of mind to
activists who know that if the guidelines are followed, outside disruption
can be controlled. These behaviors include controlling the flow of infor-

mation, such as plans for an action or only involving people on a need-to-know basis.

Another example of a social practice of concealment is the widespread use of pseudonyms or screen names, common in both Indymedia and broader social movements. Indymedia's working guidelines explicitly include respect for people's privacy when making media. Because Indymedia is operating inside a social movement, its materials are made both by and of political activism. Great pains are taken to protect the identity of political activists (who might be breaking the law) from government agencies. Because Indymedia media makers and collectives might possess materials that could be used by the state to prosecute individuals, they have found ways—both social and technical—to adapt to this situation.

Technical practices of concealment include the use of encryption algorithms that work with sets of "keys" to render a text unreadable except to the person with the other key;[18] proxy servers between a person using the Internet and the website he or she is visiting to alter the user's IP address; and secure protocols, such as Secure Sockets Layer, which secures communications on the Internet and can be used, for example, to hide a user's IP address when connecting to a chat room. These technical practices are employed to make a user's presence on the Internet anonymous, and they are part of the same system of concealment as pseudonyms and security culture. But are these concealment practices in opposition to the ideal of openness espoused by Indymedia?

THE MASK

Contemporary political and media activists know they are operating in an environment in which they are potentially always under surveillance. This environment, in and of itself, can hinder free speech because of a fear of government or institutional repression. Allowing people to participate in a way that makes them feel their identities and privacy are being protected can actually increase freedom of expression for participants who are wary of being monitored. Indymedia found ways to negotiate the seemingly incompatible ideals of openness and transparency within an environment that demands secrecy. Indymedia activists navigate these two poles, occupying concealment and openness not as two alternative territorialized spaces but as a constantly reconstituted blend. Activists play the sign system to their advantage, often occupying the mediating position I call "the mask."

Masks are used by activists around the world to hide their faces and as a symbol of resistance. Examples of masking range from the Zapatista *pasamontañas* (ski masks) to the balaclavas of the Autonomen (German autonomous movement activists) to the bandannas of the black bloc. Significantly, in these cases, the mask foregrounds a collective rather than an individual identity. The mask is at once a refusal to participate in the accumulation of information in the surveillance economy by hiding, and a practice of boldly showing oneself, an intentional act of exposure in a signifying system through semiotic subversion. As the Zapatistas have explained, "We were invisible and forgotten in Chiapas, but when the Zapatistas put on masks, all of a sudden everyone could see us."[19]

The use of pseudonyms is an example of masking. By publicly participating but taking on a different name, activists refuse to allow surveillance mechanisms to keep track of personal identities. Regular use of the same screen name allows an Indymedia participant to develop a reputation as a journalist within an activist community while maintaining distance between it and his or her real identity. Thus, participants are able to publicly express themselves without concern for the potential impact on their homes, work, schools, or family lives. The mask straddles the open and concealed positions simultaneously. It is the negotiation, the in-between place, the hybrid. The mask represents the flexible actual everyday practices of Indymedia activists rather than false dichotomies of fixed categories.

It was nearly dawn at the end of our last night working on the film *Trading Freedom: The Secret Life of the FTAA* (Free Trade Area of the Americas). I was lying half-asleep on the floor, waking every few minutes to preview another connection, another sequence, making a little change here or there. We were editing the final timeline of video segments together and had to finish in time to turn out a hard copy before four of us left to drive for six hours to the Bay Area to catch planes back to our respective homes. We were in an outbuilding nicknamed "the dojo" on two hundred acres of land in southern Oregon. We had temporarily taken over the dojo and a series of computers connected through a handmade wireless network. Families of shrews lived off our chips and coffee remains, and just miles away the largest wildfire in the United States in years burned, sometimes turning the sky apocalyptic shades of orange and purple.

Eight of us—the editorial collective for *Trading Freedom*—had gathered in Oregon. The collective possessed a unique set of skills: hotshot editor, software jockey, mental encyclopedia, anarchogeek, global networker, convivial comedian, audio wizard, hardware tamer, and wireless prodigy. We had come to this two-week encuentro to attempt to finish the film. Most of us had been in Quebec City in 2001, challenging a state establishment that was trying to push a free trade agenda at the Summit of the Americas. I had spent most of my time at the summit in the Indymedia center working on one of the video terminals, where we uploaded breaking news to the Internet while gathering contact information and log sheets—the raw material of *Trading Freedom*—from video activists. Tear-gas-clouded memories still loomed large in our minds a year later as we struggled, far away in Oregon, to tell that history to the outside world. Those memories offered us a reckoning and gave us the drive to make the project effective—because we had time to try and stop the FTAA.[20]

In Oregon we were engaging in a process that turned out to be far more significant than the film could ever be: collective production. We were working to turn an unruly archive of tapes from the far corners of the Americas—Akwesasne, Chiapas, Quebec City, São Paulo, and Tijuana—into something coherent, inspirational, and important. It seemed to be a crazy, impossible dream at the outset. We felt as if we were stumbling through a dense wood, only occasionally coming into the odd moonlit clearing. Yet our project managed to fall into place. We used and made fun of the consensus process, struggled with the desire to push our own agendas, shared common resources, felt tensions, had successes. What we did might simply be called "learning to work together" and is, of course, practiced constantly, all over the world, but through our collective labor we challenged established notions of film authorship and tried to forge what we imagined to be a better world.

When it came time to write about my experience with the collective mode of production, I approached it by interviewing most of the collective members and weaving the interview transcripts into a narrative. I was troubled by how to include my voice in the work; I didn't know how the anthropologist's voice and the editorial collective member's voice could be one and the same. I struggled through several versions, and ultimately I had someone interview me with a list of similar questions I had asked everyone else. When I transcribed the interview, I identified myself by my Indymedia screen name and added the responses to the collage as if I were just another Indymedia video editor with no annotations to my identity. All the other interviewees where identified with pseudonyms, and I suppose using my actual screen name was something of a nod to my identity beyond the use of a pseudonym, but I never added a signal to the reader to alert them to that voice as mine. It felt slightly dishonest, I admit, but through masking myself, I was able to straddle two worlds, two voices, uniting my schizophrenic experience in a way that gave respect to my work not as an ethnographer but as a collective member, and I made myself visible in the text in ways I was not able to accomplish using scholarly rhetoric. In this case, it was not a security apparatus I obscured my identity from, but rather a discipline that does not always accommodate the first-person position of the participant observer.

WHERE ARE THEY NOW?

It is increasingly difficult to remember the Internet as it was at the turn of the millennium — before YouTube, Flickr, blogs, Facebook, Twitter, and podcasting, and, importantly, before Creative Commons created a flexible copyright system that allowed for the reuse and remixing of media, but only under the conditions stipulated by the creator.[21] When Indymedia started, there were no plug-and-play video-sharing sites or templates for blogs or photo albums. Indymedia imagined them, built them, maintained them, and filled those spaces with media. That remixable media was fresh, it was exciting, and it was something that had not been seen in that way before. We had new eyes to experience it — and the attention span to match (we had to; we were reading, watching, and listening to it on dial-up modems!).

Indymedia, worldwide news of resistance at a click, but more than that, encouraged you to be a part of the story, to contribute, to participate. For many people, publishing a story to Indymedia was their first experience interacting with the Internet as a producer rather than a consumer. Indymedia built and protected public space and trained a legion of citizen-reporters on how to populate it. Indymedia was a forerunner in the web 2.0 media landscape, an Internet now centrally characterized by user-generated content, virtual communities, information sharing, and collaboration. In many cases, with almost no financing, Indymedia's reporting outshined the corporate media's coverage of the same events in terms of both production and distribution. Indymedia showed that reporting is not just a game for the moneyed elites; rather, journalism could be made (and made better) through collective action and commitment to empowered reporting.

Today these things—pictures, videos, audio, and first-person reporting—are commonplace, appropriated even. Perhaps the boldest example of this appropriation is the CNN iReport.[22] This segment features reporting via cell phone photos and video from viewers, in the first person, resplendent even with the *i* logo that is almost an exact duplicate of Indymedia's, right down to the Courier typeface. Self-publishing has become commonplace with widely available tools for uploading content to the Internet. But the focus today is more on publication as an individual experience, seen in blogs, than a collective enterprise as in Indymedia.

Many of the people I got to know during my collaboration with Indymedia can now be found in professional media-related positions. Indymedia served as an incubator where people, fueled by an intense passion to tell their stories, could learn new skills (and make mistakes). Now they make their livings as professionals, having learned to create media through the lens of first-person passionate reporting, which is inseparable from a social movement. Some of them can be found in national public media or other large media outlets, some work for media reform, some report from war zones, and some make feature films. But they all carry with them a commitment to making media in the service of social justice, a passion for the truth, the intimacy of reporting from the inside, the courage to report in dire circumstances, and perhaps even an addiction to the adrenaline rush from being in the middle of the action to bring back the images, the stories, and the connections to other places and people. Through these people, and by example, Indymedia catalyzed change in the media landscape as we know it, making it more multimedia driven, interactive, and populated with first-person reporting. These actors are the seeds that drive long-term changes to the fabric of society. The changes bear fruit slowly and may not have been the movement's goals from the outset, but through the lens of long-term engagement and hindsight we can see the results.

FIELD OR SWAMP?

Indymedia was an extremely slippery field site in which to conduct ethnographic research. It is not localizable geographically; it is not in any one place. Indymedia is a network of people and locations all over the world in constantly changing relationships with one another. It is also a network of technology: built of wires and packets of information, made of computers, cameras, and videotapes. It swells with intensity, building temporary media centers at large-scale demonstrations. It is composed of communications practices, interpersonal relationships, conventions, and subjectivities. It is in the flows of images and stories passed through wires or hand-to-hand around the globe. Indymedia is hard to circumscribe, and it is always possible to extend the connections in this network, to bring in more relationships.

Researching a fluid network left me unsettled—always feeling as if I could not say enough, could not describe all the connections I knew were there, could not get it in print before it had changed dramatically. Kim Fortun describes a similar sensation working in field sites that transcend the local—the once-bounded cultural group: "The confidence said to come with knowing your material well has been forever forestalled. Instead of cohering with time, my expertise has been increasingly dispersed. Working within such dispersion has often been frustrating and has always been overwhelming" (2001, 6). Contemporary anthropological fieldwork often involves contact with and knowledge of transnational and emergent forms of knowledge, practice, and social organization. Few traditional anthropological methods are available to the researcher engaged with a culture that refuses to be located in physical, temporal, or technological space. Emergent global phenomena such as Indymedia are, by their characteristics of dislocation and obscurement, difficult or impossible to map. Knowledge of the system, as Fortun points out, is always partial.

Doug Holmes and George Marcus (2005) have proposed that anthropologists study the "paraethnographic" works of our interlocutors in the field as a way to engage the native point of view in contemporary, multisited, and globally inscribed field sites. Such paraethnographies are works by our interlocutors about their social fields that are produced through methods similar to ethnographic methods. The concept is designed for the study of knowledge producers embedded within global institutions. In these newly conceived research locations, our interlocutors are likely to be more like our counterparts than traditional anthropological Others. Research in field sites like these goes well beyond a "when they read what we write" experience (Brettell 1996); it is more akin to a "when we write about what they write about themselves reading what we read" experience. As Holmes and Marcus note, in such fields, the anthropologist and the subject are collaborators, with porous boundaries between each other's work (see also Casas-Cortés, Osterweil, and Powell, this volume).

Indymedia activists have produced compelling self-reflexive documents, such as the "blueprints" written after large mobilizations in Seattle (N30) and Washington, D.C. (A16), which describe how the media centers were built and run.[23] More theoretical essays such as Matthew Arnison's "Open Publishing Is the Same as Free Software," and even feature-length movies such as *i: the film* (2006), offer detailed descriptions of Indymedia practices and values and can be studied as paraethnographic works. Indymedia is constantly producing paraethnographic accounts of itself and the wider global justice movement, pointing to the knowledge-producing role of social movements (see Casas-Cortés, Osterweil, and Powell, this volume), which are increasingly self-reflexive (Juris 2008a). Study of Indymedia products, including videos as paraethnographic objects, can elucidate aspects of social movements, such as their network connections, political subjectivities, material practices, goals, and commitments. I found the emphasis on paraethnographic works particularly useful for narrowing my focus in a gigantic field. This concept led me to focus on the production, distribution, and reception of Indymedia videos and the work these videos were doing in the wider global justice movement.

My work with Indymedia was complicated not only by the uncontainable vastness of a transnational network as an object, but also by the fact that I was involved in and committed to Indymedia generally, and the Indymedia global video collective more specifically. What methods are available to those, like me, who are engaged with their fields in a way that goes beyond the standard conception of participant observation? Perhaps the most important dimension of ethnographic field research is developing rapport with interlocutors. Marcus (1998) has discussed reformulations of the anthropological concept of rapport in the field, engaging Clifford Geertz's (1973) conception of the role of complicity in establishing rapport, agreeing with its utility but expanding on it. Rapport since Geertz has been reformulated through two concepts: collaboration and imperialist nostalgia. Complicity as collaboration as described by James Clifford (1988) is criticized by Marcus as a post-1960s utopian ideal that attempted to address concerns of a monologic power dynamic by replacing it with multiauthorship. Marcus suggests that Clifford's collaborative model still ultimately inscribes unequal power dynamics and does not sufficiently take the role of complicity into account.[24] In addition, complicity as reformulated by the imperialist nostalgia school of total awareness of colonial involvement left politically aware ethnographers at an impasse, paralyzed and unable to conduct so-called ethical research.[25]

The articulation of the problems associated with complicity by Marcus and others was an appropriate form of reckoning with anthropology's disciplinary legacy as a handmaiden of colonialism and projects of development. However, these scholars rely on compartmentalizing the relationship between anthropologist and subject as distant and separate. Complicity itself need not be inherently negative because many anthropologists today are personally involved with the subjects they study in ways that are distinct from the relationship between anthropology and colonialism. Complicity is articulated quite differently in my work and was in fact instrumental in my ability to build rapport and work in a field site rife with paranoia. In my case, I am complicit because I am not simply an observer; I am also an insider.

SNITCHES GET STITCHES—HYBRIDS TRESPASS

Doing my job of circulating information as an anthropologist inside a political movement put me in one of the most vilified subject positions possible—the snitch. Yet I was able to function with integrity as a researcher within paranoid worlds that saw the snitch as the enemy by not being just a collaborator,[26] as Marcus suggests, but a co-conspirator. I have experienced what it is to be a globetrotting Indymedia videographer, weaving wisps of struggle from across the globe into a digital story, a rhyme of reason, by experiencing struggle physically. I experienced the waxing and waning, the joy and terror, the successes and defeats of this movement as *my* successes and defeats, as *our* successes and defeats.

My involvement in both Indymedia and the movement for global justice provided access to knowledge that would have been otherwise unavailable. There are three main reasons for this. First, this group is composed primarily of political activists, and paranoia can be deep-seated given the history of disruption. Despite this, trust of my intentions in the network, garnered through time and commitment, allowed me to collect data with relative ease. Second, because there is no money backing Indymedia, it operates almost exclusively on volunteer labor. Through labor, I built rapport and gathered good will unavailable to researchers who had done nothing to "help out." Whether editing a film, writing grants, or cleaning bathrooms, work was the best way to interact with and learn about Indymedia. Third, Indymedia uses to a large degree its own highly technical language and referents. I had to acquire a new language and set of technical skills to be able to communicate with Indymedia activists and understand the details of practices.

Complicity made my work easier, but it also complicated things. Being a professional snitch marks me as suspect in political activist milieus; but being a conspirator marks me as unscientific in a field where distance, lack of involvement, and even objectivity are accepted as vocational norms. My experiences as both a contributing member of Indymedia and as a social scientist produced what often felt like an inescapable double bind. I was trying to negotiate my way around two competing poles: activism (being inside a movement) and academia (complete with a posture of distance). The only solution was to honestly engage all fields and audiences with a holistic approach that united my selves.

The performance artist and writer Guillermo Gómez-Peña encourages people working in cross-cultural milieus to adopt an approach he terms the "hybrid." The hybrid is a productive way to think about blurring boundaries. The concept of the hybrid is a veritable job description that fit my in-between, mediating position. Gómez-Peña explains, "At times s/he can operate as a cross-cultural diplomat, as an intellectual coyote (smuggler of ideas) or a media pirate. At other times, s/he assumes the role of nomadic chronicler, intercultural translator, or political trickster. S/he speaks from more than one perspective, to more than one community, about more than one reality, his/her job is to trespass, bridge, interconnect, reinterpret, remap, and redefine; to find the outer limits of his/her culture and cross them" (2002, 753).

Boundary crossing and trespassing can be very useful for achieving immediate instrumental ends. Multiple identity holders are able to mobilize the best identities at their disposal to achieve their desired ends. My circulation in activist and academic worlds allowed me to use my identity in a fluid way over and over again. In the aftermath of Hurricane Katrina, tens of thousands of displaced persons moved into the Houston Astrodome after being evacuated from New Orleans. Activists from Indymedia arrived at the Astrodome to hand out supplies and do media work, and we quickly learned that information was indeed the hardest resource to come by. After some discussion, what we knew would work was a radio station. A low-power station—100 watts or fewer, rather than the 50,000 or 100,000 of large commercial radio—would cover the Astrodome easily. With small radios, families could listen to updates, instructions, and hear the personal stories of other evacuees. The mayor, the governor, and the Federal Communications Commission (FCC), but not the Federal Emergency Management Agency (FEMA), were all on board. We used a loaned silver Airstream trailer as a studio, and Sony donated ten thousand radios for evacuees. After working out some snags, the station was on the air. Listeners came outside to plug into the new station as soon as it went up. Instead of waiting in long lines in the summer heat to get needed information, they picked it up over the airwaves. Evacuees got to speak out and work on policies that were failing, such as curfews that locked them out of the Astrodome.

Those days were a blur of all-nighters, red tape, media interviews, and amazing radio programming—live and uncensored on FM radio. There were many roadblocks and even more interest in our project as we beamed news, announcements, recollections, family lost-and-found stories, and music out of that Airstream trailer in the parking lot. I was a hybrid in the full sense of the word during this event. I applied to the FCC for a broadcast license under the name Houston Indymedia with the support of a coalition of grassroots media groups such as The Promethus Radio Project, I wore press credentials from Austin Airwaves that allowed me into the parking lot where the radio station was located, and I was identified by the media as a "Rice University anthropologist." Whatever worked, whatever moved us forward, whatever got me into the space I needed to get into—be it a badge, a local affiliation, or a university business card—I used it. And it worked.

The hybrid establishes a fluid place between a seeming dichotomy of fixed, opposing positions. Researchers who straddle that in-between place of complicity are, as Gómez-Peña puts it, moving between worlds, speaking "from more than one perspective, to more than one community, about more than one reality" (2002, 753). This is a more complex and realistic vision of our positionality in the field and how and to whom we report. Hybridity allows me to inhabit multiple subjectivities, slipping easily among them, rather than attempting to compartmentalize them or answering questions about whether I am an activist or a journalist, an activist or an anthropologist.

I have focused in this chapter on theorizing in-between places because, in reality, no one occupies a single, defined subject position. It may be more expedient, or even simpler, to frame the world in such stark terms, but doing so reifies dichotomies that are nothing more than conceptual categories. The fact of the matter is we occupy multiple, shifting positions simultaneously. We may mobilize the most constructive identity for a given situation, but which identity to mobilize is context dependent. I call for us to think in terms of more fluid identities, allowing for the fact that we are all of these things at once. We are hybrids. As Indymedia has changed the face of the mediascape, both intentionally by building new ways to tell stories and unintentionally by training thousands of activists to be journalists, perhaps an honest accounting of ourselves as both activists and academics will create space for others to experiment with passioned, committed ethnography. Subcomandante Marcos (2003) has written,

> A tour, even if it is merely expository, of the different resistances in a nation or on the planet, is not just an inventory. There one can divine, even more than the present, the future. Those who are part of that tour, and those who make the inventory, can discover things that those who add and subtract in the armchairs of the social sciences cannot manage to see. To wit, that the traveler and his path matter, yes, but what matters above all is the path, the direction, the tendency. In noting and analyzing, in discussing and arguing, we are doing so not only in order to know what is happening and to understand it, but also, and above all, in order to try and transform it.

For decades anthropologists have been implored to shed a tone of objectivity, to clearly state our positionality, to experiment with ethnographic form using multiauthorship and shared authority; but the fact of the matter is as a discipline we are not yet there. Indymedia critiqued mainstream media for its position of false objectivity and argued for the validity of passionate, first-person reporting, not simply by making the case, but concretely, through its modes of production, distribution, and reception. So must anthropologists engage with our discipline. With each honest declaration of our commitments and hybrid identity we make more room for future possibilities of change within the academy through our activism and within social movements through our work and support as academics.

NOTES

1 Indymedia arose out of the networking of many established media makers, activists, organizations, and geeks—from Freespeech TV to Paper Tiger and Deep Dish TV to Big Noise Films to Whispered Media and to those who brought with them the ideals and practices of the free and open-source software movement.

2 E-mail to Grassroots Media Network, "GMC Organizers Update: Progress in Austin," October 20, 1999; archived at the Homeless People's Network, http://hpn.asu.edu/archives/Oct99/0185.html (accessed December 25, 2011).

3 Errol Maitland of *Democracy Now* was interviewed at the Independent Media Center for the December 3, 1999, edition of the *Blind Spot* newspaper; excerpts are available from "WTO Media Flashback: Ralph Nader and Errol Maitland," November 25, 2009, www.reclaimthemedia.org (accessed December 25, 2011).

4 These episodes are assembled in a video called *Showdown in Seattle: 5 Days That Shook the WTO*; available at www.archive.org (accessed December 25, 2011).

5 Copies of the *Blind Spot* are archived at www.reclaimthemedia.org (accessed December 25, 2011).

6 See the "Imc History" page of the Indymedia Documentation Project website, https://docs.indymedia.org (last updated May 14, 2006).

7 Active is software developed by Catalyst, an Australian radical tech collective, for a website to provide and coordinate coverage of the international Carnival against Capitalism on June 18, 1999.

8 Subcomandante Insurgente Marcos, videotaped message to the activists in attendance at the Freeing the Media Teach-in, New York City, February 1, 1997 (my transcription); available at the A Mi Időnk website, http://amiidonk.zzl.org (accessed December 25, 2012).

9 I transcribed the quote from the segment "Breaking the No-Free Media Zone" in the fifth and final episode of *Showdown in Seattle*. The Indymedia video programs aired on Deep Dish TV during the protests in Seattle in 1999. Friedberg was also one of the series coordinators.

10 See the "About Us" page on the Indymedia website, www.Indymedia.org (accessed December 25, 2011).

11 Sheri Herndon, panel presentation at "Our Media" conference, Barranquilla, Colombia, June 2003.

12 For more on participatory democracy, see Polletta 2002.

13 http://thisisdemocracy.org (accessed December 25, 2011).

14 Norm Stockwell, "Interview with Big Noise Films," November 24, 2002; available at http://madison.indymedia.org (accessed January 1, 2012).

15 Open-source software is computer software for which the source code and certain other rights normally reserved for copyright holders are provided under a software license that meets the Open Source Definition or that is in the public domain. This permits people to use, change, and improve the software, and to redistribute it in modified or unmodified forms. It is very often developed in a public, collaborative manner (see also Juris, Caruso, Couture, and Mosca, this volume).

16 Matthew Arnison, "Open Publishing Is the Same as Free Software," March 2001 (revised June 9, 2003), available at Arnison's website, http://purplebark .net (accessed December 25, 2011).

17 The nationwide arrests of seventeen environmentalists in the United States in February 2006 (they were accused of associating with the Earth Liberation Front) launched the "Green Scare." At court hearings in Eugene, Oregon, it was revealed that the majority of the information being used by the prosecution came from a paid and planted informant known as "Anna." Anna was present at many antiglobalization and anarchist events for several years. She always carried a video camera and said she was a "video activist." She participated in Indymedia centers and posted to websites and e-mail lists.

18 These include PGP (pretty good privacy), GnuPG, and OpenPGP.

19 This quote is from a meeting between the Zapatistas and the teachers' union in Oaxaca City on February 9, 2006. http://elkilombointergalactico.blogspot .com.

20 On January 1, 2005, Venezuela, Argentina, Bolivia, and Brazil rejected the creation of the FTAA.

21 Creative Commons is a flexible copyright system that allows producers to choose how their materials can be reused (see http://creativecommons.org, accessed December 25, 2011).

22 See CNN's iReport website, www.ireport.com (accessed December 25, 2011).

23 Some of the first IMCs to get started wrote descriptions of how they organized themselves, which heavily impacted the way future event-based IMCs were organized. They also crystallized how an event-based IMC should perform. These descriptions are available at the Indymedia Documentation Project website, https://docs.indymedia.org (accessed December 25, 2005).

24 Marcus's critique of the dialogic model in anthropology is also applicable to documentarians who work on collaborative models of filmmaking. Even when documentary filmmakers feel that they have left themselves completely

out of films and simply given technology to people to tell their own stories, the technology itself is inscribed with, and inscribes, particular subjectivities and power dynamics.

25 This is at least as far as subaltern groups go. One approach to addressing this concern has been to study elites or to "study up" within institutions of power (Nader 1972).

26 The irony and problematic use of the term *collaborator* and its connotations of involvement with the security state is not lost on me and likely contributes to my desire to use different language.

14

The Cultural Politics of Free Software and Technology within the Social Forum Process

JEFFREY S. JURIS | GIUSEPPE CARUSO
STÉPHANE COUTURE | LORENZO MOSCA

This chapter examines the dynamic, contested relationship between the social forum process, new digital technologies, and the movement for free/libre and open-source software (FLOSS). Rather than a movement in the traditional sense, FLOSS is more of a heterogeneous grouping of overlapping networks of geeks and programmers brought together by the practice of "arguing about and discussing the structure and meaning of Free Software: what it consists of, what it is for, and whether or not it is a movement" (Kelty 2008, 98). Since the first World Social Forum (WSF) was held in Porto Alegre, Brazil, in January 2001 to discuss and develop alternatives to neoliberal globalization, the global social forum process has emerged as a parallel process of debate about political alternatives, contemporary politics, and the forum itself. In this sense, the global forum process shares many of the characteristics of FLOSS as a recursive public, defined as "a public that is vitally concerned with the material and practical maintenance and modification of the technical, legal, practical, and conceptual means of its own existence as a public; it is a collective independent of other forms of constituted power and is capable of speaking to existing forms of power through the production of actually existing alternatives" (Kelty 2008, 3). The forum has been more focused on organizational structure, yet the basic element of recursivity is there: a widespread preoccupation with and inclination toward endless discussion and debate around its own organizational, ideational, and technological conditions of possibility.

However, like all political processes, the forum, as a networked space of transnational encounter between different movements, ideologies, and visions, is internally divided; many participants do not view the forum as a public at all. Instead, they would like the forum to become a unified actor capable of making collective decisions and taking concrete actions, reflecting the latter position in the "space" versus "actor" debate (see Juris 2005a, 2008a; and chapters by Caruso, Conway, and Juris, this volume). Since its inception, the WSF has been conceived as an open space for civil society organizations and movements to share ideas and resources, debate alternatives, and coordinate around specific campaigns, but the WSF's charter specifically states that no one can speak in the name of the forum or all of its participants (see Sen 2003; Whitaker 2007b).[1] However, an increasingly vocal sector would like the forum to express common positions and coordinate actions (see Bello 2007). Nonetheless, the fact that this debate has been so central to the forum and that thousands of articles, essays, declarations, e-mail messages, and other documents have been written about it, many voicing concern about the organizational, ideological, and material sustainability of the process, attest to the operation of the forum as a recursive public.

Technology is a central dimension of the forum's material, technical, and organizational conditions of possibility, yet it has received less public attention. New technologies and FLOSS, in particular, are often viewed as organizational metaphors by forum actors: "a model based on free co-operation, collaborative and collective construction and open access" (Fuster Morell 2008, 3). This can be explained, at least in part, by the networking logic inscribed in the organizational architectures of the forums (see Juris 2005b, 2008a, this volume). Such a networking logic, based on horizontal coordination among flexible, autonomous nodes, resonates strongly with the more politicized factions of the free software (FS) movement.

FS activists have been most directly involved in the forums in the context of computer and software infrastructure development. Their involvement might seem paradoxical given the politically agnostic stance of many FLOSS enthusiasts (see Coleman 2004). However, the FLOSS community is broad and politically contradictory, including right-wing libertarian, radical anticapitalists, and even corporate actors. The FS movement itself is extremely diverse. As Christopher Kelty suggests, "It includes both heartfelt allegiance in the name of social justice as well as political agnosticism stripped of all ideology" (2008, 114). The critical point is that a relatively small subset of politically minded computer techies and programmers, many of whom identify with the FS movement, see a convergence between their commitment to FLOSS and the principles of the social forum with respect to openness, the free and open sharing of information, horizontal collaboration, and opposition to corporate monopolies. Likewise, many forum organizers, particularly those who are committed to the ideal of open space, see their political values reflected in the collaborative process and vision they associate with FLOSS. These connections should come as no surprise given the growing confluence between network norms, forms, and technologies within the wider global justice movements (Juris 2008a).

However, the specific sociotechnical assemblage linking FLOSS with the social forums should not be taken for granted. Indeed, there is no a priori affinity between FLOSS, the FS movement, and the social forum process, although there has been a mutual projection of values between more politically motivated FS activists and those forum organizers who espouse an open space ideal. These self-dubbed "horizontals" within the forum process, who view politics as open, participatory, processual, and collaborative, have challenged what they view as the centralized, closed, and top-down politics practiced by the so-called verticals (see De Angelis 2005; Juris 2005a, 2008a). FLOSS also generates significant resistance among forum organizers, often due to perceived inequities between grassroots activists and technical "experts" (see F. Fischer 2000; Nieusma 2007). In what follows, we specifically argue that, given the recursive nature of the forums, such conflicts surrounding technology and software reflect disagreements regarding the structure, process, and meaning of the forum itself.

In this chapter, we explore the cultural politics of technology within the social forums through a collaborative transnational ethnographic analysis of the political goals and struggles over FLOSS and wider technological infrastructures within the social forum process. By cultural politics of technology we mean "a methodological vision of a way to explore the relationship between culture, politics, and technology that emphasizes the cultural work that has to be performed in the conception, development, and implementation of new technologies" (Sørensen 2004, 189). We suggest that conflicts over specific uses and configurations of computers, software, and technologies are cultural—they reflect distinct cultural visions and understandings of what software and technology mean. On the one hand, we follow trends in science and technology studies that see technical artifacts as always already inscribed with particular tastes, values, and predilections to certain programs of action (Sørensen 2004; see also Akrich 1992; Latour 1992; Star 1999). Indeed, as James Leach (2009) argues, moral imaginations shape and are shaped by particular ways of making technology, including FLOSS. On the other hand, we also pursue a more anthropological tack in approaching the politics of technology as deeply embroiled in contests over meaning, interpretation, and communication (see Hess 1995; Sørensen 2004, 186). Similar debates over FLOSS and technology have surfaced within forums situated in different political and cultural contexts, including conflicts over efficiency, openness, and expertise. In this sense, we further contend that decisions about software and technology are political, not merely technical.

Each of us has been deeply engaged in the social forum process as a scholar and activist. Not only have we had firsthand experiences working within forum organizing spaces, we have also developed a greater depth of understanding of internal forum dynamics than would have been possible otherwise. Consequently, we hope our analysis will be of interest to activists as well as to academics, advancing knowledge about the forums while helping forum organizers to grasp the politics of free software and technology and to appreciate the struggles and exclusions often associated with their use. At the same time, as we further explain in the conclusion, our engaged perspective should be tempered by a critical reflexivity regarding the contradictions entailed by our dual positionality. Moreover, given the racial, gender, and class dynamics of the processes we address, it is also important to locate ourselves: one of us is a white, middle-class male from the United States (Juris); another is a white, middle-class French-speaking male from Quebec, Canada (Couture); and the other two are white, middle-class males from Italy (Caruso and Mosca).

This chapter is based on nearly a decade of participant observation in the social forum process. Specific events examined here include the 2004 WSF in Mumbai; European Social Forums (ESFs) in Florence in 2002, Paris in 2003, London in 2004, and Athens in 2006; and the U.S. Social

Forum (USSF) in Atlanta in the summer of 2007. We did not set out to write a collaborative paper, but by bringing together our fieldwork experiences post-facto we have ended up with something akin to a collaborative, multisited ethnography, albeit informed by cultural-political specificities in particular locales.[2] Specifically, we trace the transnational flow of struggles related to software and technology within the forums across space and over time. However, rather than physically moving across geographic sites, we remain rooted in place, taking advantage of our multiple locations to trace cross-border flows and conflicts. Together with other recent experiments in this vein (e.g., Kelty 2009; Matsutake Worlds Research Group 2009; Jackie Smith, Juris, and the Social Forum Research Collective 2008), this kind of collaborative, transnational participant observation provides a model for studying complex, emerging forms of life in a global, digitally networked world.

IDEOLOGIES AND PRACTICES AT THE INTERSECTION OF FLOSS AND THE SOCIAL FORUM PROCESS

FLOSS has been the subject of increasing interest in recent years. Many activists and progressive intellectuals, in particular, have seen FLOSS and its development model as a critique of and an alternative to top-down, monopolistic practices. It is important to recognize, though, that the social world of FLOSS is not homogeneous and to attend to the diverse "articulations, interpretations, and performances of the development of FLOSS" (Lin 2004; see also Kelty 2008). This is even more so as scholars begin to examine FLOSS projects outside Europe and the United States (see Couture 2007; Hakken 2007; Takhteyev 2009; Zúñiga 2006). Although we are primarily concerned in this chapter with the relationship between a specific sector of the FLOSS world and the social forum process, it is important to provide a broader discussion of FLOSS. In particular, a brief outline of the distinct ideological positions with respect to FLOSS can help to situate the forum-related activism surrounding software and technology explored below and to reveal the often contested, sometimes contradictory intersections between FLOSS and wider social forum activism.

The notion of "free software" is usually credited to the Free Software Foundation (FSF) and its founder, Richard Stallman, who developed a licensing model that would guarantee full access to software source code—the set of instructions that make software work. In contrast to proprietary software, free software licensing means that everyone has the right to read, use, modify, and redistribute software and its source code. Freedom for the FSF is primarily an ethical impulse to preserve the freedom of expression, modification, and distribution rather than an issue of technical efficiency or superiority. Over the last ten years, free software advocates have coalesced around the idea that the freedom of software is akin to the freedom of speech. Consequently, as Gabriella Coleman suggests, free software has been framed as the "right to make and alter technology through argument" (2009, 422). Understanding code as speech means seeing software as an ongoing cultural process rather than a tool or commodity; it means being more concerned with process than product, an idea that resonates with many forum activists.

The term *open-source software* is often used interchangeably with or to replace *free software*, both of which designate similar software technologies, people, and practices. However, these terms are associated with a key philosophical difference. *Open source* was introduced by more business-oriented programmers, such as Eric Raymond, and certain corporations, including Netscape, to avoid the morally charged discourse of *freedom*. *Open source* emphasized the pragmatic quality of the openness of the source code, which could be exploited for commercial and technological advantage. This "semantic coup d'état" (Kelty 2008, 99) was aided by the writing of Eric Raymond (1999), who outlined a "bazaar" style of developing FLOSS software, in this case the Linux kernel at the heart of the GNU/Linux operating system.[3] Raymond saw this bazaar style as technically equal, if not superior to the "cathedral" style of traditional software development.[4] The rise of the notion of *open source* has been widely seen as a break with the FS movement. Although many activists view free software as a challenge to corporate monopolies, the term *open source* was developed to denote a more corporate-friendly approach to a similar process of software development.[5]

At the same time, for many social justice activists, even those who identify with the FS movement, the process denoted by the term *open source* (if not the business-oriented impulse behind the term) offers a way to characterize a mode of decentralized, horizontal collaboration that reflects their political ideals with respect to grassroots participation and direct democracy. However, other FLOSS enthusiasts have sounded a critical note: "'Open Source' is fast becoming an omnibus framework and near-universal toolkit to tackle very diverse social issues. There is little wrong in itself with this . . . but for the fact that it tends to obscure . . . a wide gap in approach and attitude between activists and hackers that is just too critical to be easily papered away. . . . [U]nlike activists, hackers are focused on the pursuit of knowledge and the exercise of curiosity for its own sake" (Riemens 2005, 330). Indeed, many FLOSS advocates express an agnostic stance toward political association of any kind (see Coleman 2004; Couture 2007; Kelty 2008). There may also be organizational and cultural differences between FLOSS and social activist communities (see, e.g., Luke et al. 2004), and even tensions related to social justice goals, such as the inclusion of women (see Leach 2009; Nafus, Leach, and Krieger 2006).

We should thus be careful not to assume an a priori cultural-political affinity between FLOSS advocacy and social forum activism per se. That having been said, many free software activists have been deeply involved in expressly political activism related to patents, monopolies, and corporate globalization, often redefining freedom in more egalitarian terms and aligning with actors committed to developing new modes of politics that are more grassroots, bottom-up, and collaborative. Along these lines, Dominique Cardon and Fabien Granjon (2003) have identified a politicized fraction of the FS movement that participates in the social forums and brings to bear an expressivist critique, promoting collaborative, directly democratic process and means over ends. This can be contrasted to an antihegemonic critique associated with Marxist and other traditional sectors within the forums. Many forum actors refer to these contrasting logics as a divide between horizontals and verticals. The politicized fraction of the FS movement tends to align with the horizontals, viewing the forum as a vehicle for opening up new spaces of collaborative practice where everyone can (at least in theory) participate in the horizontal production of knowledge. In what follows, we examine the tensions and struggles associated with this particular vision of technology and software within the forum process.

FREE AND OPEN SOFTWARE IN MUMBAI

The 2004 WSF in Mumbai was the first time the forums ran entirely on FLOSS. Indian organizers viewed FLOSS as a way to support the struggle against marginalization and uneven distribution of information and knowledge. However, inconsistencies between the organizational structure of the forum and the ethical requirements of FLOSS arose due to distinct perceptions of the technical and political implications of software. These tensions led to conflicts between older, largely male organizers who valued the presumed efficiency of hierarchical organization and younger FS activists and other forum organizers who advocated participatory processes, reflecting a tension between ethics and efficiency. Whereas the choice to use FLOSS had been informed by ethical-political considerations, the ensuing conflicts raised doubts about previous software and technology-related decisions.

At the peak of the workload in the Mumbai WSF office, thirty-seven computers ran a free and open GNU/Linux-based operating system administered by three young volunteers from the FSF branch in India. For most of the FSF volunteers, FLOSS reflected the world that the WSF was meant to prefigure: a society without hierarchies where work would be collective and decisions made by all those affected; where social borders would be permeable and continuously crossed, generating creative hybridization; and where tensions between work and leisure, efficiency and creativity, values and practices, and responsibility and recognition would be resolved.

However, the 2004 WSF fell short of its ambition, due in part to a lack of attention to the political, ethical, and cultural dimensions of FLOSS. GNU/Linux was new to most of the workers in the office, but the FSF volunteers did not offer trainings and gave only one presentation on the political and ethical goals of free software. Their interactions with the staff were mostly restricted to troubleshooting, which created a dynamic of dependence between users and experts. This caused problems related to coordination in system design and implementation, a lack of appreciation on the part of FSF volunteers for the everyday experience of software use in the daily routines of the office, and a tendency among most office workers to view software as a technological issue. When Caruso arrived in Mumbai in early October, the WSF office was already a site of conflict. The core issue, characterized by FSF activists as a misunderstanding with respect to the relevance of free software, was a clash of political interests, ethical principles, and political-cultural values.

Specifically, these conflicts involved tensions between the older, largely male members of the WSF leadership—composed of the Indian Working Committee (IWC, decision makers), the Indian Organizing Committee (IOC, implementers), and the office coordinators (members of and appointed by the IOC)—and the younger, mostly female office staff and younger, male FSF activists. For many IWC and IOC members, software was of marginal interest. Some viewed FLOSS as a way to claim self-reliance from megacorporations, but they still saw it in technical terms. For FSF activists, software provided a way to connect with others working on similar issues at the WSF. For the office coordinators, the logistical success of the WSF was more important than such political considerations. Many office volunteers and staff failed to understand why so much energy was dedicated to learning new software and constantly tweaking an unstable system.

Compounding matters was the decision to entrust the development of the official WSF website to a company with no prior FLOSS experience. Although the use of an outside contractor had produced poor service and significant tension during the 2003 Asian Social Forum in Hyderabad, India, political pressure and practical reassurances on the part of allegedly independent consultants led to a similar arrangement this time around. The resulting technological snafus sparked fierce conflict and accusations of corruption, ineptitude, and bullying. There were also debates over transparency and openness because information was often inaccessible when the website was down for maintenance.

Ultimately, pressure by the IOC and the desire to deliver an efficient "product" generated attitudes and behaviors that many organizers and FSF volunteers considered inconsistent with the values of the WSF. According to some WSF participants, the IOC should have deemphasized FLOSS and hired professionals to deal with business-oriented website managers to solve critical issues. A consultant who was hired to evaluate website errors went so far as to denounce the WSF office for corruption, incompetence, unaccountability, hierarchy, and exclusion—the very practices the WSF was supposed to be fighting against. Political and technical errors further led to worsening social relations as well as an atmosphere of suspicion. A few days later, one of the coordinators of the WSF resigned, protesting against the lack of internal democracy.

Criticisms were raised during meetings of the IOC and other organizing bodies when the issue of software came up, but specific steps to ameliorate the situation were rarely taken due to a fear of exacerbating what seemed to be an intractable conflict. No one wanted to risk a political crisis over software. However, the information technology (IT) consultant's accusations led to worsening relations among working-group delegates, office coordinators, staff members, and volunteers. Moreover, allegations regarding the conditions of stress and uncertainty among the office staff were never discussed. On December 13, 2003, office staff members and FSF volunteers had an explosive lunchtime conversation. The FSF techies were criticized for wielding excessive power given their monopoly over the knowledge and skills required to fix computer and software problems. Office workers claimed that when asked about specific repairs, techies would offer cursory explanations using obscure technical language. In this sense, expertise and knowledge hierarchies were viewed as generating dependency and exclusion (see Nieusma 2007). As a staff member explained with respect to the GNU/Linux-based operating system, "Everyone in the office seemed to be having the same problems. . . . The technical help gave technical explanations we were unable to understand. . . . Their attitude always gave the vibe that the problem was too small to bother them and that we were [too] dumb [a] lot to solve it ourselves. The natural reaction was that the staff shifted from being polite and understanding to rude and bullying with the technical help" (personal interview, August 9, 2005). For their part, FSF volunteers felt alienated and disillusioned by the behavior of the office staff. The conflict came to a head on December 26. One of the system managers said, "The FSF was attacked from all sides because of the problems we had with the computers, servers, and website. [The finance department] eventually asked us to revert to Windows" (personal interview, December 26, 2003). This sentiment reflected the highly contentious nature of technological decision making within the WSF process. However, WSF organizers maintained their commitment to FLOSS, and ultimately succeeded in developing a widely praised GNU/Linux system. Nonetheless, the struggles reflected profound tensions between the political culture of the Mumbai office and the expressed values of the WSF.

Such tensions are at the heart of a series of ongoing debates within the forum process regarding the discourse and practice of open space. They reflect a clash between distinct ways of viewing politics: the "old" of the traditional, hierarchical, and authoritarian Left (political parties, unions, NGOs) and the "new" associated with the FLOSS movement, small anarchist groups, open-space advocates, and diverse horizontalist formations (De Angelis 2004). According to this framework, closed, centralized information systems (including closed, proprietary software) are associated with hierarchical structures, while open, accessible informational environments are seen to favor horizontal networks, peer-to-peer collaboration, and grassroots participation — the expressed values of the WSF (even if contradicted in practice). In this sense, conflicts over software and technology reflect broader debates regarding the values and practices of the social forum, which constitute the forum as a transnational recursive public. However, it is important to remember that antiauthoritarian, directly democratic politics have, at least, centuries-deep roots and are by no means a unique product of the contemporary moment. What is interesting is the way that many contemporary proponents of such politics adopt the language of, and find their political visions and preferred organizational forms reinforced by, new technological artifacts and paradigms. In addition, as we argue in this chapter, dynamics of conflict and power are at work in all social and political processes and formations, whether verticalist or horizontalist, although they may play out differently in each case.

TECHNOLOGICAL CONFLICTS WITHIN THE EUROPEAN
SOCIAL FORUM PROCESS

Contrasting understandings of the links between culture, organizational structures, and technology have also characterized the European Social Forum (ESF) process. Beyond FLOSS, this has been most clearly evident in the ESF media centers, key sites where information regarding the forum is produced and disseminated.[6] At the same time, choices related to the organization of the media centers (their locations and their degree of openness) paralleled similar debates related to FLOSS, which many FS activists view as prefiguring the egalitarian organizational arrangements that should inform the social forums. In other words, the perceived horizontal, open, and accessible nature of the FLOSS development process (despite the practical hierarchies of knowledge and expertise that define FLOSS development) is seen as a model for the forum's material, technological, and organizational infrastructure.

As with FLOSS, the organization of forum media centers has been a perpetual source of conflict. For example, the media center during the 2002 ESF in Florence was the scene of an intense struggle between two groups: one affiliated with Indymedia and grassroots radio projects, which assumed responsibility for the technical aspects of the media center, including computer connectivity, and the other associated with ESF organizers, which was in charge of circulating information and managing the website. Once again a conflict arose between techies and other forum organizers regarding the cultural understanding of technology, this time with respect to the openness of the media center. Grassroots media activists argued for completely open access, while the official ESF organizers wanted to restrict access to accredited personnel. The decision was finally made to distinguish between movement media and mainstream media, leading to distinct areas inside of the media center. However, resources were limited and nonmedia activists were ultimately denied access to the space. Grassroots media activists strongly opposed this decision, which highlighted the contradiction between the idea of the forum as an open space and the restrictive logic of a closed media center, widely understood as paralleling the restrictive nature of proprietary software.

According to one middle-aged, white male activist, this conflict escalated when a number of computers were stolen, compromising the ability of the media center to function (personal interview, January 2, 2007). Despite the forum's open-space ideal, the stolen laptops persuaded organizers to further restrict media center access at subsequent ESFs. For example, an official accreditation and pass were required to enter the media center during the 2003 Paris ESF. This prompted Zalea TV to issue a public statement against what in its view was "reproducing, in [the ESF] organizational practice, the more perverse, castrating model of the surveillance society."[7] Moreover, as we saw with the WSF's Mumbai office, the organization of the Paris media center was partially outsourced. Grassroots activists saw the reduced accessibility of the media center as mirroring other technological choices, including the decision not to use FLOSS. In response, they organized an alternative Independent Media Center with a few FLOSS-based desktops inside an autonomous space called the Métallos Médialab, where the politics of the FS movement were discussed.[8]

The management of the media center at the 2004 London ESF was even more contentious because so-called alternative media were denied access altogether. In the words of one activist: "Press passes for the ESF were to be available to 'proper' journalists with National Press Cards" (Jones 2004). As a result, grassroots media activists again established an alternative Independent Media Center with seventy FLOSS-based computers. After the contentious forum in London, a different style of management was finally adopted at the 2006 ESF in Athens, and the media center was open to everyone. Consistent with this decision, the Hellenic GNU/Linux User Group repaired old PCs for the forum and configured them with FLOSS.[9] Wireless access was also provided in the main ESF space, making Internet connection available to every laptop at the forum. Organizers ultimately recognized that the forum's ideal of open space should be reflected in the openness of its technology, media, and software.

The London ESF was characterized, even more than prior forums, by conflicts between distinct organizational cultures related to alternative understandings of technology. The horizontals called for democratizing the organizing process, emphasizing diversity, open participation, and consensus decision making. They accused the so-called verticals of hierarchical, exclusive practices and betraying the principles of the WSF's charter (see Juris 2005b; Jackie Smith et al. 2007). This conflict was also visible in the choices surrounding the forum's website, again reflecting a conflict over centralization, access, and expertise. Initially, the horizontals wanted to participate in developing the official ESF website, but the verticals outsourced website administration to a private software company at a cost of £40,000.

As Dave Jones (2004) argues, while the e-commerce functionality of the website was considered crucial, "the requirements for the other website functionalities were never opened up for public discussion; all public interactivity was rejected and too few people were trusted to participate and administer the site." For this reason, the horizontals created an alternative website based on wiki technologies. Following the London ESF, greater importance was given to the European dimension of the process and organizers agreed that a permanent ESF website would be developed under the control of the open European Preparatory Assembly. ESF event websites, which managed registration and logistic information, would continue to be administered by national organizing committees.[10]

The experience of the ESFs suggests that wider conflicts surrounding technology mirror debates over software, particularly with respect to the perceived collaborative nature of FLOSS development. As we have seen, radical tech activists associated with the horizontals view software and technology as a platform for prefiguring "another world" and implementing the idea of an open space. This view has been challenged by many verticals, who favor efficiency and central political control over the more ethical dimensions of free software and collaborative organization. These conflicts ultimately underscore the political nature of software and technology, suggesting that technological choices should not be restricted to the domain of so-called experts but should rather be subject to wider political negotiation.

The U.S. Social Forum (USSF) in 2007 was lauded by participants and observers for its diversity and efficiency. New digital technologies played an important role in terms of internal coordination, outreach, and registration, and also as a facilitator of interactive communication. The Information and Communication Technology (ICT) team, a geographically distributed network of volunteers spearheaded by a group of radical techies in New York City,[11] decided early on to run FLOSS on the roughly seventy public-access computers at the USSF and to build the website using Drupal.[12] At the same time, ICTs were also key sites of conflict, reflecting differing views of the role of technology within social struggles.

During a series of technology workshops at the USSF and through subsequent interviews, ICT team members articulated a clear vision of the political nature of technology decisions. For example, with respect to FLOSS, Ricardo, a middle-aged, Latino ICT team member who gave a presentation during one of the sessions, explained, "It seemed like anything that did not use . . . [FLOSS] would go against the whole idea of all us coming together and sharing the information in the same space" (personal interview, September 7, 2007).[13] For his part, Robbie, a young, white male ICT team member, said, "By actively using a tool you are making that tool better. . . . When you give that contribution to a proprietary tool you are helping to build a community around that tool. . . . I would like to see that community built around free tools. . . . That is a key piece of the struggle" (personal interview, September 5, 2007). FLOSS was also viewed as reflecting the broader goals of the forum. As Ricardo later recounted, "We felt the selection that the social forum makes for its software should mirror the politics of the social forum, which are about the development of a large network and community where there is genuine shared commitment, a sense of equality, respect, and collaboration, and that is what free and open-source software is" (personal interview, September 7, 2007).

Moreover, beyond FLOSS, the USSF communications system and tools were designed to encourage grassroots participation and horizontal collaboration. The USSF blog represented a clear example of a decentralized mode of bottom-up reporting. As Ricardo explained, "Blogging is a form of grassroots journalism. . . . You try to get people to write their own stories. . . . If you go onto the site you get a real live portrait of the experiences everyone had at the social forum." The blog reflected a vision of the forum as an open space for sharing ideas and experiences. Ricardo continued, "The forum is the collectivized and refined experience of masses of people, that's what the forum is about, and so, that we would blog it that way, that we would take an historical record of it that way is appropriate."

The Media Justice Center, another important site of conflict, was also meant to encourage participatory collaboration. As Robbie explained during one of the technology-themed sessions that took place at the forum on June 30, 2007, "We set up six rooms for people doing media, using open-source tools. . . . Everything for networking . . . so anyone . . . could connect their camera . . . upload [images] to a shared server, and then publish it to the [USSF] media site, which anyone could then use. . . . And it was a beautiful thing to watch!" Similarly, tech volunteers viewed the online registration system not only as efficient but also as a way to get participants involved in running the forum.[14] Ricardo pointed out that, "If you were already registered, you'd walk up to a registrar and they'd take your registration off the computer. You have already registered online, so that's empowerment. If you hadn't registered, we sent you to a bank of fifteen computers where you could register yourself" (personal interview, September 7, 2007).

However, there was also a great deal of conflict surrounding technology within the USSF process, particularly early on in the development of the website. Some members of the National Planning Committee (NPC) were less than enthusiastic about the initial proposals. They were not necessarily opposed to the goals of the ICT team, but they had little sense of the potential of new technologies. ICT team members thus had to raise awareness among other USSF organizers of the capabilities offered by new ICTs and the political nature of technical decisions, particularly with respect to FLOSS. Robbie confided during the same technology workshop on June 30, 2007, that "none of this was a foregone conclusion—these were political discussions, political struggles in some cases, and sometimes very intense [ones], to make sure that FLOSS was the standard for the social forum."

Tech volunteers also waged struggles to get NPC members to recognize them as fellow organizers. As Robbie later pointed out in an interview: "It took a while for other organizers to recognize we actually were organizers.

There's a general sense in our culture that information and communications technology work is . . . a consultant-client relationship. . . . I tell you, 'I want x, y, and z,' and you go do it" (personal interview, September 5, 2007). Indeed, some forum organizers were frustrated at the ICT team's slow pace at the beginning, but rather than emphasize efficiency, tech workers spent a lot of time addressing the political as opposed to the technical aspects of the decisions they were making. Robbie explained, "We weren't superefficient initially, because I think we all felt it was important that, you know, this is the U.S. Social Forum, it's about another world is possible, let's not replicate the consultant-client relationship, let's not replicate the status quo tool set. . . . Let's really think about how we can bring new people in; let's figure out how we can use tools we are comfortable with, that we feel we have a political affinity for."

Although most NPC members came to respect the political work of the ICT team, tensions were never very far from the surface. One particularly contentious exchange occurred on the blog, as a member of the logistics working group (age and racial background not indicated in the blog post) expressed exasperation at the way he felt he was being treated by members of the tech team while trying to get basic answers for what he thought was a mundane issue. However, his post reflected a more serious critique of the relationship between users and experts:

> I read all of these discussions of open-source code being so much more politically egalitarian than the proprietary stuff, but what good does that do when only a handful of people can deal with the open source, and the rest of us are at their mercy? So we replace our reliance on the already wealthy (who have the resources we want) with the not yet wealthy (who have the resources we want). . . . On the whole, it feels to me that the tech team acts as autocratically as any other bureaucratic organization.[15]

This unleashed series of responses by ICT team members who recognized his frustration and agreed on the need for a better relationship between techs and nontechs, but they also asked for further clarification of the specific issues involved. The original poster eventually replied in a more conciliatory tone: "While the structure of tech requests may seem natural to you who deal with them every day to many of us it's like trying to learn CAD [computer-aided design] software with no instruction manual." He then clarified: "I respect the political importance of open source code. The only thing I have a problem with is the assumption that because something is non-corporate or non-proprietary, it evades serious power differentials. At this point, tech . . . holds more control over the happening of the USSF than any other single entity."[16] Indeed, just as wider debates regarding free speech have little to say about social and political exclusion, so too the emphasis on freedom within FLOSS circles often have difficulty addressing issues of access and equality.

This gets to the heart of a key contradiction related to new ICTs, including FLOSS: despite their egalitarian goals and ability to facilitate decentralized, interactive communication, they often reproduce "knowledge hierarchies" (Nieusma 2007), including the divide between those who possess certain kinds of technical expertise and those who do not. More fundamentally, marginalized communities that lack access to basic computing resources may be excluded from technologically driven processes entirely. This is a particular concern for a forum dedicated to overcoming social, economic, class, and racial inequalities (see Juris, this volume). The 2007 USSF was widely praised for its efficiency and also for its racial and class diversity. Organizers had made a deliberate effort to ensure the USSF was led by the grassroots. It should thus come as no surprise that issues related to technology, inequality, and access also arose during the USSF.

For example, during another technology-related workshop, "Gender, Race, and Open Source," on July 28, 2007, a young, African American man said that he did not know how to access FLOSS technologies, and then noted how few people of color there were in the room. Ironically, the African American woman facilitator of the session later wrote that out of thirty-five participants, seven or eight were people of color, which was "the most diverse crowd [she'd] ever talked with or been in for an open source conversation."[17] This surely had something to do with the inclusion of gender and race in the title of the workshop, but more generally her comment also suggests that people of color, and as she further pointed out, women, are significantly underrepresented in the FLOSS movement, signaling a tension between discourses of *freedom* and *openness*.[18] There is often a slippage between the language of *free* and *open source*, pointing to a liberal blind spot within the discourse and practice of both communities.

One of the most explosive moments of the USSF came during the People's Movement Assembly on the last day of the forum when a group of Native Americans protested the silencing of an indigenous leader from Ecuador. Just after their protest concluded, a young woman of color from *Poor Magazine* denounced the lack of accessibility of the Media Justice Center. Someone from *Poor Magazine* had made this critique the day before on the blog: "We are running the Ida B. Wells Media Justice Center in a hallway. Everyone has to travel a hallway to get to a room, but when your room is the hallway, it sends a clear message, there is no room for you."[19] These anecdotes suggest that unequal access, power, and hierarchy are as endemic to technology as any social field. Indeed, part of the challenge facing both social forum and FLOSS communities is to make such resources widely available across gender, race, and class divides.

CONCLUSION

Software and technology decisions are not merely technical matters; they are also deeply political. This is particularly so in the case of the social forums, which are committed not only to building a more just, egalitarian, and democratic world but also, for many participants, to an innovative model of politics associated with the idea of open space. Many forum organizers and participants view their commitment to an open, processual, and collaborative politics as reflected in the ideals and social relations perceived to be associated with FLOSS. Foremost among these are the distributed, decentralized, and networked nature of the FLOSS production process and the novel conception of property as the right to distribute, not the right to exclude (see S. Weber 2004). It is in this latter sense that many forum organizers see a resonance between FLOSS and their own commitment to challenging the power of corporate monopolies. At the same time, a small yet active group of FS activists see the social forum as a political corollary to its own emphasis on openness and networked collaboration, and has promoted open, interactive processes with respect to media and technology within the forums more generally.

We are not suggesting that all FLOSS enthusiasts make this connection or that there is an a priori affinity between FLOSS and the social forums. Nor are we arguing that all participants view the forum as an open space. Both FLOSS and the social forums, as networked spaces of transnational encounter, are fiercely contested. Indeed, the fact that so much discussion and debate has revolved around meaning, structure, and process, as well as technical, organizational, ideational, and other conditions of possibility, is precisely why we view FLOSS and the forums as recursive publics. What we are arguing is that an important, if often overlooked, dimension of this recursivity in the case of the forums has been the recurring debates and struggles regarding technological and software-related infrastructures. Many radical forum techies are deeply committed to FLOSS and the facilitation of open, collaborative, and interactive processes with respect to technology, viewing this goal as a reflection of the wider objectives of the forum. However, software and technology have also generated a great deal of conflict within particular forum processes with respect to power, hierarchies of knowledge, and expertise, as well as racial, class, and gender inequalities. These tensions are intricately tied to meaning, interpretation, and identity, and, as such, are constitutive of a heated cultural politics of technology. In this sense, technology is a critical terrain of struggle, as conflicts over media centers, websites, computers, and software mirror contests over the nature of the forum itself.

Moreover, our research revealed striking similarities with respect to issues and conflicts surrounding software and technology within forum processes situated within vastly different social, cultural, and political contexts. Beyond simple comparison, it was precisely the transnational, collaborative, and cross-temporal nature of our ethnographic research that allowed us to trace the transnational flows of objects and struggles within the forums. In this sense, discourses and struggles surrounding FLOSS within the USSF process recalled similar debates inside the Mumbai organizing process, while conflicts between techies and nontechies regarding hierarchies of knowledge and expertise were apparent in both cases. Similarly, struggles over interactivity and accessibility with respect to media centers and websites characterized both the U.S. and European forums. At the same time, specific forum processes confronted issues unique to their local settings. Concerns about openness and horizontality were thus more prevalent in the European context, while barriers of race, class, caste, religion, ethnicity, and gender were more central in the United States and India, reflecting predominant concerns among forum organizers in each region given varying sociopolitical contexts, social movement histories, and the particularities of each forum process. Despite these place-based specificities, the issues addressed were remarkably similar across locales, pointing to the way that global problematics are re-embedded within specific local political-cultural contexts.

At the same time, social movements are not simply objects of ethnographic analysis. Each of us, to some extent, also identifies as an activist and organizer. Our long-term political engagements meant that certain experiences were available to us that would simply not have been otherwise. As well, our activist commitments greatly contributed to our practical understanding, not only of the connections between free software, technology, and the social forums but also with respect to key practices, conflicts, and tensions involving the links among domains. Directly engaging in the forums has also led to a self-critical reshaping of our research practices and dispositions. In this sense, our political engagement has informed our decision to search for new forms of collaborative writing and research that reflect the distributed, transnationally networked conditions of our political and intellectual production (see also Casas-Cortés, Osterweil, and Powell, this volume).

Ultimately, we hope our analysis will not only contribute to academic debates regarding social movements, cultural politics, and technology, but that it can also inform activist strategy (including our own). A particular challenge for forum organizers over the coming years will be to ensure that a wider set of individuals and groups can participate in technological decisions, thus avoiding a situation where a small number of expert technicians can exert disproportionate influence and control over the process. This will require a further democratization of the basic knowledge, skills, and technology needed not only to use but also to appreciate the political dimensions that are always already constitutive of technology and software. In sum, we hope our ethnographic analysis, constructed with the methodological and theoretical tools at our disposal, can contribute to an ongoing process of reflection and debate that is already occurring among forum organizers and other activists regarding the relationships between technology, organization, and the social forums. Indeed, each of us participates in these discussions within various forum-organizing bodies and working groups, and we plan to circulate this chapter among our collaborators and interlocutors.

At the same time, it is also important to recognize the limitations of our attempt to bridge the divide between academics and activists. As organizers, we know about and participate in many other spaces of activist knowledge production and distribution. Many of these other spaces—digital forums, listservs, blogs, zines, and so on—are more accessible to activists and are open and collaborative. What do we hope to achieve then by including this chapter in a copyrighted volume intended for a more academic audience? This is a vexing question, but we do not see it as a simple either-or choice. Most of us will continue to write and publish in more open, available, and largely online activist sources, yet the tone and quality of the writing is not the same. There is often little space for ethnographic, theoretically informed, and critical modes of writing in these spaces. Academic outlets remain critical for the kind of reflective and nuanced analyses we hope to produce, and they allow us to also reach a broader nonactivist audience. The point is to generate analyses that can speak to multiple audiences, sometimes in more-activist spaces, other times with university and other academic presses, and to push the boundaries of whatever venues we choose. In this sense, we hope that academic presses will consider publishing in open formats and will market to audiences that are not based at universities, and that it will be seen as economically advantageous to do so. In the meantime, we are left with the hopes, frustrations, and contradictions of our attempts to bring together ethnography and transnational activism within our organizing and academic pursuits.[20]

NOTES

1 According to the WSF's Charter of Principles, "The World Social Forum is an open meeting place for reflective thinking, democratic debate of ideas, formulation of proposals, free exchange of experiences and interlinking for effective action, by groups and movements of civil society that are opposed to neoliberalism" (WSF Charter of Principles, August 6, 2002, www.forumsocialmundial.org.br [accessed December 25, 2011]).

2 The overall chapter was collaborative, but each author contributed at least one empirical section: Stéphane Couture, "Ideologies and Practices at the Intersection of FLOSS and the Social Forum Process"; Giuseppe Caruso, "Free and Open Software in Mumbai"; Lorenzo Mosca, "Technological Conflicts within the European Social Forum Process"; and Jeffrey S. Juris, "Organizing Software and Technology within the U.S. Social Forum."

3 GNU stands for "GNU's not Unix." GNU/Linux is preferred to Linux by free software advocates in describing the entire operating system. Linux is the kernel, but GNU is the wider system. See www.gnu.org (accessed December 27, 2011). In the rest of this chapter we use GNU/Linux to reflect this distinction and to ensure that we employ the most inclusive term possible.

4 Interestingly, in Raymond's essay, the phrase *"cathedral" style of software development* is associated with proprietary software and is also meant as a criti-

cism of the top-down development style within Emacs core, led, perhaps ironically, by Stallman.

5   As Walter Scacchi (2007) points out, there are also slight pragmatic differences between free and open-source software development processes primarily revolving around the licenses used. Free software generally uses a GNU General Public License (GPL). Open-source projects may use GPL, but they may also use a license that provides for the integration of nonfree software.

6   Media centers should not be confused with the Independent Media Centers, which often coexist with the "official" ESF media centers.

7   The statement, "Communiqué de Zalea TV sur le Média Center de Forum Social Européen," is archived at the Indymedia Mailing Lists Archive, http://archives.lists.indymedia.org (accessed December 25, 2011).

8   "Media Lab at ESF in Paris." Available at www.zalea.tv (accessed December 25, 2011).

9   See the Hellenic GNU/Linux User Group website, www.hellug.gr (accessed December 25, 2011).

10 "Istanbul Report from the European Logistics Working Group." Available at www.fse-esf.org (accessed August 31, 2007).

11 The main organizations heading up the USSF ICT team were the New York City–based May First People Link, Openflows, and the Interactivist Network.

12 Although techies working on the European and global forum processes are now using the Plone content management system, and offered to provide their code, members of the USSF ICT team opted to go with Drupal because they had more experience working with that format.

13 All names of interviewees and forum participants in this section are pseudonyms.

14 The workshop was called "Radical Reference and the InterActivist Network—Using Free Software to Enable Community Based Activism."

15 "rossglover" (username), "Techno-democracy Feels Something Like Autocracy," post on the U.S. Social Forum's message board, May 30, 2007, www.ussf2007.org (accessed December 23, 2011).

16 "rossglover" (username), "I'm Doing My Best," reply to post on the U.S. Social Forum's message board, June 4, 2007, www.ussf2007.org/en/node/5063 (accessed December 23, 2011).

17 Michelle Murrain, "Gender, Race and Open Source," June 29, 2007, Zen and the Art of Nonprofit Technology (website), www.zenofnptech.org (accessed December 25, 2011). Details regarding this workshop were also gleaned from Peter J. Smith's (Athabasca University) personal fieldnotes.

18 For more on the lack of gender, race, and class diversity within the FLOSS movement, see Lin 2006 and Lovink 2003, 194–223.

19 "POOR Magazine" (username), "POOR Magazine: Reflections on My Journey to Atlanta," post on the U.S. Social Forum's message board, June 30, 2007, www.ussf2007.org (accessed December 25, 2011).

20 As we put the finishing touches on this chapter, the social forum process continued to evolve, particularly in the realm of technology. In terms of regional forums, three editions of the ESF have taken place over the past four years in Sweden (Malmoe, September 17–21, 2008), Turkey (Istanbul, July 1–4, 2010), and France (Paris, May 23–24, 2011), while the second USSF was held in Detroit, Michigan, from June 22–26, 2010. With respect to the ESF, a collaborative platform called OpenESF was created at the end of November 2007 to provide an ongoing networking space to facilitate sustainability through the use of new technologies. However, activity on the platform declined soon after the Malmoe forum (Saeed and Rohde 2010), and the OpenESF site was finally shut down in 2010. Meanwhile, similar problems to those we address here related to the cultural politics of technology resurfaced once again within the management of the official ESF website and the translation system during the latest editions of the ESF (Saeed et al. 2010).

Concerning the second USSF, unlike at the 2007 Atlanta forum, the NPC was more aware of technological issues this time, including the political significance of free software and the fact that technologists are also political organizers. This has to do, in part, with the fact that key members of the tech team were also members of the NPC this time around, but it also reflects a process of institutional learning. The main technology-related tension that came out in Detroit had to do with the use of Facebook. Members of the outreach committee wanted to post a Facebook logo and link on the USSF website. Many members of the tech team felt that it was important to avoid promoting a corporate website and to use movement tools instead. In response, members of the outreach team argued that it was important to reach people where they are. Tech team members acknowledged the point but still felt it was important to channel people from Facebook to the USSF page, not the other way around. Ultimately, outreach members took responsibility for the website, and the decision was made to use Facebook but not to post the logo on the USSF site. The registration process also ran into a technical glitch in Detroit as organizers were trying to collect more usable information this time and the system got overwhelmed. After having to shift to a manual process on the first day, however, the tech team successfully fixed the bug on the first evening, and everything went more smoothly after that.

Technology-related trends in the USSF have also resonated with the global WSF process, particularly in relation to the February 2011 WSF in Dakar, Senegal. While the debate over Facebook reappeared and was dealt with in a similar way as in the USSF (due not only to similar reasoning but also to the participation of USSF activists in the Communication Commission of the WSF International Council), a related debate revolved around the use of Skype technology for video conferencing. In this context, a concept paper released by the Communication Commission of the Dakar Organizing Committee, which addressed the technology to be used so those who could not be physically present in Dakar could participate virtually—the "Dakar Extended" process—explained that discussions would be organized via Skype or a similar "free" technology. This open and pragmatic approach gave voice to the concerns of those who are uncertain about relying only on free technology while at the same time leaving space for the development of alternative "free" technologies. In general, the technological realm is becoming increasingly discussed and politicized within the forums, as demonstrated by initiatives such as the first World Forum on Science and Democracy at the 2009 WSF in Belem (http://fm-sciences.org/?lang=en, accessed December 25, 2011), and the first World Techie Congress at the 2010 USSF in Detroit (see "Kah" [username], "Progressive Techies Declare Their Rights—and Responsibilities," APCNews, August 2, 2010, www.apc.org, accessed December 25, 2011).

CONCLUSION

The Possibilities, Limits, and Relevance
of Engaged Ethnography

JEFFREY S. JURIS | ALEX KHASNABISH

In these final pages we want to draw out some of the epistemological, ontological, and political possibilities, limitations, and tensions that have been revealed through our explorations of the insurgent encounters presented in this volume. We have sought to draw attention not only to engaged research and activism as a series of complex, diverse, and overlapping encounters (among and between researchers, activists, movements, dominant institutions, systems of power, commitments, positions, knowledges, and so on) but also to their subversive and productive potential. Indeed, as Alex Khasnabish illustrates in his contribution, networked spaces of transnational encounter give rise to unanticipated connections, radical imaginations, and political possibilities. At the same time, such spaces of encounter are always traversed by power, conflict, and inequality. In this sense, as Jeffrey Juris critically explores in his chapter, the intentionality through which spaces of encounter are constructed is always already shaped by prevailing injustices and exclusions.

Although hypermasculinist and militaristic overtones are impossible to disentangle from the language of insurgency, as noted in our introduction, we continue to invoke this discourse as a gesture to forms of intervention that unsettle dominant accounts and systems of power, clearing the way for new acts of imagination and constitution. In her chapter on the global indigenous movement, Sylvia Escárcega offers just such an "unsettling" account, describing the new paradigms that indigenous activists are proposing as a way to transform dominant understandings of humanity, the world, and nature. In her contribution, M. K. Sterpka draws on historiography and ethnography to offer a compelling depiction of early forms of transnational civil society networking before the rise of the Internet. This chapter is a testament not only to the importance of networked ethnography but also to the lesser known, yet foundational struggles for information freedom whose impact continues to resonate. These narratives subvert the authority of dominant voices that seek to legitimate what is, instead offering paths for envisioning what might be.

SUBJECTIVITY, PERIL, AND PROMISE

It is important to honestly and critically confront one of the core premises at the heart of this volume: that our politically committed ethnographic practice and the social justice struggles with which we engage constitute significant challenges to the status quo. As Manisha Desai contends in her chapter, however, ethnography's contribution to social justice struggles may not be as expansive as we might hope. Our most important role may be limited to that of the "supportive interlocutor," rethinking knowledge production, questioning the theoretical and methodological foundations of academic disciplines, and cultivating a critical awareness among students through radicalized pedagogies without taking part in frontline struggles. Perhaps, Desai provocatively suggests, given the power-laden operation of privileged and authorized ways of knowing and speaking, this limited role for scholar-activists is not a terrible thing. Janet Conway's chapter echoes this epistemologically humble approach by drawing attention to the important contributions that engaged ethnographers can make to the study of transnational social movement fields while asserting that ethnography is not "analytically self-sufficient." Not all of the contributors share this same degree of caution, but the tension between possibilities and constraints of politically engaged ethnographic research weaves its way through many of the volume's chapters and our underlying intellectual-political project.

Indeed, we are intensely aware of the fraught nature of our efforts to practice activist scholarship (or scholarly activism), particularly in relation to the gap between the work of knowledge production in privileged sites such as the academy and movements for radical social change. Compounding this divide is a more fundamental context, namely, that as social subjects we are living through a historical moment defined by an ever-more rapacious form of global capitalism and empire, a temporally and spatially unlimited "war on terror," and a geopolitical order defined by white supremacy, patriarchy, colonialism, ecological crisis, and vast social and economic inequality. Yet, not all subjects in this order and at this historical moment are equally positioned—as contributors to this volume, for example, we are all located, to greater or lesser extents, not only within privileged sites such as the university but also as relatively privileged actors in "the belly of the beast" of this patriarchal, white supremacist, globalized capitalist order.

Our positioning and subjectivities have profound consequences for our intellectual labor, the social change projects we engage in, and the possibilities, limitations, and blind spots of the activist and academic work we produce. As Vinci Daro compellingly foregrounds in her contribution, our location in relation to the perceived center of events produces very different kinds of encounters and accounts. At the edges of what are seemingly coherent and discrete zones—social, political, epistemological, methodological—varying kinds of transgressive encounters can occur, leading to dynamic, diverse, and unanticipated outcomes. Such "edge effects" provide an apt metaphor for our collective work in this volume, generating both possibilities and uncertainties.

In the introduction, we surveyed a diversity of approaches deployed in the study of social movements and sought to demonstrate how, despite the contributions of this extensive body of work, our engaged scholarship and ethnographically informed perspectives seek to push beyond it. We contend that ethnographic attention to everyday practices, cultural imaginaries, and emerging subjectivities is particularly well suited to understanding contemporary transnationally networked movements. As Geoffrey Pleyers asserts in his chapter, many conventional political process perspectives begin with the assumption that collective actors engage in global justice struggles in order to intervene within an established political arenas. In contrast, engaged ethnographic practice allows us to see and take seriously the fact that many global justice actors instead seek an exodus from the established political sphere and a space to develop forms of resistance grounded in subjectivity, everyday life, and the elaboration of concrete alternatives. This attention to experience and subjectivity facilitates abstract analysis and theorization, and it allows for engagement with social movements in all of their diversity and complexity.

Further, we have argued that our ethnographically grounded research can produce robust depictions of social movement activity, while actively contributing to movements by situating ourselves as activists and researchers within rather than outside movement spaces. However, such a position does not mean uncritically celebrating these movements or placing ourselves at their service, nor does it mean denying the tensions and contradictions of such "embedded" positions. One of our core goals has been precisely to unsettle dominant conceptualizations of social transformation, political possibility, knowledge production, and the relationship between intellectual labor and sociopolitical activism. In their collaboratively authored chapter, for example, Maribel Casas-Cortés, Michal Osterweil, and Dana Powell provide not just a potent critique of ethnography as representation and explanation but also a convincing vision of a politically relevant ethnographic practice predicated on the trope of the ethnographer as a "translator" or "weaver" of situated knowledges. Rather than being the arbiter of "truth," the ethnographer is but one knowledge producer in a "crowded field." The ethnographic challenge becomes not representation but the facilitation of communication among diverse knowledges. In another collaboratively authored chapter, Juris, Giuseppe Caruso, Stéphane Couture, and Lorenzo Mosca deploy the tools of ethnography to examine the conflicts over free/libre and open-source software (FLOSS) in the context of the social forum process. Far from uncritically celebrating FLOSS or the forums, the authors interrogate conflicts over technology and software in explicitly cultural and political terms rather than merely technical ones. In these ways ethnography itself becomes a tool for political intervention.

Through the essays collected here, we have sought to demonstrate that activist-oriented research can be rigorous and robust in academic terms while generating analytic and theoretical insights that are useful to activists. In this sense, as Caruso argues in his chapter, ethnographic practice can assist academics, activists, and practitioners in understanding and transforming conflicts, but not by offering prescriptive analysis or promising an unattainable transformative moment. Rather, it can do so by facilitating knowledge making, deliberation, and transformative action by actors situated within movements, the academy, and wider social spheres. However, politically engaged research carried out from within movement spaces is by no means a guaranteed path to ethically superior scholarship. Indeed, as David Hess points out in his chapter, ethnography often sits uneasily along the divide between academic and activist communities. Paul Routledge thus insists in his contribution that a commitment to activist ethnography can never erase power relations but instead compels us to forge solidarities based on a relational ethics with resisting others and to eschew the all-too-easy separation of knowledge from action, particularly at a moment when the realities of eco-social crisis have never been more apparent.

None of this is enough, though, to completely transcend the contradictions that constitute our academic work for and about radical movements. After all, as social subjects we are not entirely of our own making, coming into a world overdetermined by relations of power, exploitation, inequality, and violence. This is even more so with respect to dominant institutions, such as the university, extending far beyond matters of disciplinary structure and pedagogy to the very heart of how the university is configured in relation to the production and reproduction of a particular social order (see Wallerstein et al. 1996). Moreover, the very ways that scholars practicing politically committed research go about our intellectual labor with, for, and about social struggles are themselves embedded within civilizational structures of power and oppression and the cultural myths that underwrite them. For example, as Charles Mills (1997) provocatively argues, in a world characterized by white supremacy, what we think about, our goals for such thinking, and the conceptual and analytical tools at our disposal are all structured by the operation of an underlying Racial Contract.[1] This is most obviously true for scholarship rooted in dominant paradigms, but it is no less a threat to engaged, critical research, because this contract suffuses the entire sociopolitical fabric, shaping both dominations and resistances.

ETHNOGRAPHY AND POLITICAL COMMITMENT REVISITED

Although the chapters in this volume have staked out diverse positionalities with respect to the movements and spaces we examine, overall we have argued that ethnographers studying transnational social movements should not only clearly and openly align ourselves with groups in struggle but also seek, where possible, to break down, or at least unsettle, the divide between subject and object, theory and practice. The multiple strategies highlighted by our authors include the practice of a militant, activist, or transformational ethnography; the assuming of various participant roles such as facilitator, networker, mediator, accompanier, activist knowledge producer, independent media practitioner, or sympathetic interlocutor; and the enactment of diverse forms of mutual solidarity. Despite the cautionary remarks above, we argue that such politically aligned and committed ethnographic strategies allow us to contribute something concrete to our collaborators in resistance while, at their best, also producing insightful, nuanced, and sophisticated analyses. These are not the only or even necessarily the best strategies, but they are, we suggest, particularly appropriate modes of ethnographic research for grasping the dynamics of contemporary struggles such as the global justice, social forum, and other related movements that are networked in form; transnational in scale; heterogeneous in terms of political subjectivity and class, ethnic, and racial composition; and highly self-reflexive.

The extent to which our engaged ethnographies can actually make a difference to the movements we work with was extensively addressed in this volume's introduction and most of the subsequent chapters. We will not rehearse these discussions here, except to note that while we are optimistic about the contributions of our engaged ethnographies in practical and/or strategic terms, we remain aware of their significant contradictions and limitations. Nonetheless, is it still possible that we have gone too far in our explicit commitment to and engagement with the movements and groups we are studying? Can we achieve the relative distance required to be critical of our interlocutors and to produce sound scholarship? More generally, what are the consequences of our violating long-standing principles of neutrality and impartiality upon which traditional academic research has been based?

We would suggest that ethnography is always a highly subjective pursuit, reflecting in subtle and sometimes not so subtle ways the underlying assumptions, frameworks, affinities, and political predispositions of the ethnographer. Perhaps the main virtue of the Writing Culture critique was to finally question the authority on which so many traditional ethnographic accounts were based (see this volume's introduction), suggesting that the objectivity of the singular authoritative voice is more a result of specific modes, tropes, and techniques of writing than an accurate depiction of reality. Indeed, the Heisenberg principle suggests that even in the "hard" sciences observers always affect their objects of study, an effect that is multiplied in a highly subjective humanistic endeavor such as ethnography. By clearly positioning ourselves, and reflexively accounting for our own social, cultural, and political locations, we recognize the necessarily partial nature of our ethnographic accounts (see Clifford 1986; Haraway 1991), and we provide our readers with tools for critically assessing our ethnographic representations.

In addition, we would go further to argue that beyond the impossibility of objectivity, any purported neutral stance is ultimately complicit with the status quo, reproducing domination by allowing the current order of things to go unquestioned. As João Costa Vargas writes, "Neutrality is impossible—or better still, neutrality may work for the maintenance of privileges, but it does not work for all. Many forms of oppression, exclusion, and death continue to be perpetrated in the name of objectivity and detachment" (2006, 19). Indeed, the positivist logic of objectivity has long served as a mask to hide a false universality of supposedly "uninvolved scholars reproducing a social world outside themselves" in ways that support the interests of those with greater socioeconomic, political, and cultural power (Wallerstein et al. 1996, 92). In this sense, objectivity has often meant in practice the detached, god's-eye view of the white, male, European scholar, enacting a "sociology of absences" that has silenced the voices of myriad ethnic, racial, gendered, and colonized Others (Santos 2006). This critique does not have to mean a complete retreat into the solipsistic depths of subjectivity. On the contrary, once we have recognized our situatedness and go on to produce analyses that reflexively emerge from our own personal, ethical, and political locations and inclinations, we can enter into collective dialogues that allow us to make intersubjective judgments about the nature of social reality based on our observations and lived experiences (Wallerstein et al. 1996, 92).

Beyond the situated, partial, and subjective nature of our ethnographic research as well as the need to account for our sociopolitical locations through reflexivity, is it still possible that we overidentify with the movements we study, that in collapsing the distance between subject and object we remove any space for critical engagement with our interlocutors and collaborators? In other words, do we exhibit a lack of analytic distance that results in accounts that are uncritical, and thus fail to allow for complexity and contradiction? If this were the case, it would affect the quality of our analysis and also lead to ethnographies that are less politically and strategically useful for movements themselves.

With respect to these concerns, it is important to stress that we too are uncomfortable with overly celebratory accounts of social movements. In this sense, the approaches in this volume do provide room for constructive criticism of the movements we work with, as the critical strategic discussions contained in many of the chapters attest. As we argue in the introduction, one of the benefits of politically committed ethnography carried out from within grassroots movements is that it not only allows us to better understand the dynamics of such movements but it also provides us a position from which to engage in critical discussion and debate with other activists. In this sense, it is important to clarify what we mean by bridging the divide between subject and object in light of our view of political subjects as heterogeneous and internally differentiated.

Regarding the relation between subject and object, we mean to challenge and unsettle, not collapse this divide. Instead, throughout the research process, politically committed and engaged ethnographers move back and forth between deeper modes of sociopolitical identification with our collaborators and more distant moments of interpretation and critical analysis based on our embedded and embodied experiences as activists during more physically and emotionally engaged moments of participation. Even during more active, less reflexive moments, militant ethnographers are constantly reflecting on and analyzing our actions and practices. In this sense, action and reflection are inseparable; what changes is the relative degree of importance of one or the other depending on the specific moment and context of research. This is as true for other activists as it is for engaged ethnographers—indeed, relative and shifting degrees of distancing is a constitutive aspect of all political action. What is unique about militant and other forms of politically committed ethnography, however, is the relative intensity, length, and importance of the bridging moments that periodically transcend the subject-object divide, resulting in a practice perhaps better termed "observant participation," to borrow a phrase from João Costa Vargas (2006), but that is no less ethnographic for its degree of engagement.

On the other hand, it is also possible that we do not go far enough: that we are not sufficiently experimental or collaborative in our ethnographic writing, that we do not overcome the persistent inequalities and power differentials at the heart of the ethnographic endeavor, and that we remain too wedded to academic forums, formats, and processes. With regard to the first concern, we could have been more innovative and experimental in our textual practices, but, as we point out in the introduction, we are more influenced by the recent politicized turn as a response to the critique of ethnographic authority and the colonial relations that have historically characterized the ethnographic pursuit. While we are by no means averse to nonorthodox modes of ethnographic writing, we are not convinced that textual strategies, whether polyvocality, nonlinear narratives, or fictive accounts, can dispense with authorial control, unequal power relations, and underlying dominations. We are more enthusiastic about emerging collaborative forms of ethnographic writing that involve multiple authors and networks of scholars and activists—indeed, such network-based collaborations reflect the emerging logics and practices of the movements we study. However, although at least two of our chapters are collaborative in nature, we fall well short in this regard.

Along these lines, perhaps we do not go far enough in actually combating the unequal power relations and imbalances underlying the ethnographic encounter. In this sense, significant social, economic, and political hierarchies remain between researchers and our interlocutors, and, for the most part, the authors in this volume retain tight control over our research and writing projects, affording little space for our collaborators to influence either the research process or the final product. Both of these points ring true and point to additional limitations. With regard to the first, although many of us have made a conscious effort to try to minimize the social distance and hierarchies between ourselves and our collaborators, by studying processes and practices that we are an integral part of, many of which are situated outside the traditional sites of anthropological research in local communities and villages of the global South, we cannot completely overcome inequalities and imbalances with respect to power, resources, and cultural capital. The best we can do, and what we have tried to do in the preceding chapters, is to recognize and remain reflexively aware of the lingering hierarchies, inequalities, and exclusions along axes of race, class, gender, nationality, and social location that continue to shape our ethnographic engagements.

In terms of the significant control that most of the authors in this volume maintain over our research projects and products, it is true that other methodologies, such as participatory action research (PAR), go much further in terms of equalizing the relationship between researcher and collaborator (see Greenwood and Levin 1998). In PAR, for example, the group being studied helps to design the project so it addresses useful questions, and it participates in the project's implementation at every stage, including the writing. At the same time, as we point out in the introduction, PAR works best when researchers enter into relationship with a formal group or organization that has clear decision-making procedures and clearly delimited boundaries. When ethnographers study movements that are more fluid and diffuse, such as many of those addressed in this volume, and of which they themselves are a part, the relationship between the researcher and the movement is more ambiguous. Moreover, although PAR confers significant control to the participants in the research, resulting in a more directly accountable process, the same tight control may also result in projects that are useful to the groups involved but more positivist in orientation (Hale 2006), or they may generally lack the nondirectionality and open-endedness of the ethnographic encounter. By giving up their autonomy in this way, researchers may compromise their ability to produce ethnographically informed analyses that are both analytically critical and strategically relevant.

Finally, the question might arise as to why we remain committed to ethnography at all, and why we continue to situate our ethnographic writing and publishing within the academy. If we are so keen to emphasize the participation side of the participant-observation equation, why do we continue to frame our work as ethnographic? At the same time, given the increasingly crowded field where so many other movement participants are carrying out their own quasi-ethnographic research and are writing, publishing, and distributing their own movement-oriented reflections and analyses (see Casas-Cortés, Osterweil, and Powell, this volume; Juris 2008a), can politically committed ethnographers contribute anything that is unique or particularly relevant?

In some ways, the ethnographic projects featured here diverge substantially from classic ethnographic practice: the authors have always already gone native; many of our interlocutors are engaged in similar "paraethnographic" research and writing (Holmes and Marcus 2005), as Tish Stringer discusses in her chapter; many of us are studying at home; and we are more concerned with practices, processes, and problems than with particular cultures or groups. However, rather than a rejection of ethnography, these trends are very much in line with post–Writing Culture, postfunctionalist, and poststructuralist trends in anthropology and related fields. Meanwhile, our commitment to spending extended periods of time in the field, collecting and writing fieldnotes, grounding our analyses in thick description, and engaging with contemporary anthropological, sociological, and related theories and debates situates our work squarely in the ethnographic tradition.

POLITICAL PROMISES AND LIMITATIONS

Another central argument running through the volume is that contemporary social movements that are transnationally networked, internally heterogeneous, and rhizomatic require theoretical frameworks and engaged, ethnographic methods that go beyond traditional objectivist and state-centric approaches for studying social movements. We have addressed these novel frameworks with respect to subjectivities, paradigms, knowledge production, and new technologies, among other concepts. We have also explored some of the complex internal dynamics, political tensions, and tactical struggles associated with emerging networked spaces of transnational encounter. However, even though many of the chapters touch on the impact of the movements we explore, it might help to further consider the political promises and potential limitations of these forms of activism. We thus conclude the volume by reexamining the political stakes of the movements we have studied and contributed to as active participants.

Most of the movements and spaces of encounter explored in this volume are associated with the wave of transnational struggle that many activists and observers date to the Zapatista uprising,[2] and that gained widespread visibility with the mass counter-summit mobilizations against international financial institutions such as the World Bank, International Monetary Fund (IMF), and World Trade Organization (WTO), culminating in the global expansion of the World Social Forum process (Juris 2008a). Specific examples of this transnational wave of global justice activism examined in the volume are world and regional social forums, autonomous Zapatista communities and transnational Zapatista solidarity networks, feminist movements, European and North American autonomous and direct action–oriented collectives, Argentine *piqueteros* (picketers), struggles for climate justice, indigenous movements, movements of South and Southeast Asian farmers, alternative-economy pathways, and independent media and technology movements. Although these struggles vary in terms of their constituent actors, subjectivities, organizational forms, strategic and tactical repertoires, and political goals and visions, they share many common characteristics:

- relative autonomy from political parties, trade unions, and state institutions;
- flexible, network-based forms of organization;
- a focus on autonomous self-management within the sphere of daily social life;
- an emphasis on lived experience, subjectivity, and alternative models of sociality;
- the use of creative and/or confrontational direct action tactics; and
- a commitment to directly democratic and prefigurative modes of decision making.

Not all of the movements and sectors covered in this volume reflect all of these characteristics. As Geoffrey Pleyers's chapter suggests, for example, they are particularly pronounced within struggles oriented more toward radical autonomy and direct action, such as the Zapatistas in Mexico, the Argentine piqueteros, or younger global justice activists in Europe and North America. On the other hand, the global indigenous movement examined by Sylvia Escárcega has tended toward more institutional forms of politics in international forums, despite its emphasis on alternative paradigms and autonomy, but it has more recently begun to engage the social forum process. At the same time, the grassroots base-building groups surveyed in Juris's chapter tend to have more traditionally bureaucratic organizational forms with paid organizers and clearly identifiable memberships. Indeed, one of the virtues of the networked spaces of transnational encounter considered in this volume is that they bring together movements and groups with very different political and organizational visions, forms, strategies, and tactics. Nonetheless, the movements we have examined exhibit at least some, if not all, of the attributes identified above.

As we mention in the introduction, because of the proclivity of these movements toward non-state-oriented politics (if not their complete eschewal of the state) and their unorthodox forms, they tend to escape the categories of traditional social movement theories, particularly those in the resource mobilization and political process traditions. At first glance they might seem to resemble the idealized noninstitutional actors of new social movement theory, but they deviate from the new social movements typology in important ways. For example, the broader movements and spaces of encounter considered here integrate cultural and economic themes, they tend to be multigenerational and multi-issue, they are often composed of heterogeneous actors (see Feixa, Pereira, and Juris 2009), and, perhaps most importantly, they are not necessarily self-limiting (Cohen 1985). In other words, they are putting forth radical visions that challenge the underlying institutions and assumptions of modernity and would significantly reconfigure socioeconomic, political, and cultural life.

But what is the ultimate political significance of such movements and networked spaces of encounter? Can they achieve lasting political change and longer-term social transformation? Some might question their tendency toward noninstitutional, non-state-oriented strategies. Given that the state remains the primary locus of political power in modern liberal democracies, how can movements pursuing radical alternatives achieve material benefits for their constituencies? Short of revolution, what do such movements offer? We might also question the networked structure of the spaces and struggles we address here. It is often argued that to achieve political victories, movements require formal organization, clear structures of accountability, and singular strategies. The more diffuse, rhizomatic movements and spaces of encounter considered in this volume are perhaps too ephemeral, too unfocused, and too lacking in clear strategy and leadership to have a lasting political impact and to make a difference in people's lives.

Finally, many observers have noted that more informal, networked movements and spaces of encounter, particularly in the global North, tend to constitute a privileged, white, middle-class domain of politics that leaves out the poorest and most marginalized actors from working-class and people-of-color communities. As Juris suggests in his chapter, this was precisely the critique of the global justice movement that resulted in the intentional organizing strategy implemented as part of the U.S. Social Forum process. However, before addressing these reservations, it is important to remember that these also reflect internal debates, productive tensions, or "frictions" (Tsing 2005), which are constitutive of and help to determine the shape and trajectory of the networked movements and spaces of encounter considered here.

With respect to non-state-oriented strategies, first, we would like to reiterate our argument from the introduction that as activist-ethnographers we feel it is crucial to take the movements we work with seriously on their own terms. For this reason, we have tried not to impose categories that our movement collaborators would find irrelevant, instead elaborating movement-based frameworks or developing concepts from our own engaged ethnographic work. Pleyers's chapter most directly addresses this issue by arguing for the importance of subjectivity and experience for the movements and spaces he examines rather than engaging in a reductive analysis of their institutional impact. Nonetheless, this still begs the question of what these movements can achieve, particularly in terms of durable, concrete social change. Many of the movements we engage, such as the Zapatistas or the radical autonomous collectives in the North, are specifically responding to the failure of state institutions to address their needs and concerns.

The Zapatistas, for example, have been influenced by the wider movement for indigenous autonomy in Mexico, but they are also challenging the historic neglect of Mayan communities on the part of the Mexican state in spheres such as education, health, and development. Moreover, the Zapatistas began to intensify their development of their autonomous forms of government in the wake of the failure of the Mexican state to implement the San Andrés Accords that would have granted indigenous communities in Chiapas and elsewhere a modicum of autonomy, but as part of a reconfigured Mexican state (Speed 2007; see also Chatterton 2010). For their part, young European squatters have built autonomous social centers, in part, as a response to the lack of economic opportunities, affordable housing, and spaces for social interaction provided by state institutions (see Hodkinson and Chatterton 2006; Pickerill and Chatterton 2006). In other words, as much as an abandonment of the state, struggles for autonomy reflect a history of the state abandoning grassroots communities and movements "from below" (Zibechi 2010). In their efforts to organize for themselves, then, autonomist movements are meeting their own concrete material and cultural needs with respect to economic well-being, health, housing, education, media, and artistic expression.

At the same time, many autonomy-oriented movements do not seek complete separation from the state but prefer to organize their own spaces and networks outside state institutions. Indeed, the failure of so many state-oriented movements to achieve the freedom, liberation, and democracy they had promised, as well as the negative experiences of so many grassroots activists in their efforts to work with political parties and trade unions, has reinforced their emphasis on autonomous political mobilization. Rather than rejecting the state entirely, such movements often practice a "dual politics" (Cohen and Arato 1992; see Juris 2008a), strategically building up their own autonomous spaces and networks as spheres for developing new meanings, subjectivities, and models of sociality, while tactically intervening within the realm of the state through mass mobilizations, media campaigns, and direct action protests. Such reform-oriented tactical interventions are perhaps increasingly necessary to ward off the worst excesses of the current neoliberal capitalist order, even as movements continue to organize in their own spaces for more deeply rooted structural and cultural transformation.

Such movements can influence the state indirectly by making certain issues visible and influencing public opinion, and they can also serve as laboratories for the creation of alternative paradigms, identities, and models of socioeconomic organization that may gradually migrate more widely (Juris 2008a; see also Melucci 1989). In this sense, the wave of mass counter-summit actions associated with the global justice movements made visible the negative impact of multilateral institutions such as the World Bank, IMF, and WTO; the harmful effects of debt, deregulation, and free trade; and the role of global decision-making bodies such as the G8 and European Union in reproducing neoliberal policies and practices. For their part, networked spaces of transnational encounter, such as the social forums, provide more of an emphasis on alternatives, ranging from reformist policies such as financial regulation, the Tobin Tax,[3] and debt cancellation to more prefigurative proposals related to participatory budgeting, free software, and alternative monetary systems, including those addressed by David Hess in this volume. Global justice protests, social forums, and other spaces of encounter thus also allow activists to put into practice their far-reaching visions and goals. Although radicals may reject certain reformist proposals, the broader spaces and networks they take part in bring together diverse sectors and models across the radical-reformist divide. The inevitable frictions that result help generate much of the innovation and dynamism of such spaces.[4]

In addition to occupying diverse spatial terrains, the movements and networks considered here are also oriented toward multiple temporalities of struggle and transformation (Wallerstein 2008), which intersect with particular spatial domains in complex ways. In the short run, for example, activists are often focused on addressing immediate concerns, including concrete survival issues,[5] while over the long term, they can emphasize social transformation, a horizon toward which political imaginaries are oriented, and a sphere within which sociopolitical and economic alternatives become possible. Over the intermediate term, meanwhile, movements are often concerned with strengthening their own organizational networks and capacities while refining their political strategies in order to achieve longer-term social transformation, particularly with respect to the twin goals of enhancing democratization and egalitarianism (Wallerstein 2008). In spatial terms, whereas intervening within the terrain of the state is often necessary to achieve short-run goals, state-oriented mobilizations can facilitate intermediate-term movement building while providing a platform for experimenting with longer-range utopian visions and alternative modes of sociality. Likewise, organizing within more autonomous movement spheres is not oriented toward only intermediate- and long-term objectives; it can also build movement capacity for engaging in shorter-term campaigns around issues and needs of immediate relevance.

A second concern about the movements explored in this volume relates to their diffuse, networked structure. Traditional Leftists and community organizers in the Saul Alinsky tradition might fault the movements and spaces considered here for lacking clear structures of leadership and accountability, for their failure to coalesce around unified strategies and visions, and for their lack of political efficacy and sustainability.[6] With regard to the first criticism, this position would suggest that networked movements lack direction and accountability because anyone can participate, make decisions, and come and go as they please without responding to a grassroots base. Indeed, a similar critique was made of the Occupy movements in 2011–12. According to this view, movements are stronger and more democratic when formal leaders are given clearly defined roles and are held accountable by a membership base that consists of those who are most directly affected by a problem or issue. The lack of a clear organizational and decision-making structure and leadership also makes it more difficult to develop common goals and political strategies that would allow movements to accomplish specific objectives. Finally, this lack of structure, unifying vision, and coordinated strategy means that such movements are particularly susceptible to the inevitable ebbs and flows of popular mobilization, making it more difficult to sustain themselves over time, further reducing their political efficacy.

Again, we emphasize that such debates regarding organization are also internal to the movement spaces and networks examined here, as Juris's chapter on the U.S. Social Forum attests. Perhaps most fundamentally, it is important to recognize the pluralism and diversity that such movements and spaces exhibit with respect to forms of organization (in addition to diversity in terms of tactics, strategies, and visions). More formally structured organizations are perhaps better equipped to develop common programs and visions; they do have clearer structures of leadership and accountability, and in theory they are better able to respond to the needs and wishes of an identifiable grassroots base. The benefits of networked movements lie elsewhere: in their capacity for bringing together diverse movements and groups; in their flexibility and openness, which make them more strategically adaptable; in their decentralization and lack of formal hierarchy (despite their continued vulnerability to informal hierarchies; see e.g., Freeman 1972), which multiply the channels for direct participation in movement activities and decision making; and in the emotional, solidary, and pedagogical benefits of participatory, directly democratic forms of organization (Polletta 2002).[7]

Bureaucratic organizations and vertical leadership structures are not the only means of ensuring democracy and accountability, however. For example, spokescouncil models in North American direct action circles, where decisions are made by consensus among rotating delegates selected from networks of decentralized affinity groups, ensure representation and accountability in the absence of formal leadership structures. Similar systems have long been in place throughout the global South, including the traditional assemblies in Mexican indigenous communities that serve as the basis for the Zapatista Juntas de Buen Gobierno (good government councils), which are made up of rotating delegates from the municipal assemblies that comprise a particular *Caracol* (literally shell, refers to meeting point and regional seat of autonomous government).

Despite these contributions and the political paths they have opened, these movements continue to face major barriers. The years following the WTO protests in Seattle in 1999 have witnessed the rise of increasingly securitized and militarized state apparatuses, particularly in the wake of 9/11. Across the global North, an ascendant radical Right has seized state institutions and used them to deepen and entrench inequality and exploitation domestically and internationally, and around the world military forces have been deployed as police actions in defense of elite interests and an ever-more predatory system of capital accumulation through dispossession. In the wake of the global capitalist crisis that began in 2008, these tendencies have only accelerated as elites pursue strategies of accu-mulation by dispossession, no longer even bothering to cloak the realities of exploitation, injustice, and inequality in the once-celebrated language of Keynesian social welfarism or, more recently, the rhetoric of neoliberal capitalism as a tide that lifts all boats (see McNally 2011). As elites across the global North and in emerging centers of capitalist power in places like China and India deploy the state and its juridical, propagandistic, and normative orders to erode workers' rights, police racialized migrants, roll-back hard-won rights and liberties, impose austerity, and surveil and dis-rupt resistance movements, the well-worn slogan "we are winning" that appears so often at global justice counter-summit mobilizations seems increasingly hollow.

In the face of this robust pushback from the Right, many of the move-ments and spaces we engage in this volume and the broader "movement of movements" have found themselves forced into defensive postures, seemingly ill-equipped to meet this new challenge. And yet, in Septem-ber 2011, the momentum of the biopolitics of austerity was interrupted by the emergence of a new and unanticipated collective actor on the political stage. Drawing inspiration from the Arab Spring and spurred to action by a call to "Occupy Wall Street!" issued on July 13, 2011, by the culture-jamming publication *Adbusters*, starting on September 17, 2011, in New York City a wave of occupations swept cities across North America and beyond (see Juris 2012). These occupations followed in the wake of the historically unprecedented transfer of public wealth into private hands that constituted government bailouts of capitalist institutions deemed "too big to fail," as well as the rise of the austerity paradigm that promised only further impoverishment and dispossession for the vast majority — re-ferred to by the Occupy movement as "the 99 percent." Introducing a new political lexicon, the occupiers declared that their actions were expres-sions of the anger and frustration of the 99 percent against an entrenched and widening socioeconomic inequality that was devouring them to feed the monstrous wealth appropriation of the richest and best connected — named by the movement "the 1 percent."

Bursting onto the political scene at a moment when radicalized, social justice–oriented mass movements were conspicuous in their absence, the Occupy movements were remarkable in their mobilization of so many diverse groups, including, yet moving beyond, the usual suspects in ex-perienced activist circles, many of whom had earlier cut their teeth in the alter-globalization movements. Taking place across North America and around the world, these protests combined the physical occupation of public space in city centers; the establishment of camps with an assembly-based model of collective, participatory decision making (see also Pleyers, this volume); and a reticence to engage in the institutional politics of demand. Certainly not without criticism—some fair, some not—of the diverse, popular, loosely structured, and politically undetermined nature of the occupations (to say nothing of the use of the language of occupation itself and its imperialist, genocidal overtones), these eruptions of popular dissent signaled the presence of a widely shared outrage at the status quo as well as the endurance of a spirit of resistance and alternative building that had been incubated most recently in the alter-globalization movements. By the end of 2011, the vast majority of these Occupy encampments had been systematically and forcibly dismantled by agents of the state.

In the absence of physical camps, Occupy movements in many cities shifted to community organizing and networking with established organizations, periodic protest marches and direct actions, ongoing debates about whether and how to articulate concrete political demands and engage with electoral politics, and continuing general assemblies as directly democratic alternatives to the corrupted state of a representative-democratic system largely controlled by the power and wealth of the 1 percent. Regardless of what happens going forward, the Occupy movements helped to partly shift national conversations in the United States and elsewhere from an exclusive focus on budgetary deficits and austerity to include a countervailing concern for economic fairness and inequality (see Juris 2012). What the future holds for the Occupy movements is far from clear, but even without the violent evictions at the hands of state authorities, the encampments and the movements as a whole were beginning to confront hard questions about the capacity of the Occupy movements to shift beyond the spectacle of dissent to the building of a genuine counterpower.

The current political moment reveals a renewed materiality of power. At this juncture, some radical voices have begun calling for a rebirth of principles that once seemed consigned to the dustbin of history: communism, the party, insurrectionism, and revolutionary organizations, to name a few (see Badiou 2010; The Invisible Committee 2009). In the wake of the global capitalist crisis that began in 2008, even Keynesian social democracy has returned as a hope (however faint) for something modestly less rapacious and predatory than an increasingly desperate and ravenous neoliberalism. The return of these political projects points to and is made possible by the perceived limitations and failures of the political currents we have explored in this volume and that, to a significant extent, have seen their continuation in movements such as Occupy and even the Arab Spring. When elites push back against social justice struggles with the juridical, bureaucratic, and repressive apparatuses of the state while using these same apparatuses to engage in a project of accumulation by mass dispossession, our struggles can only be judged by their capacity to defend and fight back against this onslaught. In this sense, there is an urgent need to better understand what the movements and spaces can contribute and what they cannot with respect to social struggles in an age of austerity and radical right-wing mobilization, a task of immanent reflection and critique already under way within movements and spheres of politically engaged research. Interestingly, as with the previous wave of global justice activism, politically committed anthropologists played key roles as activists and observers in the Occupy movements (see Juris 2012; Juris and Razsa 2012; and Razsa and Kurnik 2012).

In practice, traditional Leftist, grassroots base-building, and more diffuse, networked organizations have all been able to coexist, interact, and coordinate within the social forums. As the Zapatistas like to say, the idea is to create a world where many worlds fit. Such broad-based formations are absolutely vital to the reconfiguration and revitalization of a powerful Left, which is nowhere more urgent than in the United States, where both neoliberalism and right-wing Tea Party populism are increasingly resurgent. Only a broad-based networked model of resistance can bring together the diversity of actors needed to confront such trends and to begin building an alternative world based on true democracy, freedom, and economic justice. At the same time, it is true that more diffuse and rhizomatic models of organization tend to be less sustainable than formal organizations, a challenge that confronted the Occupy movements. What is particularly interesting and important about spaces of encounter, such as the world and regional social forums, is that they represent an institutionalization of the networked model of movement, providing a relatively sustainable networked "movement infrastructure" (Andrews 2004) that can facilitate sustained movement building and interaction.

A final concern commonly advanced with regard to contemporary networked movements, particularly in the global North, relates to their perceived white, middle-class character. One version of this position laments their lack of diversity, another questions their underlying legitimacy given the perceived absence of those who are most directly affected by the principle issues at stake, including various forms of social, political, and economic domination. This was the main thrust behind the "Where Was the Color in Seattle?" critique following the anti-WTO protests in November 1999, and a prime motivator of the efforts to build a more diverse and racially inclusive social forum in the United States (see Juris, this volume). Similar critiques reemerged in the context of the Occupy movements in the United States (see Juris et al. 2012).

Again, it is important to recognize that this is also an internal critique expressed within many networked spaces of transnational encounter. At the same time, from a global perspective the critique is largely off base. Many southern working-class and people-of-color movements, particularly in Latin America, such as the Zapatistas, the piqueteros, the Argentine popular assemblies, and the urban popular movements in Bolivia (see Zibechi 2010), are organized through decentralized networks of community and neighborhood assemblies, involve consensus decision making, and are rooted in lived experiences and subjectivities. Moreover, grassroots popular movements from throughout the global South have long played critical roles in transnational global justice networks such as Peoples' Global Action, Via Campesina, and the social forum process.

Nonetheless, it is the case that networked movements in the global North, particularly the radical autonomy and direct action sectors, that are most likely to emphasize directly democratic decision making, experience, and subjectivity tend to be relatively more white and middle class than other kinds of movements (such as the grassroots member organizations that have headed up the U.S. Social Forum process). As Paul Lichterman (1996) suggests, white, middle-class activists in the United States tend to prefer looser, directly democratic forms of organization that facilitate a more personalized politics, while activists of color tend to practice a more communitarian politics through formal organizations that are more deeply rooted in local histories, identities, and social conditions. Whereas formal communitarian organizations are more focused on concrete issues and are more directly accountable to their memberships, informal personalized organizations are more flexible, open, and participatory. We saw this dynamic at play in the Occupy movements, despite increasing efforts to build understanding and connections across different kinds of movement organization.[8]

These differential patterns of participation can be at least partly explained by the fact that white, middle-class activists have the time and resources to spend long hours attending meetings and concerning themselves with process, while poor and working-class activists of color have more immediate concerns rooted in their daily lives. Middle-class activists also have greater access to the new technologies around which many networked movements are organized. Interestingly, similar dynamics have led many poor and marginalized communities of color in the global South, particularly where weak states have been unable or unwilling to address the needs of such communities, to organize through more informal yet locally rooted networked movements (Zibechi 2010). Beyond differences in political tradition, this may have something to do with the more pressing conditions, the more politicized context, and the lack of formal organizational resources in these communities. The important point is that there is no necessary connection between a particular organizational form and a given activist community (see Polletta 2002). Instead the links are contingent and highly contextual.

The current challenge, it seems to us, is for contemporary struggles to develop hybrid structures that can mobilize diverse communities with the goal of building the widest-possible movements. This is precisely the promise of networked spaces of transnational encounter. The process will inevitably be conflictual, but the capacity of broad-based progressive movements to reinvigorate themselves depends on their ability to work through and effectively negotiate such differences.

NOTES

1   As Mills writes, the Racial Contract is "that set of formal or informal agreements or meta-agreements . . . between the members of one subset of humans, henceforth designated by (shifting) 'racial' (phenotypical/gene-alogical/cultural) criteria . . . as 'white,' and coextensive (making due allowance for gender differentiation) with the class of full persons, to categorize the remaining subset of humans as 'nonwhite' and of a different and inferior moral status" (1997, 11).

2   It should be noted that related strands of anti-free-trade, anti-IMF, and

anticorporate activism had taken place previously and were also occurring simultaneously throughout the global South, as well as in Europe and North America.

3 First proposed by the economist James Tobin, the Tobin Tax would levy a small tax (Tobin initially suggested 0.5 percent) on all foreign exchange transactions in order to discourage speculative currency trading. In some later versions of the proposal, the tax would also be used to raise money for a global development fund.

4 With respect to observable political impacts, particular policy changes are difficult to trace to specific movements (see Diani 1997), and the likelihood of reforms will vary across political contexts. In this sense, alternatives to neoliberal policies and practices have been more noteworthy in regions such as Latin America, which witnessed a string of Leftist political victories in the 2000s in the context of widespread anti-corporate-globalization organizing and sentiment (e.g., Lula in Brazil, Nestor Kirschner in Argentina, and Evo Morales in Bolivia), than in Europe and the United States (Juris 2008a).

5 As Immanuel Wallerstein (2008) points out, decisions regarding shorter-term strategies always entail a choice between the lesser of two evils and are primarily defensive in nature, oriented toward the protection of those rights already secured or gains already achieved and against the threat of their erosion, whether that means voting for a particular party, abstaining from voting altogether, or opting to take up arms.

6 Some have also made the point that networked forms of organization were pioneered by global capital as part of an argument against the forms' liberatory potential for social movements. Indeed, as Juris has written elsewhere (2008a), there is nothing inherently emancipatory about networks or any other organizational form. Their ultimate impact depends on the specific uses to which they are put, the values that inspire their use, and the contexts within which they operate.

7 For more on direct or participatory democracy within global justice movements, see Graeber 2009; Juris 2008a; Maeckelbergh 2009; and Polletta 2002, 176–201.

8 In Occupy Boston, for example, representatives from community-based organizations with a constituency of largely working-class people of color met regularly with occupiers to build solidarity, develop common projects, and figure out how to coordinate despite differing organizational structures and logics. For their part, many occupiers fought for the implementation of anti-oppression principles and practices as a way to recognize racial and class privilege and create spaces for historically marginalized voices (see Juris 2012). In this sense, the Occupy movements shifted largely from a more indi-

vidualized "logic of aggregation" where protest camps embody the coming together of "crowds of individuals," reflecting, in many ways, the organizational logic of social media, toward a more sustained and institutionalized networking logic, where distinct movements, organizations, and groups coordinate through the general assemblies, spokescouncils, and other emergent structures (Juris 2012).

REFERENCES

Abélès, Marc. 2008. *Anthropologie de la globalisation*. Paris: Payot.

Agrawal, Arun. 2005. *Environmentality*. Durham: Duke University Press.

Agrikoliansky, Eric, Olivier Fillieule, and Nona Mayer. 2005. *L'altermondialisme en France*. Paris: Flammarion.

Agyeman, Julian, Harriet Bulkeley, and Aditya Nochur. 2007. "Climate Justice." In *Ignition*, ed. Jonathan Isham and Sissel Waage, 135–44. Washington, D.C.: Island Press.

Akrich, Madeleine. 1992. "The De-scription of Technical Objects." In *Shaping Technology, Building Society*, ed. Wiebe E. Bijker and John Law, 205–24. Cambridge: MIT Press.

Albrow, Martin. 1996. *The Global Age*. Cambridge, U.K.: Polity Press.

———. 2007. "Situating Global Social Relations." In *Frontiers of Globalization Research*, ed. Ino Rossi, 317–32. New York: Springer.

Alexander, Nadja M. 2006. *Global Trends in Mediation*. Alphen aan den Rijn: Kluwer Law International.

———. 2008. "The Mediation Metamodel." *Conflict Resolution Quarterly* 26 (1): 97–123.

Allagui, Ilhem, and Johanne Kuelder, eds. 2011. "The Arab Spring and the Role of ICTs." Special feature section of the *International Journal of Communication* 5. Available at http://ijoc.org (accessed December 27, 2012).

Álvarez, Rebecca, Erika Gutierrez, Linda Kim, Christine Petit, and Ellen Reese. 2008. "The Contors of Color at the World Social Forum." *Critical Sociology* 34 (3): 389–407.

Alvarez, Sonia E. 1998. "Latin American Feminisms 'Go Global.'" In *Cultures of Politics, Politics of Cultures*, ed. Sonia Alvarez, Evelina Dagnino, and Arturo Escobar, 293–324. Boulder, Colo.: Westview Press.

———. 1999. "Advocating Feminism." *International Feminist Journal of Politics* 1 (2): 181–209.

Alvarez, Sonia, Evelina Dagnino, and Arturo Escobar, eds. 1998. *Cultures of Politics, Politics of Cultures.* Boulder, Colo.: Westview Press.

Amenta, Edwin, and Neal Caren. 2004. "The Legislative, Organizational, and Beneficiary Consequences of State-Oriented Challengers." In *The Blackwell Companion to Social Movements,* ed. David A. Snow and Sara A. Soule, 461–88. Malden, Mass.: Blackwell.

Amin, Samir. 1990. *Maldevelopment.* New York: United Nations University Press.

Amit, Vered. 2000. "Introduction." In *Constructing the Field,* ed. Amit Vered, 1–18. New York: Routledge.

Anand, Nikhil. 2004. "Bound to Mobility?" In *World Social Forum: Challenging Empires,* ed. Jai Sen, Anita Anand, Arturo Escobar, and Peter Waterman, 140–47. New Delhi: Viveka Foundation.

Anderson, Benedict. 1991. *Imagined Communities.* London: Verso.

Anderson, Kay, and Susan J. Smith. 2001. "Editorial: Emotional Geographies." *Transactions of the Institute of British Geographers* 26 (1): 7–10.

Andrews, Kenneth T. 2004. *Freedom Is a Contested Struggle.* Chicago: University of Chicago Press.

Appadurai, Arjun. 1996. *Modernity at Large.* Minneapolis: University of Minnesota Press.

———. 2002. "Deep Democracy." *Public Culture* 14 (1): 21–47.

Arquilla, John, and David F. Ronfeldt. 1996. *The Advent of Netwar.* Santa Monica, Calif.: Rand.

———. 2001. *Networks and Netwars.* Santa Monica, Calif.: Rand.

Asad, Talal. 1973. *Anthropology and the Colonial Encounter.* Ithaca, N.Y.: Ithaca Press.

———. 1986. "The Concept of Cultural Translation in British Social Anthropology." In *Writing Culture,* ed. James Clifford and George E. Marcus, 141–64. Berkeley: University of California Press.

Atkinson, Paul, Amanda Coffey, Sara Delamont, Lyn Lofland, and John Lofland, eds. 2001. *Handbook of Ethnography.* Thousand Oaks, Calif.: Sage.

Badiou, Alain. 2010. *The Communist Hypothesis.* London: Verso.

Bale, Lawrence S. 1995. "Gregory Bateson, Cybernetics, and the Social/Behavioral Sciences." *Cybernetics and Human Knowing* 3 (1): 27–45.

Bandy, Joe, and Jackie Smith, eds. 2005. *Coalitions across Borders.* Lanham, Md.: Rowman and Littlefield.

Barabasi, Albert-László. 1999. "The Emergence of Scaling in Random Networks." *Science* (286): 509–12.

———. 2003. *How Everything Is Connected to Everything Else*. New York: Plume Press.

Barmeyer, Niels. 2009. *Developing Zapatista Autonomy*. Albuquerque: University of New Mexico Press.

Beck, Aaron T. 1999. *Prisoners of Hate*. New York: Perennial/Harper Collins.

Beck, Ulrich. 2000. *What Is Globalization?* Cambridge, U.K.: Polity Press.

Beckerman, Gal. 2003. "Edging Away from Anarchy." *Columbia Journalism Review* 42 (3): 27–30.

Beckerman, Wilfred, and Joanna Pasek. 2001. *Justice, Posterity, and the Environment*. Oxford: Oxford University Press.

Beckman, Ludvig, and Edward A. Page. 2008. "Perspectives on Justice, Democracy and Global Climate Change." *Environmental Politics* 17 (4): 527–35.

Behar, Ruth. 1996. *The Vulnerable Observer*. Boston: Beacon Press.

Behar, Ruth, and Deborah A. Gordon, eds. 1995. *Women Writing Culture*. Berkeley: University of California Press.

Bello, Walden. 2007. "The Forum at the Crossroads." *Foreign Policy in Focus*, www.fpif.org (accessed December 25, 2011).

Benasayag, Miguel, and Diego Sztulwark. 2000. *Du contre-pouvoir*. Paris: La Découverte.

Bennett, Katy. 2004. "Emotionally Intelligent Research." *Area* 36: 414–22.

Biccum, April. 2005. "The World Social Forum." *Ephemera* 5 (2): 116–33.

Blackwell, Maylei. 2006. "Weaving in the Spaces." In *Dissident Women*, ed. Shannon Speed, R. Aída Hernández Castillo, and Lynn M. Stephen, 115–54. Austin: University of Texas Press.

Bloch, Ernst. 1986. *The Principle of Hope*. Oxford: Basil Blackwell.

Bob, Clifford. 2005. *The Marketing of Rebellion*. Cambridge, U.K.: Cambridge University Press.

Bonaparte, Darren. 2000. "A Line on a Map: A Mohawk Perspective on the International Border at Akwesasne." www.wampumchronicles.com (accessed December 25, 2011).

Bornstein, Erica. 2003. *The Spirit of Development*. Stanford: Stanford University Press.

Bosco, Fernando. 2006. "The Madres de Plaza de Mayo and Three Decades of Human Rights Activism." *Annals of the Association of American Geographers* 96 (2): 342–65.

———. 2007. "Emotions That Build Networks." *Tijdschrift voor Economische* 98 (5): 545–63.

Bourdieu, Pierre. 1984. *Distinction*. Cambridge: Harvard University Press.

Bourgois, Philippe. 2001. "The Power of Violence in War and Peace." *Ethnography* 2 (1): 5–37.

———. 2006. "Foreword." In *Engaged Observer*, ed. Victoria Sanford and Asale Angel-Ajani, ix–xii. New Brunswick, N.J.: Rutgers University Press.

Boyle, David. 2004. "The Fantasy of Gold and the Survival of Life." Lecture presented at the "Local Currencies in the 21st Century Conference," Bard College, Annandale-on-Hudson, N.Y., June 26.

Breines, Wini. 1982. *Community and Organization in the New Left, 1962–1968*. New York: Praeger.

Brennan, Tim. 2006. *Wars of Position*. New York: Columbia University Press.

Bretón Solo de Zaldívar, Víctor. 2008. "De la ventriloquía a la etnofagia o la etnización del desarrollo rural en los Andes Ecuatorianos." Paper presented at the XI Congreso de Antropología de España, University of the Basque Country, San Sebastián, Spain, September 12.

Brettell, Caroline, ed. 1996. *When They Read What We Write*. Westport, Conn.: Bergin and Garvey.

Brigg, Morgan. 2003. "Mediation, Power, and Cultural Difference." *Conflict Resolution Quarterly* 20 (3): 287–306.

Buck-Morss, Susan. 2000. *Dreamworld and Catastrophe*. Cambridge: MIT Press.

Bull, Malcolm. 2005. "The Limits of Multitude." *New Left Review* 35: 19–39.

Bunge, William. 1971. *Fitzgerald*. Cambridge, Mass.: Shenkman.

Burawoy, Michael. 1998. "The Extended Case Method." *Sociological Theory* 16: 4–33.

———. 2000. "Grounding Globalization." In Michael Burawoy, Joseph A. Blum, Sheba George, Zsuzsa Gille, Teresa Gowan, Lynne Haney, Maren Klawiter, Steven H. Lopez, Séan Ó. Riain, and Millie Thayer, *Global Ethnography*, 337–50. Berkeley: University of California Press.

———. 2005. "For Public Sociology." *American Sociological Review* 70 (1): 4–28.

Burawoy, Michael, Joseph A. Blum, Sheba George, Zsuzsa Gille, Teresa Gowan, Lynne Haney, Maren Kwaliter, Steven H. Lopez, Séan Ó. Riain, and Millie Thayer. 2000. *Global Ethnography*. Berkeley: University of California Press.

Burczak, Teodore A. 2006. *Socialism after Hayek*. Ann Arbor: University of Michigan Press.

Burdick, John. 1995. "Uniting Theory and Practice in the Ethnography of Social Movements." *Dialectical Anthropology* (20): 361–85.

———. 1998. *Blessed Anastacia*. New York: Routledge.

Bush, Robert A. B. 2004. "One Size Does Not Fit All." *Ohio State Journal of Dispute Resolution* 19 (3): 965–1004.

Bush, Robert A. B., and Joseph P. Folger. 2005. *The Promise of Mediation*. San Francisco: Jossey Bass.

Cahn, Edgar, and Christine Grey-Cahn. 2004. "Time Dollars as an Instrument of Social Justice and Systems Change." Lecture presented at the "Local

Currencies in the 21st Century Conference," Bard College, Annandale-on-Hudson, N.Y., June 26.

Calhoun, Craig. 1992. "Introduction." In *Habermas and the Public Sphere*, ed. Craig Calhoun, 1–48. Cambridge: MIT Press.

———. 2008. "Foreword." In *Engaging Contradictions*, ed. Charles R. Hale, xiii–xxvi. Berkeley: University of California Press.

Callahan, Manuel. 2004. "Zapatismo and Global Struggle." In *Confronting Capitalism*, ed. Eddie Yuen, Daniel Burton-Rose, and George Katsiaficas, 11–18. Brooklyn, N.Y.: Soft Skull Press.

Callon, Michel. 1991. "Techno-Economic Networks and Reversibility." In *A Sociology of Monsters*, ed. John Law, 132–65. New York: Routledge.

Cancian, Francesca. 1992. "Feminist Science." *Gender and Society* 6 (4): 623–42.

Candea, Matei. 2009. "Arbitrary Locations." In *Multi-sited Ethnography*, ed. Mark-Anthony Falzon, 25–46. Burlington, Vt.: Ashgate.

Cardon, Dominique, and Fabien Granjon. 2003. "Les mobilisations informationnelles dans le mouvement altermondialiste." Paper presented at the colloquium "Les mobilisations alternandialistes, Foundation Nationale des Sciences Politiques, Paris, December 3–5. Available at www.afsp.msh-paris.fr (accessed December 25, 2011).

Carter, Gwendolen M., and Patrick O'Meara, eds. 1985. *African Independence*. Bloomington: Indiana University Press.

Caruso, Giuseppe. 2004. "Conflict Management and Hegemonic Practices in the World Social Forum 2004." *International Social Science Journal* 56 (182): 577–89.

———. 2005a. *Onaya Shipibo-Conibo*. Quito: Abya-Yala.

———. 2005b. "Open Office and Free Software." *Ephemera* 5 (2): 173–92.

———. 2007. "Organizing Global Civil Society." Ph.D. dissertation, School of Oriental and African Studies, University of London.

———. 2010a. "'Their Crises, Our Solutions!' The World Social Forum and the 2008 Global Crises." *World Social Forum 2011* (blog), http://fsm2011.org (accessed December 25, 2011).

———. 2010b. "Excitement to Depression and Up Again." Paper Presented at the World Congress of the International Sociological Association, Gothenburg, Sweden, July 19, 2010.

———. 2012. *Cosmopolitan Futures*. Helsinki: Into Publishers (ebook), www.into-ebooks.com (accessed December 24, 2012).

Casas-Cortés, María Isabel. 2008. "Tools and Methods to Comprehend and Reappropriate a Global City." *Transform* (blog), http://transform.eipcp.net (accessed December 25, 2011).

———. 2009. "Social Movements as Sites of Knowledge Production." Ph.D.

dissertation, Department of Anthropology, University of North Carolina, Chapel Hill.

Casas-Cortés, M. Isabel, and Sebastián Cobarrubias. 2008. "Transatlantic Translations." *Journal of Aesthetics and Protest Press, In the Middle of a Whirlwind* (blog), http://inthemiddleofthewhirlwind.wordpress.com (accessed December 25, 2011).

Casas-Cortés, María Isabel, Michal Osterweil, and Dana Powell. 2008. "Blurring Boundaries." *Anthropological Quarterly* 81 (1): 17–58.

Castells, Manuel. 1997. *The Power of Identity*. Malden, Mass.: Blackwell.

———. 1998. *End of Millennium*. Malden, Mass.: Blackwell.

———. 2012. *Networks of Outrage and Hope*. Cambridge, U.K.: Polity.

Castoriadis, Cornelius. 1991. "Power, Politics, Autonomy." In *Philosophy, Politics, Autonomy*, ed. David Ames Curtis, 143–74. Oxford: Oxford University Press.

Chabbott, Colette. 1999. "Development INGOs." In *Constructing World Culture*, ed. John Boli and George Thomas, 222–48. Stanford: Stanford University Press.

Chase-Dunn, Christopher, Ellen Reese, Mark Herkenrath, Rebecca Giem, Erika Gutierrez, Linda Kim, and Christine Petit. 2008. "North-South Contradictions and Bridges at the World Social Forum." In *North and South in the World Political Economy*, ed. Rafael Reuveny and William R. Thompson, 341–66. Malden, Mass.: Blackwell Publishers.

Chatterton, Paul. 2006. "'Give Up Activism' and Change the World in Unknown Ways." *Antipode* 38 (2): 259–82.

———. 2010. "Autonomy." *Antipode* 42 (4): 897–908.

Chatterton, Paul, Duncan Fuller, and Paul Routledge. 2008. "Relating Action to Activism." In *Connecting People, Participation and Place*, ed. Sarah Kindon, Rachel Pain, and Mike Kesby, 245–87. New York: Routledge.

Chesters, Graeme, and Ian Welsh. 2006. *Complexity and Social Movements*. New York: Routledge.

Christoff, Stefan, and Sophie Schoen. 2008. "Contemporary Currents of Quebec's Student Movement." *The Dominion*, May 31, www.dominionpaper.ca (accessed December 25, 2011).

Cleaver, Harry. 1995. "The Zapatistas and the Electronic Fabric of Struggle." Unpublished article. Available at https://webspace.utexas.edu/hcleaver/www/zaps.html.

———. 1999. "Computer-Linked Social Movements and the Global Threat to Capitalism." Unpublished article. Available at https://webspace.utexas.edu/hcleaver/www/polnet.html.

Clifford, James. 1986. "Partial Truths." In *Writing Culture*, ed. James Clifford and George E. Marcus, 1–26. Berkeley: University of California Press.

———. 1988. *The Predicament of Culture*. Cambridge: Harvard University Press.

Clifford, James, and George E. Marcus. 1986. *Writing Culture*. Berkeley: University of California Press.

Cobarrubias, Sebastian. 2009. "Mapping Machines." Ph.D. dissertation, Department of Geography, University of North Carolina, Chapel Hill.

Coenen-Huther, Jacque. 2003. "Le type idéal comme instrument de la recherche sociologique." *Revue Française de Sociologie* 44 (3): 531–47.

Cohen, Jean L. 1985. "Strategy or Identity." *Social Research* 52 (4): 663–716.

Cohen, Jean L., and Andrew Arato. 1992. *Civil Society and Political Theory*. Cambridge: MIT Press.

Cohen, Robin, and Shirin M. Rai, eds. 2000. *Global Social Movements*. New Brunswick, N.J.: The Athlone Press.

Coleman, Gabriella. 2009. "Code Is Speech." *Cultural Anthropology* 24 (3): 420–54.

———. 2004. "The Political Agnosticism of Free Software and the Politics of Contrast." *Anthropology Quarterly* 77 (3): 507–19.

Coles, Romand. 2005. *Beyond Gated Politics*. Minneapolis: University of Minnesota Press.

Collom, Ed. 2005. "Community Currency in the United States." *Environment and Planning A* 37 (9): 1565–87.

Comaroff, Jean, and John L. Comaroff. 2003. "Ethnography at an Awkward Scale." *Ethnography* 4 (2): 147–79.

Conway, Janet. 2004a. "Citizenship in a Time of Empire." *Citizenship Studies* 8 (4): 367–81.

———. 2004b. *Identity, Place, Knowledge*. Halifax: Fernwood Press.

———. 2005a. *Praxis and Politics*. New York: Routledge.

———. 2005b. "Social Forums, Social Movements and Social Change." *International Journal of Urban and Regional Research* 29 (2): 425–28.

———. 2007. "Transnational Feminisms and the World Social Forum." *Journal of International Women's Studies* 8 (3): 49–70.

———. 2008a. "Geographies of Transnational Feminisms." *Social Politics* 15 (2): 207–31.

———. 2008b. "Reading Nairobi as Place, Space, and Difference." *Societies without Borders* 3 (1): 48–70.

———. 2010. "Troubling Transnational Feminism(s) at the World Social Forum." In *Solidarities beyond Borders*, ed. Pascale Dufour, Dominique Masson, and Dominque Caouette, 149–72. Vancouver: University of British Columbia Press.

———. 2012. *Edges of Global Justice*. New York: Routledge.

Costa Vargas, João H. 2006. *Catching Hell in the City of Los Angeles*. Minneapolis: University of Minnesota Press.

Coté, Mark, Richard Day, and Greig de Peuter. 2007. *Utopian Pedagogy*. Toronto: University of Toronto Press.

Couture, Stéphane. 2007. "Logiciel libre, activité technique et engagement politique." Master's thesis, University of Quebec, Montreal.

Cumbers, Andrew, Paul Routledge, and Corinne Nativel. 2008. "The Entangled Geographies of Global Justice Networks." *Progress in Human Geography* 32 (2): 183–201.

Cunningham, Hilary. 1999. "The Ethnography of Transnational Social Activism." *American Ethnologist* 26 (3): 583–604.

Da Costa, Alcino Louise. 1976. "Third World Feature Service." In "Information and the New World Order." Special issue of *Development Dialogue* 2: 52–64.

Dag Hammarskjöld Foundation. 1975. "Introduction." In "What Now—The 1975 Dag Hammarskjöld Report on Development and International Cooperation." Special issue of *Development Dialogue* 1 (2): 3–21.

Damasio, Antonio R. 1994. *Descartes' Error*. New York: Avon Books.

Daro, Vinci. 2009a. "Global Justice Protest Events and the Production of Knowledge about Differences." *McGill Journal of Education* 44 (1): 39–54.

———. 2009b. "Edge Effects of Global Summit-Hopping in the Post-Seattle Period, 2000–2005." Ph.D. dissertation, University of North Carolina, Chapel Hill.

Daulatzai, Anila. 2004. "A Leap of Faith." *International Social Science Journal* 56 (182): 565–76.

De Angelis, Massimo. 2004. "Opposing Fetishism by Reclaiming Our Powers." *International Social Science Journal* 182: 591–604.

———. 2005. "PR Like PROCESS!" *Ephemera* 5 (2): 193–204.

Debord, Guy. 1994. *The Society of the Spectacle*. New York: Zone Books.

De Landa, Manuel. 2006. *A New Philosophy of Society*. New York: Continuum.

Deleuze, Gilles, and Félix Guattari. 1987. *A Thousand Plateaus*. Minneapolis: University of Minnesota Press.

Delgado Díaz, Carlos J. 2004. "The Political Significance of Small Things." ECO 6 (1–2): 49–54.

Delgado P., Guillermo. 1996. Barbados III: Etica y Antropología Latinamericana. La Paz, Bolivia: Ediciones Isla.

———. 2002. "The Makings of a Transnational Movement." NACLA Report on the Americas 35 (6): 36–40.

della Noce, Dorothy J. 1999. "Seeing Theory in Practice." *Negotiation Journal* 15 (3): 271–301.

della Porta, Donatella. 2005. "Multiple Belongings, Tolerant Identities, and the Construction of 'Another Politics.'" In *Transnational Protest and Global Activism*, ed. Donatella della Porta and Sidney Tarrow, 175–202. Lanham, Md.: Rowman and Littlefield.

———, ed. 2007. *The Global Justice Movement*. Boulder, Colo.: Paradigm Publishers.

della Porta, Donatella, Massimiliano Andretta, Lorenzo Mosca, and Herbert Reiter. 2006. *Globalization from Below*. Minneapolis: University of Minnesota Press.

della Porta, Donatella, Hanspeter Kriesi, and Deter Rucht, eds. 1999. *Social Movements in a Globalizing World*. New York: St. Martin's Press.

della Porta, Donatella, and Sidney Tarrow, eds. 2004. *Transnational Protest and Global Activism*. Lanham, Md.: Rowman and Littlefield.

del Valle Escalante, Emilio. 2009. *Maya Nationalisms and Postcolonial Challenges in Guatemala*. Santa Fe, N.M.: School for Advanced Research.

Desai, Manisha. 2009. *Gender and the Politics of Possibilities*. Lanham, Md.: Rowman and Littlefield.

Dewey, John. 1922. *Human Nature and Conduct*. New York: Holt.

———. 1925. *Experience and Nature*. Chicago: Open Court.

Diani, Mario. 1997. "Social Movements and Social Capital." *Mobilization* 2 (2): 129–47.

———. 2003. "Introduction." In *Social Movements and Networks*, ed. Mario Diani and Doug McAdam, 1–20. Oxford: Oxford University Press.

Dirlik, Arif. 1998. "Globalism and the Politics of Place." *Development* 41 (2): 7–14.

Dobson, Andrew. 1998. *Justice and the Environment*. Oxford: Oxford University Press.

Doherty Brian, Alex Plows, and Derek Wall. 2007. "Environmental Direct Action in Manchester, Oxford, and North Wales." *Environmental Politics* 16: 805–25.

Dombrowski, Kirk. 2001. *Against Culture*. Lincoln: University of Nebraska Press.

Donson, Fiona, Graeme Chesters, Ian Welsh, and Andrew Tickle. 2004. "Rebels with a Cause, Folk Devils without a Panic." *Internet Journal of Criminology*, www.internetjournalofcriminology.com (accessed December 25, 2011).

Doyle, Clare. 2001. "Storm in Quebec." *Socialism Today*, June, www.socialism today.org (accessed December 25, 2011).

Dubet, François. 1994. *Sociologie de l'expérience*. Paris: Seuil.

Dubet, François, and Michel Wieviorka, eds. 1995. *Penser le sujet*. Paris: Fayard.

Earl, Jennifer. 2004. "The Cultural Consequences of Social Movements." In *The Blackwell Companion to Social Movements*, ed. David Snow, Sarah Soule, and Hanspeter Kriesi, 508–30. Malden, Mass.: Blackwell.

Earle, Duncan, and Jeanne Simonelli. 2005. *Uprising of Hope*. Lanham, Md.: Altamira Press.

Edelman, Gerald M. 2006. *Second Nature*. New Haven: Yale University Press.

Eglash, Ronald. 1999. *African Fractals*. New Brunswick, N.J.: Rutgers University Press.

Ellwood, Wayne. 2001. *The No-Nonsense Guide to Globalization*. London: Verso.

Elmer, Greg, and Andy Opel. 2008. *Preempting Dissent*. 1st ed. Winnipeg: Arbeiter Ring Publishing.

El-Shaarawi, Abdel H., and Walter W. Piegorsch. 2002. *Encyclopedia of Environmetrics*. Hoboken, N.J.: Wiley.

England, Kim. 1994. "Getting Personal." *The Professional Geographer* 46 (1): 80–89.

Epstein, Barbara. 1991. *Political Protest and Cultural Revolution*. Berkeley: University of California Press.

Escárcega, Sylvia. 2003a. "Indigenous Intellectuals and Activists." *Brújula, Revista Interdisciplinaria sobre Estudios Latinoamericanos* 2 (2): 43–56.

———. 2003b. "Internationalization of the Politics of Indigenousness." Ph.D. dissertation, Department of Anthropology, University of California, Davis.

———. 2009. "Trabajar haciendo." *Intercultural Education* 20 (1): 39–50.

———. 2010. "Authenticating Strategic Essentialisms." *Cultural Dynamics* 22 (1): 3–28.

———. 2011. "Indigeneidad, migración y género desde una perspectiva internacional." In *Organización política y gobernabilidad en territorios indígenas de América Latina*, ed. Jorge Hernández-Díaz, 395–422. México City: Grupo Editorial Miguel Ángel Porrúa.

Eschle, Catherine, and Bice Maiguashca. 2007. "Rethinking Globalised Resistance." *BJPIR* 9: 284–301.

———. 2010. *Making Feminist Sense of the Global Justice Movement*. Lanham, Md.: Rowman and Littlefield.

Escobar, Arturo. 1992. "Culture, Practice and Politics." *Critique of Anthropology* 12 (4): 395–432.

———. 2000. "Notes on Networks and Anti-globalization Social Movements." Paper presented at the Annual Meeting of the American Anthropological Association, San Francisco, November 15–19.

———. 2001. "Culture Sits in Places." *Political Geography* 20: 139–74.

———. 2004. "Other Worlds Are (Already) Possible." In *World Social Forum: Challenging Empires*, ed. Anita Anand, Arturo Escobar, and Peter Waterman, 349–58. New Delhi: The Viveka Foundation.

———. 2008. *Territories of Difference*. Durham: Duke University Press.

———. 2009. "Postconstructivist Political Ecologies." In *International Handbook of Environmental Sociology*, ed. Michael Redclift and Graham Woodgate, 91–105. Cheltenham, U.K.: Edward Elgar.

Ettlinger, Nancy. 2004. "Towards a Critical Theory of Untidy Geographies." *Feminist Economics* 10: 21–54.

Ettlinger, Nancy, and Fernando Bosco. 2004. "Thinking through Networks and Their Spatiality." *Antipode* 36: 249–71.

Eyerman, Ron, and Andrew Jamison. 1991. *Social Movements*. Cambridge, U.K.: Polity Press.

EZLN. 1994. *Documentos y Comunicados 1*. Mexico City: Era.

———. 1995. *Documentos y Comunicados 2*. Mexico City: Era.

Faber, Daniel. 2005. "Building a Transnational Environmental Justice Movement." In *Coalitions across Borders*, ed. Joe Bandy and Jackie Smith, 43–70. Lanham, Md.: Rowman and Littlefield.

Falzon, Mark-Anthony. 2009. "Introduction." In *Multi-sited Ethnography*, ed. Mark-Anthony Falzon, 1–24. Farnham, Vt.: Ashgate.

Fardon, Richard, ed. 1995. *Counterworks*. New York: Routledge.

Farmer, Paul. 2004. "An Anthropology of Structural Violence." *Current Anthropology* 45 (3): 305–25.

Farrow, Heather, Pam Moss, and Barbara Shaw. 1995. "Symposium on Feminist Participatory Research." *Antipode* 27 (1): 77–101.

Featherstone, David. 2003. "Spatialities of Transnational Resistance to Globalization." *Transaction of the Institute of British Geographers* 28 (4): 404–21.

———. 2005. "Towards the Relational Construction of Militant Particularisms." *Antipode* 37 (2): 250–71.

———. 2008. *Resistance, Space and Political Identities*. Malden, Mass.: Wiley-Blackwell.

Featherstone, David, Richard Phillips, and Johanna Waters. 2007. "Introduction: Spatialities of Transnational Networks." *Global Networks* 7 (4): 383–91.

Feixa, Carles, Inês Pereira, and Jeffrey S. Juris. 2009. "Global Citizenship and the 'New, New' Social Movements." *Young* 17 (4): 421–42.

Feminist Dialogues. 2005. Report Written by Development Alternatives with Women for a New Era (DAWN), Women's International Coalition for Economic Justice (WICEJ), Articulación Feminista Mercosur (AFM), National Network of Women's Autonomous Groups (NNWAG), African Women's Development and Communication Network (FEMNET), INFORM-Sri Lanka, and Isis International-Manila.

———. 2007. "Transforming Democracy." A Report of the 3rd Feminist Dialogues for the 7th World Social Forum, Nairobi, Kenya, January 17–19, 2007. Isis International-Manila.

Fernandez, Luis. 2008. *Policing Dissent*. New Brunswick, N.J.: Rutgers University Press.

Filastine, Grey. 2003. "Not in Service." In *We Are Everywhere*, ed. Notes from Nowhere, 211–13. London: Verso.

Fischer, Frank. 2000. *Citizens, Experts, and the Environment*. Durham: Duke University Press.

Fischer, Michael M. J. 2003. *Emergent Forms of Life and the Anthropological Voice*. Durham: Duke University Press.

———. 2005. "Technoscientific Infrastructures and Emergent Forms of Life."
American Anthropologist 107 (1): 55–61.

Fisher, William. 1997. "Doing Good? The Politics and Antipolitics of NGO Practices." *Annual Reviews in Anthropology* 26: 439–64.

Fisher, William, and Thomas Ponniah, eds. 2003. *Another World Is Possible*. New
York: Zed Books.

Fortun, Kim. 2001. *Advocacy after Bhopal*. Chicago: University of Chicago Press.

Foucault, Michel. 1975. *Discipline and Punishment*. New York: Random House.

Fox, Jonathan. 2002. "Assessing Binational Civil Society Coalitions." In *Cross-
Border Dialogues*, ed. David Brooks and Jonathan Fox, 341–417. La Jolla: Center for U.S.-Mexican Studies, University of California, San Diego.

Fox, Richard G., and Orin Starn, eds. 1997. *Between Resistance and Revolution*.
New Brunswick, N.J.: Rutgers University Press.

Fraser, Nancy. 1992. "Rethinking the Public Sphere." In *Habermas and the Public
Sphere*, ed. Craig Calhoun, 109–42. Cambridge: MIT Press.

———. 1997. *Justice Interruptus*. New York: Routledge.

Freeman, Jo. 1972. "The Tyranny of Structurelessness." *The Second Wave* 2 (1):
20.

Freire, Paulo. 2000. *Pedagogy of the Oppressed*. New York: Continuum.

Friedman, Jonathan. 2004. "Globalization, Transnationalization, and Migration." In *Worlds on the Move*, ed. Jonathan Friedman and Randeria Shalini,
63–88. London: Tauris.

Fukuyama, Francis. 1992. *The End of History and the Last Man*. New York: Free
Press.

Funke, Peter. 2010. "The Global Social Forum Rhizome." Ph.D. dissertation, Department of Political Science, University of Pennsylvania.

Fuster Morell, Mayo. 2008. "Social Forums and Technology." Paper presented
at the "Networked Politics and Technology" seminar, University of California,
Berkeley, December 6–7.

Gamson, William. 1990. *The Strategy of Social Protest*. Homewood, Ill.: Dorsey.

Gandhi, Nandita, and Nandita Shah. 2005. "An Interactive Space for Feminisms." Unpublished manuscript, AKSHARA, Mumbai, India.

Geertz, Clifford. 1973. *The Interpretation of Cultures*. New York: Basic Books.

———. 1989. *Works and Lives*. Stanford: Stanford University Press.

Gerlach, Luther P., and Virginia H. Hine. 1970. *People, Power, Change*. Indianapolis, Ind.: Bobbs-Merrill.

Gibson-Graham, Julie-Katherine. 1994. "'Stuffed If I Know!'" *Gender, Place and
Culture* 1: 205–24.

———. 1996. *The End of Capitalism as We Knew It*. Cambridge, Mass.: Blackwell.

———. 2006. *A Post-Capitalist Politics*. Minneapolis: University of Minnesota
Press.

Giddens, Anthony. 1991. *Modernity and Self-Identity*. Cambridge, U.K.: Polity Press.

Gille, Zsuzsa. 2001. "Critical Ethnography in the Time of Globalization." *Cultural Studies—Critical Methodologies* 1 (3): 319–34.

Gilligan, Carol. 1982. *In a Different Voice*. Cambridge: Harvard University Press.

Giugni, Marco. 2004. "Personal and Biographical Consequences." In *The Blackwell Companion to Social Movements*, ed. David Snow, Sarah Soule, and Hanspeter Kriesi, 489–507. Malden, Mass.: Blackwell.

———. 2008. "Political, Biographical, and Cultural Consequences of Social Movements." *Sociology Compass* 2 (5): 1582–1600.

Giugni, Marco, Doug McAdam, and Charles Tilly. 1999. *How Social Movements Matter*. Minneapolis: University of Minnesota Press.

Glasius, Marlies. 2005. "Deliberation or Struggle?" *Ephemera* 5 (2): 240–52.

Gómez-Peña, Guillermo. 2002. "The New World Border." In *The Mexico Reader*, ed. Gilbert Michael Joseph and Timothy J. Henderson, 750–55. Durham: Duke University Press.

Goodwin, Jeffrey, James Jasper, and Francesca Polletta, eds. 2001. *Passionate Politics*. Chicago: University of Chicago Press.

Graeber, David. 2002. "The New Anarchists." *New Left Review* 13: 61–73.

———. 2004. *Fragments of an Anarchist Anthropology*. Chicago: Prickly Paradigm Press.

———. 2007. *Possibilities*. Oakland, Calif.: AK Press.

———. 2009. *Direct Action*. Oakland, Calif.: AK Press.

Greco, Thomas, Jr. 2004. "Building Healthy Community Economics." Lecture presented at the "Local Currencies in the 21st Century Conference." Bard College, Annandale-on-Hudson, N.Y., June 26.

———. 2009. *The End of Money and the Future of Civilization*. White River Junction, Vt.: Chelsea Green.

Greenwood, Davydd J. 2008. "Theoretical Research, Applied Research, and Action Research." In *Engaging Contradictions*, ed. Charles R. Hale, 319–40. Berkeley: University of California Press.

Greenwood, Davydd J., and Morten Levin. 1998. *Introduction to Action Research*. Thousand Oaks, Calif.: Sage.

Grubacic, Andrej. 2003. "Life after Social Forums." *Znet*, February 9, www.zcommunications.org/znet (accessed December 25, 2011).

Guerrero, Michael Leon. 2008. "The US Social Forum." *Societies without Borders* 3 (1): 168–86.

Guidry, John A., Michael D. Kennedy, and Mayer Zald, eds. 2000. *Globalization and Social Movements*. Ann Arbor: University of Michigan.

Gupta, Akhil, and James Ferguson. 1997a. "Discipline and Practice." In *Anthro-*

pological Locations, ed. Akhil Gupta and James Ferguson, 1–46. Berkeley: University of California Press.

———. 1997b. "Culture, Power, Place: Ethnography at the End of an Era." In *Culture, Power, Place*, ed. Akhil Gupta and James Ferguson, 1–32. Durham: Duke University Press.

Gutiérrez, Margarita, and Nellys Palomo. 2000. "A Woman's Eye View of Autonomy." In *Indigenous Autonomy in Mexico*, ed. Araceli Burguete Cal y Mayor, 53–82. Copenhagen: IWGIA Document No. 94.

Habermas, Jürgen. 1984. *The Theory of Communicative Action*. Cambridge, U.K.: Polity Press.

———. 1989. *The Structural Transformation of the Public Sphere*. Trans. Thomas Burgle. Cambridge: MIT Press.

Hadden, Jennifer, and Sidney Tarrow. 2007. "The Global Justice Movement in the United States since Seattle." In *The Global Justice Movement*, ed. Donatella della Porta, 210–31. Boulder, Colo.: Paradigm Publishers.

Haiven, Max, and Alex Khasnabish. 2011. "What Is the Radical Imagination?" *Affinities* 4 (2): i–xxxvii.

Hakken, David. 2007. "A Critique of Popular Political Economies of Knowledge in Cyberspace, an Alternative Political Economy of Cyberspace Knowledge, and a Demonstration of the Applicability of the Alternative to Study of Free/Libre and Open Source Software in the Malay World." *New Proposals* 1 (1): 40–80.

Hale, Charles R. 2006. "Activist Research v. Cultural Critique." *Cultural Anthropology* 21 (1): 96–120.

———. 2008. "Introduction." In *Engaging Contradictions*, ed. Charles R. Hale, 1–30. Berkeley: University of California Press.

Halleck, DeeDee. 2002. *Hand Held Visions*. New York: Fordham University Press.

Haraway, Donna J. 1988. "Situated Knowledges." *Feminist Studies* 14 (3): 575–99.

———. 1991. *Simians, Cyborgs, and Women*. New York: Routledge.

Harden, Joel Davison. 2006. "Québec Solidaire." *Canadian Dimension Magazine*, July/August, http://canadiandimension.com (accessed December 28, 2011).

Harding, Sandra. 2005. "Negotiating with the Positivist Legacy." In *The Politics of Method in the Human Sciences*, ed. George Steinmetz, 346–65. Durham, N.C.: Duke University Press.

Hardt, Michael, and Antonio Negri. 2000. *Empire*. Cambridge: Harvard University Press.

———. 2004. *Multitude*. New York: Penguin.

Harvey, David. 2005. *A Brief History of Neoliberalism*. Oxford: Oxford University Press.

Held, David. 2010. *Cosmopolitanism*. Cambridge, U.K.: Polity Press.

Held, David, and Andrew McGrew. 2002. *Globalization/Anti-globalization*. Cambridge, U.K.: Polity Press.

Hellman, Judith A. 1999. "Real and Virtual Chiapas." In *Necessary and Unnecessary Utopias: Socialist Register 2000*, ed. Leo Panitch and Colin Leys, 161–86. Suffolk, U.K.: Merlin Press.

Hemment, Julie. 2007. *Empowering Women in Russia*. Bloomington: Indiana University Press.

Henderson, James (Sa'ke'j) Youngblood. 2008. *Indigenous Diplomacy and the Rights of Peoples*. Saskatoon, Canada: Purich Publishing Limited.

Henderson, Victoria L. 2008. "Is There Hope for Anger?" *Emotion, Space and Society* 1: 28–37.

Hernández Castillo, Rosalva Aída, ed. 2008. *Etnografías e historias de resistencia*. Mexico City: Centro de Investigaciones y Estudios Superiores en Antropología Social, Universidad Autónoma Nacional de México, and Programa Universitario de Estudios de Género.

Hess, Beth, and Myra Marx Ferree. 2001. *Controversy and Coalition*. New York: Twayne Publishers.

Hess, David. 1995. *Science and Technology in a Multicultural World*. New York: Columbia University Press.

———. 1998. *Evaluating Alternative Cancer Therapies*. New Brunswick, N.J.: Rutgers University Press.

———. 2001. "Ethnography and the Development of Science and Technology Studies." In *Sage Handbook of Ethnography*, ed. Paul Atkinson, Amanda Coffey, Sara Delamont, Lyn Lofland, and John Lofland, 234–45. Thousand Oaks, Calif.: Sage.

———. 2007a. *Alternative Pathways in Science and Industry*. Cambridge: MIT Press.

———. 2007b. "Crosscurrents: Social Movements and the Anthropology of Science and Technology." *American Anthropologist* 109 (3): 463–72.

———. 2009. *Localist Movements in a Global Economy*. Cambridge: MIT Press.

———. 2010. "Declarations of Independents." *Anthropological Quarterly* 83 (1): 147–70.

———. 2011. "Electricity Transformed." *Antipode* 43 (3): 1056–77.

Hess, David, and Margaret Wooddell. 1998. *Women Confront Cancer*. New York: New York University Press.

Hesse-Biber, Sharlene Nagy, ed. 2007. *The Handbook of Feminist Research*. Thousand Oaks, Calif.: Sage.

Hewitt, Lyndi. 2005. "Reflections on the Role of Scholar-Activist in Feminist Sociology." Paper presented at the Annual Meeting of the American Sociological Association, Philadelphia, August 13–16.

Heynen, Nik. 2006. "But It's Alright, Ma, It's Life, and Life Only." *Antipode* 38 (5): 916–29.

Hirschman, Albert O. 1970. *Exit, Voice, and Loyalty.* Cambridge: Harvard University Press.

Hodkinson, Stuart, and Paul Chatterton. 2006. "Autonomy in the City?" *City* 10 (3): 305–15.

Holland, Dorothy, Gretchen Fox, and Vinci Daro. 2008. "Social Movements and Collective Identity." *Anthropological Quarterly* 81 (1): 95–126.

Holland, Dorothy, William Lachicotte Jr., Debra Skinner, and Carole Cain. 1998. *Identity and Agency in Cultural Worlds.* Cambridge: Harvard University Press.

Holland, Dorothy, and Jean Lave. 2001. "History in Person: An Introduction." In *History in Person*, ed. Dorothy Holland and Jean Lave, 3–33. Santa Fe, N.M.: SAR Press.

Holland, Dorothy, Dana E. Powell, Eugenia Eng, and Georgina Drew. 2010. "Models of Engaged Scholarship." *Collaborative Anthropologies* 3: 1–36.

Holloway, John. 2002. *Change the World without Taking Power.* London: Pluto Press.

———. 2003. "Anche un bacio può essere un movimento anticapitalista." *Carta* 5 (1): 60–63.

Holmes, Douglas, and George E. Marcus. 2005. "Cultures of Expertise and the Management of Globalization." In *Global Assemblages*, ed. Aihwa Ong and Stephen Collier, 235–52. Malden, Mass.: Blackwell.

hooks, bell. 1991. *Yearning.* Boston: South End Press.

Illich, Ivan. 1973. *La convivialité.* Paris: Seuil.

INCITE! 2007. *The Revolution Will Not Be Funded.* Boston: South End Press.

Ingold, Tim. 1996. *Key Debates in Anthropology.* New York: Routledge.

The Invisible Committee. 2009. *The Coming Insurrection.* Cambridge, Mass.: Semiotexte.

Iqtidar, Humeira. 2004. "NGO Factor at WSF Worries Activists." *Znet*, February 15, www.zcommunications.org (accessed December 27, 2011).

J-A Juanena, Coro. 2010a. "Investigando al otro cultural." Ph.D. dissertation, Universidad Rey Juan Carlos (Madrid).

———. 2010b. "La identidad política de mujeres indígenas ante los organismos internacionales." *Diálogo* 13: 10–17.

Jasper, James. 1998. "The Emotions of Protest." *Sociological Forum* 13: 397–424.

———. 2007. "Cultural Approaches to the Study of Social Movements." In *Handbook of Social Movements across Disciplines*, ed. Bert Klandermans and Conny Roggeband, 59–110. New York: Springer.

Johnston, Robert. 2003. *The Radical Middle Class.* Princeton: Princeton University Press.

Jones, Dave. 2004. "ESF Media and Communications Strategies." *Euromovements Newsletter* 4, www.euromovements.info (accessed August 31, 2007).

Juris, Jeffrey S. 2004a. *Digital Age Activism*. Ph.D. dissertation, University of California, Berkeley.

———. 2004b. "Networked Social Movements." In *The Network Society*, ed. Manuel Castells, 341–62. Cheltenham, U.K.: Edward Elgar.

———. 2005a. "The New Digital Media and Activist Networking within Anticorporate Globalization Movements." *The Annals of the American Academy of Political and Social Sciences* 597: 189–208.

———. 2005b. "Social Forums and Their Margins." *Ephemera* 5 (2): 253–72.

———. 2005c. "Violence Performed and Imagined." *Critique of Anthropology* 25 (4): 413–32.

———. 2007. "Practicing Militant Ethnography with the Movement or Global Resistance in Barcelona." In *Constituent Imagination*, ed. Stevphen Shukaitis and David Graeber, 164–78. Oakland, Calif.: AK Press.

———. 2008a. *Networking Futures*. Durham: Duke University Press.

———. 2008b. "Performing Politics." *Ethnography* 9 (1): 61–97.

———. 2012. "Reflections on #Occupy Everywhere." *American Ethnologist* 39 (2): 259–79.

Juris, Jeffrey, and Geoffrey Pleyers. 2009. "Alter-activism." *Journal of Youth Studies* 12 (1): 57–75.

Juris, Jeffrey S., and Maple Razsa, ed. "Occupy, Anthropology, and the Global Uprisings." *Cultural Anthropology Hot Spots* (web forum). www.culanth.org (accessed December 24, 2012).

Juris, Jeffrey S., Michelle Ronayne, Firuzeh Shoksoh-Valle, and Robert Wengronowitz. 2012. "Negotiating Power and Difference within the 99%." *Social Movement Studies* 11 (3–4): 434–40.

Kaldor, Mary. 2003. *Global Civil Society*. Cambridge, U.K.: Polity Press.

Katsiaficas, George. 1987. *The Imagination of the New Left*. Boston: South End Press.

———. 2006. *The Subversion of Politics*. 2nd ed. Oakland, Calif.: AK Press.

Katz, Cindi. 2001. "On the Grounds of Globalization." *Signs* 26 (4): 1213–29.

Kearney, M. 1995. "The Local and the Global." *Annual Review of Anthropology* 24: 547–65.

Keck, Margaret, and Kathryn Sikkink. 1998. *Activists beyond Borders*. Ithaca, N.Y.: Cornell University Press.

Kelty, Christopher M. 2008. *Two Bits*. Durham: Duke University Press.

———. 2009. "Collaboration, Coordination, and Composition." In *Fieldwork Is Not What It Used to Be*, ed. James D. Faubion, George E. Marcus, and Michael M. J. Fischer, 184–206. Ithaca, N.Y.: Cornell University Press.

Kezar, Adrianna. 2003. "Transformational Elite Interviews." *Qualitative Inquiry* 9 (3): 395–415.

Khasnabish, Alex. 2007. "Insurgent Imaginations." *Ephemera* 7 (4): 505–26.

———. 2008. *Zapatismo beyond Borders*. Toronto: University of Toronto Press.

———. 2010. *Zapatistas*. New York: Zed Books.

Kidd, Dorothy. 2003. "Indymedia.org." In *Cyberactivism*, ed. Martha McCaughey and Michael D. Ayers, 47–69. New York: Routledge.

Kim, Claire Jean. 2000. *Bitter Fruit*. New Haven: Yale University Press.

Kingsnorth, Paul. 2003. *One No, Many Yeses*. London: Free Press.

Kivisto, Peter. 1984. "Contemporary Social Movements in Advanced Industrial Societies and Sociological Intervention." *Acta Sociologica* 27 (4): 355–66.

Klein, Naomi. 2002. *Fences and Windows*. Toronto: Vintage Canada.

Knorr Cetina, Karin. 1997. "Sociality with Objects." *Theory, Culture and Society* 14 (4): 1–30.

Kobayashi, Audrey. 1994. "Coloring the Field." *The Professional Geographer* 46: 73–80.

Koehn, Daryl. 1998. *Rethinking Feminist Ethics*. London: Routledge.

Kuhn, Thomas. 1970. *The Structure of Scientific Revolutions*. Chicago: University of Chicago Press.

Laclau, Ernesto, and Chantal Mouffe. 1985. *Hegemony and Socialist Strategy*. London: Verso.

Lakoff, George, and Mark Johnson. 1999. *Philosophy in the Flesh*. New York: Basic Books.

Lal, Vinay. 2002. *Empire of Knowledge*. London: Pluto Press.

Lamphere, Louise. 2004. "The Convergence of Applied, Practicing, and Public Anthropology in the 21st Century." *Human Organization* 63 (4): 431–43.

Lansing, Stephen. 2006. *A Perfect Order*. Princeton: Princeton University Press.

Lassiter, Eric Luke. 2005. "Collaborative Ethnography and Public Anthropology." *Current Anthropology* 46 (1): 83–106.

———. 2008. "Moving Past Public Anthropology and Doing Collaborative Research." *National Association for the Practice of Anthropology Bulletin* 29: 70–87.

Latour, Bruno. 1992. "Where Are the Missing Masses?" In *Shaping Technology, Building Society*, ed. Wiebe E. Bijker and John Law, 225–58. Cambridge: MIT Press.

———. 1993. *We Have Never Been Modern*. Cambridge, U.K.: Cambridge University Press.

———. 1996. *The Love of Technology*. Cambridge: Harvard University Press.

———. 2000. "When Things Strike Back." *British Journal of Sociology* 5(1) 105–23.

———. 2005. *Reassembling the Social*. Oxford: Oxford University Press.

Law, John. 2004. *After Method*. New York: Routledge.

Leach, James. 2009. "Freedom Imagined." *Ethnos* 74 (1): 51–71.

Leite, José Corrêa. 2005. *World Social Forum*. Chicago: Haymarket Books.

Leyva-Solano, Xochitl. 2001. "Neo-zapatismo." Ph.D. dissertation, Department of Social Anthropology, Manchester University.

Lichterman, Paul. 1996. *The Search for Political Community*. Cambridge: Cambridge University Press.

Lin, Yuwei. 2004. "The Future of Sociology of FLOSS." *First Monday*, special issue no. 2: Open Source, October, http://firstmonday.org (accessed December 25, 2011).

———. 2006. "A Techno-feminist Perspective on the Free/Libre Open Source Software Development." In *Encyclopedia of Gender and Information Technology*, ed. Eileen M. Trauth, 1148–53. Hershey, Penn.: Idea Group Inc.

Linebaugh, Peter, and Marcus Buford Rediker. 2000. *The Many-Headed Hydra*. Boston: Beacon Press.

Linton, Michael. 2004. "LETS: An Undertaking in Accountancy." Lecture presented at the "Local Currencies in the 21st Century Conference," Bard College, Annandale-on-Hudson, N.Y., June 26.

Lorenz, Edward. 1969. "Three Approaches to Atmospheric Predictability." *Bulletin of the American Meteorological Society* 50: 345–49.

Lovink, Geert. 2003. *My First Recession*. Rotterdam: V2_/NAi Publishers.

Low, Setha M., and Sally E. Merry. 2010. "Engaged Anthropology." *Current Anthropology* 51 (2): 203–26.

Luke, Robert, Andrew Clement, Randall Terada, Dominic Bortolussi, Cameron Booth, Derek Brooks, and Darcy Christ. 2004. "The Promise and Perils of Participatory Design Approach to Developing and Open Source Community Learning Network." In *PDC 2004: Proceedings of the Eighth Biennial Participatory Design Conference Volume I*, 11–19. New York: CPSR and ACM.

Lyons, Oren. 1994. "Oren Lyons." In *Voice of Indigenous Peoples*, ed. Alexander Ewen, 31–36. Santa Fe, N.M.: Clear Light Publishers.

Maeckelbergh, Marianne. 2009. *The Will of the Many*. London: Pluto Press.

Maguire, Patricia. 1996. "Considering More Feminist Participatory Research." *Qualitative Inquiry* 2: 106–19.

Mandelbrot, Benoit. 1983. *The Fractal Geometry of Nature*. New York: W. H. Freeman Press.

Mander, Jerry. 2006. "Introduction." In *Paradigm Wars*, ed. Jerry Mander and Victoria Tauli-Corpuz, 3–10. San Francisco: Sierra Club.

Mander, Jerry, and Victoria Tauli-Corpuz, eds. 2006. *Paradigm Wars*. San Francisco: Sierra Club Books.

Mansbridge, Jane, and Aldon Morris, eds. 2001. *Oppositional Consciousness*. Chicago: University of Chicago Press.

Marcos, Subcomandante Insurgente. 2002. "Testimonies of the First Day." In *The Zapatista Reader*, ed. Tom Hayden, 207–16. New York: Thunder's Mouth Press.

————. 2003. "The World: Seven Thoughts in May of 2003." *El Kilombo Intergaláctico*, www.elkilombo.org (accessed December 27, 2012).

————. 2004. "A Death Has Been Decided." In *¡Ya basta!*, ed. Žiga Vodovnik, 593–600. Oakland, Calif.: AK Press.

Marcus, George E. 1995. "Ethnography in/of the World System." *Annual Review of Anthropology* 24: 95–117.

————. 1998. *Ethnography through Thick and Thin*. Princeton: Princeton University Press.

————. 1999a. *Critical Anthropology Now*. Santa Fe, N.M.: School of American Research Press.

————. ed. 1999b. *Paranoia with Reason*. Chicago: University of Chicago Press.

————. 2007. "Ethnography Two Decades after Writing Culture." *Anthropological Quarterly* 80 (4): 1127–45.

————. 2009. "Introduction." In *Fieldwork Is Not What It Used to Be*, ed. James D. Faubion, George E. Marcus, and Michael M. J. Fischer, 1–31. Ithaca, N.Y.: Cornell University Press.

Marcus, George E., and Michael M. J. Fischer. 1986. *Anthropology as Cultural Critique*. Chicago: University of Chicago Press.

Marcuse, Peter. 2005a. "Are Social Forums the Future of Social Movements?" *International Journal of Urban and Regional Research* 29 (2): 417–24.

————. 2005b. "Rejoinder." *International Journal of Urban and Regional Research* 29 (2): 444–46.

Markowitz, Lisa. 2001. "Finding the Field." *Human Organization* 60 (1): 40–46.

Marston, Sallie A., John Paul Jones III, and Keith Woodward. 2005. "Human Geography without Scale." *Transactions of the Institute of British Geographers* 30 (4): 416–32.

Martínez, Elizabeth. 2000. "Where Was the Color in Seattle?" *Colorlines* 3 (1), http://colorlines.com (accessed December 25, 2011).

Martinez-Torres, Maria Elena, 2001. "Civil Society, the Internet and the Zapatistas." *Peace Review* 13 (3): 347–55.

Massey, Doreen. 1994. *Space, Place, and Gender*. Minneapolis: University of Minnesota Press.

————. 2004. "Geographies of Responsibility." *Geografiska Annaler* 86 (1): 5–18.

————. 2005. *For Space*. Thousand Oaks, Calif.: Sage.

Massumi, Brian. 2002. *Parables for the Virtual*. Durham: Duke University Press.

Mathers, Andrew, and Mario Novelli. 2007. "Researching Resistance to Neoliberal Globalization." *Globalizations* 4 (2): 229–49.

Matsutake Worlds Research Group. 2009. "Strong Collaboration as a Method for Multi-sited Ethnography." In *Multi-sited Ethnography*, ed. Mark-Anthony Falzon, 197–214. Burlington, Vt.: Ashgate.

Maturana, Humberto R. and Francisco Varela. 1992. *The Tree of Knowledge*. Rev. ed. Boston: Shambhala.

Maurer, Bill. 2005. *Mutual Life, Limited*. Princeton: Princeton University Press.

Mayer, Bernard 2004. *Beyond Neutrality*. San Francisco: Jossey Bass.

McAdam, Doug, John D. McCarthy, and Meyer Zald, eds. 1996. *Comparative Perspectives on Social Movements*. Cambridge, U.K.: Cambridge University Press.

McAdam, Doug, Sidney Tarrow, and Charles Tilly. 2001. *Dynamics of Contention*. Cambridge, U.K.: Cambridge University Press.

McDonald, Kevin. 2002. "*L'intervention Sociologique* after Twenty-Five Years." *Qualitative Sociology* 25 (2): 247–60.

———. 2006. *Global Movements*. Malden, Mass.: Blackwell.

McNally, D. 2011. *Global Slump*. Oakland, Calif.: PM Press.

McNamee, Sheila, and Kenneth Gergen, eds. 1999. *Relational Responsibility*. Thousand Oaks, Calif.: Sage.

Meikle, Graham. 2002. *Future Active*. New York: Routledge.

Melucci, Alberto. 1985. "The Symbolic Challenge of Contemporary Movements." *Social Research* 52 (4): 789–816.

———. 1989. *Nomads of the Present*. London: Century Hutchinson.

———. 1996. *Challenging Codes*. Cambridge, U.K.: Cambridge University Press.

Méndez, Jennifer Bickham. 2005. *From the Revolution to the Maquiladoras*. Durham: Duke University Press.

———. 2008. "Globalizing Scholar Activism." In *Engaging Contradictions*, ed. Charles R. Hale, 136–63. Berkeley: University of California Press.

Merleau-Ponty, Maurice 1962. *Phenomenology of Perception*. New York: Humanities Press.

Mésini, Béatrice. 2003. *Anti/Altermondialisation, des mondes en volition*. Aix: Pli Zetwal.

Midnight Notes, eds. 2001. *Auroras of the Zapatistas*. Brooklyn, N.Y.: Autonomedia.

Milgram, Stanley. 1967. "The Small World Problem." *Psychology Today* 1 (1): 60–67.

Mills, Charles. W. 1997. *The Racial Contract*. Ithaca, N.Y.: Cornell University Press.

Missingham, Bruce. D. 2003. *The Assembly of the Poor in Thailand*. Chiang Mai, Thailand: Silkworm Books.

Mitchell, Stacy. 2009a. "Independent Retailers Outperform Chains over Holidays, National Survey Finds." Press release. Institute for Local Self-Reliance, January 15. www.ilsr.org (accessed December 25, 2011).

————. 2009b. "Starbucks Goes Stealth with Unbranded 'Local Cafes.'" Institute for Local Self-Reliance, July 22. www.ilsr.org (accessed December 25, 2011).

Moghadam, Valentine M. 2005. *Globalizing Women*. Baltimore: The Johns Hopkins University Press.

————. 2009. *Globalization and Social Movements*. Lanham, Md.: Rowman and Littlefield.

Mohanty, Chandra T. 2003. *Feminism without Borders*. Durham: Duke University Press.

Moore, Henrietta, ed. 1999. *Anthropological Theory Today*. Cambridge, U.K.: Polity Press.

Mosse, David. 2005. *Cultivating Development*. London: Pluto Press.

Mouffe, Chantal. 1999. "Deliberative Democracy or Agonistic Pluralism?" *Social Research* 66 (3): 745–58.

"Moving towards a New International Information Order." 1976. In "Information and the New World Order." Special issue of *Development Dialogue* 2: 8–11. Upsala, Sweden: The Dag Hammarskjold Foundation.

Muehlebach, Andrea. 2001. "'Making Place' at the United Nations." *Cultural Anthropology* 16 (3): 415–48.

Mullins, Paul R. 2011. "Practicing Anthropology and the Politics of Engagement." *American Anthropologist* 113 (2): 235–45.

Murphy, Brian. 2000. "Mapping the Prehistory of Cyberspace and the Making of Social Movement Computer Networks 1973–1993." Ph.D. dissertation, Communications Department, University of Massachusetts, Amherst.

Nader, Laura. 1972. "Up the Anthropologist." In *Reinventing Anthropology*, ed. Dell Hymes, 285–311. New York: Pantheon.

Naficy, Hamid. 2001. *An Accented Cinema*. Princeton: Princeton University Press.

Nafus, Dawn, James Leach, and Bernhard Krieger. 2006. *Free/Libre and Open Source Software*. Cambridge, U.K.: University of Cambridge.

Naples, Nancy A. 2003. *Feminism and Method*. New York: Routledge.

Narotsky, Susana, and Gavin Smith. 2006. *Immediate Struggles*. Berkeley: University of California Press.

Nash, June. 2001. *Mayan Visions*. New York: Routledge.

Nast, Heidi. 1994. "Opening Remarks on 'Women in the Field.'" *The Professional Geographer* 46: 54–66.

Negri, Antonio. 1999. *Insurgencies*. Minneapolis: University of Minnesota Press.

Nieusma, Dean. 2007. "Challenging Knowledge Hierarchies." *Sustainability: Science, Practice, and Policy* 3 (1): 32–44.

Niezen, Ronald. 2003. *The Origins of Indigenism*. Berkeley: University of California Press.

Noguera, Ana. 2002. "The Birth and Promise of the Indymedia Revolution." In *From ACT UP to the WTO*, ed. Benjamin Shepard and Ronald Hayduk, 290–98. London: Verso.

Notes from Nowhere, eds. 2003. *We Are Everywhere*. London: Verso.

Nunes, Rodrigo. 2005. "Nothing Is What Democracy Looks Like." In *Shut Them Down!* ed. David Harvie, Keir Milburn, Ben Trott, and David Watts, 299–319. Brooklyn, N.Y.: Autonomedia.

———. 2009. "What Were You Wrong about Ten Years Ago?" *Turbulence* 5: 38–39.

O'Brien, Rory. 2004. "Enabling Civil Society Participation in Global Policy Making." Association for Progressive Communications, http://www.apc.org (December 25, 2011).

Odum, Eugene P. 1971. *Fundamentals of Ecology*. 3rd ed. Philadelphia: W. B. Saunders Co.

Olesen, Thomas. 2005a. *International Zapatismo*. London: Zed Books.

———. 2005b. "Transnational Publics." *Current Sociology* 53 (3): 419–40.

Ong, Aihwa, and Stephen J. Collier, eds. 2004. *Global Assemblages*. Malden, Mass.: Wiley-Blackwell.

Oppenheimer, Andres. 2002. "Guerrillas in the Mist." In *The Zapatista Reader*, ed. Tom Hayden, 51–54. New York: Thunder's Mouth Press.

Ornelas, Raúl. 2004. "La autonomía como eje de la resistencia Zapatista." In *Hegemonías y emancipaciones en el siglo XXI*, ed. Ana Esther Ceceña, 133–72. Buenos Aires: CLACSO.

Osterweil, Michal. 2004a. "A Cultural-Political Approach to Reinventing the Political." *International Social Science Journal* 56 (182): 495–506.

———. 2004b. "De-centering the Forum." In *The World Social Forum: Challenging Empires*, ed. Jai Sen, Anita Anand, Arturo Escobar, and Peter Waterman, 183–90. New Delhi: The Viveka Foundation.

———. 2008. "Reframing the 'Activist' Research Debate." Paper presented at the 2008 Annual Meetings of the American Anthropological Association, San Francisco, November 19–23.

———. 2010. "In Search of Movement." Ph.D. dissertation, Department of Anthropology, University of North Carolina, Chapel Hill.

Pacari, Nina. 2003. "Nina Pacari." In *Contemporary Indigenous Movements in Latin America*, ed. Erick D. Langer with Elena Muñoz, 201–4. Wilmington, Del.: Jaguar.

Page, Edward. A. 2006. *Climate Change, Justice, and Future Generations*. Cheltenham, U.K.: Edward Elgar.

Patomäki, Heikki, and Teivo Teivainen. 2004. "The World Social Forum: An Open Space or a Movement of Movements?" *Theory, Culture and Society* 21 (5): 145–54.

Pavis, Theta. 2002. "Modern Day Muckrakers." *USC Annenberg Online Journalism Review,* http://www.ojr.org (accessed December 25, 2011).

Pearson, Ruth. 2003. "Feminist Responses to Globalization." In *Women Reinventing Globalization,* ed. Joann Kerr and Caroline Sweetman, 25–34. Oxford: Oxfam Press.

Phelps-Brown, Henry. 2003. The Counter-Revolution of Our Time." *Industrial Relations* 29 (1): 1–14.

Pickerill, Jenny, and Paul Chatterton. 2006. "Notes towards Autonomous Geographies." *Progress in Human Geography* 30: 730–46.

Piven, Frances Fox, and Richard Cloward. 1978. *Poor People's Movements.* New York: Vintage.

Pleyers, Geoffrey. 2004. "Des black blocks aux alteractivistes." *Lien Social et Politiques* 51: 123–34.

———. 2006. "Sujet, expérience et expertise dans le Mouvement Altermondialiste." Ph.D. diss., L'Écoles des Haute Études en Sciences Sociales.

———. 2008. *Forums Sociaux Mondiaux et défies de l'altermondialisme.* Louvain-La-Nueve: Bruylant-Academia.

———. 2011. *Becoming an Actor in the Global Age.* London: Polity.

Plows, Alex. 2008. "Social Movements and Ethnographic Methodologies." *Sociology Compass* 2 (5): 1523–38.

Polletta, Francesca. 2002. *Freedom Is an Endless Meeting.* Chicago: University of Chicago Press.

Ponniah, Thomas. 2006. "The World Social Forum Vision." Ph.D. dissertation, Department of Geography, Clark University.

———. 2008. "The Meaning of the U.S. Social Forum." *Societies without Borders* 3 (1): 187–95.

Pool, Ithiel de Sola. 1984. *Technologies of Freedom.* Cambridge: Harvard University Press.

Postero, Nancy. 2006. *Now We Are Citizens.* Stanford: Stanford University Press.

Powell, Dana E. 2010. "Landscapes of Power." Ph.D. dissertation, Department of Anthropology, University of North Carolina, Chapel Hill.

Powell, Dana E., and Andrew Curley. 2009. "*K'e, Hozhó,* and Non-governmental Politics on the Navajo Nation." *World Anthropologies Network E-Journal* 4: 109–38.

Powell, Dana E., and Dáilan Jake Long. 2010. "Landscapes of Power." In *Indians and Energy,* ed. S. Smith and B. Frehner, 231–62. Santa Fe, N.M.: School of Advanced Research Press. www.ram-wan.net.

Prigogine, Ilya. 1997. *The End of Certainty.* New York: Free Press.

Princen, Thomas, and Mattias Finger. 1994. *Environmental NGOs and World Politics.* New York: Routledge.

Probyn, Elspeth. 1993. *Sexing the Self.* New York: Routledge.

Pulido, Laura. 2003. "The Interior Life of Politics." *Ethics, Place and Environment* 6 (1): 46–52.

Rabinow, Paul, and Andrew Sullivan. 1979. *Interpretive Social Science: A Reader.* Berkeley: University of California Press.

Raghavan, Chakravarti. 1976. "A New World Communication and Information Structure." In "Information and the New World Order." Special issue of *Development Dialogue* 2: 43–50. Upsala, Sweden: The Dag Hammarskjold Foundation.

Rai, Shirin M. 2003. "Networking across Borders." *Global Networks* 3 (1): 59–74.

Raymond, Eric. 1999. *The Cathedral and the Bazaar.* 1st ed. Sebastopol, Calif.: O'Reilly.

Razsa, Maple, and Andrej Kurnik. 2012. "The Occupy Movement in Žižek's Hometown." *American Ethnologist* 39 (2): 238–58.

Reitan, Ruth. 2007. *Global Activism.* New York: Routledge.

Ribeiro, Gustavo Lins. 1998. "Cybercultural Politics." In *Cultures of Politics, Politics of Culture,* ed. Sonia Alvarez, Evelina Dagnino, and Arturo Escobar, 325–52. Boulder, Colo.: Westview Press.

Ribeiro, Gustavo Lins, and Arturo Escobar, eds. 2006. *World Anthropologies.* Oxford: Berg.

Riemens, Patrice. 2005. "Some Thoughts on the Idea of 'Hacker Culture.'" In *Anarchitexts,* ed. Joanne Richardson, 327–32. New York: Autonomedia.

Riles, Annelise. 2000. *The Network Inside Out.* Ann Arbor: University of Michigan Press.

Rivera Zea, Tarcila. 1999. *El andar de las mujeres indígenas.* Lima: Chirapaq, Centro de Culturas Indias.

Roberts, J. Timmons, and Bradley C. Parks. 2006. *A Climate of Injustice.* Cambridge: MIT Press.

Ronfeldt, David, John Arquilla, Graham E. Fuller, and Melissa Fuller. 1999. *The Zapatista Social Netwar in Mexico.* Santa Monica, Calif.: Rand Corporation.

Rose, Gillian. 1997. "Situating Knowledges." *Progress in Human Geography* 21 (3): 305–20.

Rosie, Michael, and Hugo Gorringe. 2009. "The Anarchists' World Cup." *Social Movement Studies* 8 (1): 35–53.

Routledge, Paul. 1993. *Terrains of Resistance.* Westport, Conn.: Praeger.

———. 1996a. "Critical Geopolitics and Terrains of Resistance." *Political Geography* 15 (6/7): 509–31.

———. 1996b. "The Third Space as Critical Engagement." *Antipode* 28 (4): 397–419.

———. 1997. "The Imagineering of Resistance." *Transactions of the Institute of British Geographers* 22: 359–76.

———. 2002. "Travelling East as Walter Kurtz." *Environment and Planning D* 20: 477–98.

———. 2003a. "Convergence Space." *Transactions of the Institute of British Geographers* 28 (3): 333–49.

———. 2003b. "River of Resistance." *Ethics, Place and Environment* 6 (1): 66–73.

———. 2003c. "Voices of the Dammed." *Political Geography* 22 (3): 243–70.

———. 2005. "Reflections on the G8." *ACME* 3 (2): 112–20.

———. 2008. "Acting in the Network." *Environment and Planning D* 26: 199–217.

———. 2009. "Activist Geographies." In *International Encyclopedia of Human Geography, Volume 1,* ed. Rob Kitchin and Nigel Thrift, 7–14. Oxford: Elsevier.

———. 2010. "Major Disasters and General Panics." In *The SAGE Handbook of Qualitative Geography,* ed. Dydia DeLyser, Steve Herbert, Stewart Aitken, Mike A. Crang, and Linda McDowell, 388–405. Thousand Oaks, Calif.: Sage.

———. 2012. "Sensuous Solidarities." *Antipode* 44(2): 428–52.

Routledge, Paul, and Andrew Cumbers. 2009. *Global Justice Networks.* Manchester: Manchester University Press.

Routledge, Paul, Andrew Cumbers, and Corinne Nativel. 2007. "Grassrooting Network Imaginaries." *Environment and Planning A* 39: 2575–92.

Ruby, Jay, and Barbara Myerhoff. 1982. *A Crack in the Mirror.* Philadelphia: University of Pennsylvania Press.

Saeed, Saqid, Volkmar Pipek, Markus Rohde, and Wolf Volker. 2010. "Managing Nomadic Knowledge." In *Proceedings of the 28th International Conference on Human Factors in Computing Systems,* 537–46. New York: ACM.

Saeed, Saqid, and Markus Rohde. 2010. "Computer Enabled Social Movements?" In *Proceedings of COOP 2010: Proceedings of the 9th International Conference on Designing Cooperative Systems,* ed. M. Lewkowicz, P. Hassanaly, M. Rohde, and M. Wulf, 245–64. Aix-en-Provence, France: Springer.

Sánchez Néstor, Martha. 2005. *La Doble Mirada.* Mexico City: Instituto de Liderazgo Simone de Beauvoir AC.

Sanford, Victoria. 2006. "Introduction." In *Engaged Observer,* ed. Victoria Sanford and Asale Angel-Ajani, 1–18. New Brunswick, N.J.: Rutgers University Press.

Sanford, Victoria, and Asale Angel-Ajani, eds. 2006. *Engaged Observer.* New Brunswick, N.J.: Rutgers University Press.

Santos, Boaventura de Sousa. 2004. "The World Social Forum." In *The World Social Forum: Challenging Empires,* ed. Jai Sen, Anita Anand, Arturo Escobar, and Peter Waterman, 337–43. New Delhi: Viveka Foundation.

———. 2006. *The Rise of the Global Left.* London: Zed Books.

———. 2007. *Another Production Is Possible.* London: Verso.

———. 2008. *Another Knowledge Is Possible*. London: Verso.

Scacchi, Walter. 2007. "Free/Open Source Software Development." In *Advances in Computers, Volume 69*, ed. Marvin Zelkowitz, 243–95. Amsterdam: Elsevier.

Scheper-Hughes, Nancy. 1995. "The Primacy of the Ethical." *Current Anthropology* 36 (3): 409–20.

Schiller, Nina Glick, and Georges Eugene Fouron. 2001. *Georges Woke Up Laughing*. Durham, N.C.: Duke University Press.

Schlosberg, David. 2004. "Reconceiving Environmental Justice." *Environmental Politics* 13 (3): 517–40.

———. 2007. *Defining Environmental Justice*. Oxford: Oxford University Press.

Scott, David. 2004. *Conscripts of Modernity*. Durham: Duke University Press.

Selbin, Eric. 2003. "Zapata's White Horse and Che's Beret." In *The Future of Revolutions*, ed. John Foran, 83–94. New York: Zed Books.

Selin, Henrik. 2003. "Global Efforts on Sustainable Development from Stockholm to Rio." Paper presented at the 6th Nordic Conference on Environmental Social Sciences, Abo, Finland, June 12–14.

Sen, Jai. 2003. "The Long March to Another World." Unpublished paper. Available at www.choike.org (accessed September 15, 2008).

Sen, Jai, and Peter Waterman, eds. 2007. *The World Social Forum: Challenging Empires*, 2nd ed. London: Black Rose Books.

Seyfang, Gill. 2003. "'With a Little Help from My Friends.'" *Local Economy* 18 (3): 257–64.

———. 2004. "Time Banks." *Community Development Journal* 39 (1): 62–71.

Seyfang, Gill, and Noel Longhurst. 2012. "Money, Money, Money? A Scoping Study of Grassroots Complementary Currencies for Sustainability." University of East Anglia, 3S Working Paper 2012-02, http://grassrootsinnovations .org (accessed December 27, 2012).

Shukaitis, Stevphen, and David Graeber, eds. 2007. *Constituent Imagination*. Oakland, Calif.: AK Press.

Sitrin, Marina. 2006. *Horizontalism*. Oakland, Calif.: AK Press.

Slater, David. 1998. "Rethinking the Spatialities of Social Movements." In *Cultures of Politics, Politics of Cultures*, ed. Sonia E. Alvarez, Evelina Dagnino, and Arturo Escobar, 405–14. Boulder, Colo.: Westview Press.

Smith, Jackie. 2008. *Social Movements for Global Democracy*. Baltimore: The Johns Hopkins University Press.

Smith, Jackie, Charles Chatfield, and Ron Pagnucco, eds. 1997. *Transnational Social Movements and Global Politics*. Syracuse, N.Y.: Syracuse University Press.

Smith, Jackie, and Ellen Reese. 2008. "Editor's Introduction: Special Issue on the World Social Forum Process." *Mobilization* 13 (4): 349–52.

Smith, Jackie, and Hank Johnston, eds. 2002. *Globalization and Resistance*. Lanham, Md.: Rowman and Littlefield.

Smith, Jackie, Jeffrey S. Juris, and the Social Forum Research Collective. 2008. "'We Are the Ones We Have Been Waiting For.'" *Mobilization* 13 (4): 373–94.

Smith, Jackie, Marina Karides, Marc Becker, Dorval Brunelle, Christopher Chase-Dunn, Donatella della Porta, Rosalba Icaza, Jeffrey Juris, Lorenzo Mosca, Ellen Reese, et al. 2007. *Global Democracy and the World Social Forums*. Boulder, Colo.: Paradigm Publishers.

Smith, Jay. 2005. "The World Social Forum: A Contested Space of Politics." Paper presented at the International Studies Association Annual Meeting, Honolulu, March 1–5.

Smith, Linda Tuhiwai. 1999. *Decolonizing Methodologies*. London: Zed Press.

Smith, Michael Peter. 2008. *Citizenship across Borders*. Ithaca, N.Y.: Cornell University Press.

Smith, Michael Peter, and Luis Guarnizo. 1998. *Transnationalism from Below*. Piscataway, N.J.: Transaction Publishers.

Smythe, Elizabeth, and Scott Byrd. 2010. "World Social Forum Activism in Belém and Beyond." *Journal of World-Systems Research* 16 (1): 94–105.

Snow, David A., E. Burke Rochford Jr., Steven K. Worden, and Robert D. Benford. 1986. "Frame Alignment Processes, Micromobilization, and Movement Participation." *American Sociological Review* 51: 464–81.

Solnit, Rebecca. 2004. *Hope in the Dark*. New York: Nation Books.

Somavia, Juan. 1976. "The Transnational Power Structure and International Information." In "Information and the New World Order." Special issue of *Development Dialogue* 2: 15–28. Upsala, Sweden: The Dag Hammarskjold Foundation.

Sørensen, Knut H. 2004. "Cultural Politics of Technology." *Science, Technology and Human Values* 29 (2): 184–90.

Sparke, Matthew. 2007. "Geopolitical Fears, Geoeconomic Hopes, and the Responsibilities of Geography." *Annals of the Association of American Geographers* 97 (2): 338–49.

Speed, Shannon. 2006. "At the Crossroads of Human Rights and Anthropology." *American Anthropologist* 108 (1): 66–76.

———. 2007. *Rights in Rebellion*. Stanford: Stanford University Press.

———. 2008. "Forged in Dialogue." In *Engaging Contradictions*, ed. Charles R. Hale, 213–36. Berkeley: University of California Press.

Spivak, Gayatri. 1994. "Can the Subaltern Speak?" In *Colonial Discourse and Post-colonial Theory*, ed. Patrick Williams and Laura Chrisman, 66–11. New York: Columbia University Press.

Sprague, Joey, and Mary K. Zimmerman. 1993. "Overcoming Dualism." In *Theory and Gender/Feminism on Theory*, ed. Paula England, 255–89. New York: Aldine de Gruyter.

Star, Susan Leigh. 1999. "The Ethnography of Infrastructure." *American Behavioral Scientist* 43: 377–91.

Starr, Amory. 2004. "How Can Anti-imperialism Not Be Anti-racist?" *Journal of World-Systems Research* 10 (1): 119–51.

———. 2005. *Global Revolt*. London: Zed Books.

Sterpka, M. K. 2006. "Emergent Socialities, Networks of Biodiversity, and Anti-globalization." Ph.D. dissertation, Department of Anthropology, University of Massachusetts, Amherst.

———. 2007. "An Aesthetics of Networks." *First Monday* 12 (9), September, http://firstmonday.org (accessed December 27, 2012).

Suárez Navaz, Liliana, and Rosalva Aída Hernández Castillo, eds. 2008. *Descolonizando el feminismo*. Madrid: Ediciones Cátedra.

Swadener, Beth Blue, and Kagendo Mutua. 2008. "Decolonizing Performances." In *Handbook of Critical and Indigenous Methodologies*, ed. Norman K. Denzin, Yvonna S. Lincoln, and Linda Tuhiwai Smith, 31–43. Thousand Oaks, Calif.: Sage.

Takhteyev, Yuri. 2009. "Networks of Practice as Actor-Networks." *Information, Communication and Society* 12 (4): 566–83.

Tarrow, Sidney. 1998. *Power in Movement*. Cambridge, U.K.: Cambridge University Press.

———. 2005. *The New Transnational Activism*. Cambridge, U.K.: Cambridge University Press.

Tarrow, Sidney, and Donatella della Porta. 2005. "Conclusion." In *Transnational Protest and Global Activism*, ed. Donatella della Porta and Sidney Tarrow, 227–46. Lanham, Md.: Rowman and Littlefield.

Tarrow, Sidney, and Doug McAdam. 2005. "Scale Shift in Transnational Contention." In *Transnational Protest and Global Activism*, ed. Donatella della Porta and Sidney Tarrow, 121–50. Lanham, Md.: Rowman and Littlefield.

Tauli-Corpuz, Victoria. 2010. "The Human Development Framework and Indigenous Peoples' Self-Determined Development with Culture and Identity." Document prepared for the ninth session of the UN Permanent Forum on Indigenous Issues, March 5.

Taylor, Charles. 1971. "Interpretive Sciences of Man." *Review of Metaphysics* 25 (1): 3–51.

———. 2004. *Modern Social Imaginaries*. Durham: Duke University Press.

Taylor, Verta, and Leila Rupp. 2002. "Loving Internationalism." *Mobilization* 7: 141–58.

Teivainen, Teivo. 2002. "The World Social Forum and Global Democratization." *Third World Quarterly* 23 (4): 621–32.

———. 2004. "The WSF: Arena or Actor." In *World Social Forum: Challeng-*

ing Empires, ed. Jai Sen, Anita Anand, Arturo Escobar, and Peter Waterman, 122–29. New Delhi: Viveka Foundation.

———. 2007. "The Political and Its Absence in the World Social Forum." *Development Dialogue* 49: 69–79.

———. 2008. *Democracy in Movement*. New York: Routledge.

Thayer, Millie. 2001. "Transnational Feminism." *Ethnography* 2 (2): 243–72.

———. 2010. *Making Transnational Feminism*. New York: Routledge.

Tilly, Charles. 2004. *Social Movements, 1768–2004*. Noble Court: Paradigm.

Tormey, Simon. 2005. "Not in My Name." *Parliamentary Affairs* 59 (1): 138–54.

Toscano, Emmanuele. 2011. "L'expérience italienne des centres sociaux." In *La consommation critique*, ed. Geoffrey Pleyers, 229–39. Paris: Desclée de Brouwer.

Touraine, Alain. 1981. *The Voice and the Eye*. Cambridge, U.K.: Cambridge University Press.

———. 2000. *Can We Live Together?* Cambridge, U.K.: Polity Press.

———. 2002. "From Understanding Society to Discovering the Subject." *Anthropological Theory* 2 (4): 387–98.

Tsing, Anna. 2005. *Friction*. Princeton: Princeton University Press.

Turbulence Collective. 2010. *What Would It Mean to Win?* Oakland, Calif.: PM Press.

UN Economic and Social Council document E/C.19/2010/4, "Study on the Need to Recognize and Respect the Rights of Mother Earth," from the Permanent Forum on Indigenous Issues, ninth session, April 19–30, 2010. Available at www.un.org (accessed December 26, 2012).

Urry, John. 2003. *Global Complexity*. Cambridge, U.K.: Polity Press.

Uzelman, Scott. 2002. "Catalyzing Participatory Communication." Master's thesis, School of Communication, Simon Fraser University.

Varela, Francisco J., Evan T. Thompson, and Eleanor Rosch. 1992. *The Embodied Mind, Cognitive Science, and Human Experience*. Cambridge: MIT Press.

Vargas, Virginia. 2003. "Feminism, Globalization and the Global Justice and Solidarity Movement." *Cultural Studies* 17 (6): 905–20.

———. 2005. "Feminisms and the World Social Forum." *Development* 48 (2): 107–10.

Virno, Paolo. 2003. *A Grammar of the Multitude*: Los Angeles: Semiotext(e).

Visweswaran, Kamala. 1988. "Defining Feminist Ethnography." *Inscriptions* 3/4: 36–39.

———. 1994. *Fictions of Feminist Ethnography*. Minneapolis: University of Minnesota Press.

———. 1997. "Histories of a Feminist Ethnography." *Annual Review of Anthropology* 26: 591–621.

Walker, Gordon. 2009. "Beyond Distribution and Proximity." *Antipode* 41 (4): 614–36.

Wallerstein, Immanuel. 2008. "Remembering Andre Gunder Frank while Thinking about the Future." *Monthly Review* 60 (2): 50–61.

Wallerstein, Immanuel, et al. 1996. *Open the Social Sciences.* Stanford: Stanford University Press.

Wapner, Paul. 1996. *Environmental Activism and World Civic Politics.* Albany: State University of New York Press.

Warner, Michael. 2002. Publics and Counterpublics. *Public Culture* 14 (1): 49–90.

Waterman, Peter. 1998. *Globalization, Social Movements, and the New Internationalisms.* London: Mansell.

Watts, Duncan, and Steve Strogatz. 1998. "Collective Dynamics of Small World Networks." *Nature* 393: 440–42.

Weber, Max. 1995. *Économie et société.* Paris: Plon.

———. 2004. *The Vocations Lectures.* Indianapolis: Hackett.

Weber, Steven. 2004. *The Success of Open Source.* Berkeley: University of California Press.

Whitaker, Francisco (Chico). 2004. "The WSF as Open Space." In *World Social Forum: Challenging Empires*, ed. Jai Sen, Anita Anand, Arturo Escobar, and Peter Waterman, 111–21. New Delhi: Viveka Foundation.

———. 2005. *O desafio do Forum Social Mundial.* San Paolo: Fundação Perseu Abramo.

———. 2007a. "Crossroads Do Not Always Close Roads." WSF Library, May 27, www.wsflibrary.org (accessed January 24, 2010).

———. 2007b. *A New Way of Changing the World.* Nairobi: World Council of Churches.

Whittier, Nancy. 1995. *Feminist Generations.* Philadelphia: Temple University Press.

Wieviorka, Michel. 2003. *Un autre monde.* Paris: Balland.

———. 2005. "After New Social Movements." *Social Movement Studies* 4 (1): 1–19.

Williams, Raymond. 1977. *Marxism and Literature.* Oxford: Oxford University Press.

Wilmer, Franke. 1993. *The Indigenous Voice in World Politics.* Thousand Oaks, Calif.: Sage.

Wing, Steve. 2002. "Social Responsibility and Research Ethics in Community-Driven Studies of Industrialized Hog Production." *Environmental Health Perspectives* 110 (5): 437–44.

Wolch, Jennifer. 2007. "Green Urban Worlds." *Annals of the Association of American Geographers* 97 (2): 373–84.

Woodhouse, Edward, David Hess, Steve Breyman, and Brian Martin. 2002. "Science Studies and Activism." *Social Studies of Science* 32 (2): 297–319.

Wortis, Helen, and Clara Rabinowitz, eds. 1972. *The Women's Movement*. New York: Halsted Press.

Wright, Colin. 2005. "Opening Spaces." *Ephemera* 5 (2): 409–22.

Ylä-Anttila, Tuomas. 2005. "The World Social Forum and the Globalization of Social Movements and Public Spheres." *Ephemera* 5 (2): 23–42.

Yngvesson, Barbara. 1992. "The Construction of Subjectivity and the Paradox of Resistance." *Signs* 18 (1): 44–73.

Young, Iris M. 1990. *Justice and the Politics of Difference*. Princeton: Princeton University Press.

Zibechi, Raul. 2010. *Dispersing Power*. Oakland, Calif.: AK Press.

Zuberi, Tukufu, and Eduardo Bonilla-Silva, eds. 2008. *White: Logic, White Methods*. Lanham, Md.: Rowman and Littlefield.

Zúñiga, Lena. 2006. *Voces libres de los campos digitales*. San José, Costa Rica: Bellanet International.

CONTRIBUTORS

GIUSEPPE CARUSO is a research fellow at the Centre for Excellence in Global Governance at the University of Helsinki. He received his PhD in development studies in the School of Oriental and African Studies at the University of London. He is the author of *Cosmopolitan Futures: Global Activism for a Just World* and various articles on transnational social movements and the World Social Forum.

MARIBEL CASAS-CORTÉS is a postdoctoral fellow, supported by the National Science Foundation, examining border policy in the European Union and northern Africa, as well as parallel organizing by transnational networks for migratory rights. She received her PhD in anthropology from the University of North Carolina, Chapel Hill, where she was actively involved in the Social Movements Working Group. Her writings engage social movements as knowledge producers, focusing on counter-cartography, precarious work, and the politics of care.

JANET CONWAY is a Canada Research Chair in Social Justice and an associate professor of sociology at Brock University. She received her PhD in political science from York University, and is the author of *Praxis and Politics: Knowledge Production in Social Movements* and *Edges of Global Justice: The World Social Forum and Its "Others,"* as well as numerous articles on transnational social movements.

STÉPHANE COUTURE is finishing a joint PhD in communication studies at Université du Québec à Montréal and in social sciences at Télécom ParisTech. His research interests are concerned with political and cultural aspects of science and technology, especially free software development. He is also a member of different activist groups concerned with issues of technology and democracy.

VINCI DARO is a postdoctoral scholar at the Graduate School of Education at the University of California, Berkeley. She received her PhD from the University of North Carolina, Chapel Hill, where she was a founding member of the Social Movements Working Group. Her work examines the productivity of differences in the context of social movements and other cultural spaces.

MANISHA DESAI is an associate professor of sociology and women's studies at the University of Connecticut. She is the author of *Gender and the Politics of Possibility* and is a co-editor of *Family, Gender, and Law in a Globalizing Middle East and South Asia* and *Women's Activism and Globalization*. In addition, she has written numerous articles on transnational movements and globalization. She is currently working on a book about gender, the environment, and protest in India.

SYLVIA ESCÁRCEGA has taught at DePaul University and has been a researcher at the Center of Research and Superior Studies in Social Anthropology in Oaxaca, Mexico. She received her PhD in anthropology from the University of California, Davis, and has published a book on indigenous migration and several articles on indigenous struggles at the international level. She is currently finishing a book on the global indigenous movement.

DAVID J. HESS is a professor of sociology at Vanderbilt University. His most recent books are *Alternative Pathways in Science and Industry*, which won the Robert K. Merton award for the best book in science and technology studies, and *Localist Movements in a Global Economy*.

JEFFREY S. JURIS is an associate professor of anthropology in the department of sociology and anthropology at Northeastern University. He received his PhD in anthropology from the University of California, Berkeley, and is the author of *Networking Futures: The Movements against Corporate Globalization* and the co-author of *Global Democracy and the World Social Forums*. He has also written numerous articles on social movements, transnational networks, new media, and political protest.

ALEX KHASNABISH is an assistant professor of sociology and anthropology at Mount Saint Vincent University. He received his PhD in anthropology from McMaster University and is the author of *Zapatistas: Rebellion from the Grassroots to the Global, Zapatismo beyond Borders: New Imaginations of Political Possibility*, as well as numerous articles about the radical imagination, contemporary social movements, and social justice struggles.

LORENZO MOSCA is an assistant professor of sociology of culture and communication at the University of Roma Tre. He received his PhD in political science at the University of Florence and has published numerous articles on social movements, new technologies, and the global justice movement. He is also a co-author of *Globalization from Below: Transnational Activists and Protest Networks*.

MICHAL OSTERWEIL is a lecturer in the Curriculum in Global Studies at the University of North Carolina, Chapel Hill, where she also received her PhD in anthropology. She is an active member of the Social Movements Working Group, as well as various transnational collaborations. She is a founding member of *Turbulence*, a journal of social movements and networks, and has authored various articles on the social forums and the global justice movement.

GEOFFREY PLEYERS is a Fonds de la Recherche Scientifique research associate at the University of Louvain, Belgium. He received his PhD in sociology from the École des Hautes Études in Paris and is the author of *Alter-Globalization: Becoming Actors in a Global Age*, *Forums Sociaux Mondiaux et Défis de l'Altermondialisme*, and numerous articles on the global justice movement, youth activism, and social movements in Mexico. He is also the editor of *Movimientos sociales* and *La consummation critique*.

DANA E. POWELL is an assistant professor of anthropology at Appalachian State University in Boone, North Carolina. She received her PhD in anthropology from the University of North Carolina, Chapel Hill, where she was actively involved in the Social Movements Working Group. Her research explores the sociocultural dimensions of energy development and infrastructure, environmental, and indigenous movements, with fieldwork experience on the Navajo Nation in the U.S. Southwest, in southern Mexico, and in Beijing.

PAUL ROUTLEDGE is a Reader in the School of Geographical and Earth Sciences at the University of Glasgow. He received his PhD in geography from Syracuse University. He is the author of *Terrains of Resistance: Nonviolent Social Movements and the Contestation of Place in India* and is a co-author of *Global Justice Networks: Geographies of Transnational Solidarity*.

M. K. STERPKA is an anthropologist, artist, and activist based in western Massachusetts. She received her PhD in anthropology from the University of Massachusetts, Amherst, and has published a number of articles on the intersection of globalization, biodiversity networks, and new technologies. Her recent work follows developments in transnational militarization. She is currently co-authoring a book on the cultural implications of network-centric warfare.

TISH STRINGER is a lecturer in film production and the film program manager in the Department of Visual and Dramatic Arts at Rice University. She received her PhD in anthropology from Rice University, and her dissertation explored activism, new technologies, and transnational networking within the Indymedia network.

INDEX

academia: activist ethnography and, 250–67; activist research debates in, 26–28, 203–7; ethnographic research and role of, 70–71

Accented Cinema, An (Naficy), 324–25

Acorn organization, 45

activist research, 32; academic debates over, 203–7; emergent themes in, 209–14; emotions and, 260–66; ethnography and, 23–28, 253–66; examples of, 36n.15; Feminist Dialogues and, 89, 94–104; indigenous movements and, 130–32; scholar activism and, 104–6; sites of, 149n.6; solidarity and, 251–53, 266–67; subjectivity in, 368–71; transformative ethnography and, 230–32; translocal solidarity and, 250–67. *See also* engaged ethnography

actor-network theory (ANT): global justice movements, 15–16; polycentric emergence and, 311–13

Adbusters, 384

Adivasi (indigenous peoples) movement (India), 241–42

affinity: activist ethnography and, 255–66; power relations and politics of, 259–66

African Feminist Forum, 101

Agenda 21 document, 309

agonistic democracy: race and class diversity and, 48–54; social forums as, 43–45

agonistic space, World Forum as, 42–43

aguascalientes (regional places of Zapatista encounter), 34n.1

Akina Mama wa Africa, 101

Akwesasne territory, 178–80

Alianza Amazonica, 283

Alinsky, Saul, 382

alter-activists, 114–16; emerging practices of, 124; experimental initiatives of, 116–18; spaces of experience for, 118–21

alter-globalization movements, 66–67, 87n.1, 388n.2; defined, 125n.1, 268n.5; edge effects of, 171–91; experience, subjectivity and power in, 108–24; knowledge production and, 121–23; multisited ethnography and, 110–13; terminology of, 192n.1, 226n.6; young alter-activists in, 114

alternative economies and currencies: anti-globalization movements and, 153–56; ethnography of, 151–70; localism, scale, and transnationalism, 156–61

Alternex, 309

Alvarez, Sonia, 11, 13–14

Amazon Watch, 283

Cahn, Edgar, 151–52, 161

Cahn, Jean Camper, 151

Cameron, James, 129–30, 137

Canada: activist collectives in, 70; indigenous conflicts in, 87n.5; Quebec antipathy within, 177–82; Zapatista encounters in, 18, 29, 35n.6, 66–86

Canada-Colombia Solidarity Campaign, 75

Canadian Council for International Cooperation, 306

Canadian Union of Public Employees, 77

Capital District Community Loan Fund, 159–61

Capital District Local First, 156–61

capitalism: counter-summit protests against, 31; global indigenous movements and, 142–45; hegemony of, 383–84; Northern and Southern frameworks for, 298–99

caracoles (Zapatista governing councils), as transnational encounter, 1–5, 34n.1, 34n.4

Caracol Intergaláctica (youth activist space during the 2005 World Social Forum), 120

Cardon, Dominique, 348

care theory, 228n.22

Carnival for Full Enjoyment (CFE), 183–84

Caruso, Giuseppe, 20–21, 31–34, 229–49, 342–62, 370

Casas-Cortés, Maribel, 20, 31, 199–225, 212, 370

Castells, Manuel, 12, 14

caste politics, Indian World Social Forum and, 241–46

Castoriadis, Cornelius, 72–73

Chase-Dunn, Christopher, 45

Chatterton, Paul, 266

Chávez, Hugo, 43

Chiapas Media Project, 74

civilizational crisis, indigenous activists' paradigm of, 134, 284

civil society: activist research and, 212–14;

first-wave transnational networking and, 300–303, 316n.2; in India, 241–42, 247–49; indigenous movements and, 141–45; information systems for, 307–10; insurgency in, 276–77, 291n.1; social forums and, 43–45; transnational networks and, 296; World Social Forum and concepts of, 271–72

Clandestine Insurgent Rebel Clown Army (CIRCA), 184–85, 261–63

class: collaborative research and, 36n.16; costs of diversity and, 60–64; diversity at USSF and, 45–54; engaged ethnography and, 379; localist politics and, 158–60; at U.S. Social Forum, 39–64

climate change: activist ethnography concerning, 253–55, 260–66; indigenous perspectives on, 131

Climate Change Convention, 309–10

climate justice camps, 120

Cloward, Richard, 56–57

CNN iReport, 332

Coalitions across Borders (Bandy and Smith), 11

Coca-Cola, as capitalist symbol, 2–3, 34n.3

cognitive practice, social movement theory and, 20

CONINTELPRO (FBI surveillance program), 327

Coleman, Gabriella, 347

Coles, Romand, 220

collaborative research: activist ethnography and, 250–61; class and, 36n.16; ethnography and, 24–25; of Feminist Dialogues, 96–104; Indymedia project and, 324–25; power relations in, 258–66; relational ethics and, 264–66

collective action: ethnographic research on, 68–70, 87n.3; film production and, 330–31; in Indymedia project, 325–28; media production and, 324–25; transnational activism as, 13–17

collusion, ethnographic theory and practice and, 209–14

colonialism: ethnography and, 23–28, 290–91; global indigenous movements and, 130–48, 142–45; indigenous decolonization and, 143–45; indigenous women's challenge to, 134–39; political aspects of ethnography and, 375–77

command logics, open space and, 42–45

communication networks: digital technology and, 307–10; global activism and, 12–17; second-wave transnational networking and, 303–6

communitarian politics, U.S. Social Forum and, 50, 55–58

Community Land Trusts, 161

complexity theory: global justice movements, 15; knowledge practices and, 214–19, 226n.5; network ethnography and, 315–16; representation and, 296–99; in science research, 295; social science research and, 295–96; transnational networks and, 296–316

computers. *See* digital technology

concealment practices in social movements, 327–28

conflict mediation: central and peripheral conflicts in, 242–46; transformative ethnography and, 235–39; in World Social Forum, 239–42

Consultative Network Group (CNG) (Feminist Dialogues), 98–104

consumer-based anticapitalism, 3–5

contact zones, social forums as, 54–55

contentious politics, defined, 125n.4

Continental Summit of Indigenous Women, 286–87

Convention on Biological Diversity, 309–10

convergence spaces, forging of solidarity and, 252–53

Conway, Janet, 20, 32, 269–91, 368

Coordinadora Andina de Organizaciones Indígenas (Andean Coordination of Indigenous Organizations), 284

Coordinating Group (CG), of Feminist Dialogues, 95–104

core activism, 193n.13

cosmopolitanism: first-wave transnational networking and, 300–303; in World Social Forum, 279–82, 290, 292n.9

Costa Vargas, João, 373–74

counterpower, 126n.11

counterpublics, social forums and, 54–55

counter-summit protests, 31, 171–91, 226n.6, 377, 381

Couture, Stéphane, 21, 342–62, 370

Creative Commons, 331–32

criminalization of global justice movements, 186–90

Critical Resistance, 45

cross-border collective action, 13; barriers at Feminist Dialogues to, 99–104; global activism and, 178–81, 194n.19

cross-fertilization, in transnational activism, 172–73, 176–77

cultural critique: activist research and, 204–7; class politics and, 386–88; ethnography and, 23–25, 163–69

cultural logic of networking, 21, 92–94; logic of social movements, Feminist Dialogues and, 92–94. *See also* networking logic

cultural politics of networking, 15, 21, 33–34; free/libre and open-software movement and, 342–62; indigenous women's movement and, 137–39; place-based contexts and, 297–99; resistance and, 108–24; social forum technology, 342–62

culture, transnational activism and, 11

cultures of ethnography, 163–69

Cultures of Politics, Politics of Cultures (Alvarez, Dagnino, and Escobar), 11

cumbre (summit) process, 285

Cunningham, Hilary, 13

Cunningham, Myrna, 135, 149n.9

Dag Hammarskjöld Foundation, 303–6, 316n.1

Dagnino, Evelina, 11

engaged ethnography: political aspects of, 371–77; possibilities, limits and relevance of, 367–88; subjectivity and, 368–71; transformations in, 199–225. *See also* activist research

environmental justice movements, 31, 201; activist ethnography and, 250, 253–55; communication networks for, 309–10; first-wave transnational networking and, 302–3; "Green Scare" and, 340n.17; knowledge and complexity in, 215–19

epistemological encounter, ethnography as, 9–10, 218–19

Escárcega, Sylvia, 19, 30, 129–48, 368, 378

Escobar, Arturo, 11, 15, 22–23, 220

ethical issues: activist ethnography and, 263–66; in localist politics, 161–63; in World Social Forum, 235–39

ethnographic gaze, World Social Forum research and, 275–80

ethnography: alternative economies and, 151–70; emergent theory and practice in, 208–14; encounter practices in, 214–19; language of, 9–10; of networks, 313–16; overview of research methodology in, 28–33; political aspects of, 5–10, 22–28, 371–77; of radical imagination, 83–86; scholar activism and, 105–6; story collection and, 68–69; translational aspects of, 219–25; transnational activism and, 3–5; of World Social Forum, 269–91. *See also* cultural critique; specific research disciplines, e.g., activist research

European Social Forum (ESF): activist ethnography and, 60; global activism and, 116–18, 210–11; global justice movement and, 40; technological evolution in, 352–54, 364n.20

European Union, 212

event-space, anti-globalization movements and, 183–90

"exit option" for social movements, 120–21

experience: knowledge production through, 121–23; resistance through, 115–16; spaces of, 118–21

experimentation: global activism and, 116–18; knowledge production through, 121–23

extended case methodology, 35n.8

Eyerman, Ron, 20

Facebook, 364n.20

Federal Communications Commission (FCC), 337

Federal Emergency Management Agency (FEMA), 337

Feminist Dialogues (FD), 29–30; as activist scholarship, 89, 94–104; Coordinating Group in, 92; cultural logic of social movements and, 92–94; history of, 94–95; language difficulties in, 99–100; sponsors of, 107n.6

feminist theory: activist ethnography and, 250, 260–66; epistemology and, 218–19, 226n.4; ethnographic research and, 23, 26, 290–91; indigenous women's movements and, 131–32, 134–39; scholar activism and, 89–92, 126n.11; transformative mediation and, 235; transnational activism and, 13–14, 29–30

Fernandez, Luis, 13

fieldwork: complexity of knowledge in, 214–19; in ethnographic research, 22; ethnography of World Social Forum, 270, 273–75; on Indymedia project, 332–35; transformative ethnography and, 230–32

Fifth Continental Meeting of Indigenous Women of the Americas, 136–37

Fifty Years Is Enough, 49

figured worlds, global activism in context of, 193n.14

film collectives, political impact of, 324–25

first-wave transnational networking, 300–303

Fischer, M. J., 22, 227n.12

Folger, Joseph, 235–36

Mouffe, Chantal, 43

Mouvement Souveraineté-Association (Movement for Sovereignty Association), 177–82

movement-building models: limitations of, 384–88; race and class issues and, 41; U.S. Social Forum and, 52–58, 65n.9

movement-versus-space dynamic, social forums and, 42, 52–58, 291n.5

Movimiento de Liberacón Territorial (Territorial Liberation Movement), 118

Moving the Movement Workshop, 49, 53

Multilateral Agreement on Investments, 192n.6

multilateralism, first-wave transnational networking and, 301–3

multilocal ethnography: elements of, 22; global activism and, 110–13

multiplicity, in World Social Forum, 278–80

multitude, emerging subjectivity of, 17–18

Mumbai: free/libre and open-source software in, 348–52; transnational activism in, 14; World Social Forum in, 239–42, 283

Murphy, Brian, 308

Muslim groups: exclusion at social forums of, 45; Indian World Social Forum and, 244–46

mutual solidarity, politics of affinity and, 256–66

Naficy, Hamid, 324–25

Narmada Bachao Andolan (Save the Narmada Movement) (NBA), 263–65

National Planning Committee (NPC): digital technology and, 356–59, 364n.20; openness and horizontality as goals of, 59–64; U.S. Social Forum and, 49–58

nation-state structures, transnational activism and, 71–72

Navajo Nation, 215–19

Negri, Antonio, 12, 17–18, 72–73, 121

neoliberalism: alter-globalization movement and, 173–74; ascendancy of, 383–88; ideological power of, 298–99; nongovernmental organizations and, 16–17; political impacts of, 388n.4; World Social Forum and, 107n.4

Netscape, 347

networked space: activist research and, 206–7, 210–14; complexity of, 299; cultural politics of, 15; ethnographic research on, 313–16; of Feminist Dialogues, 96–104, 107n.5; first-wave transnational networking, 300–303; free/libre and open-source software and, 342–62; global indigenous movements and, 129–48; history as, 300; of indigenous women, 136–37; Indymedia project and, 318–38; multisited ethnography and, 22–28; open space vs., 42–45; polycentric emergence in, 311–13; possibilities, limits and relevance of, 368–88, 388n.6; practice-based research on, 14–15; promises and limitations of, 377–88; second-wave transnational networking and, 303–6; social movement theory and, 199–225; transformative ethnography and, 232–39; transnational activism in, 1–5, 12–21, 35n.9; of transnational encounter, 9–10

networking logic, 12, 42, 210–11, 227n.10, 343, 388. See also cultural logic of networking

New Economics Foundation, 153

New International Economic Order, 316n.4

New International Information Order (NIIO), 296, 303–4, 307, 316n.4

New Left politics, transnational encounters and, 78–79

new politics, ethnographic research and role of, 210

New Rules Project, 156

Nicaragua, women's labor collective in, 14

nongovernmental organizations (NGOs): ethnographic research on, 16–17; feminist forums and, 13–14; information politics of, 10; UNFCCC and, 150n.12

261–63; summit-hopping and, 177–90, 194n.27

political process model, 11–12, 35n.10

politics: of affinity, activist ethnography and, 255–66; debates on research in, 203–7; ethnographic research and, 5–10, 22–28, 371–77; knowledge practices and, 201–3; promises and limitations of, 377–88; of transnational activism, 10–17

Polletta, Francesca, 62

polycentric emergence, network structures and, 311–13

Poor Magazine, 359

popular education, 254–55

postrepresentational ethnography, 200, 224–25, 225n.2

poststructuralist anarchism, 210

Powell, Dana, 20, 31, 199–225, 370

power relations: activist ethnography and, 258–66, 267n.1; in alterglobalization movements, 108–24; antipower and spaces of experience concerning, 118–21; complexity of knowledge and, 217–19; ethnographic research, 23–25; in feminist research, 90–92; imagination and, 73–74; localist politics and, 158–60; at social forums, 44–45; sociotechnical networks, 16; solidarity and, 252–53; Spinoza's discussion of, 126n.10; U.S. Social Forum formation and, 52–54; Zapatista movement and, 74–79

practice-based research, global justice networks, 14–15

Precarias a la Deriva (Precariat Adrift), 219–20, 222–23, 228n.22

precarity activism, 219–23, 226n.7; activist research and, 211–14

problem spaces, in social movement research, 207

Proceso de Comunidades Negras (Process of Black Communities), 15

production-oriented anticapitalism, 3–5

pseudonyms of Indymedia activists, 327–31

publication, of activist ethnography, 26–28

public sphere, open space ideal and, 42–45

Pulido, Laura, 265

Quebec City, FTAA summit in, 177–82

Quechua culture, 150n.10

race: costs of diversity and, 60–64; diversity at USSF and, 45–54; free/libre and open source software and, 358–59; at U.S. Social Forum, 39–64

Racial Contract, 371, 388n.1

radical environmental networks, 57

Radical Theory Forum, 210–11

Raymond, Eric, 347–48, 362n.4

Reclaim the Streets network, 119–21, 184

Rediker, Marcus, 78

Red Scares, 327

reductionist discourse, in World Social Forum, 274–75

reflexivity: in ethnographic research, 221–25; political aspects of ethnography and, 373–77; World Social Forum ethnographic research and, 270

Reinsborough, Patrick, 84–85

Reitan, Ruth, 12

relational ethics, activist ethnography and, 263–66

representation: complexity and, 296–99; distortion in transnational activism of, 172–73; in ethnographic research, 23; politics of, 221–25; in World Social Forum, 271–72, 278–80

research methodology: debates concerning, 203–7; overview of, 28–33

resistance: activist ethnography and terrains of, 251, 267n.1; embodied terrains of, 32; ethnography as form of, 35n.14

resource mobilization framework: activist ethnography and, 266–67; ethnography of transnational activism and, 10–17; social forums and, 56–57

rhizome model of activism: power and subjectivity and, 17–18; World Social Forum and, 269–72, 277–80, 291n.4; Zapatista movement and, 66, 79–83

Index | 439

knowledge categories, 20; transnational activism and politics in, 5–10

social science, alternative economies and, 151–70

soda cans, as capitalist symbol, 2–3

solidarity: activist ethnography and, 251–53, 266–67; forging of, 251–53; mutual solidarity, 256–66

Soohen, Jacquie, 66, 79, 82–83

Southeast Organizing Committee (SOC) (U.S. Social Forum), 51

So We Stand, 253–55, 267, 268n.3

space, ideal of: experience and, 118–21; indigenous women's movements and, 134–39; limits of activism and, 381–82; solidarity and, 252–53. *See also* networked space; open space

Sparke, Matt, 266

specificity in ethnography, limits of, 290–91

Speed, Shannon, 23, 36n.15

Spinoza, Baruch, 126n.10

Spivak, Gayatri, 219–21

Stallman, Richard, 346–47

Starbucks, 157

Sterpka, M. K., 21, 33, 295–316, 368

"sticky engagements," summit meetings as, 173–74

Stockholm Conference on the Human Environment, 301–3

storytelling: ethnographic research and, 68–69, 161–64; in Indymedia project, 324–25

Stringer, Tish, 21, 33, 318–38, 376

Students for a Democratic Society (SDS), 79

Studio x (radio program), 321

subalternity, at World Social Forum, 279–88, 292n.9

subjectivity(ies): in alterglobalization movements, 108–24; engaged ethnography and, 368–71; resistance through, 108–24; transnational activist encounters and, 17–18, 29

subtraction, power and logic of, 121

subversive technologies, transnational encounter and, 20–21

Summit Conference of Nonaligned Countries, 303

summit-hopping: alter-globalization protests and, 171–91, 193n.9; Gleneagles economic summit, 182–90; imaginary and, 173–74; relentless policing at, 177–82

surveillance of political activists, 327–28

Swann, Robert, 161

systemic anticapitalism, 3–5

Sztulwark, Diego, 118

Tanzanian Gender Networking Programme, 101

Tarrow, Sidney, 11–12, 84

Tauli-Corpuz, Victoria, 140–41

Taylor, Charles, 73, 227n.19

Tea Party populism, 386

technology: ethnography and, 32–33; first-wave transnational networking and, 301–3; free/libre and open-source software and, 342–63; subversive technologies, 20–21

Teivainen, Teivo, 42, 277, 291n.8

Territories of Difference (Escobar), 220, 223

Thayer, Millie, 14

Third Continental Assembly of Indigenous People, 39

Third Intercontinental Encuentro for Humanity and Against Neoliberalism, 74, 77

Third Worldism, first-wave transnational networking and, 301–3

Third World Journalists' Seminar, 303–6

This Is What Democracy Looks Like (film), 324

time banks and dollars, 151–54, 161

Tobin Tax, 381, 388n.3

"tolerant" identities, transnational activism and, 11–12

Touraine, Alain, 105–6, 107n.12, 109–11, 115

intentional space transition at, 45–54; organizing software and technology within, 355–59, 364n.20; political limitations of, 382–83; race, class, and horizontality at, 39–64

universalism, critiques of, 210–11

Universidade Federal do Pará (UFPA), 282

Universidade Federal Rural da Amazônia (Federal Rural University of the Amazon) (UFRA), 281–82, 285

University of Toronto, activist movement at, 74

Valletri Agreement, 308

Varela, Francisco, 218

Vietnam War, protests against, 79

Virno, Paolo, 72–73

Walker, Amy, 45

Wallerstein, Immanuel, 388n.5

Walmart, 157

Warrior Society (Mohawk nation), 87n.5

Weather Underground, 79

Weber, Max, 112, 124

"Where Was the Color in Seattle?" critique, 387

Whitaker, Francisco, 277

white activists: limitations of, 386–88; U.S. Social Forum and role of, 50, 52, 57–58

women: communication networks and, 317n.8; in World Social Forum, 243–46, 283–88

Women in Development Europe, 101

Women Living under Muslim Laws, 101

women's movements: in Europe, 101; indigenous women's movements, 131–32, 134–39; Nicaragua women's labor collective, 14; time banks and, 151

Woodward, Keith, 299

World Bank, 141, 175–76, 377

World Conference on Women, 135–36

World Economic Forum, 43, 92, 271

World Peoples Conference on Climate Change and the Rights of Mother Earth, 142–45

World Social Forum (WSF), 14, 60; alter-activist workshops of, 122–23; central and peripheral conflicts in, 242–46; Charter of Principles, 43, 92–94, 229, 236–38, 271–72, 291n.3, 362n.1; conflict mediation in, 236–49; ethnographic approaches to, 269–91; ethnographic gaze in research on, 275–80; Facebook and, 364n.20; factional conflicts in, 232–39; Feminist Dialogues and, 29–30, 92–104; fieldwork research on, 273–75; free/libre and open-source software and, 342–43; FTAA summit and, 177–82; history of, 40; in India, 234–46, 283, 349–52; indigenous movements and, 144–45, 147–48, 150n.15, 280–88; International Council, 40; International Organizing Committee of, 95; multisited ethnography and, 32; neoliberal cooptation of, 107n.4; networking logics and, 42, 343; networks in, 300, 311; open space concept and, 41–45, 57; organizational structure of, 94; platforms at, 44; political engagement in, 239–42; polycentric process in, 291n.2; representation in, 271–72; transformative ethnography and, 229–49; Zapatista movement and expansion of, 377

World Trade Organization (WTO), 377; alter-activists at, 116; alter-globalization protests of, 171–91; alternative media networks and, 319–23; counter-summit protests against, 31; networks in, 299; online protest resources against, 312–13; poststructuralist anarchism and, 210

Wright, Colin, 43–44

Writing Culture critique, 23, 371–72

writing machines, Marcus's concept of, 209

young activists, 377–78; antipower and spaces of experience for, 118–21; local ethnography on, 108–10; at World Social Forum, 281–82

Yunas, Muhammed, 161

S. 73

Made in the USA
Monee, IL
27 August 2020